WORKING
WITH
SELF
-
HELP

WORKING WITH SELF-HELP

NASW PRESS

National Association of Social Workers, Inc.
Silver Spring, Maryland 20910

Richard L. Edwards, ACSW, *President*
Mark G. Battle, ACSW, *Executive Director*

THOMAS J. POWELL
EDITOR

Library of Congress Cataloging-in-Publication Data

Working with self-help / Thomas J. Powell, editor.
    p.   cm.
   Includes bibliographical references.
   ISBN 0-87101-174-3
   1. Self-help groups—United States. 2. Self-help techniques—United States. I. Powell, Thomas J.
HV547.W67   1989
361.4—dc20   89-14031
                                               CIP

Printed in the United States of America

Cover and interior design by Janice Mauroschadt Design

CONTENTS

PREFACE

Social workers and other health and human services professionals might well ask: If there is a self-help movement, what is its nature? It is a movement judged by the growing strength and acceptance of self-help by the general public and by professional workers. Current estimates place the number of members of self-help groups in the United States at 6 million to 15 million.[1] Whatever the actual overall number, there is no uncertainty about the strength of individual organizations, such as the Alliance for the Mentally Ill and Alcoholics Anonymous (AA)—each of which counts its members in the hundreds of thousands.

The immediate recognition accorded AA indicates the level of acceptance it has achieved with the general public. Moreover, it and other Twelve-Step groups, such as Narcotics Anonymous, are regarded as treatment partners by professionals and treatment facilities that work with alcohol and chemical abuse. Indeed, these Twelve-Step groups are often regarded as the most important long-term resource for recovery. Further evidence of the movement is the narrowing gap between the recognition of and acceptance accorded Twelve-Step and non–Twelve-Step programs by professionals and the public alike.[2]

One early indication came from the work of the President's Commission on Mental Health. The commission's *Report to the President* on community supports recommended that community mental

---

[1]Jacobs, M. K., & Goodman, G. (1989). Psychology and self-help groups: Predictions on a partnership. *American Psychologist, 44,* 536–545.

[2]Romeder, J. M. (1989). *The self-help way.* Ottawa: Canadian Council on Social Development.

health centers maintain a list of self-help groups to be used for referral purposes.[3] Unfortunately, progress was slowed by President Carter's exit from office and the introduction of the anti-human services policies of the Reagan administration. Nonetheless, an event took place in September 1987 on the UCLA campus that moved self-help into a new era. It was the Surgeon General's Workshop on Self-Help and Public Health.[4] C. Everett Koop did much to energize the workshop through his personal and professional testimony about self-help. He referred to his experiences with self-help as a bereaved parent of a son who had been accidentally killed. He also related how, as a pediatric surgeon, he observed the families of his patients being supportive to one another. Koop's convictions about self-help made it clear that his support was neither a fashionable gesture nor a cost-cutting strategy. Instead he was a committed pioneer who made it possible for later groups of professionals to support self-help groups.

The scores of recommendations developed by the workshop's nearly 200 participants—most of whom had had firsthand experience with self-help groups—have become an important part of the national agenda for self-help programs. Continuing work on this agenda has become the mandate of the successor organization to the Surgeon General's Workshop, the National Council on Self-Help and Public Health, which is a federally funded organization made up of self-helpers, agency executives, and policy specialists. It, in turn, works closely with a federally supported sister organization, Self-Help Alliance (SHALL), comprising exclusively self-helpers.

Consistent with this agenda has been the establishment of the Center for Self-Help Research and Knowledge Dissemination at the University of Michigan. This center is studying how persons with serious mental illness can coordinate the use of self-help and professional service systems to enhance their social functioning and sense of well-being. Its sponsorship by the National Institute of Mental Health suggests that the movement and values of the professional and self-help service systems are being recognized.

---

[3] *Report to the President from the President's Commission on Mental Health* (Vols. 1 & 2). (1978). Washington, DC: U.S. Government Printing Office.
[4] *Surgeon General's workshop on self-help and public health*. (1988). Washington, DC: U.S. Government Printing Office.

At the level of everyday service delivery, the self-help clearing-houses play a major role in the movement. The many self-help clearinghouses that are in operation across the country serve not only those who seek self-help services for themselves but professionals (sometimes as many as a third of their callers) who seek information about self-help services for their clients. Sensitive to their part in the movement, the clearinghouses have formed the National Network of Mutual-Help Centers. The name of the network reflects a mission that often goes beyond the boundaries of a clearinghouse. Individual centers have engaged in a broad range of training and technical-assistance activities related to the formation and development of self-help groups. One of the leading centers, the New Jersey Self-Help Center, has developed the *Self-Help Sourcebook*.[5] This immensely useful volume could be profitably consulted by anyone who is interested in learning about the programs that exist across a range of problems, conditions, and situations.

The existence of certain basic helping mechanisms that are common to different kinds of self-help programs is another dimension of the movement. Some of these are discussed in Part 1. These common mechanisms reduce isolation by encouraging participation in organizational tasks and facilitate the development of personal networks. They take the form of structured approaches that have been derived from the experience of those who have been "there." This experiential approach unifies the movement by defining a distinctive approach to helping. It does so while complementing and enhancing professional help.

Yet this focus on common mechanisms should not imply more similarity than exists among self-help programs. The common (and unique) mechanisms interact with different constellations of people and problems to produce different types of self-help organizations. Some of these types of organizations are discussed in Part 2.

Part 3 deals with how human services professionals can work with selected parts of the movement. It discusses how the ideas in Part 1 and Part 2 can be used to enhance the effectiveness of self-help–professional interactions. Special attention is paid to ideas that

---

[5]Madara, E. J., & Meese, A. (Eds.). (1988). *The self-help sourcebook: Finding and forming mutual aid self-help groups* (2nd ed.). Denville, NJ: The Self-Help Clearinghouse [Saint Clares-Riverside Medical Center, Denville, NJ 07834].

will enhance self-help activities in minority communities, hence the chapters related to self-help in black and Hispanic communities. The lack of a chapter about the highly developed self-help approaches in lesbian and gay communities is a serious omission; the promised, but undelivered, chapter, however, may serve as a reminder that self-help must be adapted to the distinctive needs and interests of an even larger number of minorities, such as older adults and persons with disabilities. Other chapters in Part 3 call attention to the many client-centered interactions with self-help groups (Chapters 9, 12, and 14) that are possible. At the next level, Chapter 13 shows how the clearinghouse approach spans both individual/client interactions. This chapter is followed by consideration of the possible misuses of self-help (Chapter 15) and its use as an instrument for negotiating with professionals (Chapter 16). For those who want (as most should) to obtain more firsthand information about the various groups in the self-help movement, Chapter 17 should make that task less daunting and more fun.

An edited collection can be a marvelous device for networking with people who share similar interests. It can provide insight about the range and diversity of a field. This editor is deeply grateful to the chapter authors for this experience. To the reader, he wishes a similar experience.

—T.J.P.

PART ONE

UNDERSTANDING AND ENHANCING THE BASIC MECHANISMS OF SELF-HELP

EXPERIENTIAL, PROFESSIONAL, AND LAY FRAMES OF REFERENCE

THOMASINA J. BORKMAN

Despite the extensive interest in self-help groups by professional observers during the past decade (Gottlieb, 1981, Katz & Bender, 1976, Robinson & Henry, 1977, Weber, 1982), the distinctive nature and character of these groups are far from understood. What, for example, does it mean when a member of a self-help group for recovering alcoholics withdraws from psychotherapy because she says the professional therapist is jeopardizing her sobriety and recovery? How should a nurse respond when a hemophiliac member of a self-help group argues that the nurse and other hospital personnel do not know enough about his hemophilia to be trusted with providing routine care for his pneumonia unless they are monitored or educated about hemophilia? Why would a urologist ask the advice of a long-term self-helper who has had a colostomy about where to place the abdominal opening of his latest patient's upcoming colostomy? These are situations in which self-helpers have specialized knowledge about their health stemming from personal experience. This specialized knowledge, grounded in an individual's lived experience, is termed "experiential knowledge" here. The thesis of this chapter is that members of self-help groups develop experiential knowledge and problem-solving approaches about their common problem that constitute a distinctive frame of reference in comparison with those of professionals who are knowledgeable about the same problem or of lay people. Professionals obviously have their own body

The author wishes to thank Mark Jacobs, Louis Medvene, Lee Miller, Thomas Powell, and Aina Stunz for their constructive reviews of and suggestions on this chapter.

of knowledge and skills, which will be referred to as professional knowledge. This chapter considers the frames of reference used by members of self-help groups and how their perspectives differ from those of professional experts or of lay persons on the same subject. The implications of these frames of reference for the modes of helping that each can give are also considered.

BACKGROUND AND LITERATURE REVIEW

In the literature, professional observers have characterized self-help groups in many ways (see, for example, Killilea, 1976). However, they have tended to regard self-help groups as being analogous to professional forms of service and have contrasted the methods and approaches used in self-help groups with those of helping professionals. Early works (such as Mowrer, 1964, and Hurvitz, 1974) compared these groups directly to professional psychotherapy.

The literature usually distinguishes between professional services, on the one hand, and lay support, including self-help group services, on the other hand, although the terminology differs by discipline. For example, anthropologists often use the term *folk* instead of lay. They view the folk of self-help groups not as professionals or experts but as untrained lay persons. In a widely quoted article, Antze (1976) talked about the folk information and ideology used in Alcoholics Anonymous (AA); Recovery, Inc.; and other self-help groups. Alibrandi (1978), another anthropologist who studied "sponsors" (the veteran members of AA who guide newcomers in a one-to-one relationship), labeled them "folk therapists."

The literature on self-help groups, however, is no different from that of medical sociology (also known as the sociology of health and illness). Although there is a large body of literature on the differences in the knowledge, attitudes, and values of professionals in the health care system and patients–lay people, no consistent distinctions are made between categories of lay persons. It is essentially a two-category classification: professional and lay person. Lay persons are identified by their roles vis-à-vis the health care system—as consumers, patients, clients, or advocates—but there is no uniform distinction between knowledgeable and uninformed lay persons.

Thus, the knowledge and experience of patients, consumers, or lay people are regarded as similar, whatever their condition or disease.

In a 1976 article (Borkman, 1976), this author argued that self-help groups develop and transmit specialized information—beliefs and perspectives about their focal problem and its resolution that she labeled experiential knowledge. She contended that experiential knowledge, which is based on the members' reflecting on their personal experiences in living through and resolving a problem, differs extensively from professional knowledge. In the 1976 article, this author described the differences between the two forms of knowledge in terms of their formal characteristics. Professional knowledge is university based, analytical, grounded in theory or scientific principles, and abstract. In contrast, experiential knowledge is grounded in lived experience, concrete, pragmatic, and holistic.

Professional, scientific knowledge is the primary legitimated and institutionalized way of knowing in our society in the late twentieth century, whereas experiential knowledge is not well recognized other than by its knowers, much less legitimated by society at large.

Until the mid-1980s, this author followed the conventional wisdom of viewing the world in either-or categories by contrasting experiential with professional knowledge. In a 1984 article (Borkman, 1984), she broke away from the twofold classification, explicitly contrasting the experiential information of self-helpers with the lay-folk information of their families and friends and with professionals' knowledge of the relevant area in question (a threefold classification). Powell (1987) seems to be one of the few other observers of self-help groups who also saw the tripartite division: professional, experiential, and informal systems of helping.

The view presented in this chapter is that the knowledge and perspective of the experientialist who is knowledgeable about living with and coping with a disease is far different from the knowledge and perspective of the lay bystander who is unfamiliar with the disease or the newcomer who recently developed the disease and is in the initial phases of learning how to live with it. "Lay knowledge" is defined according to the definition used by sociologists and anthropologists, who refer to it as "recipe knowledge" (Berger & Luckmann, 1967), folk information, common sense of the person on the street (Holzner & Marx, 1979), or information transmitted from one generation to the next. It also includes information gleaned by bystanders from the mass media or from scientists or professionals. "Professional knowledge" refers to information, knowledge, and skills developed, applied, and transmitted by an established specialized occupation; persons who have professional knowledge have fulfilled the formal educational, training, and apprenticeship requirements of their profession and are likely to have credentials and degrees that signify their professional status.

THE "INFORMATION SOCIETY" AND THE EXPERIENTIAL PERSPECTIVE

The late twentieth-century United States is often characterized as a postindustrial society. Many scholars and analysts argue that after World War II, the United States and other advanced industrial societies began changing significantly as computers, electronics, and other forms of high technology developed and the importance of manufacturing and basic industry declined in the expanding global economy. This society has been called the Postindustrial Society (Bell, 1973) and the Information Society, among other terms. Whatever the name given to the society that is emerging, scientific, technical, and professional knowledge has so rapidly increased that people face "future shock" from the pace of change, according to Toffler (1980), and training for many scientific and technical occupations is obsolete in 5 to 10 years.

Holzner and Marx (1979) linked the emerging postindustrial society with the accompanying ascendance and increased power of science and the professions. The major legitimated producers and disseminators of knowledge in this society are now scientists and professionals. The lay person's common sense is increasingly inadequate in a high-technology society. Divine revelation does not help one obtain governmental funding, and possessors of it face obstacles in running for public office. On-the-job training by apprenticeship alone is usually no longer adequate, as it was in earlier, simpler times.

Within the context of this information-rich, rapidly changing society, the civil and human rights movements of the 1960s and the 1970s occurred. Despite the assassination of Martin Luther King, Jr., in 1968, the civil rights movement for minorities, the anti–Vietnam War movement, the women's movement, and the succeeding human rights movements for handicapped people, stigmatized people, consumers, and others all continued and energized one another. These movements fought against discrimination, prejudice, injustice, and inequality. Most visibly, the liberal and New Left political stances attempted to decrease discrimination and inequality in employment, income, public accommodations, politics, education, and so on. These objective issues of jobs, pay, schooling, voting, and the like are well understood to be major aspects of civil rights for which the movements advocated change. Less visible and less recognized or understood were the cultural rights that were also part of these movements. "Cultural rights" refers to the idea that groups, subcultures, or social entities have the right to define themselves, to give themselves a name, and to say what is valid and true for them ("Black Is Beautiful" is an example). The concept follows Starr's (1982) concept of "cultural authority," which refers to institutionalized authority to define reality, to make judgments of meaning and value, to name things, and to have these constructions of meaning and value regarded as valid and true.

Working to diminish objective discrimination was only part of the story of these movements, for participants also shared their personal experiences with each other. The participants learned how similar were the situations they had struggled through and the associated emotions and meanings for their lives. These stories of individuals being "in the world"—of having experiential knowledge or an experiential frame of reference—are presented in a different form and style than is the knowledge of the scientist or professional. The phrase "language of the heart" captures part of it.

Experiential authority is giving credence and credibility to knowledge and viewpoints gained by personal subjective experience. In these movements, people empowered themselves by claiming their experiential knowledge and authority (although they did not give it a name). Their experiential authority gave them power among themselves to take their own and their peers' stories seriously. They claimed cultural rights, along with civil and human rights.

Cultural rights, as defined here, include the right to name yourself and your characteristics. For example, physically handicapped people say it is demeaning to refer to them as "confined" to a wheelchair; instead, they say that they "use" a wheelchair. Women from the feminist movement asked male physicians and psychiatrists to stop telling women what their sexual orgasms are like—women know their own orgasms. People who stutter do not want to be called stutterers because that typifies them by only one of thousands of their characteristics; they protest when television broadcasts the cartoon of the stuttering Porky Pig, which negatively stereotypes stutterers.

An important by-product of the civil and human rights movements of the 1960s and 1970s was the development of the experiential frame of reference among many groups. Subjective stories using the language of the heart have been hammered out of the struggle of members of groups who lived through common fates and who shared their stories with each other. This process of sharing objectifies the subjective experiences of individuals as the commonly recognized experience of a group.

Recognizing the experiential frame of reference as a valid way of knowing the world, more and more groups have developed these experiential frames of reference since the 1960s. The mass media, politicians, lay people, self-helpers, and participants of the various movements recognize the experiential, although they do not give it an explicit name. For example, many television talk shows that air issues like child abuse or alcoholism routinely feature persons who have successfully overcome the problem (experientialists), along with professional experts. Similarly, congressional hearings often have individuals present testimonies of their personal experiences with the problem of interest (such as the lack of prenatal care for pregnant women in poor inner-city areas). The public at large has no agreed-upon name for it, as it does for professional and scientific knowledge. Professionals, scientists, and academics seem to be less aware of the use of experiential frames of reference and the credibility of these frames of reference among many segments of the population. Or perhaps many people are aware of experiential knowledge in particular cases but do not see it as a general phenomenon.

MULTIPLE REALITIES: WHAT YOU SEE DEPENDS ON WHERE YOU STAND

The notion that different parties to an event perceive and interpret it differently is not new. Sociologists have recently developed major theoretical perspectives on the basis of this notion. Schutz, a philosopher and sociologist, used the term "multiple realities" to describe the idea that various social units create and maintain their own perspectives and that these perspectives have an important influence on their behaviors (see Wagner, 1970). The sociological phenomenologists and social constructionists take multiple realities seriously as a point of departure for investigating social life.

The social-constructionist view of multiple realities has parallels in the theories of relativity and quantum mechanics in modern physics. A favorite illustration is that perceptions of the speed of a train on a valley floor depend on where the observer is located in relation to the train. If one is standing 20 feet from the train tracks, the train seems to go past quickly, but if one is 20 miles away on a mountain top, the train seems to crawl slowly across the valley floor.

Of interest here is the idea that the perspective an individual has of a focal problem is affected by the kind of relationships he or she has to it. Part of experiential knowledge is the special understanding that people who have been through the same experience have of each other, which forms a bond that can be as strong as family or friendship. Often nonbelievers respond to this idea with the following comment (or its equivalent): "A cancer surgeon does not need to have cancer to do surgery on his or her patient."

It is true that cancer surgeons do not need to have cancer to do cancer surgery, which is a technical medical procedure. But just because physicians know how to diagnose and surgically treat cancer, it does not follow that they know what it is like to have cancer, to live with it and with the effects of surgery and aftercare. Professionals and scientists attempt to maintain some emotional distance from their patients or the subjects of research. For example, surgeons are not supposed to perform surgery on close family members because their emotional involvement with the family members is thought to interfere with their capacity to perform competently and to deal "objectively" with their patients.

In contrast, experiential knowledge involves emotional involvement of the person with the problem of concern—being subjective, caring about himself or herself in the situation, and not being detached. Lay persons are regarded here as being in a more neutral position between objectivity and subjectivity, since they are more often bystanders to an experience or problem.

The following scenario in three parts presents points about the multiple realities that end up as different frames of reference, although, as is obvious, reality is much more complex than this simplified presentation suggests.

Before the scenario is presented, several points need to be made. Individuals can have multiple frames of reference, depending on their relationship to the focal problem. Which frame of reference is operative depends on the individual's relationship to the problem. The scenario presents only a brief cast of characters, which would be much larger in real life. In real life, additional family members, co-workers, neighbors, and friends could be involved.

SCENARIO: MULTIPLE PERSPECTIVES

The scenario involves four people: Sally Jones, a breast cancer patient, a nuclear physicist, and the wife of Bill Jones; Bill Jones, the husband of Sally Jones and a lawyer in private practice specializing in drunk-driving cases; James Smith, a physician specializing in oncology surgery and Sally Jones's personal physician and the father of John Smith, a 16-year-old high school student; and Mary Ryan, a legal secretary to Bill Jones and a member of Al-Anon (the self-help group for persons who are concerned about the alcohol or drug use of relatives or friends) and mother of Ted Ryan, an 18-year-old high school senior who is about to graduate.

PART 1

Dr. James Smith diagnosed Sally Jones as having breast cancer that requires an immediate operation. As her surgeon, Dr. Smith is completing the arrangements for doing the surgery at his favorite hospital later this week. Bill Jones, Sally's concerned husband, is trying to help Sally deal with this unpleasant reality and to make arrange-ments to go to the hospital. Mary Ryan, secretary to Bill Jones, takes his messages for him when he is home helping Sally.

What are the frames of reference of each character? Dr. Smith clearly represents the professional's frame of reference. Mary Ryan is a bystander who does not even know Sally Jones except through her boss; she represents the lay frame of reference. Sally Jones and her husband Bill Jones are personally living through the problem and represent the experiential frame of reference. Sally Jones directly has the breast cancer and has to deal with that reality and the impending surgery. Bill Jones's personal involvement is as the emotionally attached and committed husband who has to deal with the reality of Sally's disease, her impending treatment for it, and his attitudes and emotions.

Although the physician and the lay person are also having a personal subjective experience in the situation, their experience is not labeled "experiential." The physician's personal experience concerns his practice of medicine with his patient—his occupation of diagnosing and treating cancer—not his personal experience of having cancer. The physician is a close bystander to the patient's experience of illness and can observe her and collect extensive information about the patient's disease as a bystander and as a professional oncologist.

Similarly, the patient and patient's husband are bystanders to the physician's practice of his profession. Sally is personally experiencing what it is like to have cancer, to go through surgery and its recovery, and to have to adjust her life to this reality. Bill, Sally's husband, although he does not know personally about having cancer since he is a bystander to it, is emotionally involved with his wife. He subjectively experiences living through the process of his wife's cancer as a spouse and has a different form of experiential information from that perspective.

The lay person, Mary Ryan in this instance, is truly a bystander vis-à-vis the person with breast cancer and the physician. She is somewhat less of a bystander vis-à-vis Bill Jones, the concerned husband, since he is her boss.

Having located each of the persons in relation to the focal problem of breast cancer in this instance, the question then arises, What are the elements of the frame of reference along which they differ?

Major elements of a frame of reference in this context will be discussed under the following four categories:

1 What are the individuals' stakes in the situation? What do they stand to gain or lose?

2 What are the interests and concerns of the individual in this situation? What issues are pertinent to them? What is the "emotionscape" (Borkman, 1984) of this situation, that is, what meanings and feelings are troublesome or distinctive features of the situation?

3 What beliefs, values, and information about the situation affect these individuals' perspective toward it?

4 What existential/philosophical meanings and interpretations do they have in the situation?

To illustrate the specific kinds of issues that would be involved with each frame of reference, the author developed some concrete questions and ideas for each individual. These illustrative, not exhaustive, ideas are presented in Table 1-1.

PART 2

Six months later, Dr. Smith receives a telephone call from the police that his 16-year-old son John has been arrested for drunk driving that night. Dr. Smith is anxious and wants an attorney to handle his son's case. Remembering that the husband of his patient Sally Jones is a lawyer who has handled a lot of drunk-driving cases, Dr. Smith retains Bill Jones as his attorney for this situation. Dr. Smith realizes that he knows almost nothing about alcohol problems, especially among adolescents. When Dr. Smith phones Bill Jones's office, he talks to Mary Ryan, the legal secretary. Mary seems to understand what he is going through. She explains that she went through the same experience 2 years ago when her underage son Ted was arrested on a drunk-driving charge. She has attended Al-Anon, the self-help group for persons concerned about the drinking and drug problems of a family member or friend, since then. Sally Jones is not directly involved in this situation, although she hears about it from her husband.

The focal problem of Part 2 is a parent whose underage child is arrested on a drunk-driving charge. In this instance, James Smith is the father who is facing this predicament about his son. He is personally beginning to experience the process of this predicament and thereby gaining experiential information. Mary Ryan is more of a veteran with this problem and its resolution because she has attended Al-Anon for 2 years and successfully resolved her feelings about her son's situation. She has experiential knowledge about this predicament and its resolution within the context of Al-Anon. Bill Jones is now practicing his professional role as an attorney who is representing John Smith on behalf of his father. Sally Jones is not directly involved and is the lay bystander vis-à-vis this situation.

Table 1-1

Sally Jones Faces Cancer Surgery: Experiential, Professional, and Lay Frames of Reference

ASPECT OF FRAME OF REFERENCE	EXPERIENTIALIST PERSPECTIVE		PROFESSIONAL PERSPECTIVE	LAY PERSPECTIVE
	SALLY JONES	BILL JONES, HUSBAND	JAMES SMITH, M.D., SURGEON TO SALLY	MARY RYAN, BILL JONES'S SECRETARY
Stakes (gain or loss)	• To live or die • To lose breast (sexual self-image) • To gain attention in the hospital	• To keep wife or be a widower • To have wife without a breast (sexual) • Wife's functions not performed while she is hospitalized	• To perform routine breast surgery successfully and un-eventfully • To gain a fee from the patient • To gain recognition from colleagues for successful practice • To gain a schedule of operation that is convenient for the rest of my practice and personal life	• No immediate stakes • Indirect—boss may be unavailable or have emotional issues while wife has surgery • Work longer hours
Interests, concerns, and emotionscape	• How will I feel about myself with one breast? • I'm afraid of surgery. Is Dr. Smith a competent surgeon? • I hate hospitals. Will I get good nursing care? • What clothes/cosmetics do I take to the hospital? • How will Bill react to me sexually?	• I'll feel helpless. What can I do for Sally? • This will be inconvenient for me—no clean clothes. • Is Dr. Smith a competent surgeon? • How will I react sexually to a wife with one breast? • Will our health insurance cover all the bills?	• Will my favorite operating room team be available? • Are all lab tests completed? • Is Sally overly emotional about the surgery? • Sally's case is a routine standard one I've done many times. • Did my wife schedule a late night out before surgery? • Will the hospital foul up the operating room schedule like they did last month?	• Will my boss leave me with extra work because of his wife's surgery? • Mrs. Jones is older than me, so I am probably safe from getting breast cancer at my age. • My boss is upset about this; he really cares about his wife. I hope they are okay.

(continued)

Table 1-1   Continued

ASPECT OF FRAME OF REFERENCE	EXPERIENTIALIST PERSPECTIVE		PROFESSIONAL PERSPECTIVE	LAY PERSPECTIVE
	SALLY JONES	BILL JONES, HUSBAND	JAMES SMITH, M.D., SURGEON TO SALLY	MARY RYAN, BILL JONES'S SECRETARY
	• Who will wash clothes for Bill while I am in the hospital? • I am glad Bill is worrying about paying for the operation. • How will my mother and friends react?	• Who will eat my cooking?		
Beliefs, values, and information	• Controlling cancer is more important than having two breasts (value). • Medicine knows enough about this situation to take the risk out of surgery. • I trust my doctor's diagnosis that surgery is the best treatment. • My friend Carol who referred me to Dr. Smith liked him for her cancer surgery.	• Keeping Sally alive is most important to me (value). • My friend who suggested laetrile treatment in Mexico for Sally instead of surgery is crazy. • Sally knows more than I do about the risk factors for breast cancer.	• All diagnostic information suggests that the planned surgical procedure will be most effective for Sally Jones's case. • I will not try the new procedure reported in the latest journal because it hasn't been verified as effective in clinical trials. • My conservative reputation among my oncology colleagues is important for me to maintain.	• I couldn't get breast cancer because I am unique. • Having two breasts is most important to be a fully sexual woman. • That magazine article said 5-year survival after surgery is higher than 10 years ago. • Husbands should help their wives out when they are in the hospital.

(continued)

Table 1-1 Continued

ASPECT OF FRAME OF REFERENCE	EXPERIENTIALIST PERSPECTIVE		PROFESSIONAL PERSPECTIVE	LAY PERSPECTIVE
	SALLY JONES	BILL JONES, HUSBAND	JAMES SMITH, M.D., SURGEON TO SALLY	MARY RYAN, BILL JONES'S SECRETARY
Philosophical/ existential meanings and interpretations	• Why did God do this to me? Am I being punished? • Am I to blame for getting cancer? • Do I have bad genes—my mother had cancer at the same age. • Should I make a will—will I survive surgery?	• Why did this happen to Sally and to me? • Is this a malevolent universe? • I couldn't bear to be widowed after losing my mother when I was 12. • Will Sally live through the surgery?	• Modern scientific medicine still doesn't know much about cancer. How much will we ever know? • I do my work and then it's up to the natural healing of the body to recover from surgery.	• It's up to fate whether you get cancer. • Cancer is a bad disease.

James Smith's situation with his son's drunk-driving charge is presented in Table 1-2. Illustrations of the experiential, professional, and lay frames of reference are briefly outlined in the table but are presented in less detail than was given in Table 1-1.

Parts 1 and 2 of the scenario show that one's knowledge and perspective depend on where one stands in relation to the focal situation of interest. They also show that any given individual is likely to have several frames of reference on the basis of which they operate. Part 3 illustrates more vividly the key point that individuals are not solely professionals or lay persons, but that they can be professionals within their specialized occupational sphere, lay persons in most aspects of their lives, and experientialists in some ways.

PART 3

What is the situation of the four persons in the scenario 3 months later? Sally Jones attends a self-help group for women who had mastectomies. At work, she is writing a grant proposal to obtain federal funding for a special experiment in her area of nuclear physics. Bill Jones successfully resolved the legal situation for James Smith's son, but the boy appears to have serious problems with alcohol that require professional intervention. Bill is going to a support group for relatives of women who have had mastectomies. His support group is facilitated by a social worker at the hospital where Sally's surgery was done.

Mary Ryan is attending the annual conference of the National Association of Legal Secretaries this week. She took James Smith to his first Al-Anon meeting several months ago and now she often sees him at two of the meetings she attends weekly.

In the three parts of the scenario, three experiential situations and four professional occupations were presented. Each of the experiential and professional situations generates a corresponding lay perspective. Table 1-3 considers all these issues, showing the multiple frames of reference of each person involved. Table 1-3 also shows that an individual is likely to have more lay perspectives than experiential or professional perspectives about situations. What are the implications of these multiple perspectives? For one thing, the literature on self-help groups tends to categorize individuals as having one perspective—that of either a professional or a lay person. Obviously,

Table 1-2

James Smith's Son's Drunk-Driving Charge

ASPECT OF FRAME OF REFERENCE	EXPERIENTIALIST PERSPECTIVE		PROFESSIONAL PERSPECTIVE	LAY PERSPECTIVE
	JAMES SMITH, FATHER OF JOHN SMITH	MARY RYAN, MOTHER TO TED, AL-ANON MEMBER	BILL JONES, LAWYER FOR JOHN SMITH	SALLY JONES, WIFE OF ATTORNEY
Stakes (gain or loss)	• To protect son from legal harm • To protect my reputation in the community/family from my son's behavior	• To feel good helping James Smith who is going through what I did • To repay the help I received by helping another	• To gain a fee from the client • To gain good will from my wife's doctor • To gain recognition from colleagues for good work • Opportunity to keep my skills sharpened with a juvenile case	• No immediate stakes; indirect stakes of good will of her physician toward her family
Interest, concerns, and emotionscape	• I'm worried that John may have a drinking problem. • Are these legal services very expensive? • I feel guilty because I spend so little time with John. • How can we make sure John doesn't get a court record? • Will neighbors, friends, and kin think I'm a bad father?	• I remember how it felt when Ted was arrested; I was so afraid. • Al-Anon teaches me that James Smith need not feel guilty, since he can't control his son's behavior. • Thank goodness Ted is not drinking and driving anymore.	• I hope this case isn't assigned to Judge Short; he's tough on this type. • I need to check out that new procedure at the juvenile court. • Fortunately, this is John Smith's first offense; it will help that his father is stable and from the upper middle class. • I'll take extra care on this case for Sally's sake—to repay her physician.	• I hope Bill is extraconscientious for Dr. Smith's sake. • I did not even know Dr. Smith had a 16-year-old son. • I feel sorry that Dr. Smith has to go through this; it could be embarrassing. • I hope Bill's juvenile court work doesn't interfere with his cooking dinner.

(continued)

Table 1-2   **Continued**

ASPECT OF FRAME OF REFERENCE	EXPERIENTIALIST PERSPECTIVE		PROFESSIONAL PERSPECTIVE	LAY PERSPECTIVE
	JAMES SMITH, FATHER OF JOHN SMITH	MARY RYAN, MOTHER TO TED, AL-ANON MEMBER	BILL JONES, LAWYER FOR JOHN SMITH	SALLY JONES, WIFE OF ATTORNEY
Beliefs, values, and information	• My son is basically a good kid; this is probably a fluke. • I don't know anything about alcohol abuse among kids. Could John have a serious problem? • I don't know the juvenile court situation and how hard the court is on underage drunk drivers.	• Parents can't stop their adolescent kids from experimenting with drugs, but we can help them with legal situations. • Getting good legal representation helped my son Ted in juvenile court.	• The juvenile court system in this city works well overall. Judge Short is an exception. • I need information on what John's friends are like. Do they use drugs?	• Sixteen-year-olds are too young to become alcohol abusers or alcoholics. • People should not be allowed to drink until they are age 21.
Philosophical/ existential meanings and interpretations	• The universe is unfair to do this to me. I've got too much work to have such a family problem. • No wonder I don't believe in God; there are so many unfair things in this world.	• My Higher Power helped me find peace of mind when I went through the legal situation with Ted. • My son has to find his own destiny; I can help if I detach with love but don't try to control.		

Table 1-3

Frames of Reference of Each Character

CHARACTER	EXPERIENTIAL PERSPECTIVE	PROFESSIONAL PERSPECTIVE	LAY PERSPECTIVE
Sally Jones	• Self-help group for women with breast cancer	• Nuclear physicist	• Husband • Surgeon's son • Attorney • Secretary
Bill Jones	• Husband of woman who has had a mastectomy; attends support group	• Attorney with a specialty in drunk-driving cases	• Self-help group for women with breast cancer • Surgeon's son • Physicist • Surgeon • Secretary
James Smith	• Al-Anon member; father of son arrested for drunk driving	• Oncology surgeon	• Self-help group for women with breast cancer • Patient's husband • Physicist • Attorney • Secretary
Mary Ryan	• Al-Anon member; mother of son arrested for drunk driving	• Legal secretary	• Self-help group for women with breast cancer • Patient's husband • Physicist • Attorney • Surgeon

that categorization is a gross distortion of reality. The central implication that is of interest here is that both the experiential and professional perspectives are specialized and limited in relation to the focal problems about which a person is knowledgeable; this fact affects the mode of helping that a person with such perspectives can provide.

FEATURES OF EXPERIENTIAL KNOWLEDGE

Learning from the process of living through an event is, of course, a universal and undoubtedly major form of learning for everyone. It is probably the oldest form of learning used by human beings.

Such experiential learning is certainly a large part of professional training. Students in colleges and universities have fieldwork, internships, laboratory courses, and other experiential exercises that allow them to test themselves personally and to practice their future occupational work. Professionals continue to learn from their occupational experiences on the job. Occupationally based practice is, however, done within the context of the professional frame of reference.

If everybody learns experientially, why should self-helpers be singled out and why should their learning by doing be defined as experiential learning and knowledge? Here, the term is reserved for a special class of learning for several reasons. First, self-helpers explicitly rely on their own and their peers' experience. Their lived experience occupies center stage; it is not incidental to an occupation. Second, their experiential learning becomes a source of authority and power that is independent of other aspects, in contrast to the experiential knowledge of professionals, which translates into authority and power within their professional roles, not separate from them. Third, self-helpers recognize and respond to their peers' experiential authority and power, although they do not have a name for it or a language to talk about it. Fourth, since the way the knowledge is shaped and disseminated is distinctive, this form of knowledge has its own characteristics. Fifth, since it is largely unrecognized and unnamed among professionals, it needs to be singled out and discussed so the phenomenon can become visible and understood. Experiential knowledge is a descriptive name.

Are self-help groups the only places where this experiential knowledge can be generated? Certainly not. It is developed in a number of contexts. Many of the social movements of the 1960s and 1970s were noteworthy for having generated extensive experiential knowledge and perspectives among their adherents.

One reason participants of these movements no longer trusted or had confidence in the major institutions and their leaders—the government, the military, medicine, the mass media, and so on—was that they recognized the erosion of the legal and moral authority of these institutions. Young people especially could no longer accept other people's authority on the basis of their legal positions or their credentials. They challenged people in positions of power, especially the male power establishment. Things have never been the same. People who were young in the 1960s are now in their thirties and forties and are themselves in positions of influence.

If the established authority was challenged and rejected, what filled the vacuum? Whose advice and counsel seemed sensible to consider? And what was its basis?

The movements not only developed but legitimated among their participants a source of knowledge and authority different from the predominant legal-bureaucratic, scientific, or professional sources. This same phenomenon is seen across the various social movements of that era, and its influence continues.

DEVELOPING AND USING EXPERIENTIAL KNOWLEDGE IN SELF-HELP GROUPS

How do self-help groups develop and transmit experiential knowledge about their shared situation? Persons who are in a similar predicament but are unconnected to each other do not automatically or necessarily have any useful information to bring to bear on it. Especially in a new or unfamiliar situation, they are likely to depend on their regular support system or experts to interpret and cope with the situation.

Self-help groups, however, are significantly different from a collection of unconnected persons who are in an unfamiliar situation with little or no information about it. Successful, established self-help groups create, test, use, and disseminate a body of experiential knowledge about their shared problem and a workable resolution for it. In this sense, they are more fruitfully regarded as *experiential learning communities* than human services delivery systems.

Self-help groups are constantly developing and testing their perspectives about their problem and its resolution, which are referred to as templates (function 1). Simultaneously, they are applying and using that information and perspective from the group to cope with their problem (function 2). The first function, developing knowledge, is analogous to research scientists who develop new knowledge in medicine, social science, and technology. The second function is analogous to professional practitioners who apply knowledge when they provide services to clients.

The professional literature about self-help groups has focused on the second function almost to the exclusion of the first function. Thus, the literature views members of groups as learning to change their cognitions and behaviors, but it ignores the fact that what they learn (the templates) has been developed within and by the group.

Functioning self-help groups are, in effect, communities in which persons who face a similar predicament can come together voluntarily to learn about their predicament and its resolution from peers who are trying different ways of being and living with the predicament. Established groups have created a (1) template of the focal problem and (2) a template for its resolution. The *group* develops these templates and transmits them to its members. The templates are referred to by other names in the literature; for example, Antze (1976) called them ideologies and Medvene (Chapter 6, this volume) called them cognitions and behaviors.

WELL-DEVELOPED VERSUS FLEDGLING GROUPS

The group is the primary level at which the perspective of the problem and its resolution are developed, applied by members, and transmitted to others. Therefore, self-help groups need to be distinguished by the extent to which they have developed a perspective of the problem and its resolution that works for their particular members. Well-developed groups like AA need to be distinguished from fledgling local groups that do not have a workable perspective on their problem or its resolution (Weber, 1982). The differences in templates for the same issue (being overweight or having a problem with alcohol) can be easily seen if several groups for the same problem are examined carefully about their concept of the problem and its resolution. For example, Weight Watchers and Overeaters Anonymous (OA) both deal with overweight people. Weight Watchers views the problem primarily as a matter of dieting to lose weight and then maintaining the loss; it publishes a number of books of recipes for members. OA views the problem in much broader terms, recognizing its emotional, spiritual, mental, and physical aspects. Resolution depends on a food plan plus large-scale changes in one's way of living.

The OA literature includes the Big Book (based on *Alcoholics Anonymous*) and other books on the Twelve Traditions and Twelve Steps to recovery. OA does not publish recipes or talk about specific foods.

NEWCOMERS VERSUS VETERANS

Since learning from one's experience is a process that requires reflection, living time, and communication about one's experience, newcomers to a problem need to be distinguished from veterans who have had the time, opportunity, and motivation to test different ways of viewing their problem and its resolution. Established functioning groups usually contain a mixture of members at different phases of the experiential learning process. The members learn from each other like students in a one-room schoolhouse, where all eight grades are together. The most critical element in the learning process is the mixture of members, from newcomers to old timers, since so much learning occurs by living example (role models). Fledgling groups that contain only newcomers face extensive problems in learning.

Some professionals are concerned that self-help groups are made up of lay people, all of whom have the same problem but who know nothing. That situation is unlikely in a self-help group unless the group is new and has no templates for its problem and the resolution of the problem, the available templates do not work to the members' satisfaction, or only newcomers are thrown together to resolve the problem. Professionals often put cohorts of beginners together— patients who have just been diagnosed with diabetes or alcohol and drug addicts who are in treatment for the first time, for example. Often these same professional programs discourage the alumni (who are veterans with experiential knowledge) from interacting with the novices; in doing so, they cut off an excellent means for the newcomers to learn from the old-timers.

The fact that self-help groups are experiential learning communities that create, apply, and disseminate an experiential perspective and knowledge to members and to other people raises a series of major issues, some of which are briefly introduced in the following pages. Thirteen hallmarks of experiential learning communities and the learning process used in them are listed. A thorough examination of the pertinent issues would require an entire book.

HALLMARKS OF SELF-HELP GROUPS

The following list of 13 aspects of self-help groups represents a beginning, not an exhaustive, list:

1 The knowledge and frame of reference are developed among a group of people who share a common problem or predicament, not by people individually. Later, when the frame of reference is well established, an individual could develop the consciousness by reflecting on his or her experience in light of books about it or conversations with other experientialists.

2 How are the knowledge and frame of reference developed? A sociological process of several phases is started when individuals tell their personal stories to their peers in the first person, sharing their experiences, especially their pain, struggles, and feelings. The stories tend to relate the personal situation to the larger context in which it developed. (The process by which subjective information is transformed through the group process into "objectified subjective" information is described by Berger and Luckmann [1967].)

3 The individual stories include what the group members are trying or have tried to overcome the difficulties, resolve the problem, or learn to live with its reality. Thus, the members share their strength and hope with each other. Often this process can change an individual's perspective or consciousness about the problem, not only the objective circumstance. For example, a person may shed the role of victim, or a terminally ill patient may undergo a marked change in perspective that changes the quality of his or her life and relationships with others.

Complaining, whining, and self-pity ("poor me," "woe is me," or "ain't it awful") may be found in the early phases but not in a positive resolution of the predicament.

4 The members take personal responsibility for resolving their problem or changing their consciousness but with the aid of their peers. They may not assume responsibility for having caused the problem but may challenge other persons as being responsible for having caused it.

This process of taking personal responsibility within a context of mutual help empowers many self-helpers and movement people to trust what they know from their experience as interpreted by the group. Belonging to a like-minded community of peers who understand what one is going through because they are experiencing it also helps one to become empowered.

5 In the process of sharing their personal stories with their peers, the members identify the commonalities and idiosyncrasies of their experiences. Similarly, they test in their lives ideas for changing their awareness and problem solving and assess the ideas with the group (check them out with their learning community). The stories of the veterans of the problem represent a class of stories of that group that are not unique or idiosyncratic (although elements of individuality are likely to be found as well).

6 Much of the learning and awareness in the stories are in the emotional sphere, not just the cognitive or intellectual spheres. Probably many people do not think of feelings as information or knowledge. Emotions are often segregated in a place with no name. But the feelings of personally lived situations are critical. Emotional knowledge is not just how you felt when you went through the various phases of a problem but how you got the motivation to address the problem honestly and take responsibility to do something about it— how you got energized to delve into this painful or problematic situation and solve the problem. Feelings are part of the language of the heart or a language of being that are similar among peers who have talked with each other about their common predicament.

7 The existential, philosophical, or transcendental meanings of their experiences are of great interest and concern to group members. Sometimes these issues are expressed in religious terms, but more often in this secular society, the philosophical issue of why this happened to the person and the like are not framed in terms of religion. An alternative framework for the Twelve-Step groups is to discuss it in terms of spiritual concerns.

8 The raw experience of an individual has to undergo a reflexive process before it is changed into experiential knowledge. Just having gone through a situation does not ensure that the individual learns from it (Borkman, 1976). Experiential knowledge, as used here, connotes that one has undergone a reflexive internalized process that resulted in some awareness of the situation.

9 Experiential influence is demonstrated primarily in action; it is not just talked about. A role model whose actions one can observe or who demonstrates the idea in his or her own life is more influential to the newcomer than is a person who just gives advice. Therefore, such maxims as "Practice what you preach"; "Don't give advice if you are not following it yourself"; and "Utilize, don't analyze" apply.

10 A "culture" or idioculture (Fine, 1979; Ridgeway, 1983) is likely to develop if the groups persist over time. Since the experiential knowledge and consciousness they develop are grounded in their common experiences, which have been developed in a collectivity, the members are likely to develop a common language (use terminology and understand jokes, for example, that bystanders do not know about or understand).

11 Part of the resolution of the problem may involve a change in identity. The "cultural rights" of people with that problem are asserted, and they refashion their name, identity, and characteristics into others that are likely to be different from the stigmatizing stereotypes of the society at large.

12 Often the individuals extend their concern to other people like themselves who are not members of their collectivity. They may become advocates to overcome stereotypes, injustice, discrimination, intolerance, and stigmata, but the scope of that concern varies considerably. Some groups are specific. For example, divorced wives of military men protest the restrictive rules that exclude them from certain military pension benefits, but they do not fight for the general reform of all pension programs. Or proponents of natural childbirth protest the "medicalization" of pregnancy—the treatment of pregnancy as a medical problem, not as a natural life event. But the natural childbirth advocates are not general reformers who protest against all dehumanizing forms of medical treatment or even all problems with gynecologists-obstetricians.

Obviously, groups that are concerned with general reforms are more in the spirit and action of the typical political-interest groups (Hicks & Borkman, 1988). For example, the Grey Panthers advocate for better health insurance for all older people, not just for members of their group or for a certain category of old people.

13 Bystanders and outsiders cannot necessarily understand or appreciate the experiential perspective and knowledge of a group. Bystanders bring their own frames of reference to viewing others, which may preclude them from listening to what the experientialists are saying. Moreover, they may misinterpret much of the experientialists' use of the language of the heart. Outsiders, especially professionals, often assume that intelligence is conveyed primarily as rational, objective third-person knowledge, not as a first-person narrative.

Is it possible for bystanders to be so empathic that they develop vicarious experiential knowledge—that is, they understand how the people feel, what their concerns are, and so forth? Certainly, some people seem to develop vicarious experiential knowledge. However, many people quickly claim that they have such knowledge, but it is not apparent to an experientialist. For example, professionals develop extensive bystander knowledge about living with a disease (problem) and its treatment (resolution) from observing, questioning, and providing services to their clients. This bystander knowledge is not the same as experiential knowledge. Some professionals confuse the two and claim they have experiential knowledge when they do not.

EXPERIENTIAL MODES OF HELPING

What is common and what is distinctive about the experientialists' mode of helping in comparison to that of lay persons and professionals? This complex issue can be introduced but not thoroughly covered here.

Persons with *any* of the three perspectives can provide some forms of help, although they may not do so in practice. For example, many kinds of practical aid, such as driving a person to a clinic, could be done by a professional, an experientialist, or a lay person. In practice, however, most professional jobs are structured and highly delimited so that professionals only give specialized help to clients. To distinguish what types of help people with the three perspectives *could* give from what they *do give* in specific cases is an empirical issue. Litwak (1985) examined the kinds of help that different primary groups and formal service providers can and do provide. Following his view, this author believes that all the perspectives have common modes of help, as well as distinctive features of help. In other words, there is an overlap in both the kinds of help as well as the distinctiveness of the help, as shown in Figure 1-1.

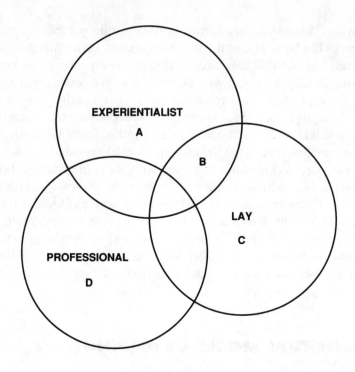

Figure 1-1   Three Frames of Reference

The general principle that Litwak (1985, p. 36) followed is that "groups will most effectively handle those tasks that are consistent with their structure." Primary groups, such as friends, neighbors, or extended family members, are classified by their structural dimensions (size, long-term commitment, affection, proximity, and so on). Tasks are then categorized by which dimensions are required to perform them (for example, borrowing "sugar" requires proximity). By comparing the requirements of a task with the dimensions of a group, one can identify which tasks are suitable for which group. This approach would be helpful in determining which tasks a self-help group could provide by empirically identifying the group's structural characteristics and comparing it with Litwak's list of tasks.

Litwak's approach would allow one to determine the forms of helping that self-help groups theoretically have in common (sector B in Figure 1-1) with families, friends, and the like, since they are all primary groups. For example, Powell (1987) pointed out that the roles of families, friends, and self-help groups are structured to be extensively available and accessible to their members or role partners.

However, Litwak's approach ignores the special experiential knowledge and perspective of the self-helper. The experiential knowledge that is developed in self-help groups is a form of specialized information and understanding that cannot be duplicated by professionals or lay social supports. Forms of help that are based on experiential knowledge and perspectives would be those that are distinctive to self-help groups. Some distinctive kinds of help from self-helpers are

■ The special bonds that form among self-helpers that lead to emotional support for the common problem.

■ Emotional reassurance of a special kind ("I've been there, too"; "You are not alone"; "You are not unique").

■ Role modeling by a veteran self-helper who manifests his or her way of resolving the problem by the way he or she lives. This form of help can provide hope and motivation to the veteran's peers that neither professionals nor lay people can give.

■ The experientialist's assessment of the applicability of professional knowledge to one's life.

■ Advocacy by experientialists who can represent the perspectives, interests, and concerns of their peers.

These preliminary ideas need to be expanded after additional analytical work is done to map out this key area. Empirical research needs to be done to establish the kinds of help that various self-help groups give.

REFERENCES

Alibrandi, L. A. (1978). The folk psychotherapy of Alcoholics Anonymous. In S. Zimberg, J. Wallace, & S. B. Blume (Eds.), *Practical approaches to alcoholism psychotherapy* (pp. 163–180). New York: Plenum Press.

Antze, P. (1976). The role of ideologies in peer psychotherapy groups. *Journal of Applied Behavioral Science, 12,* 323–346.

Bell, D. (1973). *The coming of post-industrial society.* New York: Basic Books.

Berger, P. L., & Luckmann, T. (1967). *The social construction of reality: A treatise in the sociology of knowledge.* Garden City, NY: Doubleday Anchor Books.

Borkman, T. (1976). Experiential knowledge: A new concept for the analysis of self-help groups. *Social Service Review, 50,* 445–456.

Borkman, T. (1984). Mutual self-help groups: Strengthening the selectively unsupportive personal and community networks of their members. In A. Gortner & F. Riessman (Eds.), *The self-help revolution* (pp. 205–215). New York: Human Sciences Press.

Fine, G. A. (1979). Small groups and culture creation: The idioculture of Little League baseball teams. *American Sociological Review, 44,* 733–745.

Gottlieb, B. H. (Ed.). (1981). *Social networks and social support.* Beverly Hills, CA: Sage Publications.

Hicks, F. M., & Borkman, T. (1988, September 3). *Self-help groups and political empowerment.* Paper delivered at the annual meeting of the American Political Science Association, Washington, DC.

Holzner, B., & Marx, J. H. (1979). *Knowledge application: The knowledge system in society.* Boston: Allyn & Bacon.

Hurvitz, N. (1974). Peer self-help psychotherapy groups: Psychotherapy without psychotherapists. In P. Roman & H. M. Ince (Eds.), *The sociology of psychotherapy.* New York: Jason Aronson.

Katz, A. H., & Bender, E. I. (Eds.). (1976). *The strength in us: Self-help groups in the modern world.* New York: New Viewpoints.

Killilea, M. (1976). Mutual help organizations: Interpretations in the literature. In G. Caplan & M. Killilea (Eds.), *Support systems and mutual help: Multidisciplinary explorations.* New York: Grune & Stratton.

Litwak, E. (1985). *Helping the elderly.* New York: Guilford Press.

Mowrer, O. H. (1964). *The new group therapy.* New York: D. Van Nostrand.

Powell, T. J. (1987). *Self-help organizations and professional practice.* Silver Spring, MD: National Association of Social Workers, Inc.

Ridgeway, C. L. (1983). *The dynamics of small groups.* New York: St. Martin's Press.

Robinson, D., & Henry, S. (1977). *Self-help and health: Mutual aid for modern problems.* London: Martin Robertson.

Starr, P. (1982). *The social transformation of American medicine.* New York: Basic Books.

Toffler, A. (1980). *Future shock.* New York: Bantam.

Wagner, H. R. (Ed.). (1970). *Alfred Schutz: On phenomenology and social relations: Selected writings.* Chicago: University of Chicago Press.

Weber, G. H. (1982). Self-help and beliefs. In G. H. Weber & L. M. Cohen (Eds.), *Beliefs and self-help: Cross-cultural perspectives and approaches* (pp. 13–30). New York: Human Sciences Press.

2

SELF-HELP, PROFESSIONAL HELP, AND INFORMAL HELP
Competing or Complementary Systems?

THOMAS J. POWELL

When most people are feeling blue, lonely, upset by family, or troubled by their work or school situations, they do not call on their psychotherapist. Even the majority of those with diagnosable mental disorders visit mental health specialists less than once every 6 months, according to the findings of the epidemiological catchment-area study of more than 9,000 persons in New Haven, Connecticut; St. Louis; and Baltimore (Shapiro et al., 1984). Only 39 percent of the persons with schizophrenic disorders had visited mental health specialists in the past 6 months. The percentage of those with other disorders who had visited specialists during that time was even lower: only 19 percent of those with major mood disorders, 25 percent of those with antisocial personality disorders (no indication of how many were voluntary or how many returned), 15 percent of those with anxiety disorders, and 10 percent of those with substance-abuse disorders.

Although the majority of people with problems are not running to mental health specialists, they are striving to cope. They make use of a variety of nonprofessional helping methods—some of them solitary. Prayer and private reflection or meditation are common methods. Black Americans report making frequent use of prayer to handle personal difficulties and, in this respect, they are only slightly ahead of white Americans (Neighbors & Jackson, 1984). No doubt, the use of prayer is part of looking to the church in times of trouble. But even before most people do so, they seek out their families, immediate

31

and extended (Veroff, Kulka, & Douvan, 1981). When they go beyond the family, they are most apt to seek out informal caregivers or general health care providers: physicians, nurses, clergy, teachers, co-workers, neighbors, friends, and other "natural helpers." Moreover, when they do seek out formal help, either professional help or self-help, it will usually be only because of the encouragement or at least the tacit approval of informal caregivers (Neighbors, 1984; Powell, 1981, 1987).

Perhaps it is no longer news that the majority of people who need help rely on informal methods more than on the formal mental health specialty system. But it is not so well known or even considered that when people do seek more formal help, they seem to seek out professional and self-help systems about equally. This is the reasonable conclusion that can be drawn from comparing help-seeking statistics from a general population (Lieberman, 1986) and service statistics from a database of the National Institute of Mental Health (NIMH) (Witkin, Atay, Fell, & Manderscheid, 1987). Extrapolating from a representative sample of the metropolitan Chicago population, Lieberman estimated that 6 million to 15 million people across the country participate in self-help groups. The NIMH statistics reported by Witkin et al. (1987) indicated that about 5 million people use inpatient, partial care, and outpatient services in specialty mental health organizations (mental hospitals, psychiatric wards of general hospitals, clinics, and community mental health centers). It is true that the specialty subsystem is only one of the professional subsystems that provide services. But even if the services provided by the other formal systems, the general health care system, and the chemical-dependence treatment system could be added, the relative percentage served by the formal self-help system would no doubt still be substantial.

More and more people seem to be using self-help and professional systems simultaneously. Furthermore, some professionals now view participation in a self-help program as an integral part of the overall treatment (Kurtz, Mann, & Chambon, 1987). The trend toward a more integrated use of self-help programs has not gone unnoticed by policymakers and professionals. Some view the explosive growth of professional chemical-dependency rehabilitation centers, arguably the fastest growing sector in the human services, as a partial response to the demand created by self-help organizations. And the professional organizations, in turn, or, more accurately, in back-and-forth transaction, have had an enormous impact on chemical dependence–related self-help organizations. Some may wonder, however, how these changes could occur, since Twelve-Step organizations, like Alcoholics Anonymous (AA), restrict the advocacy activities of their members. But these restrictions are often misunderstood and exaggerated. These organizations do not restrict the advocacy activities of members as long as the members do not identify themselves as members or claim to be speaking for their self-help organizations.

On the encouragement side, the self-help organizations provide a forum in which members can develop and clarify their views about gaps in services and counterproductive public policies (Ernie K., 1984). As the members' views mature and they become more confident as a result of the nurturing environment of the Twelve-Step program, they may go public, as citizens or as members of a separate organization, and advocate for more services or for changes in public policy. At the treatment level, chemical-dependency treatment centers rely heavily (some say too much) on self-help organizations for their programs. Time is set aside in the treatment program for regular self-help meetings led by volunteers from the outside. In other treatment programs, residents are transported to outside Twelve-Step meetings. Hence, to say that Twelve-Step organizations do not interact and promote professional services is to ignore all but the restriction against organized, public support for "outside causes." Alternatively, if one considers the members' private, behind-the-scenes activities or their leadership activities in related advocacy organizations and recalls that these interests were originally nurtured in the self-help organization, then it can be said that the Twelve-Step organizations play a substantial role with respect to professional services.

A watershed event in the interaction of self-help and professional organizations was the Surgeon General's Workshop on Self-Help and Public Health, held September 1987. The workshop was evidence of a growing acceptance of self-help programs by professionals and the general public. Its basic assumption was that both systems could benefit from additional interaction and coordination—an assumption that did not go unchallenged. There was a certain amount of suspicion that this proposal for a new public national agenda might contain some hidden items (see Chapter 15, this volume). Many of the participants, on both the professional and the self-help side, having suffered the Reagan administration's antipathy to human services, were suspicious of the real purpose of the workshop. As the workshop proceeded, however, it became harder to maintain this suspicion in the face of the thoughtful participation of Surgeon General C. Everett Koop.

Koop's political savvy had never been in doubt; when he began to recount his own experiences with self-help, he convinced many that the workshop was no mere effort to justify the administration's retreat from social responsibility by the magical incantation of self-help. Recalling his career as a pediatric surgeon, he noted how helpful it was for families to get together to discuss the impact of the child's illness and rehabilitation on the family. This experience led him to encourage families to form informal support groups. These were the formative experiences that sparked his interest in contributing to the development of a more formal and effective self-help movement. In a press conference after the workshop, Koop spoke in even more personal terms about self-help. He referred to what many in the workshop already knew. He had personally benefited from participation in Compassionate Friends following his son's death in an avalanche while mountain climbing.

If the workshop participants were prepared to accept the idea that both helping systems could benefit from interaction, they would not lie back while self-help services were substituted for professional services. Yet many recognized that substitution probably does occur to some extent (and thus should be studied), particularly in some health maintenance and other organizations that operate under strong incentives to lower the use of services. On balance, however, the evidence—including the earlier cited role of self-help in contributing to the demand for professional chemical-dependency services—points to a net effect in the opposite direction. This effect is a result, in part, of the awareness and motivation that self-help cultivates in its members to use professional services (National Institute of Alcoholism and Alcohol Abuse, 1983; Powell, 1979). Thus, although few will deny that there are pockets of conflict and competition between the self-help and professional-help systems, the overall effect seems to be complementary. The use of one system increases the probability of using the other system, and, more important, the use of the two together produces benefits that exceed those available from the use of a single system. This is the vision that inspired many of the follow-up activities of the surgeon general's workshop.

With this workshop as a symbol of the growing recognition of self-help and of the need for professional delivery systems to improve their coordination with self-help systems, this chapter discusses some of the means that can be used to coordinate these potential complementary systems. It proposes that these systems can complement each other when they are used simultaneously or before or after professional treatment. When it is used before professional treatment, self-help can be a kind of preparation for making better use of treatment; when it comes afterward, it can be a supportive environment in which to consolidate and extend the benefits of treatment.

To show how individuals can make discriminating use of these systems, this chapter presents some propositions about the conditions under which individuals may benefit from selective exposure to the distinctive characteristics of each of the three systems. The rationale for such an approach is that although each system shares a number of characteristics (organizational design, knowledge base, and so on) with each of the other systems, the nature of these characteristics is different for each system. Then it is assumed that different individuals or the same individual at different stages of coping will respond differently to these characteristics. In relation to the knowledge base, for example, some individuals may respond better to the experiential knowledge of the self-help system than to the more scientific, objective knowledge used in the professional system. However, it is even more likely that individuals could benefit from both kinds of knowledge for different aspects of their problem or in different stages of coping with their problem. A professional holding this point of view would be inclined to consider how he or she could assist the client to use both systems.

Yet this approach does not imply that direct contact between the professional and the other system is necessary and it certainly does not imply that the other system can substitute for professional services. Thus, its primary value is not as a means of dealing with dwindling resources. Nor does it view members of self-help organizations as nonprofessional helpers who can become "team" members once they have been "trained" by professionals. Such an approach is not compatible with the present conception of self-help as a formal helping system with its own distinctive knowledge base (Ballew, 1985; Hoch & Hemmens, 1987; Miller, 1985).

In the remainder of this chapter, the systems are compared in terms of the eight characteristics of each system. Each system, it is proposed, can be differentially helpful, depending on the overall configuration of an individual's problem, or for different aspects of a problem with which a single individual is afflicted.

CHARACTERISTICS OF THE THREE HELPING SYSTEMS

ORGANIZATIONAL BASE

Community caregivers typically do their helping informally, that is, without benefit of detailed norms or a formal organizational structure that encourages consistency in the way helping functions are carried out. Consequently, their activities are less likely to become standardized over time. One of the advantages of this lack of an explicit help-giving structure is that caregivers, such as co-workers, employers, neighbors, or coreligionists, may sometimes be able to help without the person who needs help even being aware, or at least having to acknowledge, that a helping process is operating. And it works the other way, too: Sometimes caregivers may be helpful without even being aware of it. Consider the restorative power of a neighbor's warm outreach, which neither party may interpret as anything beyond being neighborly.

The reliance of the informal system on the indirect and implicit may be especially advantageous when the individual does not wish to be reminded or constantly reminded—as she or he might say—of the need for help. This characteristic of the system is uniquely well suited to someone who does not want or is not able to acknowledge having a problem in the first place. It is important not to idealize this characteristic, however, because a realistic analysis will usually show that the informal system should not be the only resource if the individual is able to acknowledge his or her distress and could accept help. In such instances, the person who needs help would probably also benefit from using either or both the self-help and professional helping systems.

Insofar as there is a requirement that the problem should be formally acknowledged, the self-help system is closer to the professional system than to the informal system. This is one of the reasons the self-help system should not ordinarily be called an informal system. To be sure, there are exceptions, many of which are among the informal support groups and unaffiliated self-help groups (see Chapter 3, this volume). However, the typical Twelve-Step organizations or other well-developed organizations, such as Recovery, Inc., are more formal than are many professional organizations. They have explicit goals and a substantial, well-developed organization that is designed to achieve the goals. Their everyday activities are informed by a specific and detailed technology for achieving their goals. And if the definition of "formal organization" is keyed to the importance of a structured and explicit set of normative beliefs, guidelines for action, and actual procedures, these organizations might well be rated more formal than most of the professional organizations that offer generalized support or counseling services.

This is not to say there are no differences, however. One of the important differences is the sponsorship of the three types of organizations. Generally, the professional organization has a more public image owing to its support through taxes or public voluntary (United Way) contributions, whereas the others may seem more private and less open. Another important difference is the setting. Some people may feel more comfortable in a public setting or in a more personalized self-help setting. The reasons for these individual preferences may be, in one sense, as numerous as the people who seek help. Yet it may not be farfetched to imagine situations in which certain groups of persons may be inclined to judge one or the other more acceptable and accessible. Consider how some minority persons might feel. Notwithstanding the dismaying record of all helping systems in providing minorities with genuine assistance, it may be that minorities feel less estranged and more entitled to public-sector services (especially those that are tax supported) than to those offered by the self-help system. To the extent that this is so, it constitutes a great challenge to the self-help system.

FOCUS OF CONCERN

A young woman with spina bifida bursts out, "I don't want anything to do with those groups, I'm doing OK." Unfortunately, her defensiveness keeps her from realizing the enormous satisfaction she could gain from helping others in these groups while picking up a pointer or two that would be helpful in her own ongoing adaptation to her disability. Yet from another point of view, her refusal to participate is understandable because it says something about how uneasy most people become when they believe they are the only ones who need help. Surely, this belief is not surprising, but what many professionals fail to appreciate are the important differences among the systems with respect to who is defined as the focus of concern. Professional helping relationships are one-sided; they focus on the client as the one who needs help. Help via informal community systems also tends to be asymmetrical; it is not the caregiver or patron who is exposed and vulnerable, it is the patronized one.

For some, of course, these one-way relationships may be just the right prescription: "I can't be concerned with anyone else at least until I get help for myself." And beyond this, once again, there are probably countless reasons why particular individuals would not feel that it was an advantage to be in a situation in which they would be taking some responsibility—no matter how slight—for someone else. Yet, it should be recalled that the typical mutual-aid focus of self-help organizations has been found to be advantageous in other circumstances. Riessman and Gartner (1987) pointed out that cross-age tutoring and other lay helping activities tend to benefit the "helper" as much or more than they benefit the "recipient" of help. Nor are these benefits restricted to peer counselors. At some level, the awareness of possible similar benefits may be part of the constellation of motives that influences people to become professionally trained helpers. The upshot is to suggest that many people may find it desirable to become involved in self-help systems in which, gradually and at their own pace, they could enhance themselves through helping others.

KNOWLEDGE BASE

The usefulness with which people regard different kinds of knowledge depends on a number of factors. In some circumstances, only professional knowledge will do: "I want the best technical, science-based help available. I don't want to be confined by someone else's experience or limited by their prejudices. Furthermore, it does not matter whether I like the professional person; it only matters whether he or she has the technical knowledge and skills to help me out of this difficulty."

In other circumstances, the individual may be skeptical of the value of professional knowledge: "I want to know what those 'who've been there' have found to be the best way out. This is something that requires the help of someone who has had actual experience."

In still other circumstances, even the combination of professional knowledge and experiential knowledge will be insufficient. "This is an issue that is beyond the powers of both professionals and self-help groups. I need the advice of someone who has a track record for getting things done around here [in my company, school, or apartment complex]."

The differences in the attitudes about the kinds of knowledge needed raise the question about the circumstances under which each of these different kinds of knowledge would be relevant. The answer has a lot to do with making appropriate distinctions, similar to those called for in AA's Serenity Prayer. The Serenity Prayer refers to the "serenity to accept the things that I cannot change, courage to change the things I can, and the wisdom to know the difference." In the present instance, it is a matter of deciding which aspects of one's problem can best be addressed by which kinds of knowledge. No one would go to a self-help group to have surgery. But neither would one ignore the organized and accumulated experience that others have had with respect to the performance, maintenance, and longevity of the prostheses after one had certain types of surgery. Later, the know-how of an informal system might be called on to help the individual maintain her rights as an employee following a period of absence because of a disability. In such an instance, one needs to gain access to someone in the organization "who knows how this place works and can get things done." The odds are that such a person would have neither professional expertise nor personal experience with the disability.

It should be understood that the persons just referred to all have specialized knowledge, but in different spheres of problem solving. And, at least in the abstract, there is no a priori reason to place them in some hierarchical order of importance or to consider that one can substitute for the other. Moreover, since most problems manifest themselves in several different spheres, the optimum situation would be one in which the individual had simultaneous access to the different kinds of knowledge held by all three of these specialists.

BASES OF POWER

The predominant type of influence or power used in the three helping systems closely parallels their distinctive bases of knowledge. The referent power of the self-help leader parallels his or her special access to experiential knowledge. The expert power of the professional is linked to his or her technical knowledge. The social power of the informal helper is derived from his or her insider's knowledge about how particular settings work.

The referent power of the self-help leader is based on attraction and liking, which, in turn, are based on a perceived similarity between the successful old-timers (mentors) and the still-desperate newcomers. The mentor possesses a remarkably strong power that is based on "our being like you, having shared your experience, and, more generally, just being your kind of people." The mentor or sponsor uses this power by encouraging the newcomer "to refer to us, to compare yourself with us. Take special note of how badly off we were and how far we have come because you can come just as far. Yet, never forget that we need you, too; helping you keeps us from relapse by reminding us that we are just a slip [or a drink] away from that turmoil and misery of our previous lives. Follow our lead, then, because we were once like you [or, perhaps, worse], and it is because of this experience that we can offer you hope that you can become like us."

The newcomer's hope is aroused "because these people were like me and because they accept me even though they know who I am and what I've done. Despite everything, there may be hope for me yet." It is in this manner that referent power is exercised and in such a form that it can meet the needs of both the overwhelmed newcomer and the mentor who must remain ever vigilant. The hope aroused in the newcomer is palpable in the revival spirit of some self-help meetings (Stuart, 1977). Yet, it is balanced by a special kind of realism: "My peers in the ongoing struggle [or my partners in recovery] cannot be deceived by me. They know the score; they are insiders. They cannot be taken in or lured into becoming falsely 'supportive,' as my misguided friends and family sometimes are. They love me but they are tough."

Regardless of what the help seeker likes, sometimes it is important to have an expert on the case. The professional is an expert who can provide, or be a link to, whatever technical assistance is available. But even then, some problems, as was noted earlier, have aspects that are not amenable to the efforts of either technical experts or self-help specialists. With this kind of problem, community caregivers are needed who can wield social power and make legitimate demands on behalf of their protégés. These caregiver-patrons (employers, physicians, teachers, clergy, and so forth) may also be able to dispense rewards on behalf of the person who seeks their patronage (French & Raven, 1959). Most problems, it would seem, would be appropriate for judicious applications of these three types of power.

ROLE OF THE PROVIDER

Sometimes it is best to be explicit about one's need for help and to pay for it. It is cleaner that way. People who feel this way tend to prefer the professional system. But even these people occasionally feel, "Once in a while I'd like to see someone do something for me that they didn't get paid for. How can I feel worthwhile when I end up paying for something [friendship] others get free?" (Schofield, 1964). People who feel this way should consider adding a self-help program to their help-seeking activities. Those who have difficulty making an explicit request for help have the option to increase contact with selected informal helpers in the community caregiving system. Informal caregivers have the further advantage that they do not ordinarily charge for their services. Nonetheless, the potential cost to privacy of having an employer or pastor know about the problem cannot be overlooked. Sometimes the help seeker should decide that he or she is unable to afford the assistance of the potential patron.

ROLE OF THE PARTICIPANT

"Take what you like and leave the rest." With minor variations, this slogan is used by a number of self-help organizations. It is a fetching way to say that the member retains control. To be sure, the member is not free to challenge certain basic tenets about such matters as anonymity or confidentiality, but, nevertheless, the member retains a good deal of discretion. More positively, the member is enjoined to be self-directing within the mutual aid or fellowship structure of the organization. Yet he or she is not left to fend for himself or herself. The expectation is that the exact nature of each individual's participation will be worked out in a process of mutual interaction between that individual and other members of the organization. A number of options should become evident as this process unfolds within the context of a complex organization that requires diversity in its membership if it is to fill its many working niches. Thus, the individual can exercise considerable control over a mutual process that will determine how he or she will participate in the organization. And because the complex structure encourages different kinds of participation, the role of the member can be particularized in distinctive ways to suit the needs of the individual.

This openness stands in sharp contrast to the narrower definition of the client's role in the professional system. The professional system tends to be centered on self-disclosure, reflective discussion, and acquiring the resolve to think and do things differently. Its advantage is its clear focus on key problem-solving methods. Its disadvantage is its lack of options: There is one way, and it is the therapist's way. This is not to belittle the client's opportunity, indeed obligation, to "talk about whatever bothers you," but it is to highlight that it is the therapist who, however unobtrusively, defines the agenda, which calls for reflective talk about troubling issues with the express purpose of making this talk a point of departure for changing how the trouble is perceived or managed. And as befits a situation in which it is the client, not the therapist, who pays the fee, the professional system is characterized by a nonmutual, therapist-directed helping approach.

In the caregiving system, the participant's role is not so clear-cut. It depends on the type of caregiver. With a friend or neighbor, the nature of the help seeker's participation may reflect the individual's initial self-direction and subsequent mutual interactions with these persons. With the physician, teacher, or even clergy, it is likely to be different. These authorities are expected to give direction, and thus the process is not a reciprocal one. In thinking about how to interact with the potential helping systems, it may be important not to establish an automatic preference for one of these approaches. Instead, it may be better to think about a variety of person-problem-situation constellations in which one is likely to be more effective than another.

INPUTS

Systems run down without continual new inputs. To say that the self-help system is less dependent on money than is the professional system is not to say that it is free of concerns about input. One need only sit through a few listless, rambling self-help meetings, which are not a rare occurrence, to realize the truth of this ideologically discomfiting statement. It makes one acutely aware that the self-help system is dependent on "paybacks." These paybacks can be thought of as a variety of contributions from senior members that often take the general form of mentoring and organizational-development activities, which are based on the desire of the seasoned members to return to the organization some of what it has given them. It is sometimes sad to note that the availability and quality of these paybacks vary greatly from organization to organization and over time within the same organization. (As with everything else in self-help, the wide range of values for such variables reflects the voluntary nature of the organization and its utter dependence on the membership.) Still the ability of the self-help organization to be relatively independent of money can be a great advantage. It means that the volume of available services does not have to be closely tied to the availability of money. Members do not consume services in the sense of drawing against a fixed, exhaustible supply. Instead, they produce as they consume services, their consumption triggering mechanisms to produce services, hence, the term "prosumers" (Gartner & Riessman, 1977). The greatest threat to self-help may be that it will be used too little, not too much. Thus, the organizational imperative is to offer more service, not less. Unlike the professional and even the community caregiver systems, the self-help system will need to limit its helping activities only in unusual circumstances.

Another major advantage of the payback system is that the senior, successful members are retained by the organization to serve as models for the newcomers but are also able to use the affiliation to maintain their own gains. Sometimes concern is expressed, usually mistakenly, that these senior members are stunting their personal growth by their long-term "dependence" on the organization. To the contrary, many of these people have roles or jobs in the organization that challenge them far beyond any other social or vocational opportunities they may have. Like others who make a deep commitment to their church, union, neighborhood, community, or political organization, these people may create a satisfying and productive avocation for themselves within self-help organizations. And since it is not work—not something for which they need to be paid—they often perform their activities with a dedication seldom found in paid workers. It is only half in jest that they say that they could not be paid enough to do what they do for free.

The absence of this sense of personal obligation is one of the advantages of a fee system. Those who have sufficient means can pay for the service and then can get out. There are no additional obligations, no need to pay back. As far as the organization is concerned, money also has its advantages; it can be used to stabilize and enrich the services. A visible coordinating office can be rented, staff can be trained, clerical services can be purchased, brochures and marketing materials can be printed, and so on.

Like the self-help system, the informal caregiving system is not heavily dependent on out-of-pocket payments by the help seeker. The informal caregiver usually operates on some combination of altruism and personal liking for the help seeker. Without attempting to enumerate all the possible advantages and disadvantages of these arrangements, it may simply be noted that whatever the advantages of altruism, they are more likely to be evident in the short term than in the long term.

The self-interested desire to maintain a social system should be distinguished from altruism. For many caregivers, this desire is an inextricable part of their motivation. Employers, managers, teachers, and others who take a personal interest in their charges may do so, in part, to maintain the smooth and efficient operation of the workplace or educational institution. This double payoff is a strong attraction, but since the same action may not serve the best interests of both parties, it is the stuff out of which real or perceived conflicts of interest may arise. Therefore, some help seekers will choose to avoid situations in which there is even a possibility that their interests may be compromised by persons with another agenda.

SPECIFICITY OF FUNCTION

The specificity of the system can be an important consideration for help seekers. Some people do not want to engage in a broad-ranging exploration that they fear will stir up unnecessary trouble. Others start with the belief that it is naive to attempt to encapsulate problems in tight little compartments; instead, they are more inclined to believe that "everything is related to everything else." The former would find a highly specific system more congenial and the latter would be more comfortable in one that does not make highly specific assumptions about how the problem is to be defined or resolved. Some people, of course, start in one place and end up in another. Initially, some may seek a highly specific system only to discover, after immersing themselves in it, that the problem has more manifestations, more roots, and potentially more ways of being dealt with than they had at first anticipated. Many self-help organizations are able to accommodate to this evolving pattern. AA and Overeaters Anonymous lend themselves to the person who is motivated to see them as possessing a high degree of specificity. This specificity is reflected in their slogans: "Abstinence for today"; "Three meals a day with nothing in between"; "Identify, don't compare"; "Utilize, don't analyze"; and "One day at a time" are the seemingly simple and specific watchwords of these organizations. Yet as members gain a measure of control over the acute problem and are able to appreciate some of the program's more subtle insights, they learn that "Thin is not necessarily well" and that "Abstinence is not sobriety." They also hear about working on "character defects," and, coincidentally, they will find it harder to view their problems in highly specific and simple terms.

Many self-help organizations have a great capacity to accommodate to these changing interests. At first, the members are welcome to consider that the problem is just their addiction, their physical illness, their disturbing family member, or whatever. However, when they are ready to see more, that more human option is also available.

In the professional system, the help seeker may feel pressured to accept the idea that the solution will involve more than dealing with the initial presenting problem. To some, this idea will be unacceptable, and to many more, it will be off-putting. Those at the other end of the spectrum may perceive the self-help system, rightly or wrongly, as too superficial and too narrow. They may value the broader and less-specific approach of the professional system. For them, the objective often is not to allow themselves to postpone giving up the first drink or the next binge until "therapy causes something significant to happen."

The community caregiving system is more difficult to categorize in terms of the degree of specificity that characterizes its activities. It is even more variable than the by-no-means uniform self-help and professional systems. Neighbors and friends, for example, may be involved in generally caring actions that are not highly specific to the problem. However, the family physician or employer may offer highly specific help. This variability also suggests that no one level of specificity should be automatically preferred over another; instead, the task is to make appropriate matches between the help seeker's multiple needs and the three helping systems. Table 2-1 provides a convenient means to compare the variation in the characteristics of the three systems.

COORDINATING THE THREE SYSTEMS

Getting help is a process that usually involves more than one of the helping systems. Yet, many human services professionals have a myopic view of how real people get support and help in actual communities. In thinking they can be an adequate answer to the need for help, professionals succumb to the universal tendency to adjust reality to their own fields of vision. To begin with, many professionals and self-help leaders fail to appreciate that if it were not for the informal system, most clients and self-help members would not even have reached or stayed with their specialized forms of help.

Table 2-1

Characteristics of the Three Helping Systems

CHARACTERISTICS	SELF-HELP SYSTEM	PROFESSIONAL SYSTEM	COMMUNITY CAREGIVING SYSTEM
Organizational design	Formal	Formal	Informal
Focus of concern	Self and others	Self only	Self only
Knowledge base	Experiential	Professional	Social (insider)
Type of power	Referent	Expert	Social, legiti-mate, reward
Role of provider	Volunteer, explicit	Paid, explicit	Unpaid or indirectly paid, implicit
Role of participant	Mutual, self-directed	Nonmutual, other directed	Mutuality and direction vary (for example, physician versus friend)
Inputs	Paybacks	Fees	Altruism, maintenance
Functional specificity	At first high, then low	Medium	Variable

Once the person has reached the professional system, the professional needs to consider how to bring the other helping systems into play. He or she needs to consider that the other two systems have the potential to intensify the professional experience. These other systems may do so by affirming the importance of the professional service or by contributing grist to its mill. They can also be marketing areas for piloting the newly developed products of therapy. The self-help system should be explicitly dealt with in the therapy, whether it was experienced before therapy, is occurring during the professional service, or is planned as a follow-up to the service. Ideally, of course, all clients of professional helpers would participate in help-seeking activities with the other two helping systems. Ideally, too, all the members of self-help groups would participate in the other two systems. However, the informal system is different; a majority of those who participate in the informal system are not likely to need to consider participating in either the self-help or the professional system.

But concern with these three systems must go beyond simply encouraging their use. Professionals (and other formal and informal providers of care) need to become more discerning about which aspects of the problems they encounter are best addressed by which systems. Under what circumstances, for example, will an individual be most responsive to the experiential character of the self-help system, to the one-way processes of the professional system, or to the social resources available through the informal system? Thus, the goal must be a more precise matching of the client's needs and interests with the different characteristics of the three helping systems. This matching should be considered an ongoing dynamic operation, for as most people move through different stages of coping, they will show parallel changes in their response to different aspects of the three systems. For example, few neophyte copers would be likely to benefit from holding a leadership position in a self-help group. However, the seasoned coper may find the same leadership position to be a lifesaver. What must ever be kept in mind is that these helping systems will flourish only if their professional and self-help agents are careful not to compromise the integrity of their systems. If the integrity of the systems is compromised, they will have been robbed of the characteristics that make them powerful helping systems.

REFERENCES

Ballew, J. R. (1985). Role of natural helpers in preventing child abuse and neglect, *Social Work 30*(1), 37–41.

Ernie K. (1984). *90 meetings, 90 days: A journal of experience, strength, and hope.* Minneapolis, MN: Johnston Institute.

French, J. R. P., & Raven, B. (1959). The bases of social power. In D. Cartwright (Ed.), *Studies in social power.* Ann Arbor: Institute for Social Research, University of Michigan.

Gartner, A., & Riessman, F. (1977). *Self-help in the human services.* San Francisco: Jossey-Bass.

Hoch, C., & Hemmens, G. C. (1987). Linking informal and formal help: Conflict along the continuum of care. *Social Service Review, 61,* 432–445.

Kurtz, L. F., Mann, K. B., & Chambon, A. (1987). Linking between social workers and mental health mutual-aid groups. *Social Work in Health Care, 13*(1), 69–78.

Lieberman, M. (1986). Self-help groups and psychiatry. *American Psychiatric Association Annual Review, 5,* 744–760.

Miller, P. A. (1985). Professional use of lay resources. *Social Work, 30*(5), 409–416.

National Institute of Alcoholism and Alcohol Abuse. (1983, February 1). Growth of A.A. treatment cited over past 15 years. *NIAA Information and Feature Service (IFS 104),* 2.

Neighbors, H. W. (1984). Professional help use among black Americans: Implications for unmet need. *American Journal of Community Psychology, 12*(5), 551–566.

Neighbors, H. W., & Jackson, J. S. (1984). The use of informal and formal help: Four patterns of illness behavior in the Black community. *American Journal of Community Psychology, 12*(6), 629–644.

Powell, T. J. (1979). Comparisons between self-help groups and professional services. *Social Casework, 60,* 561–565.

Powell, T. J. (1981). The impact of social network on help-seeking behavior. *Social Work, 26*(4), 335–337.

Powell, T. J. (1987). *Self-help organizations and professional practice.* Silver Spring, MD: National Association of Social Workers, Inc.

Riessman, F., & Gartner, A. (1987). The surgeon general and the self-help ethos. *Social Policy, 18*(2), 23–25.

Schofield, W. (1964). *Psychotherapy: The purchase of friendship.* Englewood Cliffs, NJ: Prentice-Hall.

Shapiro, S., Skinner, E. A., Kessler, L. G., Von Korff, M., German, P. S., Tischler, G. L., Leaf, P. J., Benham, L., Cottler, L., & Regier, D. A. (1984). Utilization of health and mental health services. *Archives of General Psychiatry, 41*(10), 971–978.

Stuart, R. B. (1977). Self-help for self management. In R. B. Stuart (Ed.), *Behavioral self-management.* New York: Brunner/Mazel.

Veroff, J., Kulka, R., & Douvan, E. (1981). *Mental health in America: Patterns in help seeking from 1957 to 1966.* New York: Basic Books.

Witkin, M. J., Atay, J. E., Fell, A. S., & Manderscheid, R. W. (1987). Specialty mental health system characteristics. In R. W. Manderscheid & S. A. Barrett (Eds.), *Mental health, United States, 1987* (pp. 15–20). Washington, DC: U.S. Government Printing Office.

3

DIFFERENCES BETWEEN NATIONAL SELF-HELP ORGANIZATIONS AND LOCAL SELF-HELP GROUPS: Implications for Members and Professionals

THOMAS J. POWELL

Unaffiliated, simply structured, local self-help groups (LSHGs) appeal to the same kinds of people as do the affiliated, more complexly structured, national self-help organizations (NSHOs). LSHGs reach out to people with a broad range of difficulties, including, for example, spouses of chemically dependent persons, parents who are concerned about child abuse, single parents, and the families of persons with serious mental illnesses. People in similar situations may also choose to participate in NSHOs, such as Al-Anon, Parents Anonymous, Parents without Partners, and the Alliance for the Mentally Ill. The question is, Which one, the NSHO or the LSHG, is likely to be of greater benefit to its members? This question has important implications for professionals who refer clients to these units. The implications are compounded for clearinghouses and self-help centers that have assumed a broad mission to work with self-help units and must, therefore, establish priorities about which ones they will work with and in relation to what issues. Most of all, perhaps, it is a crucial question for self-help leaders who are involved in continuous efforts to develop their programs.

At the outset, it should be understood that there are many differences between self-help units beyond whether they fall into the NSHO or LSHG category. Consequently, this chapter does not argue that the differences between these categories outweigh all other differences. Nonetheless, this admittedly simple dichotomous concept can serve a useful analytic purpose. For practical purposes, it needs to be considered along with other factors. The choice of self-help unit should take into account a variety of factors that will receive little attention here, including the personal preferences of the prospective member and the accessibility and quality of the local program. These and other factors may well outweigh the differences between the NSHO and the LSHG in particular situations.

Within these limits, it is argued here that the NSHO—a chapter or group that is affiliated with an NSHO—offers its members greater benefits than does the unaffiliated LSHG because of its more highly developed program. Its more highly developed program is a result of its accumulated experience and the regular input of supportive communication from its organizational network, which includes other chapters or groups that are operating in a similar context. The chapters or groups in the network share goals, beliefs about personal change or coping, norms or guidelines for action, and protocols for conducting meetings and transacting business. Much of this information is funneled to the chapters through the coordinating efforts of the national office. The national network, which is coordinated by a central office, encourages individual members to consider themselves part of a large external community—a community that can be a means to become more self-accepting and a source of experiential wisdom, the insights of people who have been "there" (see Chapter 1, this volume; Powell, 1975). And in a tangible way, it is a group that can be contacted for concrete support and specific information.

Another feature of the NSHO—its relative permanency—tends to produce a structure that develops and promotes shared beliefs about conditions that are helpful and harmful to its members. Furthermore, it encourages stabilizing norms and procedures that give the program further definition and strength. These features of the NSHO inspire confidence in the members and provide a basis for channeling unfocused energy and controlling the inevitable, though it is hoped infrequent, distracting and disruptive impulses of some members. Still further, the multiple objectives of the organization (recruitment, publication of a newsletter, public relations, interchapter coordination, and the like) encourage a structure that provides for a considerable variety of differentiated roles. Thus, the NSHO can accommodate—and, indeed, must seek out—a diverse range of members who can fill these organizational niches. Last, leadership is structured within the NSHO in a way that offers newcomers greater access to seasoned members who are models of the very patterns of successful coping that the organization encourages.

SELF-HELP ORGANIZATIONS VERSUS BUREAUCRACIES

To suggest that self-help activities can flourish within a formal organizational structure may evoke the skepticism especially of those who think of organizations only as bureaucracies. Such people adhere to the popular image of organizations as highly centralized, tightly regulated bureaucracies whose remote leaders are more interested in ensuring compliance with the rules than in promoting the well-being of their members. In keeping with this image, members of bureaucracies (employees) comply because they are paid to do so, and even if their immediate compensation does not depend on doing so, they believe that their future raises and promotions will depend on their compliance. To the extent that bureaucracies adequately compensate their members for their efforts, they can operate impersonally, indifferent to the needs and interests of individual members. But, clearly, this is not how NSHOs work, and if this chapter touted this classic conception of bureaucracy as the model of organization that is most likely to be supportive of self-help, it would be proposing something that is indeed antithetical to self-help (Gartner & Riessman, 1982; Katz, 1981).

Nonetheless, although the model of organization on which this analysis rests is not a bureaucratic one, all organizations share certain common features with bureaucracies (Katz & Kahn, 1978). They have a strong orientation to goals that is supported by a systematic program that, in turn, is developed and maintained by a differentiated or complex structure. However, self-help organizations are unlike bureaucracies in that they are voluntary organizations operating in a flexible manner according to egalitarian and humanistic values. Thus, they are like a number of newer and more recently conceptualized forms of organization that differ from classic bureaucracies in that they do not rely on wages or economic incentives to obtain compliance. Instead, they rely on the moral commitment of their members to their goals or mission (Etzioni, 1975). Their members subscribe voluntarily to the norms of the organization because they personally identify with its mission. Consequently, tight vertical control is unnecessary and would be counterproductive. To the contrary, the primary direction of chapter ties is not upward to some headquarters but horizontal to other NSHO chapters and to their coordinating or general service office.

Consistent with the horizontal orientation among chapters, the substructures within chapters are aligned on an approximately equal plane, with the membership making most decisions by consent. In sharp contrast to the classic bureaucratic pattern, the members relate by engaging in face-to-face interaction and in keeping with the charge to adjust their interactions to their own needs and interests. From their earliest contacts, members are encouraged to "take what you like and leave the rest." This emphasis on the individual means that self-help organizations are anything but impersonal, even though they are regulated and made more enduring by formal guidelines.

Another feature that effectively counters any tendency toward NSHOs adopting a bureaucratic model of operation is their wide geographic dispersion. This distance, especially when combined with the few sanctions available to the central office, means that the total organization functions more like a federation of autonomous units than a bureaucracy. In summary, then, the local NSHOs can be thought of as largely autonomous units, "staffed" by volunteers, whose members engage in close personal relationships while making decisions at the level of primary action—the chapter level (Perrow, 1970). The overriding commitment of NSHOs to humanistic values and flexible operations means there is little resemblance between them and the tightly held subsidiaries of large business corporations (Rogers & Whetten, 1981).

ADVANTAGES OF AN ORGANIZATIONAL DESIGN

Still, it may be asked, Why retain the term "organization" if it is so open to misunderstanding? The reason is that the concept of organization tends to inspire stronger self-help units. The advantages of an organizational design can be considered under several headings.

BETTER-DEVELOPED PROGRAMS

Without structure, the self-help unit (and its program) is at a greater risk of remaining an underdeveloped, fledgling group of limited effectiveness. According to Weber (1982, pp. 22–23):

> [Fledgling] groups are characterized by tentative interpersonal relationships, limited sharing of norms and beliefs, and initial organizational and program activities such as arranging and conducting meetings, developing group goals, and choosing leaders. Fledgling groups may develop into well-organized ones . . . provided they develop an overriding ideology, an inspired leadership, a meaningful program for members, a strong emotional loyalty among members, and common norms and beliefs.

NSHOs are more likely to be full-fledged programs. In the beginning, it may be argued, it is possible to go too far and impose unnecessary rules and detailed procedures on the program. But, in general, this is not the weakness of self-help programs, which are more likely to suffer from underdevelopment. In only a few cases, such as Recovery, Inc., and Reach to Recovery, has there even been speculation that they are in danger of becoming less responsive because of overly detailed procedures and rigid policies (Raiff, 1982; Wechsler, 1960). Weber (1982, p. 16) again provided a succinct summary of the essential elements of what he called "well-organized groups":

> [They] consist of a number of individuals who share a common set of beliefs or norms regulating their behavior, in matters of consequence to the group. Moreover, the status and role relationships of the members are stable, particularly at a given time. Morale, solidarity or cohesiveness, and loyalty of the members are typically high.

Among the best-known examples of beliefs and norms that regulate behavior are those embedded in the "steps" and "traditions" of Twelve-Step organizations, such as Alcoholics Anonymous (AA). However, these well-known organizations are not the only ones that have converted their accumulated wisdom into norms and procedures. And all who have done so have highlighted the basic elements of their programs. Over time, these basic norms and procedures become increasingly comprehensive and tightly linked to the goals of the organizations as a result of their constant development and refinement. These organizations' evident insight about various aspects of their members' difficulties often convinces prospective members to give the programs a try.

The underdevelopment of LSHGs stems partly from their isolation, a condition NSHOs counteract with their regular substantive and morale-sustaining communication with the national office and other chapters. The benefits of a national communication network were noted by Toseland and Hacker (1982, p. 345) in their study of self-help programs in upper New York State:

> They provided the [NSHO] groups with a sense of community and a national perspective that the [LSHG] groups lacked. Through newsletters, pamphlets, and other communication channels, the national associations provided leadership and helped local groups maintain their focus and direction. Representatives from the regional and national offices of the associations met with the local self-help groups to present new information, innovations, changes in policy, and consultation on needs or problems specific to the local group. Groups that did not belong to state and national associations were often more dependent on the largess, encouragement and direction of a church, community center, or social service agency for their continued functioning than were groups that were members of a national or state association.

STABILITY AND PREDICTABILITY

Well-developed norms and procedures contribute to the stability of the organization and to its predictability for the individual member. They can also give meaning to otherwise ambiguous events and indicate the path of recovery and successful coping (Dewar, Whetten, & Boje, 1980; Hall, 1982). But even before that, they establish the preconditions for improvement. The link between organizational performance and personal well-being was explicated by Maton (1988, p. 56) as follows:

> Some minimal set of rules and norms, whether formal or informal, is necessary to maintain an orderly flow of sharing, discussion, and support at meetings, especially considering the usually high level of member distress. When order and organization are lacking, it can be expected that monopolization of discussion, negative or judgmental feedback, discontinuity in focus, and other maladaptive group process features will be present. Thus, order and organization and member well-being and group appraisal likely are related.

Maton's other point is that norms and rules tend to limit individual actions that may otherwise result in tangential or disruptive behavior. Norms and rules counteract this possibility by encouraging the establishment of a community in which members have well-defined and accepted responsibilities and privileges. It does not matter (or it matters less than elsewhere) that members are ranked differently in prestige by the larger society. In the organization, these differences are muted and harmony is fostered by the transcendent norm that principles take precedence over personalities. And faithful to its own norm, the organization is structured so that the members who embody these principles are the ones who are most apt to receive the esteem of their peers.

This indifference to status in the larger society, sometimes called "impersonality," is not to be confused with bureaucratic coldness or detachment. Actually, the "impersonal" guidelines, which are both the cause and effect of the organizational structure, are more likely to have an opposite impact. Individuals may be less threatened by close ties when the ties are regulated by certain normative practices. Buddy or mentoring relationships often work better when both parties are protected by formal "sponsorship" guidelines, which lessen the risk of impropriety while raising the participants' confidence that they can benefit from a close relationship without it going further than they want it to go or can manage. The ongoing refinement of these structural arrangements seems to be an ingredient in the success of such mature organizations as Recovery, Inc., and the many Twelve-Step organizations that model themselves on AA. The stability that results not only makes the organization predictable for the individual, but it allows the organization to engage in controlled testing of possible program developments.

DIVERSE MEMBERSHIP

Narrow-minded exclusionary practices, to which groups sometimes fall prey, are also discouraged by the multiple objectives of the NSHO. To attain these objectives, the NSHO must continually recruit new members, improve public relations, resolve grievances, publish newsletters, negotiate with professionals, and maintain communications among groups and with the national office. These functions require people in differentiated roles. They call for people with heterogenous interests and specialized skills (Van de Ven & Ferry, 1980). And there are never enough such people; the organization is perpetually understaffed. For example, consider the "bodies"—the very word suggests the value assigned to almost anyone—it takes to manage the mundane tasks of getting out a mailing, finding a meeting place, setting up the meeting room, arranging the coffee and refreshments, and cleaning up. No wonder, then, that the organization is inclined to welcome everyone who can help or who even promises to help at a later time. In this situation, tolerance of diversity and acceptance of individual differences are encouraged (Knoke, 1981). Given their constantly understaffed condition, NSHOs can ill afford to turn away willing participants even if they are "a little weird," "different from us" (read "from a lower class or different ethnic group"), "too talkative," or "too quiet." This dynamic counters parochial tendencies and fits well with the requirement that different people (and at different times, the same people) need to participate in different activities and at different levels of intensity (Hasenfeld, 1983; Hasenfeld & English, 1974; Thompson, 1967).

LEADERSHIP STRUCTURE

Another advantage of the NSHO is associated with its leadership structure. To ensure the organization for future members, the NSHO must retain and promote seasoned members to leadership roles. The opportunity to lead is considered a privilege, but it can be given a twist of obligation as it was when one NSHO member declared, "There are two reasons to participate in a self-help group: because you need it or because it needs you." And the needs are without end; there are lists (manual and computerized) to be updated, contacts to be made, sessions to be planned, transportation to be arranged, bookkeeping to be done, and on and on. Even so, members are warned not to neglect their primary personal work and if that seems to be happening, despite the warning, fellow members will remind them to pull back, invoking well-accepted norms against overinvolvement in organizational tasks. AA and other like organizations commonly caution against "twelfth step" work that is undertaken too soon or at the expense of personal work.

Referent Power

The way leadership is structured in NSHOs gives leaders a distinctive power. Although both the LSHGs and NSHOs make use of peer assistance, the NSHOs are more firmly committed to the primacy of experiential knowledge, which is being continuously developed by those like "ourselves" (Borkman, 1984). The LSHG cannot make this same claim credible if it is open to "professional facilitators." When a self-help unit opens itself to a facilitator, it squanders much of its potential for referent power by conferring high status on someone who does not share the central experience of the membership (French & Raven, 1968). NSHO leaders naturally share that experience because they have been "there," while the professional facilitators of LSHGs do not because they have not. An exception to the frequently negative effect of professionals' participation in self-help programs seems to occur in LSHGs that are organized around physical illness. When illness is concerned, the participation of professionals seems to have a salutary effect because of the technical information the professionals provide and the opportunities they can make available to pursue changes in the arrangements for medical care (see Chapter 15, this volume; Chesler & Barbarin, 1987). Another reason is that the more technically defined role of the medical provider makes him or her less likely to compete for influence with the self-help leaders.

In NSHOs, novices have much greater access to successful models than in other helping situations, including professionally facilitated groups that do not utilize the members' peers as ongoing primary leaders. Access is further enhanced by the value attached to NSHO leaders being both "givers" and "receivers" (see Chapter 1, this volume). Leaders make it plain that their own recovery or "making it" depends on giving it away, and with no one to give it away to, it would not be possible to continue "making it." A little later they may talk about the need to be reminded how miserable they were not so long ago and how easy it would be to slip back without such reminders (Ernie K., 1984). In this way the commitment of the veteran reinforces the hope of the novice, and vice versa. From a slightly different perspective, this is the climate in which helper-therapy relationships thrive (Riessman, 1965).

This point of view was well summarized by Gellman (1964, p. 135), who wrote of AA as organization therapy:

> In essence the entire program is an ameliorative device, and *participation by the alcoholic in any phase of the organization's activities is theoretically an integral part of his recovery and rehabilitation*. As a therapeutic agency Alcoholics Anonymous is intrinsically distinctive. It has usually been categorized as a form of group psychotherapy; yet it transcends the orthodox forms of treatment in certain respects. Alcoholics Anonymous is fundamentally *"organization therapy"* involving the structure and processes of the total social system of the association. [Italics added.]

Just as many problems have been substituted for alcohol in the canon of other Twelve-Step organizations (for instance, compulsive eating in Overeaters Anonymous [OA] or compulsive gambling in Gamblers Anonymous), so could many other organizations be substituted for AA in Gellman's passage. Many other organizations—such as Parents without Partners; Recovery, Inc.; Compassionate Friends (CF), for parents who have experienced the death of a child; Candlelighters, for parents of children with cancer; and the Alliance for the Mentally Ill—can also provide organization therapy.

LIMITS TO THE ADVANTAGES OF NSHOs

There are, of course, limits to the advantages of NSHOs. NSHOs will have no advantage when, for example, the national office promulgates unwise policies, imposes unnecessary restrictions, or requires excessive dues from local chapters. NSHOs also will not benefit individuals who fare better when they are free from certain aspects of organizational life. For instance, those who tend to become overly involved in organizations may fare better in a simpler LSHG program, as may those who believe that the multistranded relationships of NSHOs are more likely to be entangling than enriching. From their point of view, the opportunity to engage in reciprocal helping is, at the least, an unnecessary chore.

But going beyond these considerations of individual style and preference, there are instances in which the hypothesized advantages of the NSHO will not apply to whole groups of people. One of the primary instances is when the NSHO is compared with a culturally relevant LSHG. Separated and divorced Roman Catholics, for example, may derive more benefit from a church support group over the "organizationally richer" program of Parents without Partners. The Catholic LSHG may be perceived as offering more meaningful, value-congruent relationships than may the culturally neutral NSHO. The LSHG may be viewed as being likely to possess more acceptable remedies or the capacity to modify the member's reluctance to embrace a less desirable one. Similar considerations may explain the appeal of Dignity to Episcopalians who are homosexual or of Integrity, to their Roman Catholic counterparts. When these ethnic/cultural considerations are salient, they can imbue the LSHG with more meaning and intensity than the NSHO. Weber (1982, p. 17) put it simply: "When religion, race, or nationality become major elements in the composition of an ethnic group, the group's integration and solidarity is likely to be particularly close."

This feeling of closeness and solidarity would seem to account for much of the spectacular growth of a weight-loss group for black people in Detroit called Eat Right and Slim Easily (ERASE). In its 32 weekly meetings, which attract 1,000 participants, the message of ERASE is that "diets [are] all geared to the foods white people eat. Most of the things we as Blacks like to eat, we're taught, are fattening. That's not true. Mustard and collard greens . . . cornbread" ("Detroit Women," 1983).

Nevertheless, the success of an LSHG like ERASE is no argument against an LSHG working toward full-fledged NSHO status. Indeed, a culturally relevant NSHO should prove superior to a similarly relevant LSHG. It would be able to take advantage of its organizational capabilities, as well as its ethnic and religious identity. The importance of organization was noted by the National Black Women's Health Project (1987, p. 3) this way:

> Fundamental to the structure of membership is better organization at the grass-roots level. It is important that self-help chapters in all stages of development relate to the National Office as a standard for structuring their own work and as a readily available source of technical assistance at the outset of their formation. By working with women within their own environment, they are provided a supportive atmosphere that allows them

to trust their own perception of themselves, learn together, and emerge with a new sense of power.

Another indication that this is a viable way to operate can be seen in the example set by some of the best-established NSHOs (for example, AA; Recovery, Inc.; and Parents Anonymous), which started out as LSHGs. Women for Sobriety is a recent example of a crossover from LSHG to NSHO status. In crossing over, it took a major step toward institutionalizing its feminist cultural identity.

Although much more empirical research needs to be done to test the hypothesis of the advantages of the NSHO, two studies have added to the knowledge of the effects of organizational design on self-help programs (Leventhal, Maton, & Madara, 1988; Maton, 1988). In their study of nearly 3,000 self-help groups in New Jersey, Leventhal, Maton, and Madara found that the vast majority, some 90 percent of the groups, were "affiliated groups," or NSHOs. The "death" or discontinuation rate of NSHOs was below that of the "independent groups," or LSHGs. However, when the NSHOs that were affiliated with AA were eliminated from the analysis, the NSHOs were no longer superior. These findings, it should be emphasized, speak not to the issue of which type of program is likely to be most valuable for its members but to the issue of which is more likely to survive. Still it seems reasonable to suppose that many of the expired groups were so short lived that they would not have had time to develop strong programs. Another contribution of this study is the suggestion that affiliation should be understood in a larger context. Rather than thinking of affiliation with national organizations as the primary factor, it may be more useful to think of the availability of outside information and energy as the primary factor, regardless of its source. For besides what is available from the "nationals," the NSHOs' sustaining inputs are also available from what the authors called systemic organizational supports, namely, self-help clearinghouses, foundations, human services agencies, hospitals, and churches.

A study by Maton (1988) provided additional information that is relevant to the hypothesized advantages of the NSHO. Maton studied 15 groups, 5 each from OA, CF, and a multiple sclerosis (MS) organization. He looked at the effect on members of role differentiation ("Different members are in charge of different aspects of group functioning") and of order and organization ("There is a great deal of confusion in this group at times"). He found that OA members reported more role differentiation than did MS members, and CF members reported more order and organization in the group than did MS members. Also, both OA and CF members reported greater benefits from their participation in the groups than did MS members.

In a separate analysis, Maton (1988) estimated the effect (using multiple regression analysis) of the variables of role differentiation and order and organization on outcome variables while controlling for the type of group (OA, CF, or MS). For all 15 groups, he found that role differentiation was negatively correlated with depression and positively correlated with self-esteem. Order and organization was positively correlated with greater benefits from the group. Maton (p. 73) commented that the benefits of differentiation were consistent with the view that "meaningful roles for members may contribute to benefits and satisfaction by enhancing commitment, self-efficacy, and social rewards." He went on to say that the findings regarding order and organization were

> consistent with the view that an organized, ordered group environment is important to provide boundaries, facilitate trust and sharing, and enhance group viability over time. Disorder and disorganization in a group, manifested in members interrupting each other, monopolizing conversation, or proceeding in unpredictable fashion from one task to another, likely would limit a group's effectiveness and impact. (p. 74)

Although Maton's study provides support for the hypothesized advantages of the NSHO, it also suggests that the magnitude of the advantages is likely to vary by the type of NSHO (OA, CF, or MS). Furthermore, within a particular NSHO, the individual NSHO chapters are likely to vary in their effectiveness. Part of their effectiveness will depend on how efficient they are in utilizing the resources of the national coordinating office and the other chapters within their NSHO type or family. Table 3-1 summarizes the effects of the organizational differences between NSHOs and LSHGs.

IMPLICATIONS FOR PROFESSIONAL PRACTICE

In considering the criteria to be used in making referrals to self-help programs, professionals must not limit themselves to the

Table 3-1

The Effects of the Organizational Differences between NSHOs and LSHGs

ORGANIZATIONAL DIFFERENCES	EFFECTS	
	NSHO	LSHG
Accumulated experience	Developed program	Fledgling program
External inputs	More energy	Less energy
Membership networks	Greater sense of belonging	Less sense of belonging
Role differentiation	More diverse members	Less-diverse members
Development of norms	Better-regulated program	Less-regulated program
Structural differentiation	More stable program	Less-stable program
Number of objectives	More leadership opportunities	Fewer leadership opportunities
Relationship to professionals	Reference power uncompromised	Reference power compromised more often by the participation of professionals
Leadership structure	More seasoned models	Fewer seasoned models

differences between NSHOs and LSHGs. First, they should consider the preferences of the potential member and, more broadly, what he or she could accept if there were a good reason to do so. What the potential member will accept as a definition of the problem, as a possible remedy, as a meeting format, and as the practice for member-to-member contacts between formal sessions will go a long way toward defining the outer boundaries within which the selection of a self-help program can be made. Second, having established these boundaries, professionals should take into account such mundane but important considerations as the location and time of meetings. Thus, the more professionals are informed about the history, current leadership, and functioning of the potential self-help programs, the more they can help the prospective members assess their situation against these criteria.

A second set of criteria to be used in making referrals centers on the potential user's strengths and vulnerabilities. Some persons have little tolerance for ambiguous programs; they may feel threatened by a loss of self-control in loosely structured programs. On the program side, self-help units will vary in their tolerance for people with different degrees and kinds of social impairment. For example, some may be better able to tolerate the silent observation of passive members, while others may not be bothered by occasional, loosely connected, or "off-the-wall" remarks. Except for the more structured way such difficulties are handled in the NSHO, these criteria do not favor either the NSHO or the LSHG. Thus, the NSHO should not be an automatic first choice; it should be a first choice only if other considerations are not more important to a particular person.

But even when a specific NSHO proves to be the first choice, it may not be available in the person's community. At this point, a number of options need to be considered. One would be to take advantage of the tremendous versatility of broad-purpose NSHOs, such as AA; Al-Anon; Recovery, Inc.; Parents without Partners; and Parents Anonymous. These are some of the organizations that have worked successfully with people in a variety of problem situations. Parents Anonymous, for example, includes members who range from those who are simply worried about their adequacy as parents to those who have seriously harmed their children. Al-Anon has had long and successful experience with people of different socioeconomic backgrounds who define and strive to cope with their problems in markedly different ways; its only requirement is that the prospective member has a friend or family member with an alcohol problem. (What a great many difficulties this simple requirement includes.)

AA also is keyed to alcohol and it, too, has proved flexible in accommodating other problems, although as is true of all these organizations, its flexibility will vary from chapter to chapter. At different times and places, AA meetings have accommodated people with a variety of addictions and compulsions in addition to alcohol. Some chapters are now extending a special welcome to recovering mentally ill persons who are also alcoholics and are doing so with a special understanding of their need for psychotropic medication. In fact, AA's Twelve Steps are such a versatile, effective tool for handling a variety of problems that they have been successfully adapted by other organizations, including Emotions Anonymous, Narcotics

Anonymous, OA, and Gamblers Anonymous). Of the other types of programs, Recovery, Inc., is one that includes a broad spectrum of members. It has been a valuable resource for those who, at one end, suffer from a serious mental illness and those who, at the other end, suffer no discernible impairment, though they experience significant personal distress.

When referral to one of the broad-purpose NSHOs (or even to an LSHG) is not a viable option, the professional should consider various organizational-development strategies to increase the availability of self-help resources. Professionals have often been instrumental in getting local NSHO chapters established. The national or coordinating office of the NSHO frequently supports professionals (and others who request assistance) by furnishing "starter kits," which typically contain a manual, brochures, recommended recruitment strategies, and procedures for announcing the time and place of meetings. Sometimes they also facilitate linkages with experienced resource-members in nearby communities. Such persons can play an important role in the first few meetings and, for a limited period, they may agree to form the nucleus of the new chapter. Over the long term, they may agree to be available to consult with the founders of the new chapter.

Although another strategy is to work with a fledgling or even not-so-fledgling LSHG, care should be taken not to give this option priority over working with an NSHO. If professionals are to play a constructive role, they must ensure that they do not divert public or professional attention from the numerically superior and often-stronger programs of the NSHOs. This is a concern because some professionals, particularly clearinghouse staff, seem predisposed to work with LSHGs, rather than with new chapters of NSHOs (Leventhal et al., 1988). Sometimes this orientation is justified and sometimes it is not. The well-established NSHOs, such as AA, Al-Anon, and Recovery, Inc., may have less need for the help of professionals in developing new chapters than do the LSHGs. But even so, the clients of the professionals need these NSHOs. Thus, professionals should try to develop organizational ties with NSHOs and to seize opportunities to appreciate their work publicly (Levy, 1978). Some justification for working with LSHGs is the lack of well-established NSHO alternatives for people with certain problems, such as the victims of acquired immune deficiency syndrome and adult survivors of childhood sexual abuse. This situation is also evident in the health care sector, where new groups that are concerned with rare genetic and chronic diseases are cropping up at a phenomenal rate and are asking for assistance. It is hoped that many of these fledgling groups will aspire to become NSHO-type programs as a result of professional intervention.

The foregoing suggests that the decision about whether to work with an LSHG may rest, in part, on some estimate of the likelihood that it is a potential candidate to become an ongoing, formal, externally networked organization—that is, an NSHO. If this possibility is broached in the beginning, the professional will be free to highlight opportunities to become a more permanent, externally networked NSHO. Such a course seems to be natural and desirable for the huge number of isolated and underdeveloped LSHGs that are concerned with medical and emotional problems (Leventhal et al., 1988). If they started on this course, they would be following the lead of many present-day NSHOs, such as Recovery, Inc., and Parents Anonymous, which used professionals in their formative years to make the transition from LSHG to NSHO status. Although these and other NSHOs, such as AA, Take Off Pounds Sensibly, and Ostomy Clubs (Borman, 1979; Wheat, 1980), made significant use of professionals, they did so—and this is the crucial point—for a limited time. Therefore, contemporary professionals need to communicate that their initially intense and broad-ranging collaboration in the formative stages will become narrower and more discretionary over time. They must make it known—after they first convince themselves—that as the organization develops, they will scale back their involvement, especially in the internal affairs of the organization. The need to be chary of control, however, should not be construed as an argument for noninvolvement. Indeed, the dominant trend is in the other direction: The burgeoning number of clearinghouses at all levels evidently represents an institutional recognition of the need for more professional involvement with self-help (see Chapter 13, this volume). This is no guarantee, however, that these clearinghouses will engage in appropriate activities with self-help units.

Starting with the least-risky activities, it is appropriate for the clearinghouses to assist individual help seekers to find suitable self-help programs. A parallel, but perhaps more systematic, program may be developed to help professionals who are looking for information for their clients. Next, clearinghouses should consider a number of options in expanding their already important role in providing technical assistance to self-help programs. They might, for instance, develop modules based on the practices of established NSHOs that could be adapted to the purposes of fledgling LSHGs. Modules might be prepared in the areas of goals, organizational designs, program activities, funding strategies, incorporating procedures, obtaining nonprofit and tax-exempt status, leadership plans, and recruitment strategies, to cite a few examples. As an LSHG develops, clearinghouse professionals could also help assess the pros and cons of the LSHG either affiliating with an existing NSHO or becoming one on its own. In this way, clearinghouses could maintain a better balance between NSHOs and LSHGs and enhance their credibility with NSHOs. As it stands, they are sometimes perceived (correctly) as developing LSHGs to compete with existing NSHOs.

Ideally, some of these activities and functions will be shifted to a national self-help center, such as was envisioned by the Surgeon General's Workshop on Self-Help and Public Health, held September 1987 (see Chapter 15, this volume). But even then, because of their local character, many of these functions would have to be carried out by state and regional mutual-help centers and clearinghouses.

At the local level, professionals in clearinghouses and other settings should also consider not reaching out to something that is there, that is, not working with an existing LSHG, but starting an NSHO chapter from scratch. The opportunity to tailor the new chapter to local circumstances may be a sufficient incentive to undertake such a project. And though it has been done all too infrequently, precedents exist for tailoring NSHO chapters to local ethnic, social-class, and problem-solving styles. For example, Lofland and Le Jeune (1960) reported on a number of AA meetings that were organized along ethnic and class lines. Today, nearly every large community has AA chapters that offer a special welcome to persons who are black, gay, health professionals, recovering mentally ill patients, students, and the like. The homogeneity of membership that results in such chapters has at least two happy consequences: It enhances the cohesion of the chapter while adding diversity to the overall membership of AA.

Too few professionals, however, are aware of the actual and potential diversity of NSHOs. Their damning faint praise: "It's alright for . . . ," which is usually a code for "it is rarely right for my clients," allows them to dismiss NSHOs without having to take responsibility for their conduct. Such narrow-mindedness, no doubt, deprives many help seekers of beneficial experiences.

This analysis suggests that one of the first steps that professionals must take to become more organizationally sensitive in their interactions with self-help programs is to reconsider how they should allocate their resources between LSHGs and NSHOs. This analysis also raises questions about whether professional involvement in the day-to-day operations of even fledgling LSHGs is compatible with maintaining the distinctive features of both the professional and self-help methods of assistance. The effectiveness of both professional and self-help services may benefit if more emphasis is placed on the exchange of consultation and technical assistance (Powell & Miller, 1982). Self-help leaders could provide information about the cultural context of the problem-situation and increase the capacity of professionals to gain access to and develop meaningful working ties with their target population. Professionals could help self-help groups obtain access to the mass media and funding sources and, in a more direct way, facilitate the members' access to specialized treatment services. However, to avoid encouraging undesirable dependence, which is often a great danger for self-help programs, these exchanges should be based on explicit, arranged-from-the-beginning plans for disengaging from these collaborative agreements. Levy and his associates (see Wollert, Knight, & Levy, 1980) used this approach in their successful organizational development project, Make Today Count. They helped this NSHO for the terminally ill clarify its purpose, conduct more effective meetings, and resolve issues of eligibility for membership and did so within explicit timelines. Wollert, Barron, and M. (1982) and Wollert, Levy, and Knight (1982) developed this approach further and demonstrated that NSHOs may welcome assistance with such tasks as recruiting members, improving coordination, creating program materials, and raising funds. In so doing, they have indicated a direction in which professionals in clearinghouses and in other settings may become more involved with NSHOs that deserves a more complete exploration.

REFERENCES

Borkman, T. (1984). Mutual self-help groups: Strengthening the selectively unsuppor-
tive personal and community networks of their members. In A. Gartner & F.
Riessman (Eds.), *The self-help revolution* (pp. 205–216). New York: Human
Sciences Press.

Borman, L. D. (1979). Characteristics of development and growth. In M. A. Lieberman
& L. D. Borman (Eds.), *Self-help groups for coping with crisis.* San Francisco:
Jossey-Bass.

Chesler, M., & Barbarin, O. A. (1987). *Childhood cancer and the family.* New York:
Brunner/Mazel.

Detroit women help blacks lose pounds. (1983, February 28). *Milwaukee Sentinel,* p. 8.

Dewar, R., Whetten, D., & Boje, D. (1980). An examination of the reliability and validity
of the Aiken and Hage Scales of centralization, formalization, and task
routineness. *Administrative Science Quarterly, 25,* 120–128.

Ernie, K. (1984). *90 meetings, 90 days: A journal of experience, strength, and hope.*
Minneapolis, MN: Johnston Institute.

Etzioni, A. (1975). *A comparative analysis of complex organizations* (rev. ed.). New
York: Free Press.

French, J. R. P., & Raven, B. (1968). The bases of social power. In D. Cartwright & A.
Zander (Eds.), *Group dynamics* (3rd ed.). New York: Harper & Row.

Gartner, A., & Riessman, F. (1982). Self-help and mental health. *Hospital and
Community Psychiatry, 33,* 631–635.

Gellman, I. P. (1964). *The sober alcoholic: An organizational analysis of Alcoholics
Anonymous.* New Haven, CT: College & University Press.

Hall, R. H. (1982). *Organizations: Structure and process* (3rd ed., chaps. 4 & 5).
Englewood Cliffs, NJ: Prentice-Hall.

Hasenfeld, Y. (1983). *Human service organizations.* Englewood Cliffs, NJ: Prentice-
Hall.

Hasenfeld, Y., & English, R. A. (1974). *Human service organizations: A book of
readings.* Ann Arbor: University of Michigan Press.

Katz, A. H. (1981). Self-help and mutual aid. *Annual Review of Sociology, 7,* 129–155.

Katz, D., & Kahn, R. (1978). *The social psychology of organizations* (2nd ed.). New
York: John Wiley & Sons.

Knoke, D. (1981). Commitment and detachment in voluntary associations. *American
Sociological Review, 46,* 141–158.

Leventhal, G. S., Maton, K. I., & Madara, E. J. (1988, October). Systemic organizational
support for self-help groups. *American Journal of Orthopsychiatry, 58*(4),
592–603.

Levy, L. H. (1978). Self-help groups viewed by mental health professionals: A survey
and comments. *American Journal of Community Psychology, 3,* 305–313.

Lofland, J. F., & Le Jeune, R. A. (1960). Initial interaction of newcomers in Alcoholics
Anonymous: A field experiment in class symbols and socialization. *Social
Problems, 8,* 102–111.

Maton, K. I. (1988). Social support, organizational characteristics, psychological well-
being, and group appraisal in three self-help group populations. *American
Journal of Community Psychology, 16*(1), 53–77.

National Black Women's Health Project. (1987). *Vital Statistics* (special brochure
issue), p. 7.

Perrow, C. (1970). *Organizational analysis: A sociological view.* Belmont, CA: Brooks/Cole.

Powell, T. J. (1975). The use of self-help groups as supportive reference communities. *American Journal of Orthopsychiatry, 45,* 756–764.

Powell, T. J., & Miller, G. P. (1982). Self-help groups as a source of support for the chronically mentally ill. In H. Fishman (Ed.), *Creativity and innovation.* Davis, CA: Pyramid Systems.

Raiff, N. R. (1982). Self-help participation and quality of life: A study of the staff of Recovery, Inc. *Prevention in Human Services, 1,* 79–89.

Riessman, F. (1965). The helper-therapy principle. *Social Work, 10,* 27–32.

Robinson, D. (1979). *Talking out of alcoholism: The self-help process of Alcoholics Anonymous.* London: Croom Helm.

Rogers, D. L., & Whetten, D. A. (1981). *Interorganizational coordination.* Ames: University of Iowa Press.

Thompson, J. D. (1967). *Organizations in action.* New York: McGraw-Hill.

Toseland, R. W., & Hacker, L. (1982). Self-help groups and professional involvement. *Social Work, 27,* 341–348.

Van de Ven, A. H., & Ferry, D. L. (1980). *Measuring and assessing organizations.* New York: John Wiley & Sons.

Weber, G. H. (1982). Self-help and beliefs. In G. H. Weber & L. M. Cohen (Eds.), *Beliefs and self-help* (pp. 13–20). New York: Human Sciences Press.

Wechsler, H. (1960). The self-help organization in the mental health field: Recovery, Inc., a case study. *Journal of Nervous and Mental Disease, 130,* 297–314.

Wheat, P. (1980). Hope for the children: A personal history of Parents Anonymous. Minneapolis, MN: Winston Press.

Wollert, R. W., Barron, N., & M., Bob. (1982). Parents United of Oregon: A self-help group for sexually abusive families. *Prevention in Human Services, 1,* 99–109.

Wollert, R. W., Knight, B., & Levy, L. H. (1980). Make Today Count: A collaborative model for professionals and self-help groups. *Professional Psychology, 1,* 130–138.

Wollert, R. W., Levy, L. H., & Knight, B. G. (1982). Help-giving in behavioral control and stress coping self-help groups. *Small Group Behavior, 13,* 204–218.

4

SOCIAL NETWORKS AND SELF-HELP ORGANIZATIONS

THOMAS J. POWELL

Concepts of social networks can provide insight into the causes and resolution of personal problems, particularly into how self-help programs can resolve these problems (Ell, 1984; Erickson, 1975; Fischer, 1982; Gottlieb, 1981; Maguire, 1980; Mueller, 1980). This chapter explicates how the relationships that are formed in a self-help program can serve to correct deficiencies in the person's network. Sometimes the new relationships are directly beneficial. At other times, the benefits of these newly formed relationships are indirect; that is, they are important not so much for themselves but for the changes they stimulate in relationships outside the self-help program. Thus, the new relationships that are formed in the self-help program may be richly rewarding and therapeutic in themselves or the necessary precursors to positive changes in more permanent and consequential external relationships, such as marital or work relationships (Froland, Pancoast, Chapman, & Kimboko, 1981; McIntyre, 1986; Pilisuk & Parks, 1981; Swenson, 1979; Turkat, 1980).

Throughout this chapter, participation in a self-help program should be understood as participation in a local chapter or meeting of a national self-help organization (NSHO), as was discussed in Chapter 3. The local chapters of such NSHOs as Alcoholics Anonymous (AA); Parents Anonymous (PA); Parents without Partners; Recovery, Inc.; and Stroke Clubs are hypothesized to be more fully developed and more effective than are their ad hoc, unaffiliated counterparts, local self-help groups (LSHGs). The accumulated experience of the NSHOs, it is hypothesized, usually enables them to develop more substantive and detailed policies, norms, and practices. The unaffiliated LSHGs, in contrast, are more likely to limp along with underdeveloped programs because of their inexperience and lack of access to supportive external inputs from other units doing the same work.

To most people, the term "networking" means little more than developing relationships with one's actual or potential contacts. Those who use it in this way are, for the most part, unaware of the insights that can be gained through the use of the analytic concept. The analytic concept can help one understand how certain characteristics of a person's relationships can influence the nature of the support available from these relationships (Hirsch, 1979; Tolsdorf, 1976; Wellman, 1983). Mitchell (1969, p. 2), in an often-cited definition, referred to "network" as a "specific set of linkages among a defined set of persons with the additional property that the characteristics of these linkages as a whole may be used to interpret the social behaviour of the persons involved." Each linkage or relationship, or the entire set of these relationships, can be described in terms of these characteristics. Differences in the values of these characteristics have been correlated with different levels of support (Gallo, 1984; Perrucci & Targ, 1981). Potasznik and Nelson (1984) showed that the benefits of a self-help program were related to certain characteristics of the network. They surveyed 56 members of the Families and Friends of Schizophrenics in southern Ontario, 59 percent of whom were positive about their participation in self-help. The parents who felt positively about their participation were significantly less burdened by the disruptive symptoms of their seriously mentally ill sons and daughters; they also felt "less anxiety, worry, depression, and guilt" about the person with mental illness ($r = -.33$, $p = <.01$). And apropos of the network, the supportiveness of the self-help group was correlated ($r = .43$, $p = <.01$) with the participant's total satisfaction with his or her network.

To get an idea of how improvements in participants' networks result from self-help programs, it would be useful to see how influences from formal self-help sessions carry over into other spheres (Powell, 1981). Then it would be possible to determine whether relationships that are formed inside self-help groups lead to alterations in existing relationships or new relationships in the spheres of family, friends, neighborhood, and workplace or school. Outside formal sessions, it would be desirable to track the extra-group, mutual-aid relationships that are encouraged by organizations, such as Families and Friends of Schizophrenics, not just those that take place within the formally scheduled self-help sessions (Maguire, 1981). Although some group psychotherapists have suggested that extra-group contacts detract from the formal sessions, just the opposite has been found in self-help programs. In separate studies of self-help organizations dealing with the elderly, grieving parents, and persons with physical illness or substance abuse problems, it has been shown that outside contacts and friendly relations contributed and sometimes were essential to the effectiveness of the NSHOs that were studied (Lieberman & Gourash, 1979; Maton, 1988; Chapter 8, this volume). Indeed, one might conclude from these studies that an individual's involvement in these "outside" contacts is an indication of his or her commitment to the self-help program.

CHARACTERISTICS OF THE NETWORK

More than a dozen characteristics have been conceptualized by network theorists. Because of their number and their sometimes overlapping references, it is usually neither feasible nor desirable to monitor them all. Those who try to collect comprehensive data incur the risk of ending up with large amounts of missing and unusable data from incorrectly filled-out forms. In practical applications, it is wise to exercise restraint and not try for too many ratings or for discriminations that are too fine. Although it may seem that this advice was quickly forgotten in the ensuing discussion of seven characteristics, there will be occasion to come back to it.

Once the major characteristics have been set forth, a basis will have been established for selecting a smaller number to use in studying self-help organizations. Of the seven to be discussed here, two of the characteristics refer to the network as a whole and five refer to its individual linkages (Barnes, 1972; Boissevain & Mitchell, 1973; Bott, 1971; Mitchell, 1969; Sokolovsky & Cohen, 1981; Wellman, 1983).

Size and density, characteristics of the whole or total set, are especially useful in getting a "big-picture" understanding of certain conditions that are addressed by self-help programs. For example, it is difficult to resist the temptation to use previously abused substances if one's network is largely populated by people who are chemically dependent. Similarly, the isolation of single parents can be easily understood, and a solution readily imagined, simply by noticing these parents' small, poorly distributed, and too infrequently activated networks. Yet the deficiencies in these networks are hardly unique to single parents; individuals in other statuses who are also dealing with significant personal difficulties will manifest a similar pattern (McLanahan, Wedemeyer, & Adelberg, 1981).

As for individual relationships, five characteristics will be discussed, for in ideal situations, one would want to assess the *content, durability, directedness, frequency,* and *intensity* of all the key relationships that make up the total set. The assessment would involve judging how the characteristics of these key relationships are linked to the person's distress or overall well-being (Finlayson, 1976). Having completed an assessment of the strengths and weaknesses of the total network and its key relationships, the next step would be to consider how the individual's network can be improved through participation in an NSHO (Cohen, Adler, & Mintz, 1983; Maguire, 1981).

CHARACTERISTICS OF THE TOTAL NETWORK

Size. People often experience distress and less often seek help because of networks that are too small—that have too few ties. When a person's network is too small, he or she may suffer from a lack of information, access to concrete assistance, and emotional support. These problems will be all the more intense if the already too-few ties are poorly distributed and thus the individual has no access to specific kinds of information and assistance. To be distributed adequately, the network should include ties to kin, friends, neighbors, and work- or schoolmates. It would also be desirable to have some overlap among these people; that is, some of these ties should be to persons who belong to more than one of the sectors. Applying this analysis to an NSHO, it would be desirable for the NSHO to contain a few individuals with whom the individual interacts in other areas of his or her life. But like most things, this idea can be carried too far. It would not be desirable to draw most of one's close friends from an NSHO. Likewise, it would be undesirable to join an NSHO that is made up mostly of co-workers or others, such as neighbors, with whom one already interacts frequently. Aside from complicating existing relationships, it would almost certainly slow the formation of new relationships and inhibit change.

Strength, like distribution, is implied in the characteristic of size. It is possible to have an adequately sized, evenly distributed network that provides only weak support because the person does not engage in sufficiently strong or frequent interaction with it. Thus, adequate size implies a sufficient number of appropriately distributed ties that are activated at sufficiently frequent intervals.

NSHO members have several opportunities to alter the "size" of their networks. They can participate in frequent fellowship meetings, usually with more than one chapter of the same program. This opportunity is symbolized in the part recommendation, part slogan: "90 in 90" (90 meetings in 90 days), which is familiar to AA members (Ernie K., 1984). In addition to formal meetings, members can participate in sponsorship and telephone-network activities and in the seemingly endless variety of NSHO social and recreational activities— picnics, "afterglows" (after-the-meeting gatherings), coffees, dances, outings, and so forth. And if members want to do still more, they may display an openness to new relationships (or simply their pride in the organization) through the use of symbolic pins and bumper stickers. "Easy Does It" or "One Day at a Time" can be found on the bumpers of the cars of many AA members. Other activities are available through intergroup, regional, and national structures that offer increasingly formal opportunities for relationships beyond the local chapters.

Although most of these potential relationships will not be actualized by many members, it probably is comforting to know they can be if the need arises, for instance, when one is away from home or in the midst of a crisis. Another aspect of assessing the adequacy of a network's size involves considering whether there are sufficient "friends of friends" who can be reached as special needs arise. In this regard, the networks that are potentially available through NSHOs offer many opportunities because they contain a large and diverse supply of members who can be used as intermediaries or bridges to the desired contact.

Density. Another approach to looking for solutions to problems involves assessing a person's total set in terms of who the people in one's network relate to. Do they relate to others who are already familiar to the focal person or to fresh new "faces?" It has often been observed that one's close friends tend to be familiar or even close to one another. This situation is then cited as support for the idea that high-density relationships are warmly supportive. And up to a point, it is true; but, it should be added that too few low-density relationships can also be a disadvantage. It is then that most people will find themselves wondering about the difference between entanglement and support. They will find it difficult "to keep things simple" or "to get away from it once in a while." Perhaps too few low-density relationships make it difficult to strike out on a new course or to make major changes in one's lifestyle. Unless kin and close friends who are tightly knit are offset by others who place less value on maintaining present arrangements, they are likely to put a damper on one's new initiatives. The disadvantage of too few low-density relationships will be evident when one wants to gain access to new resources, such as a job or specialized information, that one needs social ties or social transportation to reach. In view of the advantages of both high- and low-density relationships, people, especially those who are seeking to ameliorate their problems, need to maintain a balance between them and cultivate both types.

Both the NSHO and the LSHG offer opportunities to develop high-density relationships. Thus, if one's primary need is for warm support, the LSHG may be sufficient. However, many will need the fresh inputs and the encouragement to depart from old patterns that outwardly radiating relationships provide. When this kind of support is needed, the NSHO will be superior.

Evidence to support these propositions comes from a number of empirical studies. In most of these studies, density was operationalized as the proportion of those who relate to a focal person (P) who also relate to each other. Thus, if A and B relate to each other as well as to P, they form part of P's dense or close-knit network. The assertion that high density is associated with close, enduring relationships has been supported by a number of studies (see, for example, Hammer, 1980; Hammer, 1981; Mitchell & Trickett, 1980; Snow & Gordon, 1980).

In a representative study, Hammer (1963) found that patients who were admitted to a mental hospital from high-density networks were more often accompanied by family members and friends, whereas those patients from low-density networks had to deal with psychiatrists and social workers on their own. A similar pattern was found in Horowitz's (1977a, 1977b, 1977c) study of admissions to psychiatric facilities, as well as among Potasznik and Nelson's (1984) earlier-mentioned study of participants in self-help groups for families with severely mentally ill members. These studies found that density was related to lower objective and subjective burden ($r = -.34$ and $r = -.36$, both $p = <.05$).

The dysfunctional side of high-density networks was evident in a study of one of the classic groups of participants in self-help programs—widows. Hirsch (1981) found that widows who returned to college after a long absence adjusted better to their new academic roles when they were involved in less dense (less interconnected) networks; they were more open to new relationships and experiences. Even actively bereaving people need, according to Walker, MacBride, and Vachon (1977), to be able to "get away from it and to something else" through low-density relationships, but they are not likely to be able to do so if too many of their relationships are connected to the deceased. Hence, widow-to-*non*–widow relationships are as important as are widow-to-widow ones.

A similar pattern has been observed in different areas of personal need. For example, McKinlay (1973) found that the underutilization of maternal health services was related to high-density, inwardly focusing networks, which seemed to keep pregnant women in or discouraged them from going out. Access to low-density sectors was also found to be especially important for high-risk and disadvantaged persons. Two studies conducted by Birkel and Reppucci (1983) affirmed this point. One study noted that high-risk women who were referred to a parent education program attended fewer sessions when they were from denser networks. The second study found that women who were participating in a supplementary feeding program were less likely to seek the advice of professionals when they came from denser networks. These studies underline the importance of being able "to move out and toward something else" through low-density, outwardly

radiating relationships. The unconnected ties of low-density relationships, which are sometimes called "weak," prompted Granovetter
(1973, 1983) to refer to "the strength of weak ties."

The abundance of low-density relationships in an NSHO can
be an important aid in resolving personal problems, and in this regard,
the NSHO usually has the advantage over an LSHG. It is likely, for
example, that Parents without Partners and Mended Hearts (for
cardiac-surgery patients) will offer better access to specialized legal
and medical resources than will their counterpart LSHGs. Similarly, it
is unlikely that LSHGs for spouses of alcoholics or recently bereaved
parents will offer the opportunities for low-density relationships that
exist in Al-Anon or Compassionate Friends.

The availability of low-density networks within NSHOs can be
especially significant for ethnic minorities (Gaudin & Davis, 1985;
Lofland & Le Jeune, 1960; Martineau, 1977). To a certain extent, low-
density ties can compensate for the lack of other minorities in an NSHO
chapter by forming bridges to minorities in other chapters. Similar
bridges may link women or men who are minorities in certain NSHOs.
For example, even though female compulsive gamblers are a small
percentage of Gamblers Anonymous (GA), they may be able to
connect with other women through the intergroup or national
structure. Lest there be any misunderstanding, these are not offered as
adequate solutions to the problems of gender and ethnic imbalance,
although they may alleviate some of the feelings of isolation and
alienation.

CHARACTERISTICS OF INDIVIDUAL RELATIONSHIPS

The nature of individual relationships can be inferred by
examining the values associated with five of their characteristics
(content, frequency, durability, directedness, and intensity). The
values of these characteristics seem likely to change in self-help
programs in two ways: The new relationships formed within the self-
help program are likely to follow a different pattern in terms of, to cite
one example, the directedness or reciprocity of the relationships.
Likewise, relationships that antedate the self-help program may be
affected by the member's participation; thus, for example, the member's

relationship with his or her spouse may become more reciprocal as a result of participation.

Content. A relationship may be simple or complex in content. It is complex when there is more than one basic theme, as would be the case when a relationship operates in more than one sphere (kinship, friendship, neighborhood, and workplace or school) (Boissevain & Mitchell, 1973; Hammer, 1981; Mitchell, 1969). Relationships will also be complex when they have multiple themes within a single sphere. It would not be unusual, for example, for the content of a relationship within an NSHO to include information, concrete assistance, emotional comfort, and personal affirmation. Typically, these complex or multistranded relationships are strong and stable because they are invested with multiple interests.

The complex tasks and objectives of NSHOs encourage these multistranded, complex relationships. And naturally, as the tasks change, the initiator and the salience of the strands will also change; the person may be an information giver in the immediate situation and an information receiver in the next situation. The outcome of these interdependent interactions is apt to be mutual support. Even though, or actually because, support is not the explicit aim of these interactions, these interactions can deliver impressive amounts of support.

The amount of support that results naturally and without contrivance from these interactions may exceed the amount that is available from people in nominally supportive roles, such as a counselor or a therapist. The same may be true when this more natural support is compared with support that is available through the rap- or support-group structure of a larger multipurpose self-help organization. The nonreciprocal nature of the relationship with a professional (or with the leader of a support or rap group), together with its lack of grounding in a concrete external task, may limit it as an instrument of support. This view stems from the idea that support may be more effective when it is unsolicited and implicit, for, in the very asking for support, one stirs up feelings of inadequacy and raises doubts about whether the "support" that results is a spontaneous response to the person or a dutiful response to the implicit demand for it. Thus, the support that emanates naturally and spontaneously from the multiplex relations among NSHO members may be the most effective form of support.

The negative trade-off is that multiplex relations tend to discourage frank requests for help or candid complaints that one's needs are being slighted. This situation may be due to a feeling that asking for or complaining about something would jeopardize other interests. Hence, there may be too much pressure to compromise and avoid conflict. The other person's dysfunctional behavior may also be inappropriately ignored because her or his cooperation is needed in another sphere. (This, of course, is not to suggest that behavior should never be ignored because sometimes it is necessary to do so if one is to be a tolerant person.) Thus, it may be concluded that a delicate balance must be struck between the opportunity to engage in multistranded relationships and to pursue single-stranded relationships with individuals who are not heavily connected to others in one's network.

The constructively involving operation of complexity in NSHOs can be illustrated by an example from GA, whose organizational design resembles that of a number of NSHOs. The scenario opens with the men (most members of GA are male) in the GA "room" "giving therapy" to one another.

The men take turns relating how they are working one of the Twelve Steps (previously specified by the rotating chairman) and how doing so is changing their lives. (They address three questions: "What was it like then?" "What changed?" and "What is it like now?") After the informal, and often valuable, visiting that follows the formal session, one of the men accompanies the other to his home to work on plans for the upcoming regional GA conference. While working on the conference, the men receive several calls from members who "need to check something," the last from a new member who is upset by the "deceitfulness" of his teenage son. Later in the week, the men engage in another support contact when they testify at the trial of a third compulsive gambler about the potential benefits and limitations of GA.

Despite the heavy responsibilities these men shoulder in this scenario, the relationship is more likely to be strengthening than straining because of the supportive resources available to GA members (and, in similar circumstances, to other NSHO members). But the support comes not through GA alone. The men also derive support and perceive their responsibilities to be less of a burden because of their relationship as co-workers and neighbors. However, if their responsibilities become too burdensome, the men know they can pull back gracefully by choosing to work on simpler tasks. One or both of them, for example, may elect to coordinate the distribution of publications from the General Service Office of GA.

Frequency. Frequent contact can strengthen individual relationships. NSHOs offer multiple meetings that encourage frequent contact among members. Members are encouraged to attend as many meetings as necessary to prevent "backsliding." That "Meetings Make It" is not an empty slogan was evident in an article by this title in the *Gamblers Anonymous, Life Line Bulletin.* The article hailed a member for attending more than 2,500 meetings in a 10-year period. LSHGs also encourage frequent contact though they are less likely to be able to offer as many meetings.

Durability. The multiple functions of relationships within NSHOs also contribute to their durability. If the organization is to accomplish its mission, new members must be recruited, programs recycled, procedures revised, and policies revitalized. Members are alternately cajoled and admonished to stay long enough to "pay back" the organization or to "pass it on," in the AA phrase. Paying back is a norm that has become institutionalized in some organizations by formal leadership training programs. Recovery, Inc., for example, operates a multilevel training program leading to increasingly higher levels of responsibility within the organization. The mere existence of a training program that would take several years to complete in the normal course of events is itself a statement about the value of enduring relationships (Weber, 1982).

Directedness. Directedness refers to the reciprocity of the relationship. When helping relationships are bidirectional, the person receiving help is less likely to feel uneasy about his or her indebtedness or inferior because of his or her need for help. And although both NSHOs and LSHGs attempt to foster reciprocal help by peers, the LSHGs will be at a disadvantage if they allow professionals, as they sometimes do, to play important facilitating roles. Regardless of their intentions, professionals cannot model how to engage in bidirectional relationships. The NSHO, however, has a strong incentive to encourage bidirectional relationships in that it can look only to its own membership as a source of new energy and leadership.

Intensity. The relationships of family members who remain close over a period of years, despite limited contact, are intense. The intensity is carried over from the shared emotional experiences of early life. It is strong because of the sharing that occurred during critical stages when family members were predisposed to bond with one another. As a consequence, later contacts, even after long separations, are imbued with the intensity whose source is the shared experiences that occurred during these critical periods. NSHOs have an analogous capacity to generate intense feelings during the critical early stages of recovery and affiliation that carry over and intensify what otherwise might seem like ho-hum events. This ability probably has something to do with why NSHO meetings often remind one of a family reunion or a religious revival. The vital importance of intense and confiding ties such as these was demonstrated in Berkman's (1986) and Berkman and Syme's (1979) prospective study of middle-aged adults. The study found that the presence of a confiding tie, whether to a friend, a relative, a spouse (the kind of tie that exists among self-helpers), was associated with fewer deaths over a 10-year span.

Although intense relationships are available in NSHOs, they are not compulsory; it is recognized that such relationships are not for everyone and certainly not for everyone right away. Newcomers are encouraged "to sit back and observe" and "to take what you like and leave the rest." Paradoxically, intense relationships are fostered by not insisting on them. What is stressed, instead, is that the desire for intensity is a highly individual matter and that the NSHO aims to be responsive to individual preferences.

Improvements in networks that may come about through participation in NSHOs are summarized in Table 4-1. These include the formation of new relationships within the NSHO, which, in turn, lead to the formation of new external relationships. These new relationships, together with the changes brought about by the NSHO in existing relationships, result in benefits to the individual. These improvements may be conceptualized as changes in the characteristics of the members' networks; these changes refer to both individual relationships and to the relationships as a total set.

Earlier it was averred that it will seldom be practical to measure all seven characteristics. Moreover, in many empirical contexts, several of the characteristics of individual relationships may be highly

Table 4-1

Improvements in Networks Resulting from Participation in NSHOs

CHANGES IN THE CHARACTERISTICS OF RELATIONSHIPS	IMPROVEMENTS IN NETWORKS
Total Set	
Increased size	New ties are added and the distribution and strength of the networks are improved.
Balanced density	Outwardly radiating ties and close-knit ties are added.
Individual Relationships	
Content	New relationships can be inclined toward either simple or complex themes.
Frequency	Multiple meetings and the informal network encourage more frequent contacts with people.
Durability	The ongoing mission of the NSHOs encourages enduring relationships.
Directedness	Reciprocal giving and receiving patterns are built into NSHO programs.
Intensity	NSHOs accommodate individual preferences for a range of high- and low-intensity relationships.

intercorrelated. For these reasons, it is desirable to simplify the measurement procedures. The main recommendation would be to reduce the number of measurements taken of individual relationships. After measuring size and density, as was previously discussed, it may be enough to assess the content and reciprocity of relationships. Together, these characteristics may be sufficient to indicate the effectiveness of the relationships. Multistranded relationships tend to be substantive, and reciprocal relationships tend to be satisfying. The importance of reciprocity was clearly evident in Maton's (1988) study of the members of Compassionate Friends, Multiple Sclerosis Society, and Overeaters Anonymous (OA). In all these organizations, members who both provided and received support from other members benefited more than did those who simply received or gave support. Those who engaged in two-way support relationships saw themselves as being less depressed and as having more self-esteem. They also said that the NSHOs were more personally satisfying and beneficial than did the members who did not engage in reciprocal relationships.

WHAT PROFESSIONALS CAN DO

Professionals often have or can create the opportunity to guide individuals who will be in some sequence of participation with an NSHO (Collins & Pancoast, 1976; Mitchell & Hurley, 1980). Sometimes they will work with an individual who participates in an NSHO while receiving services. At other times, they will have an opportunity to advise a client to become a member of an NSHO after the professional service has been completed. At still other times, they will work with a client who participated in a self-help program before seeking professional help. In each of these situations, the professional can use the concepts of networks to maximize the value of the self-help experience for the client. The client who is involved in a self-help program is in a laboratory for trying out new patterns of relationships that the professional can help the client assess and manage. The mutually potentiating effect was described by one member of OA (1982, p. 93) as follows: "I continued in therapy, and for the first time it was working. The therapy helped me to be open to O.A., and O.A. helped me to be open to therapy." If the self-help experience is still in the offing, the professional can anticipate how the experience may contribute to the individual's well-being. In so doing, care must be taken not to imply judgments that would be prejudicial to either form of help. It may help to have in mind the OA member who connected the two in this way: "I began therapy, and I am not sure I would have stayed alive long enough to find O.A. without it" (OA, 1982, p. 110). The person who began in self-help and now is in therapy should be encouraged to review the experience with the therapist to see what parts of it may be relevant to the current therapy.

For the client who is participating in an NSHO and in professional therapy concurrently, the professional needs to be aware of how the NSHO can function to reduce isolation, decrease the stigma, and promote a sense of community (Coates & Winston, 1983; Cohen, 1979). The professional will sometimes need to explore with his or her client the potential value of the NSHO as a positive reference group. This exploration may well facilitate a natural identification that may exist between the client and members of the NSHO. If, in the end, the client chooses to identify with members of the NSHO, he or she will not only satisfy a need to affiliate but will be in a position to identify with individuals in the reference group who are "making it." Sometimes the professional may be able to expand the client's dim awareness that many of the other members who are now making it, and making it well, were once even worse off than the client.

Professionals should also discuss with their clients the opportunity to increase the size of their networks through the NSHO. Although the small size of a client's network may not be the only problem, it is likely to be part of it. Typically, people who are experiencing difficulties relate to too few people; need more ties in certain spheres, such as friendship; or need to strengthen their ties to the people they already know (Sokolovsky, Cohen, Berger, & Geiger, 1978). They need to be aware of the importance of having enough ties to cover their major spheres of functioning and to use them with sufficient frequency. As part of this discussion, it would also be appropriate to consider whether the NSHO may be used to meet specialized needs (legal, financial, or medical) that cannot usually be met in ordinary lay networks.

In continuing to review the total network, the professional can ask the client to assess the density of his or her network. Is the network sufficiently dense to provide emotionally supportive relationships? In this regard, the professional can ask, "Do the people you relate to know enough about you as a whole person because they are also in touch with other people you know?" "And does their contact with these others you know provide an added incentive to develop their relationship with you?" Shifting to the low-density sector, the professional may ask the client whether his or her network is deficient in the outwardly radiating relationships that are so necessary for such purposes as getting a job or obtaining specialized services or information. Or perhaps the problem is more the lack of warm dense support; that is, the supply of instrumental assistance may be adequate, but there is not enough emotional support to do the follow-up. Most likely, of course, the need is for more of both high- and low-density relationships. In such situations, NSHOs can often be a valuable resource. Most NSHOs offer a range of relationships, some of which are more likely to lead to tightly knit ties within the NSHO, while others are more likely to radiate outside the organization. The aim should be to prepare the client who is also a member of the NSHO to choose among the options through discussions with his or her human services professional.

As far as individual relationships are concerned, the NSHO offers the opportunity to start from scratch, to form new relationships that are relatively uncompromised by previous experiences and patterns. The client can be helped to assess what kind of relationships he or she wants to form by a number of questions: Does the member/client need more simple or complex relationships? Does he or she need to get away from it all and maintain some relationships at a simple and uncomplicated level? Or, does the self-help member/client need more close complex relationships? And does the client appreciate that if he or she is to benefit from the self-help experience, he or she probably will need to become involved in experiences outside and in addition to the regularly scheduled formal sessions? (See Chapter 8, this volume; and Videka-Sherman & Lieberman, 1985.)

And so this review goes—on down the line. If the member/client needs to modify the frequency, intensity, directedness, or duration of his or her relationships, the NSHO will offer an opportunity to create and maintain relationships with the desired characteristics and can serve as a training ground for modifying relationships outside the NSHO. The transfer of learning can be facilitated if the professional helps the client/member consider how these new qualities may become part of ongoing outside relationships. This end will be further advanced if the professional continues to help the member/client to monitor and refine the results.

Just as the professional has a role with clients who are concurrent participants, he or she also has a role with clients who are prospective members of NSHOs at the time of their termination or graduation from a course of professional counseling. The about-to-matriculate self-help member can be advised about what to expect and how to integrate his or her new experiences into a total program of recovery and self-development. Membership in an NSHO can be made part of the client's search for a more supportive environment. Doing something as modest as encouraging a long-term client to deal with his or her frustrations through regular participation in PA may be a significant act. In so doing, the professional may help consolidate and extend the gains the client has made against his or her abusive tendencies in treatment.

A retrospective examination of a self-help experience can be a useful way to pinpoint the problems that need to be worked on in a professional relationship. If the new client, for example, complains about never getting any information despite having participated in the Alliance for the Mentally Ill or the Manic Depressive and Depressive Association, the professional will be alerted to the possibility that the problem may be with how the client/member seeks or assimilates information from these organizations. Similarly, if a former member of PA complains that he or she could never get away from the children, the professional may be sensitive to how the client used or was unable to use the opportunities that are available through the formal and informal networks of PA. As a result, both the client and the professional may come to see that the task is not so much to discover new opportunities but to make better use of existing ones. Other tasks that need to be accomplished can sometimes be brought into focus by an analysis of how the client used the potentially available network during his or her period of membership in an NSHO. This analysis is intended to encourage professionals to think about how problems can be directly ameliorated by modifying existing relationships or forming new ones. Participation in an NSHO can often be an effective means of doing so.

REFERENCES

Barnes, J. A. (1972). *Social networks.* Reading, MA: Addison-Wesley Modular Publications, Module 26.

Berkman, L. F. (1986). Social networks, support and health: Taking the next step forward. *American Journal of Epidemiology, 123*(4), 559–562.

Berkman, L. F., & Syme, S. L. (1979). Social networks, host resistance and mortality: A nine year follow up study of Alameda County residents. *American Journal of Epidemiology, 109,* 186–204.

Birkel, R. C., & Reppucci, N. D. (1983). Social networks, information-seeking, and the utilization of services. *American Journal of Community Psychology, 11*(2), 185–205.

Boissevain, J., & Mitchell, J. C. (Eds.). (1973). Network analysis: Studies in human interaction. The Hague: Mouton.

Bott, E. (1971). *Family and social network* (2nd ed.). New York: Free Press.

Coates, D., & Winston, T. (1983). Counteracting the deviance of depression: Peer support groups for victims. *Journal of Social Issues, 39,* 169–194.

Cohen, C. I. (1979). Clinical use of network analysis for psychiatric and aged populations. *Community Mental Health Journal, 15,* 203–213.

Cohen, C. I., Adler, A. G., & Mintz, J. E. (1983). Network interventions on the margin. In D. L. Pancoast, P. Parker, & C. Froland (Eds.), *Rediscovering self-help.* Beverly Hills, CA: Sage Publications.

Collins, A. H., & Pancoast, D. L. (1976). *Natural helping networks.* Washington, DC: National Association of Social Workers.

Ell, K. (1984). Social networks, social support and health status: A review. *Social Service Review, 58,* 133–149.

Erickson, C. D. (1975). The concept of personal network in clinical practice. *Family Process, 14,* 487–498.

Ernie K. (1984). *90 meetings, 90 days: A journal of experience, strength, and hope.* Minneapolis, MN: Johnston Institute.

Finlayson, A. (1976). Social networks as coping resources: Lay help and consultation patterns used by women in husband's post-infarction career. *Social Science and Medicine, 10,* 97–103.

Fischer, C. S. (1982). *To dwell among friends.* Chicago: University of Chicago Press.

Froland, C., Pancoast, D. L., Chapman, N., & Kimboko, P. (1981). *Helping networks and human services.* Beverly Hills, CA: Sage Publications.

Gallo, F. (1984). Social support networks and the health of elderly persons. *Social Work Research & Abstracts, 20*(4), 13–19.

Gaudin, J. M., & Davis, K. (1985). Social networks of black and white rural families: A research report. *Journal of Marriage and the Family, 47*(4), 1015–1022.

Gottlieb, B. (1981). *Social networks and social support.* Beverly Hills, CA: Sage Publications.

Granovetter, M. (1973). The strength of weak ties. *American Journal of Sociology, 78,* 1360–1380.

Granovetter, M. (1983). The strength of weak ties: A network theory revisited. In R. Collins (Ed.), *Sociological theory.* San Francisco: Jossey-Bass.

Hammer, M. (1963). Influence of small social networks as factors in mental hospital admission. *Human Organization, 22,* 243–251.

Hammer, M. (1980). Predictability of social connections over time. *Social Networks, 2,* 165–180.

Hammer, M. (1981). Social supports, social networks, and schizophrenia. *Schizophrenia Bulletin, 7,* 45–56.

Hirsch, B. (1979). Psychological dimensions of social networks: A multi-method analysis. *American Journal of Community Psychology, 7,* 263–277.

Hirsch, B. J. (1981). Social networks and the coping process. In B. Gottlieb (Ed.), *Social networks and social support.* Beverly Hills, CA: Sage Publications.

Horowitz, A. (1977a). The pathways into psychiatric treatment: Some differences between men and women. *Journal of Health and Social Behavior, 18,* 169–178.

Horowitz, A. (1977b). Social networks and pathways to psychiatric help seeking. *Social Science and Medicine, 12,* 297–304.

Horowitz, A. (1977c). Social networks and pathways to psychiatric treatment. *Social Forces, 56,* 86–105.

Lieberman, M., & Gourash, N. (1979). Effects of change groups on the elderly. In M. A. Lieberman & L. D. Borman (Eds.), *Self-help groups for coping with crisis* (pp. 150–163). San Francisco: Jossey-Bass.

Lofland, J. F., & Le Jeune, R. A. (1960). Initial interaction of newcomers in Alcoholics Anonymous: A field experiment in class symbols and socialization. *Social Problems, 8,* 102–111.

Maguire, L. (1980). The interface of social workers with personal networks. *Journal of Social Work Groups, 3,* 2–28.

Maguire, L. (1981). Natural helping networks and self-help groups. In M. Nobel (Ed.), *Primary prevention in mental health and social work.* New York: Council on Social Work Education.

Martineau, W. (1977). Informal social ties among urban black Americans. *Journal of Black Studies, 8,* 83–104.

Maton, K. I. (1988). Social support, organizational characteristics, psychological well-being, and group appraisal in three self-help group populations. *American Journal of Community Psychology, 16*(1), 53–77.

McIntyre, E. L. G. (1986). Social networks: Potential for practice. *Social Work, 31*(6), 421–426.

McKinlay, J. B. (1973). Social networks, lay consultation, and help-seeking behavior. *Social Forces, 52,* 275–292.

McLanahan, S. S., Wedemeyer, N. V., & Adelberg, T. (1981). Network structure, social support, and psychological well-being in the single-parent family. *Journal of Marriage and the Family, 43,* 601–612.

Meetings make it. (1981, July). *Gamblers Anonymous, Life Line Bulletin.*

Mitchell, J. C. (Ed.). (1969). Social networks in urban situations. Manchester, England: University of Manchester Press.

Mitchell, R., & Hurley, D. (1980). Collaboration with natural helping networks. *Community Mental Health Journal, 16,* 277–298.

Mitchell, R. E., & Trickett, E. J. (1980). Task force report: Social networks as mediators of social support. *Community Mental Health Journal, 16,* 27–44.

Mueller, D. (1980). Social networks: A promising direction for research on the relationship of the social environment to psychiatric disorder. *Social Science and Medicine, 14A,* 147–161.

Overeaters Anonymous. (1982). *Overeaters Anonymous.* Los Angeles: Author.

Perrucci, R., & Targ, D. (1981). *Mental patients and social networks.* Boston: Auburn House.

Pilisuk, M., & Parks, S. H. (1981). The place of network analysis in the study of supportive social associations. *Basic and Applied Social Psychology, 2,* 121–135.

Potasznik, H., & Nelson, G. (1984). Stress and social support: The burden experienced by the family of a mentally ill person. *American Journal of Community Psychology, 12*(5), 589–607.

Powell, T. J. (1981). The client's social network and help seeking behavior. *Social Work, 26,* 335–337.

Snow, D., & Gordon, J. (1980). Social network analysis and intervention with the elderly. *The Gerontologist, 20,* 463–467.

Sokolovsky, J., & Cohen, C. (1981). Toward a resolution of methodological dilemmas in network mapping. *Schizophrenia Bulletin, 7,* 109–116.

Sokolovsky, J., Cohen, C., Berger, D., & Geiger, J. (1978). Personal networks of ex-mental patients in a Manhattan SRO hotel. *Human Organization, 37,* 5–15.

Swenson, C. (1979). Social networks, mutual aid, and the life model of practice. In C. Germain (Ed.), *Social work practice: People and environments.* New York: Columbia University Press.

Tolsdorf, C. C. (1976). Social networks, support, and coping: An exploratory study. *Family Process, 15,* 407–417.

Turkat, D. (1980). Social networks: Theory and practice. *Journal of Community Psychology, 8,* 99–109.

Videka-Sherman, L., & Lieberman, M. (1985). The effects of self-help and psychother-apy intervention on child loss: The limits of recovery. *American Journal of Orthopsychiatry, 55,* 70–82.

Walker, K. N., MacBride, A., & Vachon, M. H. S. (1977). Social support networks and the crisis of bereavement. *Social Science and Medicine, 11,* 35–41.

Weber, G. H. (1982). Self-help and beliefs. In G. H. Weber & L. M. Cohen (Eds.), *Beliefs and self-help* (pp. 13–30). New York: Human Sciences Press.

Wellman, B. (1983). Network analysis: Some basic principles. In R. Collins (Ed.), *Sociological theory.* San Francisco: Jossey-Bass.

PART TWO

DIFFERENT TYPES OF ORGANIZATIONS

5

TWELVE-STEP PROGRAMS

LINDA FARRIS KURTZ

In the late 1930s, the founders of Al-
coholics Anonymous (AA) devised a singularly effective set of
principles, known as the Twelve Steps, to help alcoholics achieve
sobriety. Since then, AA's program has been applied to many other
compulsive behaviors and emotional concerns. Noting the pertinence
of the Twelve Steps to other difficulties, one clergyman, the Reverend
Arnold Lugar, wrote, "I truly believe that the Twelve-Step Program is
a Twentieth Century revelation of the Holy Spirit to counteract the
emotional problems which our present pace of living is producing in
almost plague-like proportions" (Emotions Anonymous [EA], 1978,
p. 14). This comment reflects what is distinctive about Twelve-Step
fellowships: the offering of spiritual guidance to members.

Public health professionals predicted the use of the Twelve
Steps for problems other than alcoholism early in AA's history. In 1951,
the American Public Health Association presented AA with the Lasker
Award, recognizing that the fellowship offered a "new therapy based
on kinship in common suffering; one having vast potential for the
myriad other ills of mankind" (AA, 1957, p. 301). Since AA's founding,
its General Service Office reports that more than 80 new fellowships
based on the AA example have been formed (AA, 1987b). There are
an estimated 125,000 separate chapters of Twelve-Step fellowships in
this country and abroad (Madara & Meese, 1988). AA is the largest, with
85,270 chapters worldwide and an estimated 1,734,734 members as of
early 1988 (AA, 1989).

Rather than attempt to discuss all or even most of the various Twelve-Step associations, this chapter presents an overview of the steps, traditions, and practices to which all fellowships adhere. The discussion draws on the professional literature that critically examines AA as a therapeutic movement and on literature by and about other Twelve-Step associations. Guidelines for cooperation with professionals come from the author's research on AA/professional relationships and from the AA and Al-Anon literature on cooperation with the professional community (AA, 1982; Al-Anon, 1986a; L. F. Kurtz, 1984a, 1984b, 1985).

This chapter begins with an introduction to AA's historical roots. The focus then turns to the evolution of additional fellowships, beginning with Al-Anon in 1951. The overview of how the steps are used will concentrate on their therapeutic action and the meaning of sobriety, which is a central concept of Twelve-Step programs. An examination of the meeting formats, organizational philosophy, and literature of these programs leads to an analysis of both the professional criticism and justification of the programs. The chapter ends with guidelines for professional cooperation with Twelve-Step fellowships.

THE BEGINNING

Twelve-Step groups began when Bill Wilson, a down-and-out Wall Street securities analyst, encountered Ebby Thatcher, a former drinking buddy, in 1934 (see AA, 1957, 1984; E. Kurtz, 1979). Thatcher was attending meetings of the Oxford Group. The group, whose U.S. headquarters was at Calvary Episcopal Church in New York City, was an evangelical-style attempt to recapture the ethos of primitive Christianity. Thatcher had sought a religious solution to his drinking problem after learning that Swiss analyst Carl Jung had recommended religion as possibly the only way to resolve his otherwise hopeless compulsion. Thus began a series of events that would lead Wilson to Akron, Ohio, where he met Dr. Bob Smith and where, in 1935, the two of them would form the beginning group of what would later become AA. After Wilson returned to New York, he began another group for recovering or newly abstinent alcoholics who joined the Calvary Church Oxford Group and attended an extension of the Oxford Group solely for alcoholics in Wilson's home.

In 1937, the alcoholics in New York split from the Oxford Group to meet separately. They sifted from the Oxford Group's practices those spiritual principles they thought were most helpful to them as recovering alcoholics. Then they combined these practices with diverse cultural influences, such as the pragmatic philosophy of William James (1958), the opinions of Richard Peabody (1931), and their own experiences, to form the basis of the program now known as AA (see McCarthy, 1984). Their ideas and stories were first formulated in written form for the book *Alcoholics Anonymous: The Story of How Many Thousands of Men and Women Have Recovered from Alcoholism* (AA, 1976). The newly developing program later took its name from the book's title (E. Kurtz, 1979).

AA's early beginnings in the Oxford Group are important for understanding what the Twelve-Step programs retained and discarded from that movement. From the Oxford Group came AA's independence from organized religion; its concept of the stages through which one moves, from surrender to confession to a changed life; and its practices of making restitution, using nonprofessional, unpaid members in direct assistance to those who are suffering, and obliging a member to engage in helping others to help himself or herself (E. Kurtz, 1979). The alcoholics rejected the Oxford Group's adherence to absolutes—absolute honesty, purity, unselfishness, and love— finding that the word "absolute" either unduly pressured the alcoholic or led to the unhealthy inflation of the ego. Furthermore, they replaced the aggressive evangelism of the Oxford Group with strict adherence to anonymity and with what eventually became Tradition 11: "Our public relations policy is based on attraction rather than promotion" (AA, 1952, p. 13).

The Twelve Steps, written primarily by cofounder Wilson, were thus a reflection of the Oxford Group's procedures, refined by the pragmatic experiences of the first AA members in the years 1935–39 (AA, 1957). The Twelve Steps and the Twelve Traditions now form the basis of all Twelve-Step programs and are discussed more completely later in this chapter.

FORMATION OF NEW FELLOWSHIPS

In the early 1940s, wives of the then mostly male members of AA met with their husbands in AA meetings; later, they met in auxiliary groups in various parts of the country (Al-Anon, 1966, 1986c). By 1948, 87 individual auxiliaries for family members requested listings in the AA national directory. Affiliation with outside groups, even the wives' groups, conflicted with AA's tradition of nonaffiliation, however, so the wives formed a separate fellowship in 1951. The new fellowship was officially called Al-Anon and was the first new group to follow the AA pattern. In 1957, Alateen (for the teenage children of alcoholics, as its name implies) became a part of the Al-Anon Family Groups; today, it lists over 25,000 separate chapters worldwide (Al-Anon, 1986b).

In 1953, Narcotics Anonymous (NA) was founded in response to the needs of drug users, who were not accepted in AA. Although NA uses the terms *narcotics* in its name, its program addresses any drug user. According to the most recent estimates, NA chapters numbered over 14,000 worldwide (personal communication with NA headquarters, January 1989). Another fellowship, Gamblers Anonymous (GA), which deals with compulsive gambling, was officially formed in 1957, although chapters were meeting earlier in the 1950s. GA is not large, listing only 700 chapters in 1988 (Madara & Meese, 1988), but it is one of the early pioneers that adapted the AA program to help those with problems other than alcoholism.

Between 1950 and 1983, 48 different groups requested permission from AA to use the copyrighted steps and traditions—an average of 1.45 new groups per year. From the end of 1983 to February 1987, 33 groups made the same request—an average of over 11 new fellowships per year (Madara & Meese, 1988). These figures provide a rough idea of the degree to which Twelve-Step programs and self-help groups generally grew in the 1980s.

Newer groups represent many of the illnesses and special problems that were rarely mentioned and even more rarely understood when AA first came into being. For example, sex and love addiction is the focus of at least three Twelve-Step fellowships. Sexaholics Anonymous, founded in 1979, is based in California and sponsored approximately 700 separate chapters as of December 1987 (Madara & Meese, 1988). Sex Addicts Anonymous, based in Minneapolis,

Minnesota, has no figures on the number of chapters. Sex and Love Addicts Anonymous (SLAA), the Augustine Fellowship, founded in 1976, is based in Boston and estimates there are about 500 chapters (Madara & Meese, 1988).

THE STEPS

Although they serve members with a wide variety of concerns, Twelve-Step programs have many similarities, not the least of which is their following of the Twelve Steps. Understanding how Twelve-Step fellowships define the problems they address is essential to understanding how the steps work.

In general, the focal concern for most Twelve-Step groups is the members' obsessive preoccupation with something to the point where that focus takes over a major part of their lives. For example, members of Al-Anon are obsessed with the alcoholic; Overeaters Anonymous (OA) members, with food; members of SLAA, with sex and love; and so on. These concerns, which help the person to blot out pain and anxiety, become so extreme that they make life increasingly unmanageable. The sufferer's lack of control motivates him or her to try to exercise more control, but this effort fails and pushes the person further into a cycle of efforts to control that are concurrent with feelings of unmanageability. For example, an Al-Anon member learns that his or her preoccupation with the alcoholic contributes to sustaining the alcoholic family pattern by giving the alcoholic an excuse to drink (Al-Anon, 1966, pp. 39–43). The partner's efforts to control become increasingly desperate as the alcoholic drinks more and the cycle goes around and around. Similarly, SLAA (Augustine Fellowship, 1986) points out that its members have been engaged in obsessive-compulsive patterns in sexual or love relationships either through a compulsive search for sex and romance or by entrapment in hyperdependent relationships.

AA (1976) and NA (1987) emphasize the ingredient of self-will and self-centeredness in these obsessive behaviors. Even those individuals who appear to be preoccupied with others harbor beneath their obsession a secret need for unreasonable attention from the other person (Al-Anon, 1966). The sex and love addict, for example, craves the emotional high and excitement achieved by sexual seduction and other kinds of romantic excitement (Augustine Fellowship, 1986). One reaches bottom when one becomes so defeated in the obsession that one can no longer continue it without suffering grave emotional, social, or physical consequences. Within the Twelve-Step fellowship, this is the point at which the sufferer admits powerlessness over the obsessive focus and surrenders in the struggle for control by asking for help from a Higher Power: a process contained in the first three of the Twelve Steps. Surrender is not an abdication of responsibility for self but, rather, a letting go of unreasonable efforts to control independently what cannot be controlled.

The Twelve Steps, found in the literature of all such groups, guide action (see, for example, AA, 1952, 1976; EA, 1978; OA, 1980; *Hope and Recovery,* 1987). Members observe that those who follow the path suggested by the steps eventually realize a spiritual awakening that leads to serenity. After the first three steps, one takes a moral inventory; shares this inventory with God and with another human being; asks that defects of character be removed; lists those he or she has harmed; becomes willing to made amends; and, in the ninth step, makes amends. The groups that followed AA have made few changes in the actual wording of the steps and no changes in the principles behind them. OA (1980), for example, changed only the word "alcohol" to "food" in Step 1 and "alcoholics" to "overeaters" in Step 12. A few associations, however, have changed or added to the steps, although the basic ideas are still similar; for instance, Homosexuals Anonymous (1980), for freedom from homosexuality, has 14 steps.

For the members of most Twelve-Step groups, the goal is sobriety. The term "sobriety" is commonly misunderstood to mean abstinence from alcohol (or other compulsions), but the goal in AA or any other Twelve-Step group is not merely abstinence but a fundamental change in thinking and acting. The member does not control his or her habit but rather surrenders it and learns to live a life of moderation and serenity. The steps help the person to achieve sobriety by replacing the obsession with spiritual wholeness—a recognition that once the first nine steps have been taken, one must continue to take personal inventory, continue to maintain conscious contact with a Higher Power, and continue to carry the message to those who still suffer—the tenth, eleventh, and twelfth steps. As an anonymous founder of OA (1980, p. 28) wrote, "The emptiness in my soul that I had tried to fill with men . . . food and possessions was a spiritual emptiness." Spirituality, an elusive concept, means that the member becomes able to accept life's mysteries, to infuse all his or her life with a new way of thinking, to be grateful for the freedom attained by such understanding, and to find and maintain humility (E. Kurtz, 1988b).

TWELVE-STEP GROUP MEETINGS

For those who adhere to a Twelve-Step program, studying and applying the steps to one's life requires a manner of living that demands rigorous honesty. To maintain honesty, one must attend group meetings, talk privately with a sponsor (a member with more experience), sponsor others, and engage in service to the fellowship. Much of this activity goes on not only during the meetings, which are held anywhere that is convenient but often in church basements, but at other times as well.

Most Twelve-Step associations adhere to the typical meeting formats of AA groups. There are at least two basic AA formats and minor variations within them. At speaker meetings, one person "gives a lead" by telling his or her story of "what we used to be like, what happened, and what we are like now" (AA, 1957). Stories allow the listener to identify with the speaker's initial suffering, to hear how that person hit his or her personal bottom, and how life has been changed by following the principles of the program. The second type of meeting features discussions, which can center on a step or a topic. One person chairs and starts the discussion, which then moves around the room. It is expected that each speaker will share a personal reflection on the topic and how the program works in his or her experience.

Anyone who speaks in a Twelve-Step group should be a member or a potential member. Some groups are more liberal than others, however, and practices regarding visitors vary from group to group. This writer's observations suggest that since AA is more generous than other fellowships in sponsoring open meetings, potential visitors to other fellowships should call or check with someone before attending a meeting. Meetings typically open and close with a prayer—usually the Serenity Prayer[1] or the Lord's Prayer. Following the opening, the meeting may begin with a short business session before moving on to the evening's program. In between meetings, members may talk with other members on the telephone and are expected to read the group's literature.

TWELVE-STEP LITERATURE

As Twelve-Step fellowships mature, they usually produce literature, an important contribution to carrying the message to the person who still suffers. Several programs offer a "Big Book," modeled on AA's original. The term "Big Book" in AA stems from the fact that the copies of the first edition (1939) of *Alcoholics Anonymous* (AA, 1976) were printed on the thickest paper available to convince buyers that it was worth its $2.50 price in the depression year 1939 (E. Kurtz, 1979). The AA Big Book contains a discussion of alcoholism and presents the AA program. Its best-known chapter, "How It Works," contains the steps and how to use them; the introductory paragraphs to this chapter are usually read in every AA meeting. The AA Big Book had sold over 6 million copies by early 1987, and it now sells at the rate of 1 million copies every 15 months (E. Kurtz, 1988a). The major focus of Big Books are their stories of recovering members. For example, GA's (1984) Big Book contains 33 stories of recovering gamblers and the Big Book of Sex Addicts Anonymous (Augustine Fellowship, 1986) contains 19 stories of recovering sex addicts.

Other literature supplements the Big Books, much of it in the form of pamphlets and brochures. These products include starter kits for new groups; packets for new members; and brochures on special topics, such as sponsorship, relapse, and working with professionals. The literature published by Twelve-Step associations, in keeping with Tradition 12, rarely contain the name of an author, unless the author is a nonmember, which is also rare. These items are known as "conference-approved literature." Many groups prefer that members

---

[1]God, grant me the serenity to accept the things I cannot change, the courage to change the things I can and the wisdom to know the difference.

introduce to meetings only the literature that is conference approved, while others, in the spirit of autonomy, quote from and bring to meetings a variety of inspirational literature that in some way fits with their conception of the program.

THE TWELVE TRADITIONS

More than other self-help associations, Twelve-Step programs represent a way of thinking that is alien to professionals because of their spiritual orientation and what has been called their "organizational anarchy."[2] The Twelve Traditions declare that "there is but one authority and that is God as He may express Himself through the group's conscience."[3] Furthermore, Tradition 2 states, "Leaders are but trusted servants, they do not govern." The organizational chart is an inverted pyramid, with the groups at the top connected by a system of delegates to the World Service Conference at the bottom. The World Service Conference responds to the will of the autonomous groups and makes no decisions without input from the groups.

The traditions, therefore, are guides to organization and the embodiment of AA's organizational philosophy, but they are not rigid policies that inhibit the autonomy of groups. Like the Twelve Steps, the original Twelve Traditions of AA have been adopted almost verbatim by the programs that followed AA. The Twelve Traditions emerged from cofounder Wilson's correspondence with those who, in the 1940s, began the multitude of AA groups that sprang up around the country. Using his experience and that of others, Wilson made suggestions for the development of the groups. Believing that all alcoholics are basically rebellious, Wilson specifically wished to avoid a rigid organization and central authority (E. Kurtz, 1979).

Tradition 1 states, "Our common welfare should come first; personal recovery depends upon unity." This means that the group is

---

[2]Attributed to Harry Tiebout, M.D., psychotherapist of cofounder Bill Wilson and a trustee of AA (see E. Kurtz, 1979, p. 107).
[3]The traditions are quoted as they appear in *Hope and Recovery* (1987, pp. 112–128); the wording is basically the same for all Twelve-Step associations.

more important than the individual. Despite AA's essentially nonau-thoritarian stance, its traditions require conformity to the principles of recovery so that the group, the key to recovery, will remain strong. Tradition 2, "For our group purpose there is but one ultimate authority—a loving God as that God may express Himself/Herself in our group conscience. Our leaders are but trusted servants; they do not govern," professes the basic democracy of the fellowship.

Tradition 3, "The only requirement for membership in a Twelve Step group is a desire to stop compulsive behavior," states the criterion for membership: a desire to stop drinking for AA, a problem of alcohol in a relative or friend for Al-Anon, or a desire to stop eating compulsively for OA. The reader should notice that this tradition does not require that a member has a professional diagnosis. The desire to stop the obsessive focus originates from within the member and is defined and identified ultimately by that person.

Tradition 4 states that "Each group should be autonomous except in matters affecting other groups or the fellowship as a whole." This tradition indicates that groups may make decisions on any matter that does not violate traditions, which is why one cannot generalize about, for example, the formats of meetings.

Tradition 5, "Each group has but one primary purpose—to carry its message to those who still suffer," has to do with the fact that a Twelve-Step group has only one thing to offer its members—the experience, strength, and hope of recovering from that one problem. For those fellowships that have open meetings, however, it is possible for one suffering from another problem to observe a meeting without discussing it. Thus, AA's generosity in having open meetings can be credited with aiding the recovery of thousands of nonalcoholics who first attended AA before starting a new fellowship (see, for example, OA, 1980, p. 13). Sharon Wegschieder-Cruse, a family therapist and professional in the treatment of addictions, predicted that Twelve-Step programs would ultimately merge (as quoted in O'Connell, 1988, p. 15). If this happens, Tradition 5 will mean something different and a key factor of the Twelve-Step mutual-aid approach will have been lost.

Tradition 6, "Our fellowship ought never endorse, finance, or lend its name to any related facility or outside enterprise, lest problems of money, property and prestige divert us from our primary purpose," prevents the fellowship from trying to reform the world, from associating with controversial causes, or from investing in financial schemes that may interfere with the primary goal of the program. Twelve-Step groups discourage the grandiosity that comes with politics, controversy, and finance. The spiritual antidote to self-centeredness and grandiosity is found in this and Tradition 7, which resist empire building in the association, and in Traditions 11 and 12, which deal with anonymity.

Tradition 7, "Every group ought to be fully self-supporting, declining outside contributions," prevents the fellowship from acquiring wealth, which might tempt members into struggles for power. It also prevents the association from accepting and depending on large contributions from donors who might expect to exercise control over the fellowship in return (see E. Kurtz, 1979, pp. 65–66, 92–94).

Tradition 8, "Our fellowship should remain forever nonprofessional, but our service centers may employ special workers," suggests that members of a fellowship should always freely give each other help as part of the twelfth step and that special workers in the Twelve-Step organization may be paid to provide professional services in areas outside the work of the twelfth step, such as legal or editorial assistance. Furthermore, members who are also professionals may offer professional assistance outside the program, but they may not use the fellowship to promote their professional careers. The last point is especially salient because many recovering people have become professional counselors or aspire to do so and are seeking to enter professional schools to obtain credentials. Twelve-Step fellowships, following the example of AA, distinguish between twelfth-step work, which is nonprofessional, and professional counseling. Those members who mingle the two without professional education may be violating Tradition 8 and may be jeopardizing their own recovery and that of the client. The fellowships, as organizational entities, do not encourage members to become professionals or to take over and run treatment facilities.

Tradition 9, "Our fellowship, as such, ought never be organized, but we may create service boards or committees directly responsible to those they serve," is similar to the second tradition. It prohibits management and hierarchical control of the autonomous groups.

Tradition 10, "Our fellowship has no opinion on outside issues; hence our name ought never be drawn into public controversy," warns the association to avoid internal and external disputes. In the discussion of this tradition, AA's *Twelve Steps and Twelve Traditions* (1952, pp. 182–183) cites the case of the Washingtonians, an association begun in the nineteenth century, that was similar to AA. The Washingtonians eventually died out after taking part in bitter political controversies over the abolition of slavery and over prohibition. An understanding of the causes of their demise contributed to AA's structuring of the fellowship as it is.

Traditions 11 and 12, "Our public relations policy is based on attraction rather than promotion; we need always maintain personal anonymity at the level of press, radio, and films" and "Anonymity is the spiritual foundation of our traditions, ever reminding us to place principles before personalities," direct the members of the fellowship to maintain their anonymity. Anonymity at the level of press, radio, and film means that no member of a Twelve-Step group should announce to the news media that he or she is a member. This rule protects the fellowship from negative publicity that may later befall the member and reminds him or her that, within the fellowship, principles come before personalities. Thus, anonymity, although it speaks to confidentiality, speaks even more to the importance of humility. As one member of NA wrote, "The drive for personal gain in the areas of sex, property and social position, which brought so much pain in the past, falls by the wayside if we adhere to the principle of anonymity" (NA, 1987, p. 69).

It is important that professionals who want to work with Twelve-Step groups understand the steps and traditions; awareness can help them avoid embarrassment and will be appreciated by members of the groups. The organizational philosophy of Twelve-Step programs is unusual and often runs counter to one's previous experience, which leads to frequent errors by members as well as by nonmembers. Thus, one can usually expect forgiveness if one appears to be ignorant of or unknowingly violates a tradition. Nevertheless, problems and conflicts between Twelve-Step groups and professionals do occur. The next section examines some of the issues that surround Twelve-Step fellowships and professionals and offers suggestions for cooperation.

PROFESSIONAL COOPERATION WITH TWELVE-STEP PROGRAMS

A careful examination of many Twelve-Step programs will reveal contributions by professionals to their founding and continuance. To mention them all would be impossible in the space available, but a few of them stand out as examples of how professionals have contributed to the fellowships. William D. Silkworth, the physician who treated AA cofounder, Bill Wilson, offered the encouragement and support needed in AA's beginning and wrote "The Doctor's Opinion" in the AA Big Book (AA, 1976, 1984). Many other health professionals would serve as supporters, trustees, and advisers to AA. There were also supportive clergy. Reverend Sam Shoemaker of the Calvary Episcopal Church in New York City supported AA's beginnings in the Oxford Group, which met in his church. Father Ed Dowling, a Jesuit priest from St. Louis, became Bill Wilson's spiritual sponsor and helped found AA in St. Louis (AA, 1984).

Professionals have supported recently begun fellowships in like manner. Emotions Anonymous (1978) reflects the support of physicians Walther Lechler, who wrote "The Doctor's Opinion" in that book, and from clergymen Lowell O. Erdahl, a Lutheran pastor, and Mark F. Mindrup, a Catholic priest. Theodore Isaac Rubin wrote the foreword to *Overeaters Anonymous* (1980), and the appendix to the same book contains endorsements from two physicians and an Episcopal priest. The GA Big Book (1984), in an illustrative departure from Big Books written in earlier years, includes an entire chapter on professional treatment, research, and education regarding compulsive gambling. Thus, the professional help in the founding stage of a new fellowship is in the form of emotional support to founders, assistance with places to meet, and official endorsements. These professional supporters have been open to the idea that fellow sufferers can help each other and have assisted the fellowships to begin and to continue. Professionals and academics have also been critical of Twelve-Step fellowships, as the following review of professional and scholarly opinion on these groups reveals.

SCHOLARLY RESEARCH AND
PROFESSIONAL OPINION

Most critical discussions of Twelve-Step groups by scholars and other professionals have centered on AA and its role in the recovery from alcoholism, although some of the same arguments have been directed at other self-help programs. Criticism of AA falls into four general categories: (1) that attachment to AA is an acting out of intrapsychic pathology, (2) that AA is antiscience and antiprofessional, (3) that AA has never been proved effective, and (4) that AA is culturally inappropriate for any other than middle-class white men. In keeping with its tenth tradition, AA has never responded directly to these comments. This section examines these criticism further (see also E. Kurtz, 1979; Leach & Norris, 1977).

Attempts to link AA to the intrapsychic pathology of alcoholism have suggested that the fellowship is an alternate dependence. An example of this position is Bean's (1975) article, which stated that attendance at AA meetings is an acting out of immature intrapsychic needs. Later, Bean and Zinberg (1981) thoughtfully expanded these observations in their study of AA's healing group dynamics, with an emphasis on AA as a corrective rather than a regressive influence. There is, however, a valid concern regarding the pressure that such groups place on members to remain involved, which may limit or exclude the members' participation in other activities. Does compulsive attendance at AA meetings, for example, prevent the workaholic-prone recovering alcoholic from learning to enjoy leisure-time activities or to achieve more intimacy with family members? More study is needed on this question.

AA has been accused of being antiscience, dogmatic, and intolerant of other forms of treatment for alcoholism (Kalb & Propper, 1976; Tournier, 1979). The latter criticism derived, in part, from the apparent dominance of AA ideas in treatment circles, where recovering alcoholics have filled the gap in service left open by professionals. As more professionals develop an interest in treating addictions and compulsions, these concerns will become less valid. Criticism of the disease concept of alcoholism often extends to or includes criticism of AA, with the view that AA originated or at least espoused the disease concept as a central concept of its philosophy (see, for example, Fingarette, 1988; Peele, 1989).

Although the controversy over the disease concept of alcoholism is an important and unresolved issue in scientific circles, AA, as an organizational entity, should neither be credited nor criticized for originating or even contributing to it directly. The controversy began long before AA did and, with their characteristic abhorrence of controversy, AA's founders attempted to avoid it by using the term "malady" rather than disease. Although AA members adhere to the disease concept in an effort to reduce the guilt associated with their failure to use alcohol appropriately, AA's perception of the malady— that it is a combination of spiritual, emotional, and physical factors— resembles as much the moral and psychiatric beliefs of the 1930s as it does the physiological disease concept of either that era or this one.

Critics, especially advocates of controlled drinking, also question the insistence on total abstinence that is often associated with AA (see Fingarette, 1988, p. 88; Heather & Robertson, 1981). Although AA members believe in the subtle power of one drink leading to another and thus espouse abstinence on a "one day at a time" basis, the long-range and more important goal of the program is sobriety, with its definition of temperance. It is this definition of sobriety that makes the AA program so easily suited to other compulsive and anxious people. It seems, therefore, that criticism of the abstinence objective misses the point that the primary focus of recovery in a Twelve-Step program is spiritual growth.

An uncritical acceptance of AA and other fellowships by professionals has concerned academics, who insist that Twelve-Step programs have not been proved effective empirically and that other approaches to treatment may be just as or more effective. The uncritical belief in AA, this argument goes, has circumscribed the search for better, more acceptable treatments. This position is really two pronged. First, is there empirical support for the assumption that AA, and by generalization other Twelve-Step programs, really works? And, second, has the search for other more adaptable, more efficient treatments been stymied?

AA has been evaluated extensively and, as usual, the outcomes conflict. The general consensus is that AA is an effective method of recovery for those who continue to attend beyond a few meetings (Emrick, Lassen, & Edwards, 1977; Leach & Norris, 1977). Despite the methodological flaws noted in much of the research, Emrick et al. (1977) and Vaillant (1983), among others, have concluded that AA is more effective than is professional treatment in helping alcoholics maintain abstinence. Although abstinence is not synonymous with sobriety, it renders true sobriety more likely. The second concern, that AA's ready availability has hampered the search for other treatments, is even more difficult to assess. Perhaps because of the past indifference of scientists, physicians, and other professionals to chemical dependence, the field, lacking hard data, has become intensely ideological. Many members of AA, as individuals, have expressed a dogmatic view that the AA way is the only true path to recovery and are intolerant of divergent viewpoints. AA's member-ship, like that of other organizations, holds to an organizational belief system that must be understood and dealt with by other organizational participants. It is important, however, to differentiate between the views and actions of individual AA members, who may also hold influential roles in addition to AA membership, and the AA program as an organizational entity.

Another concern is that AA reflects a white middle-class male bias and is less effective for women, the lower socioeconomic classes, and black and other ethnic populations (Robertson, 1988). These concerns have resulted in the development of new associations, such as Women for Sobriety, that are alternatives for those who are uncomfortable with AA. Special AA groups have also evolved for others—homosexuals, for example—who feel inhibited in a general meeting (Kus, 1987). Although the Twelve-Step philosophy strives to eliminate the belief in specialness, such groups are tolerated and form an avenue for new members to move gradually into approved groups.

Empirical studies of Hispanic, black, and American Indian AA groups (Gordon, 1981; Hudson, 1985–86; Jilek-Aall, 1981; Powell, 1987) and more recent trends in membership suggest that minorities and women can receive help in and establish and maintain Twelve-Step groups that meet their needs. Hudson, after studying AA in Harlem and other black areas, found that AA flourished in black communities and pointed out that the spiritual values of AA make it compatible with the traditional culture of blacks. He wrote (p. 15) that AA "transcends cultural, class and racial differences and will work consistently for Black alcoholics regardless of class." The specific makeup of a particular group in which one may feel uncomfortable must be separated from the broader concern of whether the Twelve-Step program and philosophy conflict with beliefs, religions, or lifestyles of different ethnic or cultural groups.

For ethnic groups, such as Native Americans, whose religious customs vary from Judeo-Christian beliefs, adaptation may be more difficult. The same has been true for Jewish alcoholics and for atheists. In this regard, it is significant that AA presents its program as spiritual, rather than religious. It is also more difficult to establish voluntary associations for economically deprived individuals, whose experiences do not encourage organizational activity and whose communities often do not offer safe meeting places.

In his recent update of AA's history, E. Kurtz (1988a) described AA's efforts to adapt and respond to elderly alcoholics; minorities, particularly Hispanics; and those handicapped by blindness or illiteracy. Spanish versions of AA's literature, containing stories of Spanish-speaking members, have been published. For those who are unable to read, AA World Services has produced audio cassettes of AA's literature. Similar efforts to adapt to the changing makeup of AA occurred in earlier decades. For example, the second edition of the Big Book was revised to contain more women's stories, for, by that time, one in four AA members was female (E. Kurtz, 1979). A 1986 survey of AA's members found that the number of women members had grown from fewer than one in four in 1968 to more than one in three (see E. Kurtz, 1988a). Thus, when women, blacks, and other minorities come to accept their addictions and to receive treatment, they also join AA. When more minorities participate in AA groups, minority-group newcomers feel more comfortable.

Less is known about the percentages of minorities and women in other Twelve-Step programs; however, gender differences generally reflect the stereotypes of those who seek help for a particular problem. For example, a random survey of Al-Anon groups (Al-Anon, 1984) indicated that 88 percent of Al-Anon members were female, and a small survey of 150 members of GA (1984, p. 102) revealed that 96 percent of them were male. This author's observations of an EA group over a 7-month period revealed that 84 percent of the participants were white and 58 percent were female.

In the 1980s, the scholarly literature on AA went beyond asking if AA works to analyzing how and why it works (see, for example, Bateson, 1972; Denzin, 1987; E. Kurtz, 1982; Mack, 1981; Maxwell, 1984). These explanations can be applied equally to most of the other Twelve-Step programs, particularly those that address obsessive-compulsive disorders. According to E. Kurtz (1982), AA treats the "sin" of isolation from others and the denial and self-centeredness of alcoholism by helping the alcoholic conceive of the self as limited. AA (and other Twelve-Step programs) becomes therapy for the member's shame, moving the sufferer to a position of self-acceptance. Bateson (1972) believed that AA changes the epistemology of the alcoholic from one of symmetry and competition with others to one of complementarity and cooperation. Maxwell (1984) viewed the change that alcoholics undergo in AA as a transition from a defensive, negative position to a growth-oriented, positive approach to life.

Mack (1981) took a psychodynamic approach to explain how AA assists the alcoholic to move away from a narcissistic orientation and how the group teaches the alcoholic to exercise self-governance. Denzin (1987) similarly proposed that the recovering alcoholic replaces an old, drinking self with a new spiritual self that belongs within the AA collective. To maintain the new self, the recovering person must remain within the collective, which is a nonindividualistic and noncompetitive system unlike the modern mainstream of life. In all these explanations, there is a theme of changed life and changed cognitions toward more acceptance of oneself, others, and the world—a change that occurs as a result of being a part of a collective experience centered on the spiritual path of the Twelve Steps.

The literature of professionals has not much addressed Twelve-Step programs other than AA. There are descriptive studies of some groups and several studies of Al-Anon family groups (Ablon, 1974; Bailey, 1965; Cutter, 1985; Gorman & Rooney, 1979). In her dissertation on Al-Anon, Cutter theorized that Al-Anon has been largely ignored, despite its long history and large membership because it has been seen as a "ladies auxiliary" to AA and as a predominantly women's organization and thus of little intellectual significance. Cutter's findings indicate that Al-Anon, like AA, provides cognitive therapy in which the self is redefined and the family member learns to detach from the problems of the alcoholic and from the disease of alcoholism. Thus, it appears that the associations that followed AA present the researcher with a broad arena for additional much-needed investigation. Most professionals know and refer to AA, Al-Anon, and NA (Todres, 1982). Other programs need more exposure to professionals before significant numbers of referrals will be made to them (L. F. Kurtz, Mann, & Chambon, 1987).

MAKING REFERRALS TO TWELVE-STEP PROGRAMS

Professional referrals constitute one of the most frequent ways that members learn about Twelve-Step groups (Al-Anon, 1984; E. Kurtz, 1988a). Two factors contribute to whether a professional referral to a Twelve-Step group will be successful. One is the degree to which the professional understands and appreciates the program and thus conveys to the client that the group will be helpful and why the professional thinks the group will help. The second is the effort the professional makes to get the client to the first meeting, which involves overcoming the client's fear of the unknown.

In regard to the first condition, the professional must be informed about the local groups. One way to do so is to visit their meetings. If there are no open meetings locally, one can ask for permission to observe a closed meeting. If permission is not granted, other ways to know about the groups include reading its literature and inviting members to visit the agency. Visits to the agency by group members, as well as other forms of collaboration, will be discussed further in the next section of this chapter.

Fear of the unknown activates resistance to attending the first critical meeting. This author's graduate social work students have increased her awareness of how intense such fear can be. The students are given an assignment to go alone to five open AA meetings. Many report that as the time for the meeting approaches, they are filled with dread. Their stereotypes about alcoholics, formerly hidden below the level of consciousness, arise in frightening proportions. By the time they walk into the meeting, their anxiety level has peaked. One student reported that when she was asked to say her first name in the meeting she could not remember it. The students are afraid that they will see someone they know who will think they are alcoholic or that the group will think they are not alcoholic and promptly expel them. After the first meeting, they are no longer afraid.

Many of these students have worked in agencies and have referred clients to AA meetings; they never realized how difficult it was to take that first step. They had been annoyed when the client did not follow through with a referral to AA and had attributed the lack of follow through to an unwillingness to stop misusing alcohol. The students say they will never refer a client to AA so casually again. In the future, they will provide a detailed description of the meeting, including what the client, as a newcomer, will be expected to do and not do. Usually, a newcomer is asked only to say his or her first name. Following this introduction, the group may respond in unison, "Hi, ——," and some groups applaud at this time. Newcomers are not asked to tell why they are there or to prove they have a problem. In the future, the students say, they will try to find someone to go to the first meeting with their clients or will take the clients to an open meeting themselves.

It is also a good idea to find out whether clients are more comfortable in large groups, where they can blend into the crowd, or whether they prefer small groups, where they will be noticed and responded to. It may be possible to pick a meeting that fits one or the other preference. There are enough AA groups available in most places to pick meetings that match the client's social class, age group, gender, and race. Such matters may not be important after the client has overcome his or her fear, but they increase the client's level of comfort in the beginning.

Referring clients to a Twelve-Step group can be time consuming for a professional, especially if one finds it necessary to take clients to meetings. When many clients need referrals to a Twelve-Step group, other methods of linking them to the program can be used to increase their knowledge of the group and to pave the way for their attending the first meeting.

ESTABLISHING LINKAGES

The author (L. F. Kurtz, 1985) surveyed by mail and interviewed professional alcoholism workers and directors of treatment centers about the ways in which they cooperated with AA. She also gathered AA members' opinions about their experiences with professional cooperation. For some treatment centers, the relationship was viewed as hostile and uncooperative by both sides. For others, both sides saw the relationship as harmonious or the professionals reported cooperation that their AA counterparts did not perceive.

The study attempted to sort out the activities in which both sides engaged that contributed to harmony and cooperation between professionals and AA members. The data indicated that when there was frequent interaction between AA members and professionals, when both sides held mutually congruent ideas about treatment and recovery, and when professionals engaged in appropriate linking strategies, harmony prevailed. Frequent interaction occurred when AA members were employed by the center as staff and volunteers and when staff members attended open meetings of AA. Congruence over the treatment strategy usually meant that the medical staff avoided the frequent use of tranquilizers for alcoholics or, at least, explained the reason for the use of psychotropic drugs when they prescribed the drugs for a coexisting mental illness. The linking activities most associated with successful cooperation included holding AA meetings in the agency, arranging for AA members to visit potential clients at the treatment center, and having AA members serve as volunteers.

A later survey (L. F. Kurtz et al., 1987) of mental health professionals' linking activities with mental health self-help groups, including EA, revealed that professionals were much less familiar with these groups and less inclined to refer clients to them. Furthermore, they were much less likely to have personal contact with the groups or their members than were professionals at alcoholism treatment centers.

Although frequent interaction and close cooperation seem to be a key to working together, professionals and group members must be able to do so without violating the traditions. This usually means that cooperation must not lead to affiliation, actual or apparent. The treatment center should not advertise that it is a Twelve-Step facility, place the name of a Twelve-Step group member on a letterhead as a representative of the Twelve-Step program, or ask for written agreements between itself and the fellowship. Members of Twelve-Step groups do their volunteer work as individuals, not as representatives of the Twelve-Step program, unless they do so as part of the service work of the program. Because it is difficult to tell the difference, the best approach for the professional to take is to call the group's headquarters, tell a representative what he or she wants to do, and ask how the group may help him or her to do it.

Two activities that some Twelve-Step programs officially offer as cooperation with professionals are the holding of institutional meetings and "meetings on wheels." An institutional meeting is a regularly held meeting of the group within the facility for the clients of that facility. Typically, a few members of the group will come to the facility to hold what may be called a beginners' meeting. The potential members who attend have an opportunity to ask questions, discuss their troubles, and see how a group operates. An AA brochure (AA, 1987a) reported that over 1,052 institutional meetings were being held in treatment centers nationwide (see also Huppert, 1976).

If there are not enough clients for a regularly held meeting, the agency may request what Al-Anon (1985) calls a "meeting on wheels." A meeting on wheels is a brief, one-time meeting held in a treatment center for the benefit of staff, clients, or both. Experienced members come to the agency and relate their stories, after which those in attendance may ask questions. Professionals and Twelve-Step groups can also promote cooperation by sponsoring a workshop. In a workshop, professionals and members meet in small-group discussions to talk over what the group does, what the professionals do, and how cooperation can be improved (AA, 1982).

If there are no groups for a particular population in an area, how may a professional begin one? The best method is to call the headquarters of the association in question and ask where the nearest chapter is located and request literature from the association that can be used by a beginning group. If there is a nearby group, members from that area may be able to travel to help start a new group. The professional assists by arranging a temporary meeting place and by gathering the clients who are interested in the group. The professional should stay in the background and withdraw from the facilitating role as soon as possible. The author knows of one case in which a psychiatric hospital wished to begin an EA group. Local AA members offered to help, and EA members from a city several hundred miles away drove to the community, where they stayed for several days helping the hospital and its clients begin the group.

Al-Anon (1976) offers some advice to professionals who work with a Twelve-Step program. Professionals, whether they are visiting or attending a meeting as full-fledged members of the groups, should refrain from using professional terms, diagnostic labels, and jargon in the meeting. Twelve-Step groups have their own understanding of the problem and how it should be dealt with; the addition of professional knowledge, however valid, will confuse the discussion and take it outside the experience of the assembled participants. If a professional observes a meeting to gain knowledge for personal reasons, he or she should simply introduce himself or herself as a visitor. If the professional is conducting research or if the meeting is closed, he or she should inform the group of the purpose of the visit and ask permission to attend. Individual members, on the other hand, are free to participate in research in any way they choose. Professionals should not use the confidential AA World Service directories to make referrals or to mail materials. They should not solicit clients or hand out business cards in group meetings. Professionals who are also members of the group must always remember which role they are playing. In general, they should not "twelve step" (tell their own story to) a client on the job or give professional advice in a meeting.

As a professional who has attended many meetings of Twelve-Step groups, this author recommends the foregoing as the best way to gain an understanding of how the program works. Students and colleagues agree. It is also a good idea to, as they say in AA, "take the cotton out of your ears and stuff it in your mouth" at your first few meetings.

THE SPIRITUAL DIMENSION

Twelve-Step programs offer a spiritual method for dealing with a variety of obsessive behaviors and addictions. As Lugar (EA, 1978, p. 14) wrote, "Our present pace of living is producing [these problems] in almost plague-like proportions." Most of the fellowships pattern their groups after AA and use the same Twelve-Step path and Twelve Traditions with little or no change in wording, suggesting that the addictive, compulsive behavior of alcoholism does not differ much from many of the other ills of modern society.

Professionals, such as William Silkworth and Walther Lechler, have helped to found Twelve-Step associations; others have criticized them as being cultlike and unscientific and as having a middle-class white male bias. Recently, scholars and researchers have given consideration to the philosophical and psychological healing dynamics in Twelve-Step groups, and continued analyses of trends in the membership of various groups indicate that the Twelve-Step approach is less culturally biased than was previously thought. Most academic attention has centered on AA and the ways in which the subculture and beliefs of the fellowship arrest the alcoholic pattern and replace it with a sober set of rules and life principles. More study of other Twelve-Step associations is needed.

Twelve-Step groups hold in common the idea of spiritual growth as an antidote to unhealthy and obsessive efforts to control pain and anxiety. Anxiety seems to increase with the rapidity of technological change. Thus, over time, the number of Twelve-Step programs for those who sedate anxiety with forms other than alcohol—food, sex, money, and religion (the possibilities seem endless)—have risen. Following a spiritual path is a time-honored remedy for anxiety, fear, and pain. Twelve-Step fellowships are a twentieth-century invention for showing a way to spiritual peace.

Professional cooperation with AA has occurred routinely for alcohol treatment centers, which provide well-developed patterns and rules for professional linkages with Twelve-Step programs. Other professionals, except for the clergy, have been less inclined to consider spiritual growth as a means of healing when consulting with clients. Thus, understanding and working with Twelve-Step fellowships can add a missing spiritual dimension to professional practice.

REFERENCES

Ablon, J. (1974). Al-Anon family groups: Impetus for change through the presentation of alternatives. *American Journal of Psychotherapy, 28,* 30–45.

Al-Anon. (1966). *Al-Anon family groups.* New York: Al-Anon Family Group Headquarters.

Al-Anon. (1976). *Al-Anon and professionals.* New York: Al-Anon Family Group Headquarters.

Al-Anon. (1984). *An Al-Anon/Alateen member survey.* New York: Al-Anon Family Group Headquarters.

Al-Anon. (1985). *Planting a seed.* New York: Al-Anon Family Group Headquarters.

Al-Anon. (1986a). *Al-Anon guidelines for cooperating with the professional community.* New York: Al-Anon Family Group Headquarters.

Al-Anon. (1986b). *Al-Anon: Then and now a brief history.* New York: Al-Anon Family Group Headquarters.

Al-Anon. (1986c). *First Steps: Al-Anon . . . 36 years of beginnings.* New York: Al-Anon Family Group Headquarters.

Alcoholics Anonymous. (1952). *Twelve steps and twelve traditions.* New York: Alcoholics Anonymous World Services.

Alcoholics Anonymous. (1957). *Alcoholics Anonymous comes of age.* New York: Alcoholics Anonymous World Services.

Alcoholics Anonymous. (1976). *Alcoholics Anonymous: The story of how many thousands of men and women have recovered from alcoholism* (3rd ed.). New York: Alcoholics Anonymous World Services.

Alcoholics Anonymous. (1982). *CPC workbook.* New York: Alcoholics Anonymous World Services.

Alcoholics Anonymous. (1984). *Pass it on.* New York: Alcoholics Anonymous World Services.

Alcoholics Anonymous. (1987a). *AA in treatment facilities.* New York: Alcoholics Anonymous World Services.

Alcoholics Anonymous. (1987b). Fellowships modeled on A.A. (unpublished list). New York: Alcoholics Anonymous World Services.

Alcoholics Anonymous. (1989). *Final report of the 1988 General Service Conference.* New York: Alcoholics Anonymous World Services.

Augustine Fellowship. (1986). *Sex and Love Addicts Anonymous.* Boston: Augustine Fellowship, Sex and Love Addicts Anonymous Fellowship-wide Services.

Bailey, M. (1965). Al-Anon family groups as an aid to wives of alcoholics. *Social Work, 10,* 68–74.

Bateson, G. (1972). The cybernetics of the "self": A theory of alcoholism. In G. Bateson, *Steps to an ecology of the mind* (pp. 309–337). New York: Ballantine Books.

Bean, M. (1975, February–March). Alcoholics Anonymous, Parts I and II. *Psychiatric Annals, 5,* 7–61.

Bean, M., & Zinberg, N. E. (1981). *Dynamic approaches to the understanding and treatment of alcoholism.* New York: Free Press.

Cutter, C. G. (1985). How do people change in Al-Anon? Reports of adult children of alcoholics. (Doctoral dissertation, Brandeis University, 1985). *University Microfilms International,* 8518894.

Denzin, N. K. (1987). *The recovering alcoholic.* Newbury Park, CA: Sage Publications.

Emotions Anonymous. (1978). *Emotions Anonymous.* St. Paul, MN: Emotions Anonymous International.

Emrick, C. D., Lassen, C. L., & Edwards, M. T. (1977). Nonprofessional peers as therapeutic agents. In A. S. Gurman & A. M. Rozen (Eds.), *Effective psychotherapy* (pp. 120–160). New York: Pergamon Press.

Fingarette, H. (1988). *Heavy drinking: The myth of alcoholism as a disease*. Berkeley: University of California Press.

Gamblers Anonymous. (1984). *Sharing recovery through Gamblers Anonymous*. Los Angeles: Gamblers Anonymous Publishing.

Gordon, A. J. (1981). The cultural context of drinking and indigenous therapy for alcohol problems in three migrant Hispanic cultures: An ethnography report. *Journal of Studies on Alcohol, 9* (Suppl. 9), 217–240.

Gorman, J. M., & Rooney, J. F. (1979). The influence of Al-Anon on the coping behaviors of alcoholics. *Journal of Studies on Alcohol, 40,* 1030–1038.

Heather, N., & Robertson, I. (1981). *Controlled drinking*. London, England: Methuen.

Homosexuals Anonymous. (1980). *Homosexuals Anonymous: A Christian fellowship*. Reading, PA: Homosexuals Anonymous Fellowship Services. •

Hope and recovery: A twelve step guide for healing from sexual behavior. (1987). Minneapolis, MN: CompCare.

Hudson, H. L. (1985–86). How and why Alcoholics Anonymous works for blacks. *Alcoholism Treatment Quarterly, 2,* 11–30.

Huppert, S. (1976). *The role of Al-Anon groups in the treatment program of a V.A. alcoholism unit*. New York: Al-Anon Family Group Headquarters.

James, W. (1958). *Varieties of religious experience*. New York: Mentor Books. (Original work published 1902)

Jilek-Aall, L. (1981). Acculturation, alcoholism, and Indian-style Alcoholics Anonymous. *Journal of Studies on Alcohol, 9* (Suppl. 9), 143–158.

Kalb, M., & Propper, M. (1976). The future of alcohology: Craft or science. *American Journal of Psychiatry, 133,* 641–645.

Kurtz, E. (1979). *Not-God: A history of Alcoholics Anonymous*. Center City, MN: Hazelden.

Kurtz, E. (1982). Why A.A. works: The intellectual significance of Alcoholics Anonymous. *Journal of Studies on Alcohol, 43,* 38–80.

Kurtz, E. (1988a). *A.A.: The story*. New York: Harper/Hazelden.

Kurtz, E. (1988b, August). *Spiritual rather than religious: The contribution of Alcoholics Anonymous*. Paper presented at the 35th International Congress on Alcoholism and Drug Dependence, Oslo, Norway.

Kurtz, L. F. (1984a). Ideological differences between professionals and A.A. members. *Alcoholism Treatment Quarterly, 1,* 73–86.

Kurtz, L. F. (1984b). Linking treatment centers with Alcoholics Anonymous. *Social Work in Health Care, 9,* 85–94.

Kurtz, L. F. (1985). Cooperation and rivalry between helping professionals and A.A. members. *Health and Social Work, 10,* 104–112.

Kurtz, L. F., & Chambon, A. (1987). Comparison of self-help groups for mental health. *Health and Social Work, 12,* 275–283.

Kurtz, L. F., Mann, K. B., & Chambon, A. (1987). Linking between professionals and mental health mutual-aid groups. *Social Work in Health Care, 12,* 69–78.

Kus, R. J. (1987). Alcoholics Anonymous and gay American men. *Journal of Homosexuality, 14,* 253–276.

Leach, B., & Norris, J. L. (1977). Factors in the development of Alcoholics Anonymous (A.A.). In B. Kissin & H. Begleiter (Eds.), *Treatment and rehabilitation of the chronic alcoholic* (pp. 441–543). New York: Plenum Press.

Mack, J. E. (1981). Alcoholism, A.A., and the governance of the self. In M. H. Bean & N. E. Zinberg (Eds.), *Dynamic approaches to the understanding and treatment of alcoholism* (pp. 128–162). New York: Free Press.

Madara, E., & Meese, A. (Eds.). (1988). *The self-help sourcebook: Finding and forming mutual aid self-help groups* (2nd ed.). Denville, NJ: New Jersey Self-help Clearinghouse.

Maxwell, M. A. (1984). *The Alcoholics Anonymous experience: A closeup view for professionals*. New York: McGraw-Hill.

McCarthy, K. (1984). Early alcoholism treatment: The Emmanual movement and Richard Peabody. *Journal of Studies on Alcohol, 45,* 59–74.

Narcotics Anonymous. (1987). *Narcotics Anonymous* (4th ed.). Van Nuys, CA: Narcotics Anonymous World Service Office.

O'Connell, T. (1988, February). Pioneer sees merger of 12-step programs. *U.S. Journal,* p. 15.

Overeaters Anonymous. (1980). *Overeaters Anonymous*. Torrance, CA: Author.

Peabody, R. (1931). *Common sense of drinking*. Boston: Little, Brown.

Peele, S. (1989). *The diseasing of America: Addiction treatment out of control.* Lexington, MA: Lexington Books.

Powell, T. J. (1987). *Self-help organizations and professional practice.* Silver Spring, MD: National Association of Social Workers.

Robertson, N. (1988). *Getting sober: Inside Alcoholics Anonymous.* New York: William Morrow.

Thigpen, M. J. (1989, November/December). The not-so-serene origins of the serenity prayer. *Professional Counselor, 4,* 51–52, 83.

Todres, R. (1982). Professional attitudes, awareness and use of self-help groups. *Prevention in Human Services, 1,* 91–98.

Tournier, R. E. (1979). Alcoholics Anonymous as treatment and as ideology. *Journal of Studies on Alcohol, 40,* 230–239.

Vaillant, G. (1983). *The natural history of alcoholism.* Cambridge, MA: Harvard University Press.

FAMILY SUPPORT ORGANIZATIONS
The Functions of Similarity

LOUIS J. MEDVENE

$\mathbf{G}$roup members' perceptions that they share similar problems are one of the foundations of the helping processes that occur in self-help groups. These perceptions can promote exchanges of affection, acceptance, and understanding (of love in the broadest sense) and can activate social influence processes that lead to changes in participants' thoughts, feelings, and behaviors. Mental health professionals can promote these kinds of helping by assisting with the group process—by teaching self-helpers how to create a safe atmosphere for self-disclosure, for example—and by aiding them with decisions about the group's composition—by identifying techniques for accommodating diversity, for instance.

These tentative conclusions are based on a variety of evidence, including (1) an in-depth case history of a local chapter of the National Alliance of the Mentally Ill (NAMI) in Hamden, Connecticut (hereafter called the Hamden AMI); (2) interviews with 17 mental health professionals associated with the Connecticut Self-Help/Mutual Support Network, all of whom helped organize self-help groups for various types of problems, ranging from specific chronic physical or

The study and interviews in Connecticut that are reported in this chapter were supported by Grant F32-MH08995—an Individual Postdoctoral Research Fellowship—to the author from the National Institute of Mental Health. The research in California on Common Concern was supported by a grant from the California Department of Mental Health. The author wishes to thank Vicki Spiro Smith, coordinator of the Connecticut Self-Help/Mutual Support Network, for facilitating contact with the mental health professionals who were working with self-help groups; David Krauss, for his help in collecting and analyzing the Connecticut data; and Jerry Goodman and Marion Jacobs for sharing their expertise in group process.

mental illnesses, to widowhood or divorce, to child abuse, and to alcoholism; and (3) analyses of data on group process, based on direct observations and tape recordings of meetings of self-help groups. This chapter discusses the implications of these conclusions for "one step removed" self-help groups—groups for people who are supporting or taking care of others with disabling health or mental health problems.

EVOLUTION OF GROUP PROCESS

A clinical social worker employed by the Hamden Community Mental Health Center was instrumental in organizing and facilitating the growth of the Hamden AMI. The social worker was especially helpful in teaching members basic communication skills in self-disclosure and advice giving. The testimonials that follow give evidence of the group's success with these process issues. In these statements, three parents describe what it was like for them to attend their first AMI meeting during the group's second year:

> I was just my usual downtrodden self, I suppose you'd say. It was a support meeting and the leader started in the beautiful, beautiful way he does, talking about his kid. And I couldn't believe, as I said, that it happened to me. I was up on my feet giving, for the first time, saying I have a schizophrenic son. Not only just in front of family or close friends, but in front of perfect strangers. You know, it was just 180 degrees, and I spoke a lot. And I was amazed; I didn't have to explain things after that and people would talk and share. And you don't have to get into nitty-gritty details. I have not had that experience with anyone else.

> _____

> What's it like? Well, you've been carrying this problem for two years, more than that, three probably, and there's no end in sight, you know, there's nowhere to go. The people who are supposed to be helping you don't. Then you walk into a room with people with the same kind of problem you have and who understand, who have a feeling and give it back to you.

> _____

> So I went there and, at first, I just sat and listened and felt that here were people who had suffered as I had, and that was an eye opener because I hadn't talked about it. I never even talked much to my mother, my brother, or anyone. I had been so totally alone with this, all of the years. But here were

people talking about their kids and their problems, and I could, too, at last, after 29 years. And I did. I told them openly why I was there. And they were wonderful, God, they were wonderful. They told me that they couldn't tell me what to do, they couldn't make my decision for me, but that they would give me ideas and then I could sort them out and use what would be helpful.

Two of these parents said they talked publicly about their family member for the first time. What in the group atmosphere made this disclosure possible? First, the newcomers listened to other group members model disclosure before they spoke. In the first case, the group leader talked about his son "in the beautiful, beautiful way he does." That is, the leader talked about his son comfortably, without conveying a sense of stigma or guilt. By being open, the leader conveyed the sense that others could be trusted with this information. Second, the newcomers did not feel pressured to disclose and thus could be spontaneous. Third, they did not feel pressured to take the advice offered by others. As one parent said: "They would give me ideas, and then I could sort them out and use what would be helpful."

These parents also described the experience of getting something back from the group: a sense of being understood. How did others in the group communicate that they understood? The quotes suggest that the newcomers felt understood both because the others did not ask a lot of questions that required them to explain themselves and because the others shared similar experiences, that is, they offered matching "me-too" self-disclosures (Goodman & Esterly, 1988; Goodman & Jacobs, 1986).

However, extensive personal interviews with the social worker and the group's organizers revealed that a great deal of hard work was required to bring the group to this level of functioning. Throughout the group's first year, its process was marked by repeated arguments about how it could be helpful to newcomers and about the causes of mental illness. Some members believed that to be helpful, they needed to become "experts" who would provide "the answers" to others' problems—to give definitive advice about what others should do. Regarding causes, some members endorsed the megavitamin hypothesis that schizophrenia is the result of vitamin insufficiencies, while others endorsed an organic attribution that schizophrenia is caused by a biochemical illness.

The social worker helped the group members understand that they could be helpful even if they did not have the "answers" and to resolve their arguments about causes. Effective techniques included encouraging the open expression of disagreements and suggesting that group members work out their differences in smaller committees. The committees carried out a survey of what participants wanted and developed ground rules for respecting differences of opinion. Over time, the group reached a consensus about the kind of support it wanted to provide to members; it decided to try to be nondirective and sharing. One of the ground rules it adopted was that newcomers should not be pressured to disclose information about themselves. The group also reached a consensus about its beliefs regarding the causes of mental illness—that it is the result of a biochemical disease.

That these ground rules had the intended effect is indicated by the finding that 87 percent of the respondents said that participation in the Hamden AMI involved listening and sharing and 84 percent said that personal problems were frequently talked about openly.

RESEARCH ON PROCESS

Evidence from studies of other self-help groups provides some support for the idea that self-disclosure is an important feature of process in self-help groups. Analyses of Common Concern (CC) groups (Goodman & Jacobs, 1986), programmatic self-help groups for women in their forties and fifties who are going through a divorce, and meetings of GROW groups, an organization for former psychiatric patients, indicate that self-disclosures occurred with various degrees of frequency in both groups.

The CC program was developed by Gerald Goodman and Marion Jacobs, codirectors of the California Self-Help Center at UCLA and psychologists in UCLA's Department of Psychology. The program consists of a set of audiocassette tapes and written materials that guide small groups through 12 meetings, each 1 1/2 hours long. The tapes are intended to teach communication and group management skills to lay people; a mental health professional is not present. Analyses of the tape-recorded meetings of the seven CC groups sampled over 12 meetings (a total of 80 minutes of audiotapes were coded per group and a total of 6,260 speech acts were coded) indicated that self-disclosure was the most frequent verbal behavior (approximately 28 percent of all the speech acts) and that "attenders," such as "umm hum" and "go on," which communicated that others were listening were also frequent (18 percent of the responses) (Medvene, Goodman, Jacobs, & Burney, 1988). However, a lower rate of self-disclosure was reported in the study of GROW groups. Observers' ratings of 529 meetings of 15 different GROW groups over a 2-year period indicated that self-disclosures constituted only 7 percent of all verbal behavior (Toro, 1988).

It is likely that much of the discrepancy in these findings is due to the broader definition of self-disclosure in the CC study. In the CC study, self-disclosures included telling personal narratives and stories, as well as revealing highly intimate information. In the GROW study, only statements revealing highly personal feelings or events were coded as disclosures. The more structured format of GROW meetings may account for another portion of the difference. Thus, standardized criteria for defining self-disclosure should be used in future research so that differences between self-help groups can be measured more accurately.

However much rates of self-disclosure may differ from one self-help group to another, a comparative study of self-helpers and professionals suggests that self-helpers disclose significantly more than do professionals. Comparing the talk of self-helpers, professional helpers, and lawyers, all of whom were working with divorcing women, Toro (1986) found that self-helpers disclosed significantly more frequently: 12 percent versus 1 percent. In a subsequent analysis of the same data using sequential analysis techniques (Bakeman & Gottman, 1986), Tracey and Toro (1989) reported that self-helpers used "me-too" disclosures and shared their experiences more with similar others, while mental health professionals were more likely to draw others out by using gentle probes or interpretations.

PERCEPTIONS OF SIMILARITY AND SELF-DISCLOSURE

Perceptions of similarity were one consequence of the Hamden AMI participants' self-disclosures. In their personal interviews and in their responses to questionnaire items, the participants indicated that they felt similar to one another and valued this relationship. More than 60 percent of the respondents reported strong feelings of "belonging-ness" and similarity to others in the group, as well as feelings of closeness and unity. For example, 70 percent identified "feeling good just being in the same room with others with the same problems" as a rewarding aspect of participation. Participants in the Hamden AMI rated two other aspects of participation as more rewarding: "learning what experts think about mental illness" (77 percent) and "learning about the availability of community resources" (71 percent).

That feelings of group cohesiveness were consequences of self-disclosure was evident to the researchers-observers throughout the study. The immediacy of the experience of being cared for, expressed in the quotations at the beginning of this chapter, only hint at the strong feelings of affection and acceptance that were often expressed, especially toward newcomers.

These findings suggest that if groups succeed in creating an atmosphere in which participants feel safe about disclosing intimate information, thoughts, and feelings, then perceptions of similarity and group cohesiveness will be strengthened. The findings also suggest how much professionals have yet to learn about process in self-help groups, specifically about the impact of perceptions of similarity on communication. These issues are of special importance to both practitioners and researchers.

FACTORS THAT PROMOTE SELF-DISCLOSURE

It is likely that the participants' self-disclosures are promoted both by their initial perceptions of similarity to old-timers and by the group facilitators' modeling of disclosure. Initial perceptions of similarity can be gained simply by attending a meeting for others with the same problem or from the contents of the meeting's agenda. Self-disclosures modeled by group facilitators can further reinforce percep-tions of similarity. It is likely that such initial perceptions are often linked to subsequent self-disclosures in positively reinforcing feed-back loops. In such situations, the initial perceptions increase the likelihood that people will make self-disclosures; if the content of these self-disclosures is consistent with the initial expectations, then the sense of similarity is heightened, and the likelihood of future self-disclosures is greater. This sequence of psychological processes may also be related to findings that, under certain circumstances, people's self-disclosures follow a reciprocal pattern whereby self-disclosures beget disclosures from others.

That perceptions of similarity make self-disclosures more likely could be the result of people's assumptions that similar others will be more responsive to their needs, more accepting, and more empathic. If these assumptions are validated, then one would expect high rates of self-disclosure and a heightened sense of group co-hesiveness in self-help groups; these are the results reported.

Such explanations of research findings suggest that shared experiences are self-helpers' most valuable personal resource in their ability to help similar others. One implication is that professionals ought not to assume that self-helpers should be trained to communi-cate and help in exactly the same ways that they have been trained. For example, because it appears that self-helpers use "me-too" self-dis-closures to communicate empathy, professionals should validate these untrained and spontaneous responses; to do otherwise might under-mine self-helpers' ability to draw on their shared personal experiences to help others.

COMMUNICATION OF EMPATHY AND UNDERSTANDING

Especially important is the identification of others' responses to self-disclosures that lead participants to feel they have been understood. A body of practice literature suggests that therapists rarely communicate understanding through self-disclosures (Yalom, 1975). However, the early research on process in self-help groups suggested that self-helpers communicate empathy by sharing a similar experi-ence (Goodman & Jacobs, 1986). The communication of empathy is an especially important area for future research because an often-repeated assumption of self-helpers is that they can understand each other—better than professionals—precisely because of the similarity of their experiences. It would be useful, as a practical and theoretical matter, to learn more about how self-helpers' perceptions of their similarities influence the ways in which they communicate empathy and understanding to similar others.

Equally important is the issue of how perceptions of similarity influence recipients' judgments of the accuracy of others' attempts to empathize with and understand them. What are the factors that lead people to perceive that others are being accurately empathic? Social psychological research (Goethels, 1986) has demonstrated that perceptions of similarity on one dimension of personality or experience can lead to false assumptions of similarity on others. Perceptions of the similarity of the type of problem may lead people to overestimate the extent to which "similar" others understand and empathize with them. Thus, it may be that responses from "similar" others are perceived as being more accurately empathic than are the same responses from dissimilar others.

But whether people's perceptions of the degree to which others actually empathize and understand them are accurate, their perceptions that they are receiving empathy and understanding undoubtedly have important positive consequences. Findings from several different areas of social psychological research suggest what some of these positive consequences may be.

Social psychological research on helping relationships (Fisher, Nadler, & DePaulo, 1983) indicates that those who give help have positive reactions when their help is valued by others and that recipients of help feel better when they have opportunities to reciprocate. Thus, the perception of similarity can lead to a series of helping exchanges that are mutually reinforcing and promote future helping behaviors, whether or not they are based on accurately empathic responses. Clearly, such exchanges promote the development of cohesive groups.

Several other areas of social psychological research are also relevant. The work of Byrne (1971) and others (Davis, 1981; Neimeyer & Mitchell, 1988; Werner & Parmelee, 1979) on the similarity attraction paradigm has demonstrated that perceived similarities in attitudes, preferences for activities, and cognitive structures lead people to be attracted to each other. It would be expected, then, that participants' perceptions of the similarities of their profound personal problems would, in and of themselves, strengthen a group's cohesiveness (Cartwright, 1968). In addition, Foa and Foa's (1974) work on resource exchange suggests that perceptions of similarity can promote the exchange of love, which is the most personal resource; money, in contrast, is the least personal. That is, although strangers can exchange money, only those who know something specific and intimate about each other can feel and express strong feelings of affection.

If only half these psychological phenomena occur in self-help groups, one could easily understand why people participate and devote extraordinary amounts of their personal resources to keep such groups going. People who feel socially isolated and anxious or uncertain about how to cope with a difficult personal problem would be expected to be that much more attracted to self-help groups.

FOSTERING PERSONAL CHANGE

Perceptions of similarity can also generate forces that can lead to personal change. Self-disclosures play a role here as well. For example, the women who organized a self-help group for caretakers of patients with Alzheimer's disease developed a sense of solidarity only after they risked talking about the incompetent behaviors of their spouses. With these disclosures, the women realized that although they had wanted to talk about these behaviors previously, they had not done so because they felt that in doing so they would be disloyal to their husbands. Sharing these feelings enabled them to dispel their guilt and to begin to cope more effectively with the realities of caring for their husbands. Similarly, the parents who organized a support group for people whose children had juvenile arthritis began to bond only after they risked telling each other about their feelings of guilt at being powerless to help their children. Sharing these feelings enabled them to get beyond their guilt and to begin lobbying collectively for better medical resources for their children.

It is striking that in each case, the experience of disclosing previously inhibited thoughts and feelings was followed by attitudinal and behavioral changes. This was the pattern for the wives of the Alzheimer's patients and for the parents of children with juvenile arthritis, as well as for the newcomers to the Hamden AMI. It may be that group cohesiveness began to develop as a result of the members' discovery that others had similar feelings and reactions to common problems. It may also be that the participants' collective overcoming of their inhibitions about self-disclosure was their first act of developing new coping behaviors and group norms.

Such speculations are consistent with reference group theory and social comparison theory, which state that people are strongly influenced by norms that "similar" others develop. Social comparison theorists suggest that people are highly motivated to find others who are similar to them for comparison purposes, especially when they are uncertain about the meaning of their situation or status or about how to act. In such circumstances, social comparisons may be motivated by a variety of purposes: (1) to establish social reality (Festinger, 1954; Schachter, 1959), (2) to evaluate how well one is doing (Pettigrew, 1967), and (3) to enhance self-esteem (Wills, 1983). Theorists also contend that such processes are heightened for people in a marginal, stigmatized group—with reference to the normative culture—who are facing a problem about which there is a lack of consensus on the cause and how to cope. Thus, it would be expected that people could be influenced by the norms developed by groups of people with similar problems, whatever these problems would be.

Antze (1976), among others, wrote about self-help groups from this perspective. Antze's analysis of belief systems in Alcoholics Anonymous (AA) and Recovery, Inc., suggests that these self-help groups provide people with norms for coping with the problems of alcoholism or "nervous symptoms." Antze characterized these groups as cognitive-behavioral interventions that persuade participants to adopt the group's beliefs about how they should think and cope with their problems.

The findings from the Hamden AMI study provide empirical support for the idea that self-help groups can function as reference groups that persuade participants to adopt new beliefs and coping behaviors. Medvene and Krauss (1989) found that participation in the Hamden AMI was associated with changes in the parents' attributions about the causes of their offspring's schizophrenia, as well as the quality of their relationships with their offspring. Comparisons of retrospective and current self-reports suggested that parents endorsed the organic attribution (that biochemical illness is a primary causal factor) more strongly [$F(1,50) = 21.3$, $p < .0001$] and the psychogenic attribution (that deficits in parenting are a primary causal factor) less strongly [$F(1,49) = 98.56$, $p < .0001$] as a result of their participation. Thus, after participating in the Hamden AMI, parents were less self-blaming.

Medvene and Krauss also found that the parents who endorsed the organic attribution most strongly were the ones who felt most similar to other group members. Endorsement of the organic attribution was positively associated with an index of the group's homogeneity, while endorsement of the psychogenic attribution was negatively associated with this index. The index of homogeneity included three items: (1) "I think my own goals are very similar to the goals of other AMI members," (2) "I think everyone in AMI faces pretty much the same problems with mental illness," and (3) "There is a strong feeling of belonging in AMI."

Comparisons of retrospective and current responses further suggested that parents changed their behaviors with their disabled offspring. After participating in the Hamden AMI, parents reported fewer arguments with their offspring [$F(1,53) = 51.19$, $p < .0001$], a greater ability to influence their offspring [$F(1,54) = 13$, $p < .0006$], and greater comfort with their offspring [$F(1,55) = 39.1$, $p < .0001$]. They also believed they were better able to understand what was going on with their offspring [$F(1,56) = 56$, $p < .0001$].

Medvene and Krauss speculated that AMI parents learned an illness schema for schizophrenia that involved a reattribution of the cause of the problem to an organic illness instead of blaming their ill relative or blaming themselves for handling their offspring's problems poorly or even causing the problems in the first place. The concept of illness schema (Leventhal, Nerenz, & Steele, 1984) refers to information about causes, patterns of symptoms, treatments, and probable outcomes. Leventhal et al. proposed that an illness schema makes it possible for people to develop effective techniques for coping with the practical and emotional tasks associated with an illness.

In the Hamden AMI, parents learned this information through experts who spoke at group meetings and through their library of resource materials. Included in their library was NAMI's guide, *Coping with Mental Illness in the Family: A Family Guide* (Hatfield, undated), which contains the following explanation:

> Scientists believe that at least some mentally ill individuals may have deficits either in the way their senses gather information or in the way their brains process it. . . . Mentally ill persons may be easily distracted, have trouble concentrating, respond to questions slowly, and complete tasks only with difficulty. . . . Experts believe that withdrawal may be a reaction to over-stimulation. (pp. 12–13)

The guide recommends the following four ways to reduce stress: (1) develop a predictable schedule and structure for daily routines, (2) communicate clearly and calmly, (3) maintain minimal realistic expectations, and (4) make sure that the mentally ill person takes his or her medication.

Observations of group meetings and anecdotes from inter-views illustrate some of the thoughts and feelings associated with this learning. For example, acceptance of the idea of an illness enabled parents to become empathic toward their children, as this statement illustrates:

> My daughter says that suffering mental illness is like going to war. But she says once you get past the acuteness of it, no one puts any medals on you like they do a soldier who has been through a wounding experience.

Several parents noted that, for the first time, they were able to read their family member "like a book." They now noticed such cues as glazed eyes or a peculiar gait, which were signs of great stress that often preceded or accompanied symptomatic behavior. Instead of trying to control their offspring's symptomatic behavior, they inter-vened to reduce the stress before further deterioration occurred. They spoke about taking their family members to emergency rooms to get changes in medication at such points and about taking time out or talking about an upcoming job change for the family member, such as a promotion that might be the source of the additional stress.

The parents also reduced their confrontive coping behaviors. For example, one parent stated,

> At one time I would just kinda keep going along with him, you know, bickering with him. Now, there are still times when I would like to keep the battle going, but I just sorta walk away from it; it'll be better tomorrow.

These findings from the AMI study resemble the findings from psychoeducational family treatment programs that, in conjunction with medication, have proved significantly effective in decreasing the likelihood of relapse and of increasing social functioning (Anderson, Hogarty, & Reiss, 1981; Falloon, Boyd, McGill, Strang, & Moss, 1981; Goldstein & Kopeikin, 1981; Leff, Kuipers, Berkowitz, Eberlein-Vries, & Sturgeon, 1982). These interventions reduce the rates of relapse by lowering expressed emotion (EE). High EE refers to a set of attitudes and behaviors of relatives of mentally ill persons that are critical, hostile, or emotionally overinvolved and have been repeatedly demonstrated to be associated with relapse.

Medvene and Krauss (1989) speculated that AMI groups may have the same impact as do psychoeducational groups by teaching parents the illness schema of schizophrenia, along with alternate coping behaviors. In addition, through participation in AMI, parents may come to endorse a caretaking norm that legitimates their entitlement to meet their own social and emotional needs and not always feel they must first meet the needs of their disabled offspring.

Although these preliminary findings will need to be confirmed by studies using experimental designs, they illustrate the kind of impact that self-help groups can have on participants' thoughts, feelings, and coping behaviors. Generalizing to other groups, the findings suggest that people in Al-Anon learn the disease model of alcoholism and a new set of coping behaviors for living with someone with the disease of alcoholism. Similarly, in groups for wives whose husbands have Alzheimer's disease and for parents coping with diabetic children, these caretakers learn new ways of thinking about their common concern, which leads to changes in their feelings and behaviors. Given that newcomers in such groups identify with and feel similar to established members, social comparison theory suggests that powerful forces of persuasion will be activated.

GROUP COMPOSITION

Group composition is another factor that influences perceptions of similarity. It would be expected that there would be greater potential for positive interactions and social influence when participants resembled one another with regard to their type of problem, the circumstances surrounding the onset of their problem, the severity and expected duration of their problem, and their emotional reactions to the problem. However, the Hamden AMI case study, as well as the interviews with mental health professionals, suggested that self-helpers also need diversity in their groups. The strongest evidence of this need was the disappointment expressed by the Hamden AMI chapter when Medvene and Krauss (1985) reported their findings that group members were similar to one another with regard to their type of problem and demographic characteristics.

Medvene and Krauss (1985) found that the Hamden AMI participants resembled one another with respect to their personal characteristics and the life circumstances of their disabled offspring. Ninety-eight percent of the respondents were parents, most of whom were white, middle-aged, middle-class mothers. Most of the respondents' disabled offspring were young high school-educated men who had been hospitalized at least twice and who had diagnoses of schizophrenia. In more than half the families, the offspring were living at home. Other surveys of the composition of local (Shapiro, Possidente, Plum, & Lehman, 1983), statewide (Sommer, Williams, & Williams, 1984), and national AMI groups (Spaniol, Jung, Zipple, & Fitzgerald, 1985) reported similar findings, especially that 90 percent of NAMI's members are parents of psychiatrically disabled family members.

It was clear to the researchers that a number of positive consequences resulted from such multiple similarities among members. One such consequence was that a predictable set of problems was raised at group meetings. The findings from the Hamden AMI study, as well as research from other studies, indicate that whether parents live in Connecticut or California, they have a predictable set of concerns. The author recently surveyed the 18 AMI support groups in Los Angeles County and found that essentially the same problems came up in meetings in California as in Connecticut.

The concerns expressed in group meetings are those that one would expect of middle-aged parents who are beginning to face their mortality but who continue to have major caretaking responsibilities for their adult offspring. They include (1) what will happen to their disabled offspring after they die, (2) difficulty gaining access to treatment during crises (such as when the family member is symptomatic), (3) learning more about mental illness (to understand more about diagnoses, causes, symptoms, and treatment), and (4) specific suggestions for how to live with their disabled offspring and respond to their symptoms (hallucinations and social withdrawal). The researchers concluded that because of the members' common concerns, the group was able to focus on a specific set of problems and to develop expertise and experiential learning (Borkman, 1976) in these areas.

However, participants in the Hamden AMI expressed keen disappointment when they were given feedback that they were so similar to one another. Their disappointment was based on several motivations. For one thing, they wanted to help everyone who had a family member with schizophrenia—not just parents, but siblings, spouses, and children. They also wanted to reach out to families whose members were suffering from manic-depressive disorders. Furthermore, they wanted to appeal to black and Latino, as well as to Caucasian, families. The group leaders wanted to build the membership by recruiting newcomers and to retain old-timers. They wanted to satisfy the needs of some members for support and of others to do advocacy work. Finally, as a self-help group that was part of a national organization (NAMI), members of the Hamden AMI wanted to increase their legitimacy and political power by developing as large and diverse a constituency as possible. It is interesting that both the evolution of NAMI and the history of large self-help organizations like AA illustrate how the need for diversity can be accommodated by creating "special groups."

The researchers were unable to salve the disappointment of the Hamden AMI chapter with explanations that their similarities contributed significantly to their effectiveness. And, although the leaders continued to recruit new members, their success in recruiting more diverse participants was limited. Their only success in this regard was in organizing a special group for siblings. After Medvene and Krauss's (1985) study, the same social worker who helped organize the "parent" group also helped a sibling who had been active in the chapter to organize a special group for siblings. This effort exemplifies the recent national trend to organize special groups for siblings under the NAMI banner, rather than to combine parents and siblings in the same groups.

AA's history illustrates the efficacy of the special-group solution. Since its inception, AA has insisted on all members having only one "fundamental common identity"—a weakness for alcohol—and has encouraged diversity with regard to personal strengths (Kurtz, 1979, p. 151). Yet throughout its history, AA has had to contend with the problem of "special groups": "groups claiming to be AA but restricted in attendance according to some shared factor in the lives of their members other than alcoholism" (Kurtz, p. 147). The earliest divisive opposition was raised by groups of coreligionists in AA who "believed they could explore the 'spiritual depths' of the AA way of life more deeply with others who shared their religious conviction" (Kurtz, p. 147). In the 1970s, the problem of "dual addiction" groups developed, and special "over-30" groups were formed that excluded younger dual-addicted alcoholics (Robertson, 1988). Most recently, special AA groups for gay people have formed. In addition, since 1984, AA has had a Latino staff member in its General Service Office who functions as a consultant for committees and groups that provide services to the Latino population. Although little has been written about this issue, the General Service Office of AA apparently dropped its opposition to some of the "special groups" during the late 1970s. The problem of accommodating an increasingly diverse membership is a source of strain between old-timers and newer members of AA, but the organization seems to be tolerating multiple principles of identity (Robertson, 1988).

Other examples of the special-group phenomenon in the AA tradition are the formation of Al-Anon, for the wives of alcoholics; Al-Ateen, for teenage children of alcoholics; and Adult Children of Alcoholics. In each case, with AA's sanction, a separate organization, each with its own chapters and groups, was created. Similarly, there are specialized groups within Compassionate Friends, a national self-help organization for parents of children who committed suicide.

ACCOMMODATING DIVERSITY

The foregoing discussion suggests that self-helpers and professionals who work with them can benefit by taking a flexible and creatively experimental approach toward how much diversity groups should attempt to accommodate. Professionals can help self-help groups appreciate that a highly homogeneous group with respect to the type of problem and the personal characteristics of members can promote group cohesiveness and effective problem solving that will be responsive to members' needs. Professionals can also help groups develop techniques for accommodating a diversity of needs in the same organization. If the experiences of AA, NAMI, and the Compassionate Friends are generalized to other groups for families who are coping with health problems, such as Alzheimer's disease, Parkinson's disease, or arthritis, it suggests that these groups will need to allow and encourage participants in different family roles to develop their own agendas and formats. Examples of mechanisms that groups have already developed include the following:

■ Setting aside time during a meeting for participants in different family roles to go to separate rooms (for example, one room for people with Parkinson's disease and another for their spouses).

■ Holding separate meetings with different formats within the same chapter (for instance, holding a small, informally structured support-group meeting one week and a large, more formally structured education and advocacy meeting the next week).

■ Forming special chapters in the same self-help organization.

■ Developing different, although allied, self-help organizations for people in different family roles.

Much sharing of experiences and conscious experimentation with different formats and techniques needs to occur if the possibilities for creative self-help group process are to be fully articulated and explored.

HOW PROFESSIONALS CAN HELP

To be helpful, self-help groups depend on members' perceptions that they share similar problems. Group process is undoubtedly the primary mechanism through which such perceptions are generated and reinforced. Specifically, self-disclosures and the ability of others to communicate their understanding and empathy foster the sense that everyone "is in the same boat." Mental health professionals can be enormously helpful to self-helpers by reinforcing their untrained communication skills or by teaching them new skills that enable them to create a group atmosphere in which participants feel safe making disclosures. With regard to group process, a better understanding is needed of the interconnectedness of participants' perceptions of their similarities with others, their willingness to make disclosures, and their perceptions that others accurately understand and empathize with them.

With regard to their need for diversity, self-helpers often want to help everyone else who has the same problem, regardless of their economic, racial, or ethnic characteristics. Such intentions create strains in their groups and organizations. Professionals can help self-helpers to accommodate these diverse needs by promoting the use of a variety of techniques, such as (1) using multiple meeting formats, (2) forming special groups, and (3) promoting the formation of parallel national organizations that are linked by a common cause. Professionals who work with family self-help groups and organizations need to be especially alert to the different needs of people in different roles in a family: parents, spouses, siblings, and children. Mechanisms may have to be developed that promote affiliation based on the fulfillment of common roles, such as parenthood or spousehood.

Although not discussed here, possible negative outcomes also need to be considered. For example, it is possible that subsequent self-disclosures will lead some members to perceive that they are different from others and do not fit in the group. Such perceptions may be one reason why people leave a self-help group or form a special group. In some cases, such people may also be among the casualties of self-help groups. This is an important issue that requires much more study.

There is also the general issue of the kinds of diversities that are desirable and functional in self-help groups. For example, veteran self-helpers have different attitudes and coping skills than do newcomers, and, undoubtedly, some people voice more optimism about their circumstances than do others. These differences enhance the possibility that people will learn helpful things from each other. However, more needs to be learned about the kinds and combinations of similarities that are supportive or stultifying and about the kinds and combinations of diversities that promote growth or are divisive.

It should be clear from this chapter that self-help groups and organizations are highly protean social inventions. Professionals can be especially helpful to the continuing evolution of such groups and organizations by assisting the members in their attempts to reconcile their opposing needs for both similarity and diversity. As a result, more and more people may come to experience the relief most commonly reported by self-helpers as "no longer feeling alone."

REFERENCES

Anderson, C. M., Hogarty, G., & Reiss, D. J. (1981). The psychoeducational family treatment of schizophrenia. In M. Goldstein (Ed.), *New developments in interventions with families of schizophrenics* (pp. 79–94). San Francisco: Jossey-Bass.

Antze, P. (1976). Role of ideologies in peer psychotherapy groups. *Journal of Applied Behavioral Science, 12,* 323–346.

Bakeman, R., & Gottman, J. M. (1986). *Observing interaction: An introduction to sequential analysis.* Cambridge, England: Cambridge University Press.

Borkman, T. S. (1976). Experiential knowledge: A new concept for the analysis of self-help groups. *Social Service Review, 50,* 121–129.

Byrne, D. (1971). *The attraction paradigm.* New York: Academic Press.

Cartwright, D. (1968). The nature of group cohesiveness. In D. Cartwright & A. Zander (Eds.), *Group dynamics: Research and theory.* New York: Harper & Row.

Davis, D. (1981). Implications for interaction versus effectance as mediators of the similarity-attraction relationship. *Journal of Experimental Social Psychology, 17,* 96–116.

Falloon, I. R. H., Boyd, J. L., McGill, C. W., Strang, J. S., & Moss, H. (1981). Family management training in the community care of schizophrenia. In M. Goldstein (Ed.), *New developments in interventions with families of schizophrenics* (pp. 61–78). San Francisco: Jossey-Bass.

Festinger, L. (1954). A theory of social comparison processes. *Human Relations, 7,* 117–140.

Fisher, J. D., Nadler, A., & DePaulo, B. M. (1983). *New directions in helping: Vol. 1. Recipients' reactions to aid.* New York: Academic Press.

Foa, G., & Foa, E. B. (1974). *Societal structures of the mind.* Springfield, IL: Charles C Thomas.

Goethels, R. (1986). Fabricating and ignoring social reality: Self-serving estimates of consensus. In J. M. Oslon, C. P. Herman, & M. P. Zanna (Eds.), *Relative deprivation and social comparison: The Ontario symposium* (Vol. 4). Hillsdale, NJ: Lawrence Erlbaum Associates.

Goldstein, M. J., & Kopeikin, H. S. (1981). Short- and long-term effects of combining drug and family therapy. In M. Goldstein (Ed.), *New developments in interventions with families of schizophrenics* (pp. 5–26). San Francisco: Jossey-Bass.

Goodman, G., & Esterly, G. (1988). *The talk book: The intimate science of communicating in close relationships.* Emmaus, PA: Rodale Press.

Goodman, G., & Jacobs, M. (1986). *The common concern program.* Sacramento: California State Department of Mental Health.

Hatfield, A. (undated). *Coping with mental illness in the family: A family guide.* Prepared for the Maryland Department of Health & Mental Hygiene, Mental

Hygiene Administration, & The National Alliance for the Mentally Ill. Arlington, VA: National Alliance for the Mentally Ill.

Kurtz, E. (1979). *Not-God: A history of Alcoholics Anonymous.* Center City, MN: Hazelden Foundation.

Leff, J. P., Kuipers, L., Berkowitz, R., Eberlein-Vries, R., & Sturgeon, D. (1982). A controlled trial of social intervention in the families of schizophrenic patients. *British Journal of Psychiatry, 141,* 121–134.

Leventhal, H., Nerenz, D. R., & Steele, D. J. (1984). Illness representations and coping with health threats. In A. Baum, S. Taylor, & J. Singer (Eds.), *Handbook of psychology and health: Volume 4. Social psychological aspects of health* (pp. 219–252). Hillsdale, NJ: Lawrence Erlbaum Associates.

Medvene, L. J., Goodman, G., Jacobs, J., & Burney, E. (1988). *Using programmatic materials to organize self-help groups for divorcing women.* Paper presented at the symposium on Conceptual and Methodological Innovations in Social Support Research, 96th Convention of the American Psychological Association, Atlanta.

Medvene, L. J., & Krauss, D. (1985). *An exploratory case study of a self-help group for families of the mentally ill.* Unpublished manuscript, Yale University, New Haven, CT.

Medvene, L. J., & Krauss, D. (1989). Causal attributions about psychiatric disability in a self-help group for families of the mentally ill. *Journal of Applied Social Psychology, 19,* 1413–1430.

Neimeyer, R. A., & Mitchell, K. A. (1988). Similarity and attraction: A longitudinal study. *Journal of Social and Personal Relationships, 5*(2), 131–148.

Pettigrew, T. F. (1967). Social evaluation theory: Convergences and applications. In D. Levine (Ed.), *Nebraska symposium on motivation.* Lincoln: University of Nebraska Press.

Robertson, N. (1988). *Getting better: Inside Alcoholics Anonymous.* New York: William Morrow.

Schachter, S. (1959). *The psychology of affiliation.* Stanford, CA: Stanford University Press.

Shapiro, R., Possidente, S. M., Plum, K. C., & Lehman, A. F. (1983). The evaluation of a support group for families of the chronically mentally ill. *Psychiatric Quarterly, 55,* 236–241.

Sommer, R., Williams, P., & Williams, W. A. (1984). Self-survey of family organization. *Psychiatric Quarterly, 56,* 276–285.

Spaniol, L., Jung, H., Zipple, A. M., & Fitzgerald, S. (1985). *Families as a central resource in the rehabilitation of the severely psychiatrically disabled: Report of a national survey.* Boston: Center for Research and Training in Mental Health, Sargent College of Allied Health Professions, Boston University.

Toro, P. (1986). A comparison of natural and professional help. *American Journal of Community Psychology, 14*(2), 147–159.

Toro, P. A. (1988). Systematic behavioral observation of ongoing mutual help groups. Paper presented at the Symposium on Conceptual and Methodological Innovations in Social Support Research, 96th Convention of the American Psychological Association, Atlanta.

Tracey, T. J., & Toro, P. A. (1989). Natural and professional help: A process analysis. *American Journal of Community Psychology, 17,* 443–458. Unpublished manuscript, University of Illinois at Champaign-Urbana.

Werner, C., & Parmelee, P. (1979). Similarity of activity preferences among friends: Those who play together stay together. *Social Psychology Quarterly, 42*(1), 62–66.

Wills, T. A. (1983). Social comparison in coping and help-seeking. In A. Nadler, J. Fisher, & B. DePaulo (Eds.), *New directions in helping: Vol. 2, Help-seeking* (pp. 109–141). New York: Academic Press.

Yalom, I. D. (1975). *The theory and practice of group psychotherapy.* New York: Basic Books.

7

HEALTH AND DISABILITY
SELF-HELP ORGANIZATIONS

ALFRED H. KATZ AND CARL A. MAIDA

Groups for the chronically ill, for
those with physical and mental disabilities, for sufferers from rare
diseases and conditions, and for family members and caregivers of
physically and mentally ill persons have existed since the 1940s and
1950s, but in more recent years, they have reached a crescendo of
growth, comprehensiveness, and acceptance by health professionals
and the public. The 40-year development and the status of such
individual self-help groups in the United States has been uneven,
however, subject to such idiosyncratic factors as the nature, extent,
and fear of the health problems they deal with, the degree and kinds
of the needs of sufferers and their families that are not met, the quality
of the group's leadership, the existence of an established voluntary
agency in their field, and so on. Nevertheless, the generally rapid
growth and present importance of these groups are unquestionable.
The groups have evoked a considerable body of descriptive observations, along with some research findings and analyses.

Other chapters in this volume analyze processes that take
place in self-help groups generally, and some deal specifically with the
functions served by and the interactions that occur in such health-
oriented self-help groups as Alcoholics Anonymous and the Candlelighters.

This chapter discusses two important types of health-oriented
groups—those organized for sufferers from a particular chronic
disease and the cross-diagnostic, multifunctional federations of the
disabled, known as independent living centers (ILCs). A third,

increasingly prominent variant form, self-help groups formed by and for caregivers of the severely ill and disabled, is covered in another chapter and, therefore, is not included here.

This discussion of self-help groups for a specific chronic disease is based on the authors' recent study of lupus; the account of the ILC movement is based both on the literature and on first-hand contacts with it by the first author. The case-study expositions will highlight in more detail than is usual in general accounts what actually takes place in representative health-oriented self-help groups, so that professional health care workers can understand and work with them better, make more appropriate referrals, and interpret their functions to others.

SYSTEMIC LUPUS ERYTHEMATOSUS

Systemic lupus erythematosus, or lupus, is estimated to affect more than 500,000 people in the United States (Phillips, 1984). A chronic, inflammatory, autoimmune disease of unknown etiology, it damages the connective tissues and can affect any organ of the body. Sufferers from lupus develop blood-cell abnormalities, including overproduction of the antibodies that normally help protect the body against infectious environmental bacteria and viruses (Phillips, 1984). In the absence of outside infectious agents, these antibodies attack the body's healthy cells, setting off an allergylike reaction. In effect, the body's immune system turns against the body itself, attacking and sometimes destroying bodily tissue (Dubois, 1976).

Lupus occurs in all races and ethnic groups and is more prevalent than such diseases as muscular dystrophy, cystic fibrosis, and multiple sclerosis. It is far more common in women than in men; 80–90 percent of the known cases are women. Typically, the onset of the disease occurs during the childbearing years, ages 15–40. More than 16,000 new cases are diagnosed annually in the United States (Smith, 1988), and approximately 1,000 lupus-related deaths occur each year (Hochberg, 1985).

Like arthritis, lupus causes swelling and inflammation of muscles and joints. It often affects the kidneys, but it can also involve the heart, lungs, central nervous system, liver, or other organs or systems. Patients experience extreme fatigue, lose hair, develop mouth sores and skin rashes, and run low-grade fevers. Swelling of the hands and feet; pain in the joints; and sensitivity to the sun, heat, and cold are also common.

DIAGNOSTIC ISSUES

To date, no cause of lupus has been established. Because there is no single pattern of onset and no single set of symptoms, the diagnosis may take several years. Lupus is difficult to diagnose because early indicators of the disease are vague and diffuse. Patients often experience symptoms long before there is physiological evidence from blood tests or other clinical assessments.

If there is no change in organ functioning or abnormal blood tests, physicians may conclude there is no real disease. Until a definitive diagnosis is made, patients receive no specific corroboration that something is physically wrong with them. The subjects of the authors' study reported that some physicians described them as "hysterical," "nagging," "inquisitive," "demanding," and "anxious." Before the diagnosis, patients may thus doubt their own judgment and feel that their problems are psychosomatic or self-induced (Shapiro, 1984). In 1982, 11 criteria were established for diagnosing lupus. These criteria include both the results of blood tests and physical symptoms. If a patient has four or more of the signs and symptoms on the list, a diagnosis of lupus is made (Phillips, 1984).

SYMPTOMS: MEDICAL AND SOCIAL-PSYCHOLOGICAL

The symptoms of lupus are unpredictable and erratic, and their severity can vary widely over time. One day, the patient feels relatively well and energetic, but the next day, he or she feels ill and enervated. This erratic course tends to evoke counterproductive behavior in patients. On "good" days, patients attempt to accomplish as much as possible to compensate for past and future "bad days." The tendency to overdo things exacerbates their symptoms, causing them to feel ill for several days afterward. This "vicious cycle" may even be life threatening, and it usually prevents sufferers from achieving a relatively normal way of life.

Especially because of the cyclical exacerbations and remissions, lupus creates psychosocial stress for patients and their families. The chronic stress with which patients live helps create episodic flare-ups of the disease and adds to the discomfort of the symptoms. For example, the physical pain can cause severe fatigue and interrupted sleep.

The usual medications alleviate or control specific symptoms but often produce adverse physiological and emotional changes, side-effects that are experienced as distressing. It is difficult to differentiate between the physical and psychological symptoms caused by the disease and those caused by its treatment (Blumenfeld, 1978).

Corticosteroids, such as cortisone, are most frequently prescribed. Their side effects include mood swings, insomnia, depression, nausea, weight loss and gain, increased appetite, bloating, water retention, personality changes, anxiety, memory impairment, mood lability, mental deterioration, obsessive reactions, and sometimes psychosis (Rogers, 1983). If the dosage of the corticosteroid is changed, abnormal behavior is apt to occur, ranging from "steroid psychosis" to physiological withdrawal symptoms. Cortisone also detracts from the body's natural ability to counteract stress and to maintain the fight/flight response. It both simulates and stimulates bodily stress.

Lupus is a serious and presently incurable illness. To a great extent, the prognosis depends on the patient's psychosocial adjustment, since state of mind, emotional stress, and immunological factors are closely linked in the disease process. Patients frequently have psychological or technically psychiatric symptoms. These symptoms are of two kinds: a mild form of emotional distress that is manifest in neurotic depression, anxiety, tension, phobias, or obsessional behaviors, and a severe form that manifests in such florid symptoms as hallucinations, delusions, disorientation, and psychosis.

Depression is pervasive. As was just noted, medications used in the treatment of lupus have depressive effects. Some clinicians believe that the patients' anger at having lupus is expressed in a depressive style or in self-destructive behavior: anorexia, the tendency to be suicidal, noncompliance with medical regimens, the abuse of medication, and the denial of the physical limitations imposed by the disease. Patients experience a loss of positive self- and body image, lowered self-esteem, heightened stress, and depression. They fear that they will be rejected by others and hence, isolated.

People with any chronic illness have periods of reactive depression. At the point of diagnosis, patients with lupus may need help in coping with the unpredictable assaults of the disease on the body and with the associated psychological distress. Anxiety, fear, and stress tend to be greater when the causes and nature of the illness and its prognosis are unknown. Lupus is mysterious and unpredictable, and many nonpatients react negatively to it. Some withdraw because they are afraid of "catching" the disease; others deny its impact on the patient.

Withdrawal by others is not the only form of isolation the patients with lupus experience. Because of physical pain, exhaustion, and emotional fatigue, these patients may isolate themselves. Divorce rates among patients with lupus are higher than the norm, in part, because of the limitations or inability to engage in sexual relations, either owing to pain or to the tendency of medications to suppress the libido (Aladjem, 1982). Sexual dysfunction may add to reluctance of unmarried patients to socialize or to become involved in intimate relationships.

Many patients with lupus experience anxiety and distress about the financial burdens that the disease imposes, both the direct medical costs and the loss of income arising from the erratic course of the disease, which makes regular employment difficult. Patients who are employed full-time fear the consequences of missing too much work. Those who can no longer work full-time experience distress about having to rely on others for financial help. Those with family obligations may feel they have failed when they cannot provide consistent financial support for their dependents.

SELF-HELP GROUPS

The social-psychological aspects of this chronic disorder have been only minimally investigated by clinicians and social science researchers. The greatest attention to them has been paid by self-help groups organized by patients, such as the Lupus Foundation of America. From the reported experience of such groups and data from the patients' participation in the self-help discussion groups that constituted the treatment intervention in the study, the authors found indications that participation in regular group meetings/discussions with other patients with lupus is beneficial to the morale, self-esteem, and coping abilities of patients who either lack a satisfying and intact social support network or who seek additional emotional/coping help through interactional sharing with fellow patients (Katz & Maida, in press).

The Lupus Foundation of America recognizes the need for understanding of the disease and for support for and self-help by sufferers and their families. With a membership of over 20,000 in some 75 chapters throughout the country in 1988 (personal communication with Sally Gardner, executive vice president, Lupus Foundation of America, February 11, 1989), the foundation's goals are (1) to educate patients and their families about the nature of the disease, (2) to provide support in the form of one-to-one counseling, self-help groups for patients, and telephone crisis lines, (3) to focus lay and professional attention on lupus by encouraging educational programs for physicians and other health professionals in hospitals, and (4) to advocate for biomedical research with governmental agencies, such as the National Institutes of Health, and for social policies, such as for changes in employment practices for sufferers, with legislative bodies.

Local chapters of the foundation hold regular meetings and organize leaderless support groups for patients. They also develop and implement community outreach programs for the general public and work with such nonprofit organizations as the Arthritis Foundation to support their mutual interests in the rheumatic diseases. Members of these local self-help organizations work with hospital staffs, professional schools of health and professional personnel, and representatives of the mass media in educational efforts. The goal of these efforts is to transmit accurate scientific information. Local chapters publish newsletters and distribute publications of the national organization that cover the medical, legal, and social-psychological aspects of the disease. At local and national conferences, patients come together to exchange ideas and problem-solving techniques in such areas as public relations, membership, legal information, the organization of chapters, and social action. The local chapters, in sum, help the individual members through traditional self-help techniques that support peer relationships dyadically and in group settings. They develop a cadre of members who, despite their illness, develop and use skills in community organization, mutual support, and education of patients; thus, they are a model of the self-help principles of the importance of activity to overcome stress and anxiety and of the reciprocity of giving and receiving help.

In the study, the self-help groups were set up in two locations: a large urban neighborhood (Group A) and a smaller suburban community (Group B). The authors observed the groups for eight months during the regular group meetings.

The data from the study suggest that groups of lupus patients may be dichotomized into two main types that function differently according to the characteristics and needs of their members. The first type, which may be termed "primary support" groups, are made up of members who, for a variety of reasons, are not receiving support from other social systems, such as their immediate families and intimate friends. The second type, which may be termed "supplementary support" groups, consist of people with relatively intact and satisfying primary supports but who wish to establish and maintain contact with peers who are experiencing a similar problem.

The data on the group sessions indicate that this dichotomy may be a useful conceptualization, since the urban Group A was largely a "primary support" group and the suburban Group B was mainly a "supplementary support" group. Differences between the two types of groups were found in such aspects as the breadth of participation, the proportion of trivia to significant content, and the frequency of conflicts or disagreements. Probably because of the greater homogeneity and personal security of its members, Group B allowed for rapid and intense discussions of significant issues surrounding the illness, rather than for a focus on procedural and status questions, as was observed in Group A. A related finding was the more positive mood at the end of the sessions and the members' greater satisfaction with the group process in Group B than in Group A.

Group A had a higher proportion of small talk than "significant" talk during its sessions compared with Group B. In fact, group procedures was the second most frequent topic of significant interchanges in Group A. These "procedural" issues, nonsubstantive so far as the disease is concerned, involved such questions as who should be invited to address the group, who should do the inviting, the frequency of meetings, and so forth. Furthermore, the startups of the discussions were more difficult in Group A than in Group B, and fewer members participated in Group A's meetings than in Group B's. Antagonistic/critical or indifferent moods were observed at the end of 25 percent of Group A's sessions, but in none of Group B's.

The authors speculate that such differences in the content, level, and intensity of the group discussions and group functioning as a whole are related to differences in the composition of the two groups, as well as to the general climate of the meetings. The majority of Group A's members were single, separated, or divorced women, most of whom had to work. Their various kinds and levels of situational life stresses were substantial and continuous, and this situation was reflected in the often-acrimonious group sessions. In contrast, Group B's members were mostly married, lived in middle-class suburbs, and generally had supportive husbands; fewer of them worked, not because they were too ill but because they chose not to. The implications of these factors for the creation of groups have not been heavily explored in the literature; they seem to warrant further study.

EMOTIONAL "SELF-CARE"

The popular concept "self-care" refers to activities that are carried out by an individual, sometimes with the help of others, to deal with somatic/psychological problems arising from an illness or to prevent an illness from occurring. There is general agreement with Fry's (1975) list of the major constituents of self-care, namely, the maintenance of health, the prevention of disease, self-diagnosis, self-medication and other forms of self-treatment, and patients' participation in professional care. In their account of self-care, Levin, Katz, and Holst (1976) expanded Fry's list, emphasizing an additional and different kind of action that individuals take to meet the objectives of self-care, that is, the participation in health-oriented self-help groups. The purposes of such participation are several: to get information from fellow sufferers about how to cope effectively with somatopsychic difficulties; to obtain emotional/social support by sharing problems in a group setting; and to bolster self-esteem and self-reliance, both in understanding one's illness and in relationships with the health care system and its professionals.

The effects of this form of self-care, stimulated or achieved through participation in self-help groups, are the subject of more and more studies. Reliable data have been collected to suggest that self-care, stimulated and motivated through the group, has greater penetrance and effectiveness than does individually practiced self-care.

Indications from the authors' small-scale study suggest that health professionals who deal with lupus patients should recognize that the severe social-psychological problems of the disease can be partially alleviated through participation in a self-help group. Although conscious self-care, in the form of necessary changes in lifestyle is required to improve their physical and social adaptations, the lupus patients' major problems seem to be in the mental health sphere. Self-care cannot "cure" the disease or change its course, but participation with other sufferers in self-help activities seems to alleviate the greatest stresses of lupus and to improve the patients' ability to cope with the disease. Self-care is not a substitute for needed medical interventions; rather, it is a desirable form of parallel social treatment for this severe, often life-threatening, chronic disease.

THE INDEPENDENT LIVING MODEL

The 1970s brought about the creation of a new type of self-help group—the independent living type of organization, which quickly showed that it had significant potential. This type of organization, usually originated by young adults always crosses specific diagnostic categories. As they developed, these new cross-diagnosis self-help groups for persons with a disability offered many of the services of established health and welfare agencies and added some innovative ones. They took a critical posture toward the conventional forms of service delivery and had a strong orientation to advocacy and social action to achieve changes in policies.

The groups organized according to this model are now numerous, varied, and highly effective in the localities in which they are found. In Berkeley, California, the prototypical center for independent living (CIL) originated in 1970 among a group of physically disabled students at the University of California, who organized to obtain more accessible buildings, classrooms, laboratories, and other academic facilities so they would not be hampered in pursuing an education. The students' success in bringing about changes in the university's facilities led them to extend their activities into the community, on behalf of other persons with disabilities. By the mid-1970s, the Berkeley CIL had become a major resource for independent living, jobs, and personal services for young adults with disabilities who were living in the San Francisco Bay Area (Kirshbaum, Harveston, & Katz, 1976). It had done so through a combination of remarkable organizational effort, imaginative leadership, "streetwise" practicality, and a nurturing social climate at the time, which made it possible to obtain numerous grants and contracts for specific service projects. One of the founders of the organization was appointed state director of rehabilitation for California in 1975, and he was quickly able to influence the state legislature to create and fund 14 additional CIL organizations in other localities in California. Similar groups arose in Boston, Houston, and other cities in the mid-1970s.

At about the same time, lobbying and legislative pressure, as well as litigation instituted first in Pennsylvania and then in other states by parents of children who were excluded from public education because of their disabilities, resulted in the passage of amendments to the Federal Rehabilitation Act of 1973 (Title V). These amendments emphasized the concepts of "normalization" and the "least restrictive environment" for disabled persons. The most influential section of the 1973 act was the one-sentence Section 504, which prohibits discrimination against "otherwise qualified handicapped individuals under any program or activity receiving Federal financial assistance" and provided for the imposition of sanctions against discrimination in many employment situations. These legislative developments reflected the important efforts of the self-help groups and laid a basis for achieving fuller integration of persons with disabilities into this society.

RANGE OF ACTIVITIES IN ILCs

The significance of the ILC type of self-help organization goes beyond their early demonstrations of clinical benefits to participants. These organizations are active on two fronts. First, they are concerned with all the personal needs of their members, including medical and attendant care and physical restoration; vocational rehabilitation, including assessment, training, counseling, and placement; and the members' entitlement to various public assistance programs (including the special housing allowances authorized under Section 8 of the Housing and Urban Development Act of 1965). They also carry out activities leading to the education of professionals, as well as of their own members, in such areas as sexuality, which were formerly ignored. For example, the Berkeley CIL provided an educational program for members in conjunction with a university; the courses that were offered led to degrees in rehabilitation counseling and in health services administration. Other CILs currently offer courses in computer programming and other practical vocational fields.

While carrying out these and other activities, such as peer counseling and self-help groups for individual members, the CILs emphasize the broader field of advocacy and social action to achieve changes in policies. They combat various barriers to independent community living; work for the provision of ramps, wider doorways, or elevators in public transportation and buildings; promote specialized housing and adaptations to equipment for self-care; and campaign against negative attitudes of and discriminatory practices by employers. Using this dual approach, the CILs and other self-help organizations of disabled people have displayed a readiness to engage in forms of community and social action that go far beyond the more cautious approaches of the "established" disease-specific voluntary social and health agencies. Thus, they have shown a concurrent concern for the disabled people's *civil* rights and rights to *benefits*. As Varela (1983, p. 43) pointed out,

> Persons with mobility impairments argue that architectural barriers deprive them of their civil rights when these barriers prevent their participation in the political life of the community. In like fashion, disabled persons have become aware that benefit rights are prerequisites to living in a community setting. Without income assistance benefits or attendant care benefits, many disabled persons would be involuntarily confined to long-term care facilities.

As was noted, the Rehabilitation Act of 1973 became a landmark for the existing CILs and a stimulus to the creation of new ones. It was important not only to disabled persons who were looking for jobs, but to those who wanted to use the same clinics, have the same choice of apartments as everyone else, and get to polling places on election day.

Using the legislative framework of the act, the most active CILs have worked for the optimal enfranchisement of disabled persons. In doing so, they have directly challenged, on a self-help basis, and reversed, to some extent, the *professional* domination of rehabilitation policy and practice. For example, as DeJong (1983, p. 12) noted,

> In vocational rehabilitation, the professional counselor no longer necessarily has the final word in case planning. Instead, the Rehabilitation Act of 1973 provides for an individualized written rehabilitation plan (IWRP), to be drawn up jointly by client and counselor. Advocacy centers to advise disabled persons of their legal rights and benefits are another product of the IL movement. Because of the awareness generated by the movement, many disabled persons are better informed about governmental benefits and regulations than are their professional counterparts in the human services system.

The doctrine of consumer sovereignty, sometimes referred to as consumer involvement, is now a basic tenet of the ILC movement. The doctrine asserts that because disabled persons are the best judges of their own interests, they should have the larger voice in determining what services are provided in disability programs. This doctrine is illustrated by the CIL organizations' concern with the quality of the personal attendant care that many severely disabled persons need to function in school, work, recreation, political life, and other community activities. Financed by various public programs, especially Medicaid, the selection, training, and supervision of attendants had been done solely by professionals before the emergence of CILs. Now these functions have been largely taken over by CILs in their localities.

Not all CIL organizations have the self-help structure and activist consumerist stance as those patterned on the Berkeley CIL. Some were professionally established and dominated. But even the professionally controlled organizations increasingly reflect the influence and self-help concepts and policies of the more militant CILs. An important element in their influence is that the latter embody the self-help principle of structural self-management by requiring that their governing bodies and staffs have a majority of persons with disabilities.

Perhaps more so than in any other self-help sector, organizations of the physically disabled have been able to unite and take action around common issues. Thus, it is accurate to speak of the National Council of Independent Living Centers, the American Coalition of Citizens with Disabilities, and like groups as constituting a social movement. These groups have emphasized coalition building on specific issues at the local, state, and national levels. An early manifestation of their effectiveness occurred at the 1978 White House Conference on Handicapped Individuals, where they submitted a minority report that far exceeded the bland recommendations of the professionals at the conference and has become the blueprint for improvements in policies.

The many-sided important and irreversible achievements of the CIL movement would not have been possible without the creation of a particular transcendent reality—a sense of community among persons with disabilities. This community comprises persons with all forms and degrees of disability and is a point of reference, a fellowship, and a sense of common needs and purposes for all who identify with it. No longer are isolation, suffering, and discrimination in all aspects of living seen as inevitable accompaniments of the individual experience of growing up with a disability or of adapting to a newly acquired one. Locally, nationally, and internationally, there is now a community of peers to relate to, draw strength from, and work with. Although many problems remain, this is an optimal pattern of living and a desirable result of participation in health-oriented self-help activities.

OTHER SELF-HELP GROUPS OF THE DISABLED

The CIL type of self-help organization generally attracts adolescents and young adults. The past 10–15 years have also seen the creation of self-help programs and organizations that are pertinent to other age groups in the disabled population, including young children and their parents, persons who acquire a disability in middle life, and the elderly. Many of these self-help groups are disease specific, but some—such as Siblings for Significant Change, which trains siblings of handicapped persons to advocate for themselves and their relatives; the National Shut-In Society, which promotes networks and communication among homebound disabled persons; United Together, a national helping and advocacy network, based on local groups of disabled persons—are cross-diagnostic.

The rapid rise of these self-help organizations and activities among several populations—parents of handicapped children, adolescents, and young adults; persons in middle life; and the elderly— demonstrates that these organizations are meeting needs that professional services have been unable to identify or satisfy. The continual growth in the number, types, programs, and influence of these vital self-help instrumentalities seems beyond question. These groups exemplify self-help principles by providing the means for persons with disabilities and their families to share experiences and to learn from each other, rather than through individual trial and error. They also demonstrate how essential and effective it is for those who are most directly involved to have a primary and major voice in the formulation and solution of their problems. And in learning and working together, these populations, once regarded as passive and dependent victims, have shown that they can combine their power to influence social and political decisions that affect their lives.

REFERENCES

Aladjem, H. (1982). *Lupus: Hope through understanding*. St. Louis, MO: Lupus Foundation of America.

Blumenfeld, M. (1978). Psychosocial concepts of systemic lupus erythematosus. *Primary Care, 6,* 213–219.

DeJong, G. (1983). Defining and implementing independent living. In N. Crew & I. Zola (Eds.), *Independent living for physically disabled people*. San Francisco: Jossey-Bass.

Dubois, E. (1976). *Lupus erythematosus* (2nd ed.). Los Angeles: University of Southern California Press.

Fry, J. (1975). *Role of the patient in primary health care: The viewpoint of the medical practitioner*. Paper presented at the Symposium on the Role of the Individual in Primary Health Care, Institute of Social Medicine, University of Copenhagen.

Hochberg, M. (1985). Descriptive and clinical epidemiology of systemic lupus erythematosus in the United States. *Arthritis and Rheumatism, 28,* 80–86.

Katz, A. H., & Maida, C. A. (in press). Self-help in a life-threatening chronic disease: A study of lupus. In A. Kutscher (Ed.), *Life-threatening illness and self-help*. Philadelphia: Charles Press.

Kirshbaum, H., Harveston, D., & Katz, A. (1976). Independent living for the disabled. *Social Policy, 7*(2), 59–64.

Levin, L., Katz, A. H., & Holst, E. (1976). *Self-care: Lay initiatives in health.* New York: Prodist.

Phillips, R. (1984). *Coping with lupus.* Wayne, NJ: Avery.

Rogers, M. (1983). Psychiatric aspects in clinical management of systemic lupus erythematosus. In P. H. Schur (Ed.), *Clinical management of systemic lupus erythematosus.* New York: Grune & Stratton.

Shapiro, H. (1984). *The physician's ordeal on becoming a patient.* Unpublished manuscript.

Smith, W. (1988). A profile of health and disease in America: Rheumatic and skin disorders. New York: Facts on File Publications.

Varela, R. (1983). Changing social attitudes and legislation regarding disability. In N. Crew & I. Zola (Eds.), *Independent living for physically disabled people.* San Francisco: Jossey-Bass.

8

BEREAVEMENT SELF-HELP ORGANIZATIONS

LYNN VIDEKA-SHERMAN

This chapter addresses self-help organizations for bereaved people, focusing on two distinct types of bereavement: widowhood and the death of a child. Descriptions are given for several types of self-help organizations that highlight the interface between the bereaved person's particular needs and the purpose, format, and function of the particular self-help organization. The following are also discussed: who joins bereavement self-help organizations and the impact of such organizations on their members, roles for human services professionals, and the fit between the developmental tasks of bereavement and what self-help organizations have to offer.

DEFINITIONS AND APPROACHES

DEFINITION OF SELF-HELP

The debate about the competing definitions of self-help centers on the presence and role of human services professionals in self-help organizations. On one end of the continuum, professionally led support groups may be labeled self-help groups, reasoning that the main therapeutic agent in such groups is the mutual aid that occurs among members. On the other end of the continuum, those such as Lieberman and Borman (1979) define self-help organizations as self-governing and self-regulating, emphasizing self-reliance without professional leadership. Schwab's (1986) distinction between support groups and self-help organizations is useful. According to Schwab, support groups are sponsored or sustained, to some degree, by professionals even though they facilitate mutual aid among group members. Examples of support groups are hospital-based groups for parents who have experienced a stillbirth and bereavement-support groups sponsored by a hospice. This chapter focuses on autonomous self-help organizations as defined by Lieberman and Borman (1979, p. 2). Examples of autonomous self-help organizations for the bereaved include NAIM (named after a biblical city where Jesus comforted a bereaved woman), a Roman Catholic organization for widows; They Help Each Other Spiritually (THEOS); Widow-to-Widow programs; and Compassionate Friends (CF), a self-help group for parents who have experienced the death of a child.

Self-help organizations for the bereaved are proliferating at a rapid pace. Organized on the assumption that "the person best qualified to understand and help with the problems of a bereaved person is another bereaved person" (Parkes, 1980, p. 5), they emphasize interaction among peers that is based on experiential knowledge as opposed to professionally based knowledge (Borkman, 1975). Experiential knowledge, which is gained from living a life event rather than studying it, is more intuitive than rational and is intimately involved with the phenomenon at hand, not emotionally detached.

APPROACHES TO SELF-HELP

Bereavement self-help organizations may be classified on three dimensions: purpose, format, and helping processes.

Purpose

The purpose of some self-help organizations is to provide support for their members, whereas the aim of others is to engage in social action. One of the core functions of support-oriented organizations is to reach out to newly bereaved people to offer service. Examples of support-oriented organizations include Widow-to-Widow programs, THEOS, and CF. The goal of social advocacy and political action organizations is to change or improve social systems; their activities may include fundraising, lobbying for legislative changes, and media campaigns to enhance public awareness about the loss around which the group is organized. Organizations that are committed primarily to social advocacy and political action include Mothers Against Drunk Driving (MADD) and sudden infant death syndrome (SIDS) organizations.

Format

The format of self-help activities varies. Support-oriented organizations meet weekly or monthly in face-to-face interaction, which is either information oriented and structured or less structured, to facilitate interpersonal exchanges among members. CF combines both formats in its monthly meetings; presentations by guest speakers (often professionals) on some aspect of grieving are followed by an open discussion period. Some bereavement self-help organizations provide support services on a one-to-one basis, rather than in group meetings. In Widow-to-Widow programs, for example, persons who have been widowed for some time visit newly widowed people to offer comfort and support.

Social action and advocacy organizations sometimes sponsor face-to-face meetings, but they also rely on networking through mailings (such as the periodic fundraising campaigns of MADD) or the interface between members of the organization and groups that the organization would like to influence. One example of the interface between a self-help organization and social institution was the appearance of Grace Monaco, former president of Candlelighters, before a U.S. Senate committee to describe the impact of living with a child with cancer on the American family, highlighting the strengths and the weaknesses of the systems for delivering and financing health care.

Helping processes

The helping processes vary considerably from group to group. Some organizations, like CF, provide their members with opportunities for altruism (by helping other newly bereaved parents). Some organizations for widows provide opportunities for their members to socialize, rather than to have interpersonal discussions of the problems of bereavement. Some social action organizations (such as MADD) give individuals the chance to change the system as a means of reducing the likelihood that others will experience a similar loss.

Others (such as SIDS organizations) work to make professionals or professional services more sensitive or more available to families who will face the same loss in the future.

WHO JOINS THESE ORGANIZATIONS?

Several studies have investigated the affiliation with bereavement self-help organizations. Lund, Diamond, and Juretich (1985) found that younger rather than older widowed persons were most likely to join self-help organizations. They also found that joiners were more likely than were nonjoiners to have a confidant, but that the joiners perceived that their confidant was less available to them throughout the 2-year bereavement period. Joiners were also better educated, more depressed, reported lower levels of satisfaction with life, and perceived their coping abilities less positively. Gender, religious affiliation, socioeconomic status, helpfulness of the informal support network, physical health, the degree of perceived stress, and self-esteem did not influence the choice to join.

Bankoff (1979) found that widows who joined NAIM were more likely to have sought professional help for problems of widowhood and were more active in neighborhood activities and other social and community groups than were nonjoiners. Although the characteristics of the networks (size, persons included, and structure) of joiners and nonjoiners were similar, she noted that the joiners reported their networks to be less helpful and available to them than did the nonjoiners.

Videka-Sherman and Lieberman (1985) found that bereaved parents who joined CF were more distressed at the time of their joining the group than were those who did not join. Lieberman and Videka-Sherman (1986) found that the widowed persons who joined THEOS were similar to nonjoiners in age, sex, education, religious affiliation, living arrangements, self-reported level of grief, and current standards of living. However, the members were different from the nonmembers in that they were more recently bereaved, more likely to be employed outside the home, more likely to turn to unmarried rather than married friends for help, and more actively involved in social organizations and clubs.

Although there are some discrepancies, these studies point to correlates of the choice to seek out self-help organizations. In contrast to nonjoiners, joiners tend to be younger, better educated, more distressed about the loss, and dissatisfied with the other social supports that are available to them. They join more organizations and seek more help for their difficulties, especially from professional sources.

Using a different approach, Lieberman (1979a) compared members' self-reported reasons for joining different types of self-help groups. He found that the reasons for joining bereavement self-help groups were different from the reasons for joining other groups. The members of NAIM most often reported that they joined the group for the following reasons (in rank order):

- To make friends
- To be with people I could feel comfortable with
- To learn how other widowed persons cope with problems
- To become more active
- To get involved in social activities
- To have fun
- To share thoughts and feelings about being widowed (p. 139)

Bereaved parents ranked the following as the most important reasons for joining CF:

- To talk with others who had the same experience
- To learn how other bereaved parents cope with problems
- To share thoughts and feelings about the loss of my child
- To get relief from things or feelings that are troubling me (p. 138)

To be with others who shared the same life experience and to learn how they coped were among the most important reasons for joining both groups. In addition, the members of CF stated that they joined the organization to get relief from the troubling feelings associated with parental bereavement, whereas the members of NAIM were more interested in rebuilding their social lives. The members of both groups were clear that they did *not* join the groups to get psychological help. "To get psychological help" was rated as a reason for joining by only 10 percent of the members of CF and 8 percent of the members of NAIM. "Wanted help for marital problems" was indicated by only 7 percent as a reason for joining CF. Paradoxically, although members of CF deny joining the group to get psychological help, several of their most frequently cited reasons for joining (such as learning how others coped and sharing and getting relief from painful thoughts and feelings) are components of psychological help. One of the attractive features of CF is the availability of role models and a source of sharing and relief from troubling thoughts and feelings without the stigma of labeling these needs as psychological help. The self-help group normalizes the need for help, labeling it as a result of the trauma of a child's death, rather than as a psychological problem of the parent.

THE IMPACT OF PARTICIPATION

An important question raised by many human services professionals is, What are the effects on members of participating in a self-help organization? Some professionals have considered self-help groups to be alternative mental health resources. Although this view may be applicable to other problems, it seems unlikely for bereavement self-help, given the findings on the patterns of help seeking that were just presented. Those who join bereavement self-help organizations tend to seek more help from formal (professional) sources as well as from informal (family and friends) sources. Although they may be less satisfied with the help they receive from their informal networks, no studies have found that dissatisfaction with professional help led to joining a bereavement self-help organization. In fact, members of self-help groups differentiate their reasons for joining self-help organizations from their reasons for seeking professional help. Nevertheless, many researchers have been interested in the impact of participation on the mental health of members of self-help groups.

Questions have also been raised about the iatrogenic effects of long-term participation in such organizations for the bereaved (Kirshenbaum & Zeanah, 1984). Skeptical professionals have asked whether participation fosters a preoccupation with the deceased person and the mourning process and thus retards the resolution of grief.

Some authors have viewed the outcomes of self-help organizations as akin to grass-roots community organizing efforts. With this point of view, one might consider the outcomes of MADD to include tougher legal sanctions on driving while intoxicated and the greater presence of programs to prevent drinking and driving. Similarly, participation in Candlelighters might result in legislation to provide services or financial support for families of children with cancer. This section examines studies of the outcome of participation in self-help organizations. The studies have focused on identifying the benefits of participation to individual members and ignored the impact on the community.

NOMOTHETIC STUDIES

Several studies investigated the impact on members of participation in bereavement self-help groups from a mental health perspective. Three studies explored the effect of self-help organizations for widowed persons (Lieberman & Videka-Sherman, 1986; Vachon et al., 1980; Walls & Meyers, 1985).

Lieberman and Videka-Sherman (1986), in a quasi-experimental year-long panel study of participants in THEOS, found that actively involved members who developed friendships in the organization were better adjusted than were self-selected nonmembers and less actively involved members on a variety of mental health indicators, including self-esteem, depression, anxiety, and well-being. Actively involved members used less psychotropic medication and were rated as showing greater improvement in their most pressing problems. These authors concluded that it is not sufficient to attend meetings of THEOS to derive mental health benefits from participation. They attributed their findings to the salutary effects of using the self-help group to develop social linkages and relationships.

Vachon and her colleagues (1980) experimentally tested a combination of the one-to-one Widow-to-Widow program followed by a support group with a control group of those who were on the waiting list. Widows were randomly assigned to the two treatment conditions. They found that participants in the program were better psychologically adjusted than were those in the control group at 6 months, better interpersonally adapted at 12 months, and better on all measures of the Goldberg General Health Questionnaire at 24 months.

Walls and Meyers (1985, p. 134) compared self-help intervention (an unstructured intervention in which "the group facilitator worked to prompt and aid discussion of topics generated by group members") with behavioral therapy and cognitive therapy for widowed women. They found that self-help intervention was not demonstrably superior to either the control, the cognitive, or the behavioral treatment conditions in reducing depression, social anxiety and distress, and irrational beliefs or in increasing satisfaction with life or the experiencing of pleasant events. The cognitive restructuring approach was the most effective intervention. This study was limited by the small sample, questions regarding the accuracy of the definition of the "self-help" treatment condition, and the attrition of subjects during the study (26 percent).

In a quasi-experimental study of bereaved parents' participation in CF, Videka-Sherman and Lieberman (1985) found that over a 1-year period, there was little demonstrable effect on the mental health, marital functioning, or parental functioning of participation in CF. Both members and nonmembers remained substantially more distressed on a variety of standardized indicators of functioning 2 years after the death than was a demographically matched sample of nonbereaved parents. Participation in CF did alter the attitudes of its most involved members, however. Highly involved members were more likely to externalize their anger that resulted from bereavement and to become less tolerant of the insensitivity of others to the experience of bereavement.

MEMBERS' PERSPECTIVES OF THEIR EXPERIENCES

An alternative approach to understanding the effects of participation in a self-help organization is to ask the members about their experiences. This "consumer-oriented" approach has been shown in studies of psychotherapy to yield more positive outcomes than does the performance of subjects on standardized indicators. To what extent this difference reflects a bias in reporting the therapeutic impact of these organizations and to what extent it reflects differences in the perspectives of clients and researchers is frequently debated.

Members of self-help organizations rate the impact of participation positively. Videka-Sherman and Lieberman (1985) found that although no effect of participation in CF could be demonstrated, bereaved parents cited many positive benefits of their participation.

They rated themselves as feeling freer to express feelings (77 percent), more in control of their lives (72 percent), more self-confident (64 percent), happier (61 percent), less depressed (60 percent), and less isolated (50 percent) as a result of their participation. Lieberman and Videka-Sherman (1986) found that members' self-reports of the impact of their participation in THEOS correlated with findings on the standard mental health measures.

Gottlieb's (1982) study of members' perceptions of the effect of their participation in self-help organizations found that members of "loss and transition groups," which included organizations for widows and organizations for bereaved parents, participated unintensively. One-third attended group meetings or had contact with other members once a month or less, one-third had contact with other members a few times per month, and only one-third attended meetings weekly or biweekly. Attendance and interpersonal contact in "loss and transition" groups was half that of participation in behavior-control groups (Alcoholics Anonymous or Gamblers Anonymous). Members of all self-help groups rated their participation positively and reported more change in their attitudes than in their behavior, a finding that was consistent with Videka-Sherman and Lieberman's (1985) findings. "Meeting others with a similar problem" was rated the most important benefit of participation. Members of loss and transition organizations stated that the organizations were less central to their lives and their adaptation than did members of other types of groups.

In another study Lieberman (1979b) investigated members' reports of mechanisms for change (experiences in the organization that members thought were helpful) in several different self-help organizations. In CF, finding individuals in similar circumstances and the support and understanding afforded by the organization were rated as the most helpful aspects of participation in the organization. Other highly rated mechanisms for change included the inculcation of hope, the acceptance of the loss, and the salutary effects of altruism— that the organization helped because it allowed the parent to help others who were also suffering from the death of a child. The *giving* of help was rated as tremendously important in helping the bereaved parents deal with their own grief. Riessman's (1965) classic article included a discussion of this process, which he termed the "helper-therapy principle." Cognitive and rational elements of group functioning, such as learning about the process of grieving and changing one's thinking about grief, were not as centrally helpful to members, despite the organizations' emphasis on it.

In NAIM, the normalizing functions of the group were rated as most helpful. These functions included "realizing my problems are not unique," not feeling "different," and not feeling like a "fifth wheel." Other helpful mechanisms included the inculcation of hope and feeling supported. Other positively rated aspects of participation in NAIM focused on opportunities for socializing, including "places to go for fun," and describing the group as "upbeat and uplifting." As in CF, the mastery of the loss through cognitive restructuring was not central to members' perceptions of what the organization has to offer.

The distinguishing features of organizations for bereaved parents versus organizations for widows included the emphasis in CF on altruism (absent in NAIM) and the focus in NAIM on rebuilding a social life. If one conducted a similar study of other self-help organizations for widows, such as Widow-to-Widow, one would expect to find altruism identified as a more central helping mechanism. No studies of helping mechanisms have been conducted with organizations like MADD that concentrate on social action.

ROLES FOR PROFESSIONALS

There is considerable variation in the relationships between self-help organizations and professionals. Therefore, it is useful to view the involvement of professionals in self-help organizations as being on a continuum. On one end of the continuum are professionally sponsored and facilitated support organizations that are dependent on the ongoing involvement of professionals. On the opposite end of the continuum are organizations that operate with no contact with professionals or their agencies. These organizations can be antiprofessional or aprofessional, that is, operate outside the professional aegis but without a policy or ideology on the role of professionals in the organization. Most research indicates few, if any, organizations adopt an antiprofessional stance. Figure 8-1 illustrates some roles of human services professionals on this continuum.

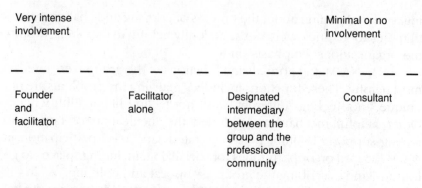

Very intense   Minimal or no
involvement   involvement

Founder   Facilitator   Designated   Consultant
and   alone   intermediary
facilitator   between the
                                  group and the
                                  professional
                                  community

**Figure 8-1   Roles for Professionals in Bereavement
Self-Help Organizations**

FOUNDING SELF-HELP ORGANIZATIONS

The founder-facilitator role involves intense and usually
ongoing efforts to set up a recruitment mechanism either by contacting
potential members directly or by setting up a referral system. The
professional in a hospice who establishes a bereavement program for
surviving family members exemplifies this role. This professional may
contact potential members for the group and then may or may not plan
to remain involved on an ongoing basis. Thus, the professional may
plan to establish the group by identifying a core group of members,
by providing space and supplies for the group, and by facilitating all
or some of the sessions for a certain period. The professional may
expect that peer leaders will emerge and enable the group to operate
under its own aegis. Fieldwork with several organizations has demonstrated that the transition of leadership is often difficult with this model;
typically, the organization collapses when the professional withdraws
from hands-on involvement.

Haber (1983) described two alternative methods for initiating
self-help organizations. The first is through professional sponsorship
of conferences that bring together activist individuals who share the
same loss. The conference provides an arena for the activists to band
together and found a group for others who are facing the same loss.
Haber gave a detailed account of how such conferences in Tampa,

Florida, spawned seven separate bereavement self-help organizations. The second mechanism is to use short-term training programs to transfer leadership skills and responsibilities to potential organization leaders. The establishment of Widow-to-Widow programs and volunteer training programs sponsored by many hospices are examples of this approach.

Another commonly observed variation on this professional-dependent model involves professionals who have experienced a loss playing a major role in the founding and running of a self-help organization devoted to that loss. One example is the bereaved parent who is a member of the clergy who founds and leads a new chapter of CF. Another example is the widowed person, who happens to be a social worker, who founds a Widow-to-Widow program. Although no statistics are available, Borman (1979) described this pattern as being frequent in the establishment of self-help organizations. There are advantages to having a professional leader who also shares the life experience around which the group is formed. Professionals often have access to knowledge about establishing an organization, running group meetings, and networking with the professional human services organizations. It is interesting to note that the professional who also shares the experience of loss usually does not found the group as a professional per se, but rather is using his or her professional skills and experience as a lay person in the role of the group's founder and leader.

MEDIATING PROFESSIONAL AND SELF-HELP NETWORKS

Intermediaries between bereavement self-help organizations and the professional community may be formally or informally designated. For example, many chapters of CF now have community boards that include professionals who specialize in grief work. As board members, the professionals usually have some formal responsibility to assist the chapters to interface with the professional community. Examples of such activities include obtaining a speaking engagement for a representative of the self-help group at a meeting of the county pediatric society, providing information to the organization regarding the activities of professional agencies, and giving feedback from a professional's perspective on a particular self-help group activity.

Professionals also give and receive referrals from self-help organizations. They provide therapeutic services for group members who need more help or different types of help than the self-help organization can provide. Most bereavement self-help organizations are careful to separate their mission of support, education, and normalization from professional mental health services. Self-help organizations frequently arrange for professionals to accept referrals made by the organizations for members who need or desire professional as well as self-help intervention. Some organizations also rely on professionals to refer bereaved persons to the organization. The quality of the referral link can make an important difference in the strength of a bereavement self-help organization, which usually has fluid and open membership boundaries and therefore relies on an influx of new members to remain vibrant.

CONSULTING

Professionals can also be consultants to self-help organizations. The types of professional consultation that are frequently used include speaking at meetings, assisting the group to plan programs by suggesting topics and individuals to speak at future meetings, and training the leaders in leadership skills. Professionals may also be called on to consult about organizational issues.

SELF-HELP ORGANIZATIONS AND BEREAVEMENT

MEETING THE PSYCHOSOCIAL NEEDS OF THE BEREAVED

Bereavement self-help organizations meet the psychosocial needs of grieving people in several different ways. Raphael (1983) described two universal adaptive tasks of bereavement: to relinquish one's attachment to the deceased person and to reinvest in life and in the future. Self-help organizations offer opportunities to master both tasks.

One way that self-help organizations provide help for the bereaved is through their ideologies, which act as "antidotes" for messages that bereaved persons encounter from informal and professional social networks (Antze, 1979). A hallmark of the belief systems of most bereavement self-help organizations is tolerance for the open expression of grief (Sherman, 1979). This permission is particularly comforting for individuals who are receiving subtle or not-so-subtle messages from their own social networks to suppress the emotional expressiveness that is part of normal grieving. The expression of grief and coming to terms with the pain that is associated with relinquishing the emotional attachment are facilitated by certain rituals, such as CF's ritual in which each member introduces himself or herself by stating his or her name, age, and the circumstances of death of the child.

Self-help organizations also support a time frame for grieving that seems more realistic to parents than the 6 weeks originally described by Lindemann (1944), to which many professionals and lay people still subscribe. Bowlby (1980), Kübler-Ross (1969), and Raphael (1983) described grief as extending for 1 to 2 years. In some research, bereaved individuals have emphatically stated that grief is never completely over—that it becomes a part of one's life. Although it subsides into the background over time, it is always there (Osterweis, Solomon, & Green, 1984; Videka-Sherman & Lieberman, 1985).

The opportunity for contact with another person who has experienced a similar tragedy is one of the most attractive features of self-help organizations and is perceived by members to be one of the most helpful aspects of participation. Self-help organizations are unique in their ability to offer this type of support, since the informal social networks of bereaved persons are often devoid of others who have experienced a similar loss.

Self-help organizations also assist with the second task of bereavement, which is to help the bereaved to reinvest in life. Many widowhood organizations provide opportunities for socializing. Hope is instilled by seeing more "senior" members of the group who have worked through much of their grief. Acutely grieving persons may model their own grief after the admired "survivors." Even more important, many organizations allow for the transformation from the status of the highly pained newly bereaved to that of an altruistic helper or activist who assists others to adapt to their losses or who prevents such losses from occurring in the future. They offer the opportunity to act in memory of the person who died by taking on a new, valued role in life—helping others facing similar tragedies.

Rarely will one self-help organization serve all the functions just outlined. Different organizations offer different approaches and potential benefits for members. It is important for human services professionals to be knowledgeable about the unique benefits that particular organizations can offer their members.

Knowledge about the bereavement process indicates that there are factors that make the process of grieving more difficult and increase the risk of poor adaptation by the survivor (Kübler-Ross, 1969; Osterweis et al., 1984; Raphael, 1983). Risk factors include certain circumstances of the death (such as sudden, unexpected, or untimely deaths and death after a prolonged deteriorating illness); the quality of the preexisting relationship with the deceased person (with strained or ambivalent relationships related to more difficulty grieving); social resources, including the social network's supportiveness and encouragement of grief; and other stressors and previous losses, particularly the death of parents when the person was a child. Individual self-help organizations address some of these factors. There are groups for family members and friends of suicide victims and of dead children—two losses that often result in the poor adaptation of surviving family members and friends.

It is also noteworthy that individuals who are more distressed during their grief tend to join self-help organizations at a higher rate than do those who experience less distress. Younger widows are more likely to experience more psychosocial difficulties than are older widows; they also join self-help organizations at a higher rate than do older widows. It appears that self-selection into self-help organizations works well. Those who have the greatest need tend to join.

PROVIDING SOCIAL SUPPORT FOR BEREAVEMENT

Researchers have found that social support mitigates the negative effects of bereavement. In their review of research on widowhood, Windholz, Marmar, and Horowitz (1985) concluded that the variable that has most consistently been found to predict better adjustment to widowhood is the perception of social support. The nature of social support and the manner in which it actually affects the process of grieving are unknown, since the definition of social support has not been consistent across studies. Most studies used global perceptions as measures of social support. Since perceptions are influenced by the person who experiences them, as well as the stimulus perceived, the actual amount and type of support that are available is not known.

Maddison and Walker (1967, p. 1065) found that

> good outcome subjects perceived permissive support in their environments as helpful, appreciating more active encouragement from the environment. Bad outcome subjects tended to perceive the environment as actively unhelpful, the relevant interchanges usually involving either the blocking of a widow's expression of affect, or covert or overt hostility directed towards her. Attempts to focus her attention to the future and to discourage her thinking of the past tended to be found unhelpful by the bad outcome subjects.

Raphael (1977) found that widows perceived that they had little social support available to them. In addition, widows whose husbands died from traumatic causes and who perceived limited social support had poorer outcomes. Bornstein, Clayton, Halikas, Maurice, and Robins (1973) identified some more-specifically operationalized indicators of social support that distinguished between depressed and nondepressed widows. They found that depressed widows less frequently lived with families and did not attend church.

Self-help organizations appear to offer social support that can mitigate some of the stress of widowhood. They provide a community affiliation that is similar in some ways to religious affiliation. Some self-help organizations are either directly affiliated with a religious organization (like NAIM) or are partly spiritual in mission (like THEOS). Many self-help groups for the bereaved explicitly support the belief that members need to express their grief and have a time to reflect on and talk about the person who died (Lieberman, 1979b; Sherman, 1979).

Self-help organizations augment social support for the bereaved person if the bereaved person becomes actively involved in the group. Since numerous studies have shown that social support can reduce the negative health and mental health sequelae of bereavement, self-help organizations have an important role to play in preventing psychological and physical morbidity in bereaved persons. If members take advantage of what the group has to offer, it is the social support mechanism that produces the positive personal outcomes.

GAPS IN SELF-HELP

There are two major gaps in the knowledge about self-help for the bereaved. The first has to do with the availability of self-help organizations. Self-help organizations have served a disproportionate number of middle-class persons compared with lower-class persons. This situation is ironic, since mortality statistics show that poorer individuals experience higher mortality rates throughout the life cycle.

There is also little information on self-help alternatives for particular ethnic groups. Related work in the area of natural helpers in low-income neighborhoods (Norton, Morales, & Andrews, 1980) and in church organizations as a helping resource for the elderly should be used as models for future research on bereavement self-help organizations to broaden our horizons on social supports and mutual helping for the bereaved.

Finally, little attention has been paid to social action-oriented self-help organizations for the bereaved. Research should be undertaken to broaden and deepen our knowledge of these organizations. Outcomes other than mental health outcomes for participants in groups also need to be considered in future research.

In conclusion, self-help organizations for the bereaved are proliferating at a rapid pace and provide positive benefits for certain members. There is evidence that these organizations work compatibly with professional services and should be perceived as important sources of comfort and help for their members.

REFERENCES

Antze, P. (1979). Role of ideologies in peer psychotherapy groups. In M. A. Lieberman & L. D. Borman (Eds.), *Self-help groups for coping with crisis*. San Francisco: Jossey-Bass.
Bankoff, E. A. (1979). Widowhood groups as an alternative to informal social support. In M. A. Lieberman & L. D. Borman (Eds.), *Self-help groups for coping with crisis*. San Francisco: Jossey-Bass.

Borkman, T. (1975). Experiential knowledge: A new concept for the analysis of self-help groups. *Social Service Review, 50,* 445–456.

Borman, L. D. (1979). Characteristics of development and growth. In M. A. Lieberman & L. D. Borman (Eds.), *Self-help groups for coping with crisis.* San Francisco: Jossey-Bass.

Bornstein, P. E., Clayton, P. J., Halikas, J. A., Maurice, W. L., & Robins, E. (1973). The depression of widowhood after thirteen months. *British Journal of Psychiatry, 122,* 561–566.

Bowlby, J. (1980). *Attachment and loss: Vol. 3. Loss, sadness and depression.* New York: Basic Books.

Gottlieb, B. H. (1982). Mutual help groups: Members' views of their benefits and roles for professionals. *Prevention in Human Services, 1,* 55–68.

Haber, D. (1983). Promoting mutual aid groups among older persons. *The Gerontologist, 23,* 251–253.

Kirshenbaum, K. S., & Zeanah, P. D. (1984). Repeated participation in a bereaved parents' group: Two case studies and implications for clinicians. *Children's Health Care, 13,* 64–70.

Kübler-Ross, E. (1969). *On death and dying.* New York: Macmillan.

Lieberman, M. A. (1979a). Helpseeking and self-help groups. In M. A. Lieberman & L. D. Borman (Eds.), *Self-help groups for coping with crisis.* San Francisco: Jossey-Bass.

Lieberman, M. A. (1979b). Analyzing change mechanisms in groups. In M. A. Lieberman & L. D. Borman (Eds.), *Self-help groups for coping with crisis.* San Francisco: Jossey-Bass.

Lieberman, M. A., & Borman, L. D. (1979). Overview: The nature of self-help groups. In M. A. Lieberman & L. D. Borman (Eds.), *Self-help groups for coping with crisis.* San Francisco: Jossey-Bass.

Lieberman, M. A., & Videka-Sherman, L. (1986). The impact of self-help groups on the mental health of widows and widowers. *American Journal of Orthopsychiatry, 56,* 435–449.

Lindemann, E. (1944). Symptomatology and management of acute grief. *American Journal of Psychiatry, 101,* 141–149.

Lund, D. A., Diamond, M., & Juretich, M. (1985). Bereavement support groups for the elderly: Characteristics of potential participants. *Death Studies, 9,* 309–321.

Maddison, D., & Walker, W. L. (1967). Factors affecting the outcome of conjugal bereavement. *British Journal of Psychiatry, 113,* 1057–1067.

Norton, D., Morales, J., & Andrews, E. (1980). *The neighborhood self-help project.* Occasional paper No. 9. Chicago: University of Chicago, School of Social Service Administration.

Osterweis, M., Solomon, F., & Green, M. (Eds.). (1984). *Bereavement: Reactions, consequences and care.* Washington, DC: National Academy Press.

Parkes, C. M. (1980). Bereavement counselling: Does it work? *British Medical Journal, 281,* 3–6.

Raphael, B. (1977). Preventive intervention with the recently bereaved. *Archives of General Psychiatry, 34,* 1450–1454.

Raphael, B. (1983). *The anatomy of bereavement.* New York: Basic Books.

Riessman, F. (1965). The "helper" therapy principle. *Social Work 10*(2), 27–32.

Schwab, R. (1986). Support groups for the bereaved. *Journal for Specialists in Group Work, 11,* 100–106.

Sherman, B. R. (1979). Emergence of ideology in a bereaved parents' group. In M. A. Lieberman & L. D. Borman (Eds.), *Self-help groups for coping with crisis.* San Francisco: Jossey-Bass.

Vachon, M. L. S., Sheldon, A. R., Lancee, W. J., Lyall, W. A. L., Rogers, J., & Freeman, S. J. J. (1980). A controlled study of self-help intervention for widows. *American Journal of Psychiatry, 137,* 1380–1384.

Videka-Sherman, L., & Lieberman, M. A. (1985). The impact of self-help and professional help on parental bereavement: The limits of recovery. *American Journal of Orthopsychiatry, 55,* 70–81.

Walls, N., & Meyers, A. W. (1985). Outcome in group treatments for bereavement: Experimental results and recommendations for clinical practice. *International Journal of Mental Health, 13,* 126–147.

Windholz, M. J., Marmar, C. R., & Horowitz, M. J. (1985). A review of the research on conjugal bereavement: Impact on health and efficacy of intervention. *Comprehensive Psychiatry, 26,* 333–340.

PART THREE

CONSIDERATIONS AND APPROACHES RELEVANT TO WORKING WITH SELF-HELP ORGANIZATIONS

9

PROFESSIONALLY FACILITATED SELF-HELP GROUPS
Benefits for Professionals and Members

CHRISTINE M. COMSTOCK AND
JOYCE L. MOHAMOUD

Many statements have been made about the superiority of "pure" self-help, that is, self-help without professional involvement. This presumed superiority would seem to perpetuate the belief that self-help and "professionalism" are antagonistic, not complementary, and that human services professionals are overly professionalized. Furthermore, many professionals and some members believe that when professionals and self-helpers interact, the professionals, not the members of the self-help groups, are the center of change. However, the authors contend that in self-help groups, both the members and the professionals gain when they maintain respect for individual differences and internalize the self-help philosophy and ethos.

Further insight may be gained by looking at the trends in the larger society. There is a growing awareness and acceptance of movements and groups that Lieberman, Borman, and Associates (1979) described as providing "information about self-reliance and individualism." Over the past few decades, associations and task forces of individuals and organizations that are concerned with health and mental health issues have proliferated almost as rapidly as have self-help groups. Among these associations and task forces are such diverse groups as clubs for minority businesspersons, the California Governor's Task Force on Wellness, spiritualist churches, proponents of EST, holistic health associations, and Reiki healers. Millions of "self-help" books, such as *Love Is Letting Go of Fear* (Jampolsky, 1979), *Dianetics* (Hubbard, 1983), *Women Who Love Too Much* (Norwood,

1985), and *Learning to Love Yourself* (Wegschider-Cruse, 1987), have
been sold.

As a result, many people, regardless of their training or
inclinations, are increasingly taking personal responsibility for their
physical, emotional, and spiritual health. This "responsibility" can be
expressed by joining self-help groups or obtaining professional
services to the extent that is necessary to accomplish the desired
changes, or both. A sense of personal responsibility in professionals
and members of self-help groups can facilitate positive change for
both, as long as both respect each other's individuality.

Respect for individual differences is a cornerstone of group
interactions in self-help. Such respect can occur only when one
constantly evaluates and reevaluates one's personal preferences,
prejudices, and beliefs and accepts those of others. Jones (1989), a
senior field consultant at the Child Welfare League of America,
developed this point when discussing the relationship between racism
and child protective services. She stated,

> Intervention cannot facilitate or promote practices that diminish the integrity
> of any group. Any intervention must see differences as neither good nor bad,
> but simply different. The choice of intervention must neither be guided by
> our individual prejudices or perceptions, nor directed by institutionalized
> policies that ignore cultural and ethnic differences. Accessibility to and
> availability of services cannot be predetermined by the color of one's skin,
> the language one speaks or the culture in which one lives.

Although Jones spoke within a context of racism and prejudices, the
value of accepting individual differences in a nonjudgmental way
cannot be ignored by anyone. Members of self-help groups have long
recognized this necessity, and professionals who act as facilitators
have little success until they are able to incorporate this philosophy.

BENEFITS FOR PROFESSIONALS

When one interviews professionals who are interested in
facilitating self-help groups (as both authors have done to select
leaders for Parents Anonymous [PA] groups), it soon becomes apparent that they have more than altruistic reasons for wanting to become
involved. Professionals know that they will grow professionally and

personally by facilitating self-help groups. In most cases, "facilitation," actually means participating, sharing, and making gains from a different, but no less personal, stance than that of the members.

The helper-therapy principle (Riessman, 1965) has been advanced as one explanation of why members of self-help groups are helped. Borkman (1987, Part 2, Sec. F, p. 2) postulated nine mechanisms, based on Gartner and Riessman's (1977) discussion, that explain this principle:

1 The helper feels an increased level of interpersonal competence as a result of making an impact on another's life.

2 The helper feels a sense of equality in giving and taking between himself/herself and others.

3 The helper often receives valuable personalized learning while giving to the other.

4 The helper often receives social approval from the helpee.

5 Helpers persuade or reinforce themselves in the messages they are trying to communicate to the helpee.

6 The helper becomes less dependent.

7 The helper is struggling with the same problem as the helpee.

8 The helper obtains a feeling of social usefulness by playing the helping role.

9 The helper role may act as a distracting source of involvement, diverting attention from the helper's own problems.

With the exception of the seventh mechanism, all the mechanisms describe benefits that professionals may derive from working with self-help groups when they "join" with the group in the spirit of acceptance described above. Compassionate Friends is an example of a self-help group in which professionals are active in the formative or active stages of a chapter of the organization. Because of the role played by the professional in the PA self-help model, the authors are able to address the issue of professional participation in self-help groups by describing the way professional facilitators in PA—called sponsors—interact and work with the groups and by analyzing the personal and professional payoffs to them.

As is perhaps the case with no other self-help group, professionals are intimately involved in PA. Ironically, Silverman (1980) described PA as having developed as a result of the failure of professional therapists to treat cases of child abuse effectively. (This view is likely to be truer for self-help groups that actively prohibit professional involvement than of PA, which embraces the partnership between professionals and parents.) The mission statement of PA states that "Parents Anonymous is a professionally facilitated self-help program for parents experiencing child-rearing difficulties." In PA, professionals coordinate with the member leaders (chairpersons) of the individual groups. The chairpersons stay in touch with other parents between meetings, lead the groups, and assume other group-leadership responsibilities, such as opening the meeting places and bringing refreshments. The effectiveness of this program in reducing abusive behavior, increasing knowledge about normal child-rearing skills, and instilling self-esteem and social skills has been well documented elsewhere (Behavior Associates, 1976). The validity of the program is exemplified by the increase in referrals by professionals to it from 3 percent in 1976 to 41 percent in 1988 (PA Chartered State Organizations, 1988). However, the ways in which professional facilitators interact with and benefit from participation in PA and other self-help groups has not been considered.

In PA, professionals may work on the national, state, or local levels to help develop and stabilize local chapters. Professionals may also act as consultants, providing technical assistance in the development of programs and in public relations, and as fundraisers. As group facilitators, or sponsors, professionals participate at the grass-roots level. Sponsors meet with their chapters weekly and participate in groups at their own level. The *Parents Anonymous Chairperson-Sponsor Manual* (1982) discusses the need for professionals to be comfortable with their role as parents. The manual further states,

> It is critical for the [professional] sponsor to serve as a positive model, to impart to the group some of the pleasure he/she realizes from parenting, to support the parenting skills group members do have (and they will have some), and to provide them with alternatives to the not-so-comfortable ways in which they parent.
>
> Too often, professionals believe that in order to work effectively with people who have problems, they must maintain a certain personal emotional distance. They don't let their own fears, anxieties, angers, uncertainties, and vulnerabilities show because to do so is unprofessional. Parents Anonymous sponsors, on the other hand, are encouraged to become more comfortable with shortcomings, needs and failures. This gives the parents in the chapters role models who are both more human and more accessible.

> For some parents in a Parents Anonymous group, a sponsor may be the first professional they have ever come into contact with and been free to relate to up close. Often, parents with abuse problems are afraid to make use of community services that could be valuable to them simply because they don't want to deal with the professionals who staff them. The image of a warm, caring, responsive individual may change their minds, and the presence of the professional sponsor can make a noticeable difference in how the parent is perceived and treated by agency personnel and can go a long way toward making the parent feel more relaxed. (p. 22)

Professional facilitators receive extensive training before their direct involvement with the groups. This training includes information about child abuse and neglect and information about group process and the role of the chairperson and professional sponsor. Within the context of a PA group, professional sponsors have an opportunity to become more broadly involved, for example, by driving parents and/ or other volunteers to and from meetings, by sharing foods made at home, and, perhaps, by sharing personal information with members of the group.

Professionals who are involved with PA groups increase their repertoire of personal and professional skills, their knowledge base, and often their reputation as competent therapists. By incorporating the self-help ethos and philosophy, they learn to relate to group members in a way that enhances the development of the group, its members, and themselves.

L. Gomorrah, who has been a PA sponsor for 13 years, is an example of how a professional can grow from involvement in PA (personal communication, 1986). When she started, she was the new director of a Head Start child care center in a rural area and the new recipient of a bachelor of social work degree. She is currently a respected researcher in her area of expertise, the developer of a new self-help model, and a member of a national board of a prominent self-help group. She would be the first to acknowledge that involvement in a PA group helped shape her professional career. By providing an egalitarian atmosphere of support and acceptance within which she could develop her personal and professional skills, PA helped her to achieve her goals.

Self-help groups not only provide treatment resources but are an unparalleled source of clinical information that has directly influenced the practice of psychotherapy and the normative patterns for society in general. Abusive out-of-control parents, once regarded as "monsters," now are viewed differently by both professionals and the general public. It was in self-help groups that parents first talked with each other about child abuse and about their own experiences as children. In the past, parents met together almost in spite of the professionals, many of whom warned against participation in self-help groups, fearing that abusive parents might give each other ideas about innovative ways to abuse their children and egg each other on. The reality has been far different. As parents shared their experiences as children and their struggles to parent their children, the then unknown information about the intergenerational cycle of child abuse emerged. Now, the concept of parenting as a learned behavior is widely accepted in both the professional and lay communities.

It was also through self-help groups that the subject of incest was discussed openly and comprehensively. When victims of incest began talking with each other, more complete stories about the families, the violence, and the victims emerged. The sense of shame has lessened as a result of this sharing, and the clinical information gained from these discussions has enabled professionals to help survivors work through their experiences far more effectively than when the professionals were dependent on the sparse information available through individual sessions.

SELF-HELP GROUPS AND PROFESSIONAL THERAPY

Professional attitudes toward self-help groups differ markedly from those that prevailed just 20 years ago. Today, many psychologists will not treat problem drinkers who are not committed to attend Alcoholics Anonymous, many psychiatrists strongly encourage patients to joint Adult Children of Alcoholics, many nurses recommend various self-help groups, and many professionals from various other disciplines recognize that self-help groups are an important addition to traditional psychotherapy and add self-help groups as adjunctive therapies to their treatment plans (see, for example, Ganzarain & Buchele, 1988; Putnam, 1989).

Self-help groups can add specific information about a particular subject, provide general support for the individual, and encourage the member to risk growth. They accelerate therapy with 24-hour-a-day support that a therapist neither can nor should provide. Suggestions of the coping strategies that others have found to be successful lessen the member's sense of helplessness, and the dramatic increase in social contacts immediately expands his or her world. Cognitive understanding is increased as the members share information, conceptual frameworks, and reading material. Even the "simple" experience of watching other members express their feelings—of pain, anger, despair, hopelessness, and joy—helps the individual to feel his or her own pain, as well as to begin to deal with the feelings of helplessness for not being able to "fix" it.

Pressure by the group to "conform" to the group's norms usually encourages a person to "work the program." Those who are most apt to rebel against such pressure generally drop out. The failure to adhere to the group's norms eventually results in the other members' exclusion and discounting of the person, rather than giving him or her more attention. People who seem to have expectations of "special" treatment from the world and from the therapist may at first perceive the group's expectations that they will get better to be an injury or an attack, but as they continue in the group, they have the chance to come to terms with the reality of the limited benefits of helplessness.

Members who join groups want to be included. The intensity of the desire to be part of a group means at least some revival of an individual's need to merge with or be included with others. This need alternates with the need to separate-individuate in both group and individual therapy. The experiences of Mrs. B illustrate the conflicts between these polarities and the way a self-help group helps a person to resolve them.

Mrs. B, a 30-year-old divorced professional woman, entered therapy because she felt anxious, depressed, and lonely. During the first 3 years of her life, she was cared for in her large extended family. A younger sister was born when she was 2 and a brother when she was 5. When she was 15, her parents divorced and she moved with her younger sister, brother, and mother into an apartment. Her mother was overwhelmed, and Mrs. B received no help with her feeling of loneliness other than to be encouraged to eat. From that time on, with neither her extended family nor her father to help her, she settled into a pattern of eating to relieve her loneliness.

At age 30, after 2 years of individual therapy, she agreed to attend Overeaters Anonymous and found herself immediately aware of the conflict she felt between the warm welcome she received and her unconscious certainty that the other members would inevitably leave her. Overeaters Anonymous helped her to refocus her self-care from food to other self-nurturing behaviors, and in therapy, she worked through her feelings about being abandoned by her family. She could then reinterpret her relational world more accurately and could see which of her responses to others were actually based in present-day reality and which were merely a reenactment of her past. Without the tangible warmth and support of the group, it would have taken her much longer even to recognize, no less do something about her simultaneous desire for and fear of intimacy—intimacy she did not learn from her own family.

Self-help groups provide more relationships through which to recognize transferential responses as the members learn to see patterns in themselves and in each other. Many members of self-help groups are sophisticated therapy clients, ready and able to confront their own pasts, their present patterns, and themselves.

RISKS FOR MEMBERS OF SELF-HELP GROUPS

The potential risks of group participation are usually controlled by the normative structure of the program. Each of the Twelve-Step programs, for example, promotes a strong task orientation that protects the integrity of the group process and discourages acting out. Although self-help groups are difficult for individual members at times, members seem to be less likely to have difficulty in groups that are professionally facilitated. It is inevitable that some groups (Twelve-Step programs and others) will establish negative patterns of interaction that are based on the unresolved childhood experiences that members bring to them. For example, a group may unknowingly collude with a member to replicate some of the same dysfunctional patterns toward a member that the member experienced with his or her family of origin. At such times, a therapist or facilitator is invaluable in helping to process the situation and, thereby, in helping clients to learn about themselves, about their families, about their expectations, and about relationships in general. Through the therapist, the negative experience can be changed into one in which the member, the group, and the therapist have the potential to grow.

Groups that have neither a professional facilitator nor a Twelve-Step format are most apt to get bogged down in difficulties, although many of them are excellent, sound, and stable groups. Survivors of incest, having been so repeatedly and so traumatically violated, have never had the opportunity to learn appropriate boundaries and appropriate caretaking behaviors (both for themselves and for others). These groups are particularly prone to both the under- and overinvolvement of their members.

On the one hand, clients who use the group's advice to avoid dealing with their own issues in therapy, to criticize the therapist, or to argue with a therapist's observation or interpretation generally use input from family members and friends in the same way. On the other hand, the group may give a client such a strong sense of additional backup and safety that the client may begin to address even more difficult issues in therapy.

SOME STICKY ISSUES

As the members of a self-help group share with each other, they may discover that they see the same therapist—a discovery that may seem to create an immediate bond among them. Their sharing of information and experiences about their therapist may seem supportive at first, but it may not always stay that way. Narcissistic injuries may abound as clients vie with each other for the supposed favored place with the therapist—whether the therapist is aware of the competition. Clients must adjust to the fact that the assumed sanctity of their therapy relationship has changed and that they must adjust to the fact that the therapist sees other people, even though they would certainly have said they "knew" that.

The discovery that others from the same group see the same therapist creates an immediate and irrevocable change in the therapeutic relationship. Boundary issues, confidentiality, safety, and importance may all have to be renegotiated and reworked. Members may develop a subgroup, believing that all members should see "their" therapist, who is the "best" therapist, and pressure those who see other therapists to switch. This situation presents members who are committed to their own therapies with the opportunity to learn to take a stand. The "best" (of the moment) therapist must check referral sources carefully at this time to avoid further complicating an already complicated relationship.

A therapist's strong commitment to self-help groups over time ensures that he or she will experience being perceived and not being perceived as the "best" therapist. This experience can help the therapist to remember that, barring the obvious feedback of reality, the client is rarely talking about the therapist, but is rather providing information about his or her internal universe and the way in which he or she has fit the therapist into that reality. A group with many members who are in individual therapy will be enriched by the offerings of many different therapists as members share in group what they have learned in their individual therapies. In turn, therapists will be influenced by the group and by other therapists as their clients recount suggestions or interpretations that the therapists may then find to be helpful for other clients.

REFERRAL CONCERNS

Assessments of clients for referral to a self-help group cannot be based solely on the *Diagnostic and Statistical Manual of Mental Disorders* (Third Edition–Revised [DSM-III-R]) (American Psychiatric Association, 1987). People who are judged to be in all the DSM-III-R categories will succeed or fail in self-help groups. Because some clients who were not considered to be "appropriate" referrals have done well in self-help groups, referrals should be made routinely to problem-specific self-help groups on the basis of information that is revealed in therapy. Twelve-Step programs do not screen their members and they help a diverse group of individuals. Many members of self-help groups came from dysfunctional families in which they learned to relate naturally and succinctly to people with problems and can be comfortable, direct, and effective with them. Groups function well with members who have some ability to respond to logic, regardless of the severity of their condition. For example, persons with schizoid and avoidant tendencies often do well in groups, as do persons with depressed and borderline features. Although persons with bipolar disorder have exhausted groups and sometimes leave a string of tired people behind them, an exciting new group, the Manic Depressive and Depressive Disorders Association, is offering new hope to people with these disorders.

People with strong paranoid ideation can exhaust a group, since group members relate first to one and then to another paranoid fantasy. Sometimes a group will eventually tire of explanation, feel helpless to defend against the delusion, and feel powerless to decipher the meaning of it. Yet, actively psychotic clients have made good group members in such organizations as Alliance for the Mentally Ill, Schizophrenics Anonymous, GROW, and Recovery, Inc. These groups have devised ways of not being overwhelmed with the delusional systems of their members and have found ways to work effectively with these individuals.

In sum, therapists benefit from self-help groups both in the professional knowledge they gain and in their personal and professional growth, which, of course, is what should happen, according to the self-help mutual aid philosophy. All participants—members and professionals—should gain. A better understanding, incorporation, and acceptance of the self-help philosophy and ethos by members, interested professionals, and the general public would generate enormous benefits for all who are involved in this still-evolving process.

REFERENCES

American Psychiatric Association. (1987). *Diagnostic and statistical manual of mental disorders* (3rd ed., rev.). Washington, DC: Author.

Behavior Associates. (1976). *Parents Anonymous: A self-help program for child-abusing parents.* Tucson, AZ: Author.

Borkman, T. (1987). *Self-help mutual aid groups: A different helping paradigm?* Paper prepared for the Surgeon General Workshops on Self-Help and Public Health.

Ganzarain, R. C., & Buchele, B. J. (1988). *Fugitives of incest: A perspective from psychoanalysis and groups.* Madison, CT: International Universities Press.

Gartner, A., & Riessman, F. (1977). *Self help in the human services.* San Francisco: Jossey-Bass.

Herbruck, C. C. (1979). *Breaking the cycle of child abuse.* Minneapolis, MN: Winston Press.

Hubbard, L. R. (1983). *Dianetics: The evolution of a science*. Los Angeles: Bridge Publications.

Jampolsky, G. (1979). *Love is letting go of fear*. Millbrae, CA: Celestial Arts.

Jones, B. (1989). Minority issues in child protection. Paper presented at the Law Enforcement/Child Protection Consensus-Building Conference, American Enterprise Institute, Washington, DC.

Lieberman, M. A., Borman, L. D., & Associates. (1979). *Self-help groups for coping with crisis*. San Francisco: Jossey-Bass.

Norwood, R. (1985). *Women who love too much*. New York: St. Martin's Press.

PA Chartered State Organizations. (1988). *Data-based survey report*. Los Angeles: Parents Anonymous National Office.

Parents Anonymous chairperson-sponsor manual (rev. ed.). (1982). Los Angeles: Parents Anonymous National Office.

Putnam, F. (1989). *Diagnosis and treatment of multiple personality disorders*. New York: Guilford Press.

Riessman, F. (1965). The "helper" therapy principle. *Social Work, 10*(2), 27–32.

Silverman, P. R. (1980). *Mutual help groups: Organization and development*. Beverly Hills, CA: Sage.

Wegschider-Cruse, S. (1987). *Learning to love yourself: Finding your self-worth*. Rutherford, NJ: Health Communications.

10

SELF-HELP AND BLACK AMERICANS
A Strategy for Empowerment

HAROLD W. NEIGHBORS, KARIN A. ELLIOTT, AND LARRY M. GANT

The Committee on Policy for Racial Justice defines *black self-help* as "that tradition of individual and group efforts aimed toward building institutions (without the assistance of the larger society) for the purpose of making racial progress and defending against a hostile society" (Joint Center for Political Studies, 1987, p. 4). The committee also wrote that the recent expansion of the government's role in helping black Americans had diminished black self-reliance, resulting in a gap between those who are in the best position to take advantage of the opportunities opened up by the civil rights movement and those who are not.

This chapter explores a number of important themes present in strategies for the progress of black people. Because so many problems that black people face are viewed as being caused by a racist social system, the majority of black self-help organizations use collective efforts aimed at economic and social change. However, the black self-help tradition has always emphasized increasing personal competence for the purpose of individual upward mobility within the system as it is presently structured. As a result, the authors discuss the implications of various combinations of self- and system responsibility for the cause and modification of the disadvantaged status of black Americans. It is their contention that the attributions utilized to understand racial oppression have important implications for how black Americans choose to cope with discrimination.

Self-help organizations will be useful for black Americans in overcoming the erroneous assumption of a simple and direct relationship between causal attributions of blame for disadvantaged status and attributions about who has responsibility to work toward changing this condition. Through the use of self-help principles, it should be possible for black Americans to develop a more complex view of their position—a view that places the blame on systemic factors, but lays the responsibility for solving those problems on the shoulders of the victims themselves. Such a perspective is not only consistent with the philosophy of black self-help but is an excellent route to black empowerment.

During the late 1960s and early 1970s, social scientists wrote that it was adaptive for black Americans to blame the system for their disadvantaged status. These writers thought that an external attribution of causality to explain the black condition was a beneficial means of coping with the lack of upward social mobility. First, it put the responsibility for solutions on the "system," that is, on federally funded economic development and welfare programs. Second, because external attributions are ego protective, they could allow the disadvantaged to retain their self-respect by being cast as "victims" of racial oppression and thereby being absolved of responsibility for their low status. As a result, many black Americans now view their disadvantaged status as heavily influenced by structural factors that are rooted in an unjust social system.

The assumption on which this chapter is based is that over the past 25 years, the excessive extension of the "system-blame" perspective for black Americans may have diminished individual feelings of self-determination that were so essential to the civil rights and Black Power movements. The discussion shows that this overemphasis on blaming the system runs counter to the traditional ideology of black self-help. Black self-help organizations can be excellent forums for fostering the development of a more critical and adaptive perspective on the black economic condition. The development of this new perspective will call for returning to the values of personal, organizational, and community control that have been inherent in the black self-help tradition.

Any action that aims to enhance a person's or group's control over situational circumstances is relevant to the theme of empowerment. People who help themselves (self-help) and who help others (mutual aid) are indeed attempting to take more control, and if they are successful, are said to be empowered. Given that self-help is a potential mechanism for attaining personal and community empowerment (Riessman, 1987), the self-help movement is a viable mechanism for developing the kind of critical awareness that black Americans need to make progress in the coming decades.

HISTORICAL OVERVIEW

Two thorough accounts of the black self-help tradition provide valuable insights into a historically developed perspective on the self-help movement among black Americans: Martin and Martin (1985) and Thomas (1987). This section, which is based on these two sources, briefly outlines this history as a foundation for a typology of black self-help organizations.

Foremost among organized self-help efforts in the black community was the black church. The Free African Society, organized in 1878, grew out of the first black churches and became one of the best models of mutual aid. It provided material support in cases of sickness and death. In addition, early black churches laid the foundation for black insurance enterprises, educational institutions, and other social and economic development projects.

Fraternal organizations rivaled black churches in the development of the self-help philosophy. For example, the Free Order of the Masons, organized in 1775, became the model for future black fraternal self-help associations (Thomas, 1987, p. 4). Throughout the eighteenth and nineteenth centuries, these fraternities encouraged and facilitated cooperative economic efforts to protect black people from poverty.

From the 1830s to the 1890s, black Americans held state and national conventions to discuss solutions to their problems. These "Negro conventions" provided a forum to discuss several critical issues, including moral education, politics, business, and the labor movement. The late nineteenth century was also marked by the rapid institutionalization of black self-help, represented by organizations like the Hampton Institute and Tuskegee Institute.

Booker T. Washington contributed significantly to the black self-help tradition by establishing the National Negro Business League

(NNBL) in 1900. The NNBL organized local business leagues throughout the country, emphasizing that black Americans could survive and progress through economic growth. Although they expressed clear ideological differences, W.E.B. DuBois and Booker T. Washington shared the basic belief that black people should participate in their own improvement, which could be achieved by economic development and financial independence.

Marcus Garvey, founder of the Universal Negro Improvement Association (UNIA) in 1921, was also a noteworthy contributor to the black self-help tradition. UNIA set up an array of businesses, including laundries, restaurants, grocery stores, small factories, and printing establishments. It was one of the first to advocate racial pride and black solidarity as the underlying philosophy of black self-help.

History also indicates that black women played a fundamental role in the development of an organized black self-help tradition. During reconstruction, black women's groups raised funds to build schools and opened centers to house and serve poor black people. In 1892, the Colored Women's League of Washington, DC, became the first black women's club to focus on organizing black women on the national level. Other early black women's organizations included the National Federation of Afro-American Women, the National League of Colored Women, and the National Association of Colored Women.

Many other groups and people should also be listed as key contributors to the black self-help tradition. They include (1) the Father Divine Peace Mission Movement (1930s), (2) the Nation of Islam (1930s to 1970s), (3) The Reverend Leon Sullivan's Opportunities Industrialization Center (OIC), (4) Martin Luther King's Southern Christian Leadership Council (SCLC), which utilized nonviolent political protest during the civil rights movement of the 1960s, (5) The Reverend Jesse Jackson's People United to Save Humanity (Operation PUSH), and (6) the many black leaders, such as Malcolm X, Franz Fanon, Ron Karenga, and Imiri Baraka, who instilled a sense of racial solidarity and collective consciousness in the black community during the black cultural movement.

On the basis of this historical overview, the following characteristics can be useful to define self-help from a black perspective. First, there is a repeated emphasis on economic development and political empowerment. Second, there is a strong tradition of church-based social support. Third, there is the presence of community uplift projects and resource-mobilization efforts, many of which were organized by women's groups. Fourth, there is also a deep concern for and active involvement in educational achievement. Finally, there is the development of social and political groups that are ideologically grounded in racial consciousness, black pride, and group solidarity.

Viewing formally established social institutions as self-help organizations is contrary to many definitions of "traditional" self-help. But the foregoing review clearly demonstrates that the black church has played a fundamental role in the historical development of black self-help. Similarly, the establishment of black-owned schools, universities, and businesses have been acknowledged as major self-help achievements in the evolution of the black self-help tradition.

CURRENT EFFORTS

The profile of black self-help just outlined serves as an underlying paradigm for a typology of black self-help organizations. However, it is necessary to add additional categories to this classification scheme to account for newly emerging black self-help organizations. This section summarizes some of the currently active black self-help organizations; the examples used are primarily from the Detroit metropolitan area, since the authors are most familiar with these organizations. The categories used to classify these groups are presented in Table 10-1.

Self-help for economic, political, and social development. These organizations take a social action approach to self-help that seeks social change, as well as individual and community empowerment. Such goals are achieved, in part, through economic independence and the mobilization of collective resources. Organizations representing this form of black self-help include People United to Save Humanity, Southern Christian Leadership Council, most of the welfare rights organizations founded in the 1960s, the Nation Of Islam, the National Association for the Advancement of Colored People, the Urban League, the Booker T. Washington Business Association, the United Negro College Fund, and Detroit's Ujama Club.

Table 10-1

A Typology of Black Self-Help Organizations

1. National and community-based self-help organizations concerned with the economic, political, and social development of black America.
2. Community-based self-help organizations instituted to enhance and strengthen black families and community life.
3. Church-based self-help organizations concerned with community development.
4. Social institutions as black self-help.
5. Black self-help groups for coping with physical illness and death.
6. Self-help organizations focused on strengthening black families and youths.
7. Self-help organizations founded by black women.
8. Self-help organizations for black professionals.
9. Black chapters of "mainstream" self-help organizations.
10. Self-help organizations for special-interest groups in the black community.

Source: Elliott (1988).

Neighborhood-based groups for community development. These black self-help organizations are formed by people who are indigenous to black neighborhoods to secure the safety and well-being of the community. In addition, they sponsor cultural enrichment programs that teach black history and culture to promote racial pride and consciousness. Such black self-help organizations include the Inner City Sub-Center (seven principles of blackness), Operation Get Down, Detroit Association of Black Organizations, Save Our Sons and Daughters, the Metropolitan Anti-Crime Coalition, and the Watts Health Foundation in Los Angeles.

Church-based organizations for community development. These groups are similar to the secular-based black self-help organizations founded to promote community development and to secure neighborhood safety. Model church-based self-help organizations include the following, which are based in Detroit: Greater Grace Educational Center (which uses a Montessori method of educating black youths), Hartford Memorial Baptist Church (which established a range of indigenously run services and programs that provide clothes, a food co-op, boutiques, bookstores, legal consultation, a credit union, and college scholarships), and Bethel African Methodist

Episcopal Church (which provides clothing for poor mothers and a credit union and organizes speakers to teach children about drugs, alcohol, and sex education).

Black social institutions as self-help. Many of the self-help traditions of early black America have been institutionalized and now function within more formal organizational settings. These self-help organizations may reflect an educational, social, or economic orientation, or they may use any combination of these approaches. Examples in this category include the Detroit-based Lewis College of Business and the Payne-Pulliam School of Trade and Commerce (founded to create a class of socially conscious entrepreneurs whose primary aim would be to create wealth in the black community), black universities and colleges (such as Howard, Tuskegee, Morgan State, and Morehouse), and the Southwest Detroit Hospital (the last remaining of 10 black hospitals that once served the city of Detroit).

Self-help groups for coping with physical illness and death. These self-help organizations offer emotional support, information, and, in some cases, advocacy to members who are confronted with illnesses that are prevalent in the black community. Some examples are the Sickle Cell Detection and Information Center, local Sickle Cell support groups throughout the country, Babies Inalienable Right to Health (an organization that addresses infant mortality and morbidity in Detroit), diabetes support groups, bereavement support groups for parents whose babies have died from sudden infant death syndrome, the National Black Women's Health Project (a health education and advocacy group), and the National Black Alcoholism Council.

Groups to strengthen black families and youths. These self-help organizations have recently organized to recapture and strengthen the traditional values of black unity in the family and community. They focus on strengthening family functioning, as opposed to promoting a particular family structure. Many of these organizations profess a strong commitment to training and socializing black youths to understand, respect, and benefit from the traditional cultural values of black America. Examples of this form of self-help include Delta Teen Lift (which provides training on career awareness and college preparation), Project Elite (designed as a first step toward encouraging black single mothers to obtain an education and train for careers), the Detroit Urban League's Male Responsibility program (which provides support and training in parenting for teenage fathers), Black Family Development, Inc. (a prevention program for child abuse and neglect), Simba and Star programs (indigenously run rites-of-passage programs in which adults prepare black children for adulthood), Black Fatherhood Collective, and the Male Parenting Telephone Connection.

Self-help organizations founded by black women. Although most of these groups fit into several other categories of black self-help, they are characterized by their black female-oriented membership, leadership, or both. Examples include Save Our Sons and Daughters (for black mothers whose children were killed by other children), Debtors Anonymous (organized by the National Council of Negro Women), National Black Women's Health Project, National Black Women's Political Leadership Caucus, Women's Conference of Concerns, Single Mothers of Color, Single Women United, Black Single Women's Connection, and a variety of black sororities.

Self-help organizations for black professionals. These self-help organizations provide their members with the opportunity to network for personal support and to develop proactive professional initiatives whose goal is to enhance the black community. Examples of such organizations include the National Association of Black Social Workers, Metropolitan Detroit Alliance of Black School Educators, National Association of Black Accountants, National Organization of Black Law Enforcement Executives, National Association of Negro Businesses and Professional Women's Clubs, Organization of Black Scientists, Wolverine Bar Association, Wolverine Dental Society, and Black Professional Singles.

Black chapters of mainstream self-help organizations. Several self-help organizations, which were founded by and still maintain a predominantly white middle-class membership, have begun to attract people of color. As a result, they have established racially integrated and all-black chapters. Such organizations include Alcoholics Anonymous, Narcotics Anonymous, and acquired immune deficiency syndrome support groups.

Self-help for black special-interest groups. These groups are defined by their membership. They share a common experience, concern, or interest that is collectively addressed through advocacy and mutual support. Examples of this type of organization include the National Caucus and Center on Black Aging, Successful Sixties Plus support groups, Office of Black Catholic Affairs, and the Detroit Coalition of Black Lesbians and Gays.

This classification scheme differentiates among the many diverse self-help organizations that operate in the black community. However, as is evident from the appearance of some groups in more than one category, a distinctive set of criteria that neatly classifies all these organizations into mutually exclusive categories does not exist. One shortcoming of this typology is that it does not adequately address the lack of black members in the traditional self-help organizations.

THE STRUCTURALIST VIEWPOINT

The argument that emphasizes the social causation of black problems via racism, discrimination, and an unjust opportunity structure, referred to hereafter as the structuralist viewpoint (see Murray, 1984, pp. 26–29), usually leads its advocates to state that the solution to problems that plague black communities is to change the system, not to change the individual to fit more easily into the system (Carter, 1981; Hilliard, 1981; Mayfield, 1972). For example, Brooks (1974, p. 491) contended that social workers should not help black clients adjust to the situation but should work toward changing the true causes that usually lie in the social conditions. Similarly, Glasgow (1972, p. 59) stated that for too long, social work has patched up the afflicted and ignored the primary causes of their troubles, which grow out of society's basic social structures. Finally, Newsome (1973, p. 52) noted,

> Blacks now conclude that their fundamental problems are systemic and structural and that these problems are generated by oppressive features of the country's major political, economic, and social institutions. No longer do blacks want their problems defined solely in terms of individual social maladjustment or inadequacies.

This viewpoint leaves one with the impression that individual black Americans need not be held primarily responsible for any solutions to the problems of discrimination or poverty. In short, many black people advocate a social causation ideology that blames the system and, as a result, advocates changing the system as the solution.

The appeal of the structuralist viewpoint seems to be linked to a number of hypothesized positive outcomes, as well as to the assumed negative outcomes of self-blame, although this idea has not been tested empirically. It has been argued that it increases the likelihood that social change efforts will be directed toward eliminating structurally based obstacles to racial advancement (Gurin, Gurin, & Morrison, 1978). In addition, it is said to place more responsibility on representatives of the system to correct the problems they created, often by providing funds from federal, state, and local governments for human services programs. Finally, because the viewpoint de-emphasizes self-blame for one's disadvantaged status, it is thought to be ego protective and, therefore, to obstruct the development of disempowering negative psychological effects, such as self-hate, depression, and low self-esteem.

This idea has led a number of epidemiologists in the field of social psychiatry, such as Neff (1985) and Veroff, Douvan, and Kulka (1981), to use the structuralist viewpoint as a post hoc hypothesis in an attempt to explain the lack of racial differences in psychological distress. These epidemiologists believe that blaming the system is an adaptive way for black Americans to cope with stress because this perspective explains the disadvantaged status on the basis of external forces and thereby allows the holders of this status their integrity.

Given that low-income black people are disadvantaged on measures of self-esteem, locus of control, and personal efficacy in comparison with poor white people, and both white and black middle-class people (Kessler & Neighbors, 1986; Porter & Washington, 1979), it seems necessary to subscribe to one of two competing explanations. Either the majority of the members of the lower classes do not blame the system for their disadvantaged status or they adhere to this view, but the concept does not operate in the manner predicted by the structuralists. Data from the National Survey of Black Americans speak directly to this point. Results from interviews with 2,107 adult black Americans indicated no relationship between blaming the system and personal efficacy or blaming the system and self-esteem (Hughes & Demo, 1988).

Thus, despite much speculation about the positive implications of the system-blame perspective for poor people and for black people, there is practically no empirical evidence on the topic. The one quantitative analysis reported found no relationship between blaming the system and personal efficacy or self-esteem. Thus, if blaming the system is indeed an adaptive perspective for the disadvantaged, its positive effects remain to be demonstrated.

The argument that an external orientation leads to negative psychological outcomes usually states that such an orientation lowers self-sufficiency by undermining the importance of individuals' exertion of control over their personal existence (Jones & Matsumoto, 1982, pp. 208–209; see also Auletta, 1983, p. 38, for a description of what he termed "victimism"). The argument also contends that an external orientation leads to a heightened sense of hopelessness if individuals engage in social change efforts and find the system to be unresponsive. Finally, epidemiologists in social psychiatry have found evidence that an external orientation results in a fatalistic attitude that reduces efforts to cope with adversity (Ross, Mirowsky, & Cockerham, 1983; Wheaton, 1980). As Caplan and Nelson (1973, p. 209) noted,

> A dogmatic system blame orientation has its own dangers in addition to being part of the truth. Reifying environmental factors as causal agents may deny and thus have the effect of dampening the autonomy and dynamism of the individual. This raises the serious question of people's attitudes toward their responsibility for their behavior. Unless counterbalanced in some way, an excessive system blame perspective carries with it the potential for providing the individual with a ready explanation for avoiding responsibility for his own behavior. One of the most serious problems of our age may be to provide a view of man and his surroundings that recognizes the validity of situational causality without leaving the individual feeling helpless and unable to shape his fate.

Research on learned helplessness has demonstrated that expectations about future success in coping with difficult experiences depends on attributions about what caused those difficulties (Seligman, 1975). It has also shown that attributing the cause of adverse negative personal situations to either stable internal factors (the lack of ability, for instance) or stable external factors (such as an unresponsive social system) results in expectancies of failure in future tasks

(Abramson, Seligman, & Teasdale, 1978; Dweck, 1975). In addition, such research has concluded that although self-blame for adversity may result in feelings of negative affect, the assumption of personal responsibility (as a result of internal attributions) for coping with adversity can counteract feelings of helplessness and generalized expectancies of failure (Brockner, Mahan, & Thomas, 1983).

Social psychology has a rich tradition of empirical investigations of the outcomes related to attributions about success and failure (Abramson et al., 1978; Lefcourt, 1982; Phares, 1984; Rotter, 1966). For example, Janoff-Bulman's (1982) important distinction of behavioral and characterological self-blame is particularly useful in clarifying the issues addressed in this chapter.

Briefly, Janoff-Bulman found that high self-esteem was related to behavioral self-blame (in which the individual focused on his or her behavior), while low self-esteem was related to characterological self-blame (in which the individual focused on his or her personality or identity). Thus, blame that focuses on unstable personal behavior may not necessarily be a problem. Conversely, blame that focuses on an individual's stable, enduring personal characteristics creates a stigma that could neutralize personal empowerment.

Although the studies that have produced these findings are biased in that the samples were white middle-class college students, they are an important addition to a literature that is too dependent on essays that rest on theoretical formulations and anecdotal observations. Furthermore, recent applications of this attributional model to the problem of discouragement in searching for a job have proved to be a fruitful way of looking at the motivation of black people (Bowman, 1983).

DEFINITIONS OF SELF-HELP

The same internal-external attributional (self-blame–system-blame) dichotomy that is observed in discussions of black people's approaches to progress can also be seen in typologies of self-help organizations. Vattano (1972) divided self-help organizations into those with a clinical focus and those with a social perspective. The former are concerned with the treatment of emotional and behavioral problems and interpersonal growth, while the latter are concerned with inadequacies of the environment and social institutions. Powell (1987, pp. 12–14) noted that some organizations attempt to change society while others try to change their members. He also stated that self-help is not a solitary activity but involves social transactions, the exchange of mutual aid, and the mobilization of outside community resources. Self-help addresses people with personal difficulties (such as physical illnesses and disturbances of habits), as well as difficult social situations like discrimination and social injustice. In short, self-help organizations are mechanisms for coping with difficult situations. As one of the most discriminated-against ethnic minorities in this country, black Americans have had to deal with tremendous adversity. Thus, self-help is an especially appropriate topic for a discussion of the situation of black Americans.

The meaning of self-help in the black community has been hotly debated. Although some supporters of black self-help view this strategy as a means of empowering the black community (Gilinsky, 1987; Rouse, 1987; Smith, 1987; Thomas, 1987; Wright, Green, & Gibson, 1984), others wonder whether the push for black self-help is a limited, conservative tactic that may result in decreased demands for social assistance and social change (see, for example, Gartner & Riessman, 1977; Powell, 1987). If one uses Powell's (1987) typology of self-help, the majority of black self-help groups fit into what he termed "lifestyle" organizations. Lifestyle organizations pay close attention to human and civil rights and engage large constituencies in campaigns against injustice. Other activities of lifestyle organizations include advocacy, providing social support, mobilizing communities, conducting networks, developing political campaigns, and initiating legal actions (Powell, 1987, p. 194). All these activities are conspicuously present in the black self-help literature.

But there is another side to black self-help. When one critically examines the ideological bases of black self-help organizations over time, it is readily apparent that there has been a strong emphasis on individual responsibility and the importance of personal competence. Sometimes this philosophy is pejoratively referred to as "bootstrapping" or, even worse, "victim blaming." The unfortunate outcome of this emotional language has been skepticism about the utility of a self-help approach to the progress of black people (Newsome, 1973; Spiegel, 1982; Withorn, 1980).

Historical accounts of the black self-help tradition in the United States (Martin & Martin, 1985; Thomas, 1987) have revealed that mutual aid and social support have always existed as fundamental strengths and critical survival strategies in the black community. Self-help organizations that take the form of local neighborhood and community development groups, social action groups, and advocacy groups are all characteristic of existing and traditional black self-help organizations (Thomas, 1987; Withorn, 1980). The focus on mobilizing material resources to meet the basic needs of the community is intrinsic to most forms of black self-help. Furthermore, the emphasis on changing the system, which involves challenging existing political structures to respond to the needs of communities and of holding officials accountable for providing equitable services and access to resources, is also a common practice among black self-help organizations. In addition, black self-help advocates the development of personal and community empowerment that will enable self-help organizations and their communities to flourish independent of the outside social structure.

In sum, some elements of self-help in the black community are advocacy; empowerment; a tolerance for diversity in membership; racial consciousness; a broad definition of self-help, including the development of formal organizations (such as black churches and black schools); and a conception of the system as a legitimate target for defining problems and developing solutions. Implicit in these elements is an emphasis on personal responsibility for advancing oneself as well as the group.

THE CASE AGAINST SELF-HELP

The largest obstacle to the acceptance of the personal approach inherent in the self-help ideology is the belief that self-help will result in the social system shirking its responsibility to provide financial assistance to disadvantaged black people. The concern is that the self-help initiative is a ploy that would allow the government to flee from its responsibility for providing adequate services and the resources needed to promote mental health and community development. Along these lines, self-help is viewed as a "bootstrapping" approach that encourages individuals to take personal responsibility for their life circumstances and to rely on their personal resources, talents, and skills to create a lifestyle of their choice.

The other major roadblock to the acceptance of self-help among the black community is the argument that self-help is just another form of "victim blaming." A victim-blaming perspective views self-help as assuming that people in disadvantaged situations have created their negative circumstances by personal behaviors and attitudes. Ryan's (1971) construct suggests that the causes of the social problem may be erroneously thought to lie in the qualities and characteristics of the victims, rather than in any structural defects in the environment. Ryan was optimistic in assuming that if the negative effects of situational forces that oppress the disadvantaged were alleviated, disadvantaged people would do as well (or as poorly) as their more fortunate counterparts. Ryan (pp. 26–30) charged liberals (who were thought to have a vested interest in maintaining present structural arrangements) with placing too much emphasis on correcting the socially determined "defects" of the disadvantaged and ignoring the social forces that produced those deficits in the first place.

Much of the confusion attending the victim-blaming debate has to do with the assumption of a direct relationship between attributions of the cause of problems and attributions of responsibility for correcting them. As Caplan and Nelson (1973, p. 200) pointed out, these two processes are often not distinguished from each other. Thus, most people assume that if individuals are to blame for the circumstances they find themselves in, they are also responsible for pulling themselves out of those situations. Similarly, if these situations are the result of an unjust system, then the system is the only unit that can alleviate the problem. The tendency is to view blame and responsibility as inextricably and directly linked. This simplistic assumption suggests that advocates of individual-level solutions to problem situations explicitly declare that the blame also resides at the personal level. Thus, the mistaken application of the label, "victim blame."

The tendency to confuse cause with remedy results in the mistaken view that individually focused solutions to problems imply individual-level causality, whereas in reality, to encourage someone to enroll in a skill-development, educational, or training program has nothing to do with attributing cause or blame for his or her situation. Rather, it merely assigns some responsibility to the individual to help create a solution.

Hence, it is more appropriate to view self-help as a "personally responsible" approach to advancement than as a victim-blaming approach, which it is not. Self-help seeks to place more control in the hands of the less fortunate who have been the victims of racism, discrimination, and oppression. In other words, the self-help ideology is a vehicle for personal empowerment. The distinction between shared responsibility for creating social injustices that breed poverty and poor health in the black community and black self-help as a means of improving conditions in the black community is the key to understanding and resolving the seemingly conflicting concerns of black empowerment and the fear of the government's abandonment under the guise of self-help.

No one disputes the limits of black self-help strategies in combating the structural causes of the poverty of black people in declining industrial cities. As a result, black self-help should be considered "only a part of the overall strategy to uplift and empower those segments of the black community still trapped in poverty" (Thomas, 1987, p. 25). Although the authors advocate that more black Americans should get involved in solving the problems that plague black communities, this does not mean that the public and private sectors should be let off the hook. Protests against racism are still needed, and pressure on the government is still required.

THE FUNCTIONAL UTILITY OF BLACK SELF-HELP

Empowerment is one of the most critical and highly valued benefits that members of the black community can attain by participating in self-help organizations (Boxill & Beverly, 1986; Fagan, 1979; Gray, Nybell, Gant, & Moffett, 1986; Mayfield, 1972; O'Connell, 1978; Pernell, 1986; Pinderhughes, 1983; Powell, 1987; Rappaport, 1987; Reischl, Zimmerman, & Rappaport, 1986; Riessman, 1985; Rouse, 1987; Smith, 1987; Solomon, 1976; Wolff, 1987; Ziter & Politi, 1987).

The empowerment and self-help literatures describe empowerment as the process of increasing personal, interpersonal, or political power (or all three) so that individuals or collectives can take action to improve their life situations (Gutiérrez, 1988, p. 3).

Empowerment operates at multiple levels. Personal empowerment is an internal process in which one develops a feeling of increased power or control that is unrelated to actual changes in the social structure (Pernell, 1986; Pinderhughes, 1983; Sherman & Wenocur, 1983; Stensrud & Stensrud, 1982; Solomon, 1976; Ziter & Politi, 1987). Interpersonal empowerment involves the negotiation of power relationships that allows one to function effectively and independently in social situations. At this level, empowerment is the ability to ward off the controlling influence of others. Political empowerment attempts to deal with direct blocks to power (inadequate resources and the denial of opportunities by social institutions). This level of collective empowerment is commonly initiated when powerlessness is externally imposed and reinforced.

Many of the components of empowerment are operationalized within the context of self-help organizations. According to the self-help literature, the empowerment process is potent. Personal empowerment increases energy; motivation; effective coping; problem-solving skills; decision-making power; and internal resources such as self-esteem, self-sufficiency, and self-determination (Boxill & Beverly, 1986; Gary, 1985; Gruber & Trickett, 1987; Pinderhughes, 1983; Powell, 1987). At another level, social and political empowerment in self-help organizations are represented by collective efforts to fight systematic discrimination and oppression by the larger society. For example, indigenously formed self-help community groups have used social action strategies to fight against redlining real estate practices and miserable public services (Asch, 1986; Fagan, 1979; O'Connell, 1978; Sherman & Wenocur, 1983; Solomon, 1976; Wolff, 1987).

Contemporary self-help approaches and traditional black self-help strategies acknowledge the reciprocal relationship between personal and group empowerment. These organizations stress how individual empowerment can contribute to group empowerment and, in turn, how increasing the power of groups can enhance the functioning of individuals (Asch, 1986; Gutiérrez, 1988; Kahn & Bender, 1985; Rappaport, 1987; Zimmerman, Reischl, Toro, & Rappaport,

1986). In sum, self-help organizations that empower participants on the individual, interpersonal, and collective/political levels provide comprehensive intervention that is consistent with the historical roots and contemporary needs of the black community.

A common element of the definitions of empowerment is the concept of control, either the control of self or the ability to influence others who may exert control over others. What is most relevant to this chapter is the notion that some organizations can be empowering to their members, that is, can provide opportunities for gaining control over their lives. This idea suggests a reciprocal relationship for disempowered black people to become empowered by joining self-help organizations, while recognizing the possibility that an organization can become empowered through the efforts of individuals who already feel personally efficacious. It is not clear which comes first: personal empowerment or organizational empowerment. Although this is an important question, a more important issue is how to bring black people together to develop the kind of critical perspective that allows them to gain some position and understanding of attributions of cause (self-blame–system blame), attributions of responsibility (internal-external), and the relative importance of the two.

As has been pointed out, black self-help is controversial because structuralists are skeptical of this individual-level focus and because many black people want to hold the system responsible for both the cause of the problems of black people and the solutions to those problems. But it should now be clear that black self-help, even though it emphasizes individual-level coping strategies, is not necessarily antithetical to a system-blame perspective. At first glance, this statement may sound contradictory. How can the self-help ideology simultaneously hold a system-blame perspective and emphasize individual-level solutions? The answer lies in the realization that attributions of blame do not, by themselves, produce solutions and in an appreciation of the complexities inherent in the black perspective of self-help.

The literature indicates that black self-help is not antithetical to blaming the system or to individual responsibility. The key is to figure out how to reconcile the two concepts of system blame and personal responsibility. As Gurin and Gurin (1970, pp. 101–102) wrote, in regard to understanding the problem of poverty,

The problem of learning new expectancies is no longer one of changing from an external to a more internal orientation. Rather, poor people are presented with the much more difficult problem of learning to make very complex judgments as to when internal and external interpretations are realistic, when an internal orientation reflects intrapunitiveness rather than a sense of self efficacy, when an external orientation becomes defensive rather than a realistic blaming of the social system. Moreover, these judgments must be made when objective opportunities are in flux, making an accurate picture of reality all the more difficult to determine.

Can a person hold both perspectives (system blame and individual responsibility) simultaneously? The authors think the answer is yes. What they do not know is the prevalence of this perspective and the implications for behavioral outcomes and strategies of coping.

In providing an initial framework for understanding the fundamental relationships that characterize styles of help seeking, Brickman, Rabinowitz, and Karuza (1982) developed an attributional model of coping. By crossing high and low levels of attributions for the causes of problems with high and low levels of attributions for the resolution of problems, these researchers obtained four distinct models of helping and coping: enlightenment, compensatory, moral, and medical (see Table 10-2). The existence of these models in social services agencies was corroborated (Gant, 1986; Harvey, 1980; Holland & Brickman, 1979), providing a plausible categorization of agencies based on the implicit endorsement of attributions of responsibility.

Table 10-2

Models of Helping and Coping, Based on Attributional Model of Coping Developed by Brickman, Rabinowitz, & Karuza (1982)

ATTRIBUTION OF RESPONSIBILITY	ATTRIBUTION OF THE CAUSE OF A PROBLEM	
	LOW	HIGH
Low	Medical Model	Enlightenment Model
High	Compensatory Model	Moral Model

Source: Adapted from Gant (1986).

According to Karuza, Zevon, Rabinowitz, and Brickman (1982, pp. 111–112), the compensatory model encourages people to see themselves as having to compensate personally for environmental constraints imposed by others. It is an optimistic view that assumes a certain amount of potential for human development, especially if disadvantaged people are given an equal opportunity to do so. The compensatory model is consistent with themes of empowerment in that clients are expected to adopt an active problem-solving ori entation in overcoming difficulties and redefine personal problems in a way that heightens their sense of personal control over difficult situations. At the same time, according to Karuza et al., the compensatory model allows clients to discount past failures and, in so doing, to maintain self-respect by avoiding feelings of guilt and incompetence.

Work now in progress is applying this model to the categorization of black and nonblack self-help organizations (Gant, 1988, 1989). The preliminary results suggest that the proactive stance of many black self-help organizations is consistent with an orientation that minimizes attributions of personal blame and maximizes attributions of personal responsibility for solving problems (the compensatory model). In contrast, nonblack self-help groups seem to be more evenly distributed across modalities (compensatory, enlightenment, moral, and medical). It is plausible that the self-help groups reflect world views that have proved most adaptive at a given time for a given population or subgroup. Historically, advances and options for the black community in the United States have emerged as a function of advocacy, demonstration, and struggle—not through passive activities (the medical model) or victim-blame activities (the enlightenment and moral models).

These themes are similar to notions developed by Gurin, Gurin, Lao, and Beattie (1969) as a result of research on black college students during the 1960s. These researchers pointed out that the collective protests in which black student activists engaged reflected an attempt to remove barriers to individual upward mobility, rather than a desire to operate outside the traditional system. Thus, individual responsibility and collective attempts to achieve social change that were based on blaming the system were not polarized among black activists. These researchers speculated that the relationship between "individual-system blame" (a measure of attributions of causality varying between self-blame and system blame) and "personal control" (a psychological construct that varies from internal to external and is similar to attributions of responsibility) may not be polarized, at least not among college students. Specifically, they speculated that it was indeed possible for black Americans simultaneously to blame the system for their disadvantaged status while looking to individual-level solutions to that same disadvantaged status. But these researchers also wondered whether these two strategies would be polarized among black youths who were not college students and who lacked the personal skills necessary to take advantage of the opportunities that were becoming available as a result of the civil rights movement.

In other words, this latter group's disenchantment with personal progress could lead to the development of the more typical popular conception of directly linking attributions of causality with responsibility at the same level (internal to internal and external to external). In Brickman et al.'s (1982) terminology, a medical orientation is characterized by the absence of self-blame, as well as the absence of a sense of personal responsibility for solving the problem. On the one hand, this is precisely the perspective that could explain disempowerment (low personal efficacy, fatalism, and helplessness) among poor black people. On the other hand, the moral model (high self-blame and personal responsibility) could be the kind of perspective that leads other disadvantaged people to be overly intrapunitive, which results in feelings of low self-esteem, self-hatred, and hopelessness.

Many black Americans have been raised with the message that they had to be "twice as good to earn half as much" as white Americans. This is an example of compensatory coping. It is critical of the system in that it is sensitive to racial injustice. But it also looks ahead to future solutions, clearly placing responsibility on the individual for self-development as a solution to the problem of racism. Many black Americans have begun to wonder whether such a perspective is decreasing among certain segments of the black population (Clark, 1965; Joint Center for Political Studies, 1987; Wilson, 1987; see also Auletta, 1983, p. 36). It is not known whether this speculation is valid, precisely since there has been no research on causal attributions (particularly system blame) among representative samples of the black population.

But it is an issue that is worthy of more research. In the meantime, the authors feel confident enough of the functional utility of the compensatory ideology to advocate its use within black self-help organizations. The critical issue is how to foster the development of a perspective among black Americans that is critical of the system but that enhances their feelings of personal efficacy so that more black people will feel empowered enough to solve their own problems. There is a clear role for self-help organizations in this process (see Withorn, 1980, p. 21).

Thus, many black Americans are asking themselves what happened to the notions of black self-determination and self-sufficiency that were so popular in the late 1960s and early 1970s. They wonder whether structurally based governmental interventions like welfare and affirmative action have inadvertently dampened individual-level responsibility for solving the problems of black people. Furthermore, black Americans need answers to the question of what separated those black individuals who were able to move successfully into the middle class and those who remained poor or, worse, became members of the underclass. Was it the removal of structural barriers only that separated the upwardly mobile from those who were not, or did it have more to do with the individual skills that some possessed that others were never able to develop? Has black self-help's emphasis on personal initiative been undermined by a well-intentioned but misapplied system-blame ideology?

These are difficult questions that can be answered only by sensitive, systematic programs of research. These questions are, however, deserving of critical discussion among black Americans from all walks of life, as well as of the support and direction that can be provided by academic social research. It is the authors' position that black self-help organizations can be excellent forums to air such issues. In so doing, self-help participants should keep the following points in mind.

First, black Americans agree that feelings of efficacy and self-esteem must be elevated in oppressed groups. Yet, when they encounter intervention approaches that focus on psychological empowerment, black people often argue that these approaches are based on a conservative victim-blaming ideology that absolves the government of its responsibility for helping the disadvantaged.

Second, and similarly, many black Americans argue that a system-blame perspective should be fostered, yet there is no empirical evidence to show that positive outcomes are associated with this viewpoint. Furthermore, there is much empirical information to suggest that an external attributional perspective that focuses on stable external factors, such as an unresponsive social structure, is more likely to lead to disempowerment. Finally, one must consider the possibility that individual empowerment increases the likelihood of group-based collective efforts that can work toward changing the system.

The time has come for black people to discard the simple one-to-one relationship between internal and external attributions of cause and solution and to look for methods to develop more critical ways of viewing their situation. Specifically, black Americans should find a way to hold themselves more personally responsible for solving their own problems and reject debilitating forms of extreme self-blame. Furthermore, they should not embrace a system-blame orientation to the point that it becomes a form of radical social reductionism, negating all the benefits of personal empowerment.

CONCLUSIONS

The history of the progress of black people in this country has often been compared to a struggle or a battle for rights, opportunities, and participation. Perhaps it is not surprising, then, that the nature of the black struggle in the United States has produced numerous proactive action-based self-help organizations. Several points that were made in this chapter can be viewed as clear theoretical propositions that may guide future research, discussions, and programs:

■ The development of a theoretical taxonomy of self-help programs within the black community is practical, desirable, and essential. Black self-help organizations, regardless of the origin of their formation, predominantly reflect the categorizations of problems and attributions of responsibility that are consistent with a compensatory model of helping. The other helping modalities (moral, medical, and enlightenment) may be found only in small percentages of indigenous black self-help organizations.

■ Systematic, comprehensive, and longitudinal research that is directed toward the etiology, maintenance, and success of black self-help organizations is imperative. The technology and procedures exist for the empirical investigation of these groups at all levels of analysis (see, for example, Brisbane & Stuart, 1985; Gary & Gary, 1985; Gray et al., 1986).

■ The principles of self-help should be embraced by all segments of black communities because self-help organizations can be useful vehicles for developing an adaptive perspective on the social problems facing black Americans. Specifically, three important issues need to be addressed by black self-help organizations: (1) black self-help organizations should develop a critical perspective that takes into account the relative importance of individual and systemic factors as causes of and solutions to the problems of black people, (2) black self-help organizations should work toward the infusion of a strong racial-group identity within their members, and (3) black self-help organizations should be involved in the development of competence-building life skills.

This last point is important because successful experiences are crucial for the development of feelings of personal efficacy, positive expectancies, and high self-esteem. It is difficult to develop group power and collective efforts without a certain level of personal empowerment. Given the consistently conflicting themes of self-blame–system blame and individual versus social change throughout this discussion, the authors find it necessary to address the difficult question of what level of empowerment to focus on first. Although it is likely that the different levels of empowerment (personal, organizational, community, and so on) operate simultaneously, the authors believe that black self-help organizations should begin by ensuring that black Americans become personally empowered by focusing their efforts on helping individuals to acquire and increase their skills. This position is based on the premise that a collection of powerless individuals is a disempowered group, containing little potential for effective collective efforts. It is also based on the assumption that empowered individuals will be more likely to come together to make systematic attacks on structural obstacles to the progress of black people as a whole.

There is no doubt that many victims of oppression are relatively disadvantaged. Yet, the fact that certain social problems have a higher prevalence among certain segments of the black population is not justification for indicting the whole group as pathological and deviant. It does, however, suggest a direction for moving closer to the root cause of problems that need to be addressed. That members of low-income minority groups are disadvantaged with respect to personal efficacy and self-esteem is evident by the fact that more often than not, it is members of the black middle class (or liberal white middle-class people) who go into low-income black communities for community organizing and development. It is people who feel personally empowered and who have somehow developed a political perspective that motivates them to use collective methods to cope with black racial oppression—in short, those who feel personally empowered—who usually try to help the powerless.

Such efforts probably will be started by one or a small number of empowered individuals who have some understanding of the relative importance of individual and structural processes in the oppression of black Americans. If this position is correct, then there is a risk that black self-help organizations will be formed by middle-class blacks (on the basis of similar values, attitudes, and behaviors) to meet the needs and concerns of the middle class, not necessarily to work toward empowering poor blacks. Therefore, skin color alone may not be strong enough to forge close relationships across social class within the black community. If self-help organizations can produce personally empowered black individuals who can also identify with other black Americans with dissimilar needs and life circumstances, then black self-help organizations may not become segregated by social class.

A strong black identity that facilitates the feeling of closeness with similar as well as dissimilar others is a necessary but insufficient component of this self-help strategy. It is necessary because it is hoped it will provide the social glue that will bring black Americans together in search of a solution to the problems plaguing their larger group. A strong black identity can also foster a sense of responsibility and concern for less fortunate black citizens. But although it brings people together, it does not necessarily lead people to act, nor does it provide the direction necessary to suggest a specific strategy.

As a result, it is also crucial that empowered black individuals possess a well-developed perspective on the issues of blame and responsibility addressed in this chapter. As was suggested, this process can be facilitated by the discussion of difficult questions in black self-help organizations. But equally important, it is necessary to help black Americans develop the individual skills that are required to have successful experiences in educational and job settings, thereby allowing them to develop feelings of personal empowerment. It is hoped that the combination of personal empowerment, group iden-tification, and an understanding of systemic factors will result in collective efforts that are aimed at social change to make organizations more responsive to black individuals.

REFERENCES

Abramson, L., Seligman, M., & Teasdale, J. (1978). Learned helplessness in humans: Critique and reformulation. *Journal of Abnormal Psychology, 87,* 49–74.

Asch, A. (1986, Winter). Will populism empower the disabled? *Social Policy, 17,* 12–18.

Auletta, K. (1983). *The underclass.* New York: Vintage Books.

Bowman, P. (1983). *A discouragement-centered approach to black youth unemploy-ment: Hopelessness, attributions and psychological distress.* Paper presented at the 91st Annual Convention of the American Psychological Association.

Boxill, N. A., & Beverly, C. C. (1986, Spring). A black self-help development program. *Social Policy, 17,* 37–38.

Brickman, P., Rabinowitz, V., & Karuza, J. (1982). Models of helping and coping. *American Psychologist, 37,* 368–384.

Brisbane, R. L., & Stuart, B. L. (1985). A self-help model for working with black women of alcoholic parents. *Alcoholism Treatment Quarterly, 3,* 199–220.

Brockner, J., Mahan, T., & Thomas, B. (1983). The roles of self-esteem and self-consciousness in the Wortman-Brehm model of reactance and learned helplessness. *Journal of Personality and Social Psychology, 45,* 199–209.

Brooks, C. (1974). New mental health perspectives in the black community. *Social Casework, 55,* 489–496.

Caplan, N., & Nelson, S. (1973). On being useful: The nature and consequences of psychological research on social problems. *American Psychologist, 28,* 199–211.

Carter, J. (1981). Treating black patients: The risks of ignoring critical social issues. *Hospital and Community Psychiatry, 32,* 281–282.

Clark, K. (1965). *Dark ghetto: Dilemmas of social power.* New York: Harper & Row.

Dweck, C. (1975). The role of expectations and attributions in the alleviation of learned helplessness. *Journal of Personality and Social Psychology, 31,* 674–685.

Elliott, K. (1988). *Self-help and empowerment in the black community: Five essays.* Unpublished manuscript, University of Michigan School of Social Work, Ann Arbor.

Fagan, H. (1979). *Empowerment.* New York: Paulist Press.

Gant, L. M. (1986). *Helping and coping styles as moderators of psychological and somatic strains.* Unpublished doctoral dissertation, University of Michigan, Ann Arbor.

Gant, L. M. (1988). *Toward a typology of self help programs.* Unpublished manuscript, University of Michigan, Ann Arbor.

Gant, L. M. (1989, September). *Models of attribution and typologies of self help programs in African-American communities.* Paper prepared for the Annual Conference, National Black Child Development Institute.

Gartner, A., & Riessman, F. (1977). *Self-help in the human services.* San Francisco: Jossey-Bass.

Gary, L. E. (1985). Attitudes toward human service organizations: Perspectives from an urban black community. *Journal of Applied Behavioral Science, 21,* 445–458.

Gary, L. E., & Gary, R. B. (1985). Treatment needs of black alcoholic women. *Alcoholism Treatment Quarterly, 2,* 96–114.

Gilinsky, R. M. (1987, May 10). Minorities sought for self-help. *New York Times.*

Glasgow, D. (1972, May). Black power through community control. *Social Work, 17,* 59–64.

Gray, S. S., Nybell, L., Gant, L. M., & Moffett, J. (1986). *Wayne County Black Family Preservation Project: A final report.* Detroit, MI: Homes for Black Children.

Gruber, J., & Trickett, E. (1987). Can we empower others? The paradox of empowerment in an alternative public high school. *American Journal of Community Psychology, 15,* 353–372.

Gurin, G., & Gurin, P. (1970). Expectancy theory in the study of poverty. *Journal of Social Issues, 26,* 83–104.

Gurin, P., Gurin, G., Lao, R., & Beattie, M. (1969). Internal-external control in the motivational dynamics of Negro youth. *Journal of Social Issues, 25,* 29–53.

Gurin, P., Gurin, G., & Morrison, B. (1978). Personal and ideological aspects of internal and external control. *Social Psychology, 41,* 275–296.

Gutiérrez, L. (1988). Coping with stressful life events: An empowerment perspective. *Working Papers.* Ann Arbor: University of Michigan School of Social Work.

Harrington, M. (1984). *The new American poverty.* New York: Penguin Books.

Harvey, J. C. (1980). *Therapists' and counselors' perceptions of their clients: Effects on the helping relationship.* Unpublished master's thesis, Temple University, Philadelphia.

Hilliard, T. (1981). Political and social action in the prevention of psychopathology of blacks: A mental health strategy for oppressed people. In J. Joffee & G. Albee (Eds.), *Prevention through political action and social change.* Hanover, NH: University of New England Press.

Holland, A. E., & Brickman, P. (1979). *Helping on a hotline: A study of parental stress service.* Unpublished manuscript, Northwestern University, Evanston, IL.

Hughes, M., & Demo, D. (1988). *Self-perceptions of black Americans: Personal self-esteem, racial self-esteem, and personal efficacy.* Unpublished manuscript, Virginia Polytechnic Institute and State University, Blacksburg.

Janoff-Bulman, R. (1982). Esteem and control bases of blame: Adaptive strategies for victims versus observers. *Journal of Personality, 50,* 180–192.

Jason, L., Tabon, D., & Tait, E. (1988). The emergence of the inner-city self-help center. *Journal of Community Psychology, 16,* 287–295.

Joint Center for Political Studies. (1987). *Black initiative and governmental responsibility.* An essay by the Committee on Policy for Racial Justice. Washington, DC: Author.

Jones, E., & Matsumoto, D. (1982). Psychotherapy with the underserved: Recent developments. In L. Snowden (Ed.), *Reaching the underserved: Mental health needs of neglected populations*. Beverly Hills, CA: Sage Publications.

Kahn, A., & Bender, E. (1985). Self help groups as a crucible for people empowerment in the context of social development. *Social Development Issues, 9*, 4–13.

Karuza, A., Jr., Zevon, M., Rabinowitz, M., & Brickman, P. (1982). Attribution of responsibility by helpers and recipients. In T. Wills (Ed.), *Basic processes in helping relationships* (pp. 107–129). New York: Academic Press.

Kessler, R., & Neighbors, H. (1986). A new perspective on the relationships among race, social class and psychological distress. *Journal of Health and Social Behavior, 27*, 107–115.

Killilea, M. (1976). Mutual help organizations: Interpretations in the literature. In G. Caplan & M. Killilea (Eds.), *Support systems and mutual help: Multidisciplinary explorations*. New York: Grune & Stratton.

Lefcourt, H. M. (1982). *Locus of control: Current trends in theory and research*. Hillsdale, NJ: Lawrence Erlbaum Associates.

Martin, J. M., & Martin, E. P. (1985). *The helping tradition in the black family and community*. Silver Spring, MD: National Association of Social Workers, Inc.

Mayfield, W. (1972). Mental health in the black community. *Social Work, 17*, 106–110.

Murray, C. (1984). *Losing ground: American social policy, 1950–1980*. New York: Basic Books.

Neff, J. (1985). Race and vulnerability to stress: An examination of differential vulnerability. *Journal of Personality and Social Psychology, 49*, 481–491.

Newsome, M. (1973). Neighborhood service centers in the black community. *Social Work, 18*, 50–54.

O'Connell, B. (1978). From service to advocacy to empowerment. *Social Casework, 59*, 195–202.

Pernell, R. (1986). Empowerment and social group work. In M. Parenes (Ed.), *Innovations in social group work: Feedback from practice to theory* (pp. 107–117). New York: Haworth Press.

Phares, E. J. (1984). *Introduction to personality*. Columbus, OH: Charles E. Merill.

Pinderhughes, E. (1983). Empowerment for our clients and for ourselves. *Social Casework, 64*, 331–338.

Porter, J., & Washington, R. (1979). Black identity and self esteem: A review of studies of black self concept. *Annual Review of Sociology, 5*, 53–74.

Powell, T. J. (1987). *Self-help organizations and professional practice*. Silver Spring, MD: National Association of Social Workers, Inc.

Rappaport, J. (1987). Terms of empowerment/exemplars of prevention: Toward a theory for community psychology. *American Journal of Community Psychology, 15*, 121–143.

Reischl, T., Zimmerman, M., & Rappaport, J. (1986). *Mutual help mechanisms in the empowerment of former mental patients*. Paper presented at the Annual Meeting of the American Psychological Association, Washington, DC.

Riessman, F. (1985, Winter). New dimensions of self help. *Social Policy, 15*, 2–4.

Riessman, F. (1987). Foreword. In T. Powell (Ed.), *Self-help organizations and professional practice*. Silver Spring, MD: National Association of Social Workers, Inc.

Ross, C., Mirowsky, J., & Cockerham, W. (1983). Social class, Mexican culture and fatalism: Their effects on psychological distress. *American Journal of Community Psychology, 11*, 383–399.

Rotter, J. B. (1966). Generalized expectancies for internal versus external control of reinforcement. *Psychological Monographs, 80*(1, whole No. 609).

Rouse, D. (1987). One health professional's experience with self-help. *Social Policy, 18,* 30–31.

Ryan, W. (1971). *Blaming the victim.* New York: Vintage Books.

Seligman, M. E. P. (1975). *Helplessness: On depression, development and death.* San Francisco: Freeman.

Sherman, W., & Wenocur, S. (1983). Empowering public welfare workers through mutual support. *Social Work, 28,* 375–379.

Smith, D. P. (1987, June). Self-help shown as empowerment tool. *New Jersey Afro-American.*

Solomon, B. (1976). Empowerment: In search of the elusive paradigm. In B. Solomon (Ed.), *Black empowerment: Social work in oppressed communities* (pp. 11–29). New York: Columbia University Press.

Spiegel, D. (1982). Self-help and mutual-support groups: A synthesis of the recent literature. In D. E. Biegel & A. J. Naparstek (Eds.), *Community support systems and mental health.* New York: Springer.

Stensrud, R., & Stensrud, K. (1982). Counseling for health empowerment. *Personnel and Guidance Journal, 60,* 377–381.

Thomas, R. W. (1987). *The black self-help tradition in Detroit. The state of black Detroit: Building from strength.* Detroit: Detroit Urban League.

Vattano, A. (1972). Power to the people: Self-help groups. *Social Work, 17,* 7–15.

Veroff, J., Douvan, E., & Kulka, R. (1981). *The inner American: A self-portrait from 1957 to 1976.* New York: Basic Books.

Wheaton, B. (1980). The sociogenesis of psychological disorder: An attributional theory. *Journal of Health and Social Behavior, 21,* 100–124.

Wilson, W. J. (1987). *The truly disadvantaged: The inner city, the underclass, and public policy.* Chicago: The University of Chicago Press.

Withorn, A. (1980). Helping ourselves: The limits and potential of self-help. *Social Policy, 11,* 20–27.

Wolff, T. (1987). 1985 Division 27 Award for Distinguished Practice in Community Psychology: Thomas Wolff. *American Journal of Community Psychology, 15,* 149–165.

Wright, H. H., Green, R. L., & Gibson, M. (1984, Spring). The role of the self-help group in the delivery of health services to underserved populations in the 1980's. *Psychiatric Forum,* 42–45.

Zimmerman, M., Reischl, T., Toro, P., & Rappaport, J. (1986). *Expansion strategies of a mutual help organization: A multimethod assessment.* Unpublished manuscript, University of Illinois at Urbana-Champaign.

Ziter, M. L. Politi. (1987). Culturally sensitive treatment of black alcoholic families. *Social Work, 32,* 130–135.

SELF-HELP AND THE
LATINO COMMUNITY

LORRAINE GUTIÉRREZ, ROBERT M. ORTEGA, AND ZULEMA E. SUAREZ

Latinos, people of Latin American descent, make up the fastest-growing segment of the American population, yet relatively little is known about them, partly because of their relative "invisibility" and partly because of the challenges presented by their demographics. The group described as Latino is heterogeneous. It includes, for example, new immigrants and descendents of some of the original inhabitants of this continent, resident aliens and American citizens, English and Spanish speakers, people of different national origins, and people who identify closely with their ethnic heritage and those who do not. In fact, there has been considerable debate over whether the label "Latino" is a meaningful ethnic term (Nelson & Tienda, 1985; Portes & Truelove, 1987).

The Latino population also presents a challenge for the human services. Statistics on Latinos reveal that they have a low mean level of education and a high rate of unemployment and are overrepresented in agencies of social control, such as the criminal justice system (Moore & Pachon, 1985; Nelson & Tienda, 1985). Yet, as a group, Latinos underutilize traditional services (Greene, 1982; Rogler et al., 1983). Thus, if the human services are to meet the challenge of the growing Latino population, new models must be developed that can better serve their needs.

Existing models of human services practice with Latinos have focused primarily on cultural factors. For example, the development of models for ethnic-sensitive or transcultural counseling have begun to identify ways in which Latinos can be helped without violating their cultural norms and expectations (Gibson, 1983; Greene, 1982; Rogler, Malgady, Constantino, & Blumenthal, 1987). However, these new models of practice are incomplete because they have paid little attention to how the low status and power of Latinos has shaped their experience. Empowering practice, which concentrates on the process of increasing personal, interpersonal, or political power, is one way in which issues of oppression can be brought into practice with Latinos (Gutiérrez, 1987; Pinderhughes, 1983; Solomon, 1976).

The literature suggests that self-help could contribute to the empowerment of Latinos. Self-help occurs when individuals or groups come together to work on a shared issue or problem. It can range from informal networks of loosely linked individuals who give one another social support to formal and structured organizations that provide a wide range of assistance. What differentiates self-help from other forms of help is its emphasis on linking individuals who are experiencing the same problem or status and on peer, rather than professional, forms of help. Paid helping professionals can play either an active role in self-help groups or no role (Powell, 1987).

Self-help groups and organizations create an ideal atmosphere for empowering Latinos. By coming together to talk about and work on an issue or series of issues, Latinos can begin to understand the commonality of their experience, which helps them understand the social nature of their individual problems and motivates them to change.

Involvement in self-help groups often affirms members' strengths and capabilities. Thus, contact with other Latinos also provides individuals with a mechanism to increase their personal, interpersonal, and political power—that is, to understand and use the power they may have to overcome personal or interpersonal problems. If the members identify issues of common concern, they may also take on group projects that will increase their political power within an organization or community.

However, most of the literature on self-help describes it as a form of help that appeals primarily to the white middle class. Self-help groups are considered to have had an abysmal record in recruiting and maintaining members from racial and ethnic minority groups (Powell, 1987). This poor record has been attributed to the nature of self-help groups and their emphasis on the values and behaviors of the dominant culture and to the characteristics of the members of minority groups and individuals' disinclination to discuss their problems (Powell, 1987). However, few question the proposition that members of minority groups underutilize self-help groups.

The authors believe that the perceived underutilization of self-help groups by Latinos may be an artifact of the ways in which self-help has been defined. When self-help is defined as participation in such groups as Alcoholics Anonymous, Parents without Partners, or Weight Watchers, Latinos may make up a small proportion of such groups. However, when other groups, such as church groups, mutual-aid organizations, and political groups, are included under the rubric of self-help, the involvement of Latinos becomes more apparent (Delgado & Humm-Delgado, 1982; Georges, 1988). By expanding the idea of what constitutes a self-help organization and removing it from its association with the dominant culture, one sees that Latinos have participated in their own form of self-help for centuries.

The history of self-help and Latinos mirrors the history of these groups in the United States. Given the lack of organized social services for most Latinos, self-help has often been the form of help most available. Churches, both Roman Catholic and Protestant, have taken a strong role in this regard by bringing together Latinos to improve their daily lives. A tradition of mutual-aid associations has also existed in the Hispanic community. These groups, run for and by Latinos, have provided concrete and other supportive services for new immigrants (Delgado & Humm-Delgado, 1982; Georges, 1988). Political organizations have also played a self-help role, and individual and family issues have often been considered coextensive with community and political issues (Guzman, 1973). Therefore, groups, such as Mujeres Latinas en Accion or the United Farm Workers, have included both support and advocacy for individuals in their agendas while working toward social change in the larger community (Baca-Zinn, 1975; Chavez, 1973; Padilla, 1985). All these organizations have been based on the concepts of mutual aid and peer, as opposed to professional, helping, which also characterize "mainstream" self-help efforts.

This brief discussion suggests that the self-help model can be useful in work with Latinos when it is organized around culturally appropriate structures and values. This chapter proposes a number of ways in which this organization can be achieved. First, it looks at Latino groups in this society and identifies a set of cultural values that differentiates them from the majority group. Next, it evaluates the compatibility of the self-help perspective with aspects of the Latino culture. Then, it concludes with suggestions for practitioners who are interested in developing self-help groups for Latinos. Since this chapter is one of the first attempts to address the topic of Latino self-help, much of what is presented is based on observation and analysis, rather than on data from empirical studies. The chapter does, however, provide a starting point for those who want to increase the involvement of Latinos in self-help groups.

A CULTURAL PERSPECTIVE

The literature differs widely in its assessment of help seeking by Latinos. From a cultural standpoint, the formal and informal social networks within Latino subgroups directly and indirectly provide the kind of support necessary to satisfy multiple personal needs and buffer individual members from daily stressors (Vega & Kolody, 1985). Social support networks that exist naturally in the Latino community are typically dense and are often relied on to meet both expressive and instrumental needs (Valle & Vega, 1980). Such natural supports have long been used to account for the low utilization of mental health services by Latinos (Delgado & Humm-Delgado, 1982; Madsen, 1972).

Despite their wide recognition in the Latino literature, the availability, accessibility, and supportive functions of natural support networks are not well understood (Vega, Hough, & Miranda, 1985). However, there is substantial evidence of the curative effects of natural support networks, and the presence of natural support among Latinos is consistent with important values that are often associated with this culture. For example, Murillo (1976) viewed traditional Latinos as being part of a social network from birth to death, relying on others and allowing others to rely on them. Interdependence and symmetry ("You do for me, and I do for you") are expected in social relationships, as are sharing and cooperating, rather than competing. The concept of *confianza* (mutual generosity) characterizes this notion (Velez,

1980). Another concept, *personalismo* (relating with and trusting people rather than institutions) is also emphasized in the Latino's social world. Latinos are known to turn away from human services bureaucracies because they consider these organizations to be impersonal, insensitive, and alienating. Instead, they may obtain help from formal non-mental health-related services (medical and religious) and from indigenous (folk) healers, such as *curanderos, herbalistas,* or *espiritistas,* particularly in rural areas. The traditional Latino view of psychological and emotional problems is based on notions of the imbalance in one's physical and social well-being (Delgado, 1981). The healthy individual is one who is in harmony with herself or himself and with the social environment.

This orientation differs greatly from that of the dominant American society, which values functional independence and autonomy and frowns on dependence on others, that is, on the ability to do things for oneself, which is necessary for one's "free spirit." Within the American context, the ideal is to be independent from relationships, events, and links to external systems. Socialization practices encourage separation ("standing on one's own two feet"), geographic mobility, and job changing. In psychotherapy and other human services interventions, the push is toward independence, and a prolonged dependency on others is discouraged. Welfare programs are often criticized because they foster dependence, and welfare recipients are stigmatized because they are assumed not to want to take charge of their lives. Institutionalization (in retirement homes, foster care and other forms of residential care, and long-term hospitalization) is feared and disliked because, as the term implies, individuals are socialized to an institutional life, which interferes with their reliance on their own skills and resources, however limited. At first glance, the extensive use of self-help appears to contradict the individualism and autonomy that the dominant society stresses. However, it probably reflects tension in the society between the values of individualism and interdependence. It also reflects the "mainstream" pioneer tradition, perhaps long buried, that is exemplified by barn raising and quilting bees. Thus, it may suggest that, in times of need, a natural response for some is to band together rather than separate, to seek communion rather than disunity.

In contrast, the Latino endures through the strength of collectivism and social harmony, rather than through individualism (Triandis, 1983). Whereas the individualist proceeds through life obtaining inner strength, skills, and resources so he or she will not have to rely on others, the Latino proceeds through life receiving strength, skills, and resources from the family and the community as a whole. The Latino's emphasis on politeness, manners, and courtesy; the avoidance of conflict; and guarding against offending others in interpersonal relationships reflect the Latino's concern with good relations and harmony (Burma, 1970; Kagan, Night, & Martinez-Romero, 1982; Madsen, 1972; Murillo, 1976). Triandis, Marin, Lisansky, and Betancourt (1984) presented data from three samples of Latinos and non-Latinos, as well as from samples of Latino monolinguals and bilinguals, which indicated that Latinos are more likely than are non-Latinos to expect high frequencies of positive social behaviors and low frequencies of negative social behaviors in associative situations. They characterized the Latino pattern of social interaction as *simpatía,* which represents the Latino focus on and concern for social relationships and the feelings attached to such relationships. Other related concepts, such as *respecto* (respect for one's dignity, for those in authority, and for the elderly) and *dignidad* (maintaining a sense of worthiness) emphasize the avoidance of negative behaviors and encourage broad personal and social responsibilities.

The authors suggest that Latino cultural ideals, such as interdependence, symmetry, mutual generosity, loyalty, cooperation, affiliation, collectivism, and social harmony, are representative qualities of the Latino self. They are transmitted intergenerationally, as part of the socialization process, and become essential to the Latino individual's *orgullo* (personal and cultural pride) (Chavez, 1986). The ideal Latino self, then, refers to the self in relation to others and involves taking the role and perspective of another. The Latino is not expected to be undifferentiated, but individuation and independence must not compromise his or her awareness of the needs of others.

This perspective illustrates how self-help is philosophically compatible with the Latino culture. However, the authors would de-emphasize "self-help" and emphasize "mutual aid." Demonstrating an ability and willingness to share, cooperate, and become interdependent is indicative of the expectations of the Latino participant in the self-help (mutual-aid) effort. Not to achieve these expectations most likely reflects a lack of caring or belonging. Allocentricism is characteristic of traditional Latinos, and the expectation is that the inner strength, skills, and resources of individuals will be offered to the primary group, extending outward to the community as a whole. The underlying assumption is that participation is based on communal concerns in which each participant is valued as an individual and as a representative of his or her social network. Among Latinos, this collective spirit is an important component of the helping that occurs in the self-help–mutual-aid group.

The reader is cautioned that although the authors write about Latino groups as though the groups are one, they do so for the sake of brevity. The fact is that there are considerable regional, historical, political, and socioeconomic differences within and among Latino subgroups. Because of these subcultural variations, it becomes imperative to explore further the bicultural meaning of self-help–mutual aid with regard to Latinos. For example, the bicultural Latino must juxtapose opposing orientations: the individualistic orientation of the dominant American society (see, for example, Williams, 1979) and the more social orientation of the traditional Latino culture. This discussion is surely not unique to the topic of self-help–mutual aid. It pervades the vast majority of the literature on the utilization of health and mental health services by Latinos.

ORGANIZING SELF-HELP WITH LATINOS

Although, as has been mentioned, self-help is philosophically compatible with the Latino culture, environmental barriers may inhibit the Latinos' use of such groups. Being members of an oppressed ethnic minority group or recent immigrants, Latinos are confronted with many issues of survival (Lum, 1986). With these realistic concerns in mind, they may not have the energy or inclination to seek out a self-help group. They may also not know that these groups exist or understand their function, since self-help groups in this country emanate from a white middle-class environment. Of the numerous problems confronting Latinos in this country, two that may prevent them from attending mainstream self-help groups are language and transportation.

Latinos who are recent immigrants or who live in ethnic enclaves may have difficulty with English. Obviously, not understanding the language precludes any participation in an Anglo self-help group. Those who do speak English, however, may be inhibited from participating in such groups because they feel self-conscious about their Spanish accent (personal communication from Louise Jimenez-Taibi, a participant and organizer of self-help groups, January 1988).

Because meetings of self-help groups are generally held in central locations outside Latino communities, potential Latino members may have difficulty attending them because of problems with transportation. For Latinos, who tend to be poor, the lack of money for carfare may present an obstacle, as can the lack of facility with English, which makes it difficult to negotiate a complex transportation system. Furthermore, because their low socioeconomic levels relegate Latinos to living in inner-city areas, those who do own a car may be discouraged from attending group meetings because they cannot find a parking space near their homes late at night. Parking far from home can be unsafe in a dangerous urban neighborhood.

Child care and household responsibilities may prevent women from participating in self-help groups. Since role definitions tend to be stricter in first-generation Latino marriages (Rogler & Santana-Cooney, 1984), the husband may not be involved with the management of the household or with baby-sitting. If in addition to her homemaking duties the woman works outside the home, she will spend evenings and weekends doing chores. In this case, the lack of time, energy, and money to pay for baby-sitters would be a barrier to attending meetings of a self-help group.

Finally, immigrants who are trying to succeed may have to hold two jobs to provide for their families. Once again, the lack of time would preclude their participation in a self-help group.

Moreover, the obstacles to participation may vary, depending on whether potential members are being recruited for Spanish-speaking chapters of mainstream groups, such as Alcoholics Anonymous, Latino-only groups, or Latino-sensitive groups. An awareness of the difference between Latino subgroups and mainstream groups may help leaders anticipate and avert potential sources of conflict. The following sections briefly discuss specific issues that relate to these three types of groups.

MAINSTREAM GROUPS

It has been suggested that Latinos may be timid about joining groups that do not consist of Latinos (L. Jimenez-Taibi, personal communication, 1988). Thus, when attempting to include Latino members in an English-speaking group that is based on mainstream cultural norms, professionals or group leaders must be aware of ethnic differences among group members. According to McGoldrick (1982, p. 4):

> Ethnicity patterns our thinking, feeling, and behavior in both obvious and subtle ways. It plays a major role in determining what we eat, how we work, how we relax, how we celebrate holidays and rituals, and how we feel about life, death and illness . . . cultural values and assumptions are generally outside of our awareness.

More specifically, Latinos, it has been suggested, differ from Anglo-Americans according to Kluckhohn and Strodbeck's schema of value orientations (Delgado, 1981; Szapocznik, Scopetta, & King, 1978). These value orientations refer to perceptions of (1) human qualities and their susceptibility to metaphysical forces (human nature orientation), (2) the interface of human beings with their environment (person-nature orientation), (3) internal versus external judgments about behavior (activity orientation), (4) the importance of time (time orientation), and (5) the value of social roles and social relationships (relational orientation) (Delgado, 1981). Therefore, Latino relational values may both clash with and complement those of mainstream self-help groups. Although the Latino cultural ideals of symmetry and interdependence are compatible with the self-help ethos, the cultural trait of lineality may pose a problem in mainstream groups. Latino relationships are said to be lineal and "influenced by relative status within a hierarchical structure" (Delgado, 1981). Hence, Latino members may attempt to thrust the leader of a self-help group into a position of authority and to expect the leader to provide or suggest possible solutions to their problems (Delgado, 1981). This expectation may be perplexing to and uncomfortable for mainstream leaders who would want to take less of an active role. If this issue arises in the group, it may be addressed by clarifying, with sensitivity and understanding, the norms of the group for the Latino member.

Another cultural factor that would be of particular importance in a group is the leader's awareness of differences in emotional expressiveness. Latinos tend to be emotionally expressive. The mainstream culture, on the other hand, seems to value self-control and "keeping a stiff upper lip" (McGill & Pearce, 1982). Ignorance and the nonacceptance of this fact can lead to conflict and misunderstanding between mainstream and Latino group members. The mainstream members may view the Latino members as being histrionic and out of control and may find it difficult to empathize with them; in turn, the Latino members may feel alienated. Recognition and acceptance of these differences can prevent tension and alienation among both members.

On a more concrete level, participants and leaders of a mixed group should keep in mind that, depending on their level of acculturation, Latinos may prefer different foods, and their preferences should be respected when organizing activities in which food is to be served. Depending on the size of the Latino membership, typically American foods from various ethnic groups may be alternated or served concurrently with Latino dishes.

SELF-HELP FOR LATINOS ONLY

Traditionally, Latinos become involved in self-help by mobilizing informal resources. Referral to more formally organized self-help organizations usually follows a standard referral process after the available natural-support resources have failed. The Latino first attempts to alleviate problems or distress through his or her own initiatives (Delgado & Humm-Delgado, 1982). If the results are unsuccessful, the next step is to look to his or her support network. Delgado and Humm-Delgado (1982) described four important components of Latino social support: (1) *the extended family*, which consists of blood relatives as well as "adopted relatives," such as close friends, special neighbors, and others who have proved that they are willing to become involved in important family matters and activities; (2) *folk healers*, such as the *santero* (visible in Cuban communities), the *espiritista* or *herbalista* (in Puerto Rican communities), or the *curandero* (in Mexican communities), who use unique culture-specific methods to diagnose and treat ailments; (3) *religious institutions* (especially the Roman Catholic Church and churches of alternative religions, including the Pentecostal and Seventh-Day Adventist), which offer both social and psychological support; and (4) *merchants and social clubs*, which are unique in that they fulfill formal and informal roles by providing credit, information, and referrals, as well as recreational activities, opportunities for socializing, and orientation for new members of the community.

Several aspects of the services of natural support networks can be applied to self-help groups that are specifically targeted to the needs of Latino individuals. They include the following:

- Cultural familiarity. Leaders should be aware of acceptable ways of expressing and resolving problems, expressing empathy (for example, touching and hugging), asking questions, and providing feedback to Latino members.

- Linguistic familiarity. Leaders should also understand verbal and nonverbal styles of communication and associated nuances (for instance, maintaining eye contact, using more formal language to show respect for elders, and the appropriate interpretation of pauses and moments of silence).

- Members should have knowledge of and access to indigenous lay-referral systems.

- The coordination of services should be in line with the Latino community's needs.

- Support from local religious and indigenous political leaders should be obtained.

- Actions that evolve *from* the group should be in accordance with the cultural characteristics of Latinos.

These are perhaps the most essential features of the natural support system. They assume Spanish to be the preferred spoken language, some degree of or desire for social integration, and relevant ways of addressing the identification and alleviation of problems. If they are incorporated into the more formally organized self-help groups, these groups can become a viable alternative service, particularly for recent immigrants or less-integrated Latinos whose support system is not dense and who do not know about relevant resources. The self-help group then becomes a way to achieve some degree of social integration while maintaining the preferred spoken language in a culturally relevant context.

LATINO CHAPTERS OF MAINSTREAM GROUPS

Another way in which Latinos can become more involved in self-help groups is through the development of special Latino chapters of existing self-help organizations. These chapters would adapt the structure and methods of an existing self-help group to the needs of the Latino community. Some organizations, such as Alcoholics Anonymous, have simply set up groups that offer their services in Spanish, while other groups have attempted to make their organization more culturally relevant.

Practitioners who are interested in founding specific Latino chapters of an organization should first learn about the local Latino community by approaching agencies that serve Latinos, by meeting with staff members and clients of community organizations, and by speaking with people at public agencies, such as schools or clinics. These contact persons can provide valuable information about the Latino community's need for the particular group and any special needs. Critical questions would concern the level of acculturation in the local community, the predominant language spoken, mass-media outlets (newspapers and local television and radio stations) that are popular among Latinos, and suggested locations for group meetings. They can also act as future sources of referrals.

An important second step would be to take a critical look at the format and structure of the "mainstream" group and their compatibility with the Latino culture and values. This analysis would suggest ways in which the group could be modified to serve the Latino community. Some specific concerns would be the degree to which members are held accountable for solving their problems, the degree to which members are encouraged to rely on family members or friends, and the role of help from peers. A format that encourages members to help one another and to utilize existing social networks would be more compatible with Latino values than would one that encourages individual efforts. By building on the tradition of *mutualista* among Latinos, a practitioner could form a special chapter of an existing organization that would be culturally relevant.

Latino members of existing chapters of an organization could be particularly helpful in founding specific Latino chapters. They could be consulted as "experts" on the ways in which special chapters could modify their structure or practice to accommodate more Latinos. They could also provide invaluable insider information regarding how the organization's services could be made more attractive and accessible to Latinos. These members could be most valuable as organizers or leaders of Latino chapters, for they could effectively explain to potential members how the Latino chapters were developed to meet their needs.

The National Alliance for the Mentally Ill, a national organiza- tion of friends and family members of mentally ill persons, is an example of such efforts. It focuses on family and community educa- tion, as well as advocacy for improvements in mental health services. In areas with large concentrations of Latinos, special chapters have been set up specifically for this population. In these chapters, meetings are conducted in Spanish, outreach fliers and announcements are printed in Spanish, and issues are addressed that are of specific concern to Latinos and their community.

PRACTICE PRINCIPLES

DEVELOPING THE ROLE OF PROFESSIONALS

The proliferation of mutual-aid groups in the Latino commu- nity cannot readily come about without the significant involvement of professionals. Although natural helping resources may already exist in the indigenous communities, professionals can intervene to provide some initial leadership and structure.

Mental health professionals familiar with the Latino commu- nity can begin by identifying what Valle and Bensussen (1985) called "linkpersons." Linkpersons in the Latino context could include friends, neighbors, and indigenous healers, such as herbalists (*yerberos*), masseuses (*sobradores*), and spiritual counselors (*espiritistas*). Other linkpersons would be religious leaders, local merchants, and members of social clubs (Delgado & Humm-Delgado, 1982). These natural helpers have traditionally provided Latinos with instrumental support or nurturance. (According to Swenson, 1979, p. 218, "instrumental social support is assistance in accomplishing a task: showing someone how to do something, providing goods or services, giving directions or financial assistance." Nurturance is emotional support, including listening, encouragement, giving advice, and being present.) The professional can then inform and educate the linkpersons about the potential benefits and operations of the mutual-aid groups so that they may act as sources of referral. Natural helpers who express enthusiasm for and a commitment to the self-help concept can be trained by the professional to become group leaders.

As an alternative, the professional can form the group and then withdraw after the first few meetings. For example, a Latino public health nurse in Chicago (Eva Hernandez, personal communication, February 1988) has facilitated the development of several mutual-aid groups (Why Me? for women with breast cancer, and Compassionate Friends, for bereaved parents who have lost a child) in the Latino community, drawing from the pool of patients in the community health clinic in which she works. To start a group, she generally calls a meeting of patients with similar problems and tells them that they are meeting to discuss how they can help each other (not how they can help themselves). Once the members are engaged in a mutual helping process, she stops attending and the group continues without her presence.

DEVELOPING CULTURALLY RELEVANT GROUPS

As was noted earlier, Latinos have a tradition of seeking help from various systems in their social support networks that have provided them with instrumental support and nurturance. Although some of these systems have been transported to this country, they may not be readily available to those who need them, such as immigrants. According to Valle and Bensussen (1985, p. 159),

> Immigrants may find themselves in a crisis situation and in need of support while living far from their original home. Frequently immigrants have had insufficient time to develop supportive ties where they currently reside. If they have developed these new socially supportive ties, their request for

assistance may not be met because the potential supportive significant others
are themselves currently overwhelmed with their own needs and problems.

The problems noted in this quotation can be addressed by
establishing mutual-aid groups that are patterned after the natural
helping networks traditionally found in Latino culture. Doing so not
only makes the groups more culturally relevant, but it ensures that the
processes that have been taking place naturally continue to do so
informally, yet systematically, through mutual-aid groups and that
better and more equal access to the benefits provided by select
indigenous community groups are promoted.

Mutual-aid groups would provide both expressive and instrumental help with the burden shared among group members so that
resources would not be exhausted. The leaders of these groups could
be community linkpersons, who could also act as cultural brokers to
connect group members to the mainstream society. Mothers Against
Gangs (MAG) is an example. Although it evolved in the Latino
community, it adopted the bylaws of a mainstream group, Mothers
Against Drunk Driving (MADD), and eventually accepted non-Latino
members. Founded by Frances Sandoval, a mother whose son was
killed by a gang member, the group later expanded to include mothers
whose children are gang members ("Fighting Back," 1988).

Started in Chicago about 5 years ago, MAG has 700 members
in 2 chapters, Chicago and Aurora, Illinois. Like MADD, it provides its
members with support not only through groups and a telephone
network but through an escort service for all court appearances.
Advocacy is also an integral part of the group's mission. MAG's goal
is to raise consciousness about the seriousness of gangs in Chicago on
the local, state, and federal levels.

The success of MAG may be attributable to the community's
immense need for such services. However, it may also be attributable
to its founder's untiring dedication and commitment to continue to
provide group members with "leadership support" and a personal
service. For example, when mothers in a neighborhood are nervous
about calling public officials to voice their concerns, Sandoval will ask
them to make the call but she will accompany them to the meeting.
This type of personalized leadership, which can be shared among a
cadre of members, seems to be an essential element of successful
Latino self-help groups.

BROADENING THE FOCUS OF THE PROBLEM

If self-help groups are to provide an alternative to formal services for Latinos, then the focus of the problem must also be expanded. One of the major problems for Latinos in gaining access to formal services is that agencies are restricted in the types of services they offer to clients. Latino clients tend not to understand this specialization. Therefore, those who are turned away from an agency because their request does not fit the agency's parameters or because they do not live in the "catchment area" may interpret this denial as rejection. They may then walk away with the idea that the agency is not helpful and that approaching other institutions would be just as futile.

In the authors' work with Latinos in the Midwest and on the East Coast, they have found that Latinos turn to agencies for help if the agencies have a reputation in the community of being helpful. When Latinos need help, they seek it at reputable agencies without stopping to think whether the requests are "appropriate." Similarly, Latinos must view self-help groups as places where people can turn for help. The life model, described by Gitterman and Shulman (1986), provides a framework for the development of groups for different life stages or transitions. Thus, instead of focusing on one problem, members would work with clusters of problems related to a specific life or transitional stage. For example, a mutual-aid group for immigrants would provide a vehicle for dealing with problems related to immigration and settlement, such as adjusting to the community and negotiating new social systems. This application differs from Gitterman and Shulman's model in that the groups would not be professionally led. Instead, the professional could use the model to conceptualize which groups may be needed in the community, encourage the development of such groups, and then withdraw leaving the leadership to the group members.

MAKING SELF-HELP WITH LATINOS WORK

In the absence of accessible mainstream human services for Latinos, self-help has historically been the form of help most available. For many Latinos, self-help represents an effective means of personal, interpersonal, and political empowerment. In this chapter, the authors have presented what they believe to be cultural ideals of the traditional Latino and argue that such ideals as mutual aid are clearly in line with the philosophy of self-help. They have pointed out important cultural considerations and barriers that need to be recognized if existing self-help groups are to be made more accessible to Latinos. They have also provided basic practice principles that, if incorporated into human services efforts, will demonstrate a serious concern for the multiple needs of Latinos.

The importance of examining existing Latino organizations and natural support networks as the beginning task of the professional cannot be overemphasized. Latino self-help is typically organic, evolving from within the Latino community around what Latinos view as the central issues of concern. Also, Latino self-help groups may initially focus on specific issues and evolve into those that serve multiple purposes within both the expressive and instrumental domains. Although this flexibility is expected by Latinos, it may be disconcerting to the mainstream member, particularly one who prefers to be task oriented. Actions are often carried out as a collective since it may be difficult for less acculturated Latinos to manage the elaborate service network and any other organization that requires redress. Accompanying each other also makes it clear to the members that they are not alone in their attempts to seek change.

What has been presented here is clearly not the final word on Latino self-help. The authors prefer to think of it as a contribution to a necessary discussion of Latino self-help at a time when self-help has become the service of choice of millions of people, both nationally and internationally.

REFERENCES

Baca-Zinn, M. (1975). Political familism: Toward a theory of sex role equity for the Chicano family. *Aztlan, 6*, 113–126.

Burma, J. H. (1970). *Mexican-Americans in the United States: A reader*. Cambridge, MA: Schenkman.

Chavez, C. (1973). An organizer's tale. In R. Rosaldo, R. Calvert, & G. Seligman (Eds.), *Chicano: The evolution of a people*. San Francisco: Reinhart.

Chavez, N. (1986). Mental health service delivery to minority populations: Hispanics—A perspective. In M. Miranda & H. Kitano (Eds.), *Mental health research and practice in minority communities*. Washington, DC: U.S. Government Printing Office.

Delgado, M. (1981). Hispanic cultural values: Implications for groups. *Small Group Behavior, 12*(1), 69–80.

Delgado, M., & Humm-Delgado, D. (1982). Natural support systems: Sources of strength in Hispanic communities. *Social Work, 27*(1), 83–89.

Fighting back: Frances Sandoval and her mothers' crusade take aim at gangs. (1988, October 16). *Sunday Chicago Tribune Magazine,* pp. 10–24.

Georges, E. (1988). *Dominican self help association in Washington Heights: Integration of new immigrant population in a multi-ethnic neighborhood.* Working Paper No. 1. Austin: Committee for Contemporary Latino Issues, Inter-University Program, Social Science Research Council, University of Texas.

Gibson, G. O. (1983). *Our kingdom stands on brittle glass.* Silver Spring, MD: National Association of Social Workers.

Gitterman, A., & Shulman, L. (1986). The life model, mutual aid, and the mediating function. In A. Gitterman & L. Schulman (Eds.), *Mutual aid groups and the life cycle.* Itasca, IL: F. E. Peacock Publishers.

Greene, J. (1982). *Cultural awareness in the human services.* Englewood Cliffs, NJ: Prentice-Hall.

Gutiérrez, L. (1987). *Toward a model of empowerment for social work practice.* Unpublished manuscript, University of Michigan.

Guzman, R. (1973). Politics in the Mexican American community. In R. Rosaldo, R. Calvert, & G. Seligman (Eds.), *Chicano: The evolution of a people.* San Francisco: Reinhart.

Kagan, S., Night, G. P., & Martinez-Romero, S. (1982). Culture and the development of conflict resolution style. *Journal of Cross-Cultural Psychology, 13,* 43–49.

Lum, D. (1986). *Social work practice and people of color: A process-stage approach.* Monterey, CA: Brooks/Cole.

Madsen, W. (1972). *Mexican-Americans of southwest Texas* (2nd ed.). New York: Holt, Rinehart & Winston.

McGill, D., & Pearce, J. K. (1982). British families. In M. McGoldrick, J. K. Pearce, & J. Giordano (Eds.), *Ethnicity and family therapy.* New York: Guilford Press.

McGoldrick, M. (1982). Ethnicity and family therapy: An overview. In M. McGoldrick, J. K. Pearce, & J. Giordano (Eds.), *Ethnicity and family therapy.* New York: Guilford Press.

Moore, J., & Pachon, H. (1985). *Hispanics in the United States.* Englewood Cliffs, NJ: Prentice-Hall.

Murillo, N. (1976). The Mexican-American family. In C. A. Hernandez, M. J. Huag, & N. N. Wagner (Eds.), *Chicanos: Social and psychological perspectives* (pp. 15–25). St. Louis: C. V. Mosby.

Nelson, C., & Tienda, M. (1985). The structuring of Hispanic ethnicity: Historical and contemporary perspectives. *Ethnic and Racial Studies, 8,* 49–73.

Padilla, F. (1985). *Latino ethnic consciousness. The case of Mexican Americans and Puerto Ricans in Chicago.* Notre Dame, IN: Notre Dame University Press.

Pinderhughes, E. (1983). Empowerment: For our clients and for ourselves. *Social Casework, 64,* 312–314.

Portes, A., & Truelove, C. (1987). Making sense of diversity: Recent research on Hispanic minorities in the United States. *Annual Review of Sociology, 13,* 359–385.

Powell, T. J. (1987). *Self-help organizations and professional practice.* Silver Spring, MD: National Association of Social Workers.

Rogler, L., Cooney, R., Constantino, G., Early, B., Grossman, B., Gurak, D., Malgady, R., & Rodriguez, O. (1983). *A conceptual framework for mental health research on Hispanic populations*. New York: Hispanic Research Center, Fordham University.

Rogler, L., Malgady, R., Constantino, G., & Blumenthal, R. (1987). What do culturally sensitive services mean? The case of Hispanics. *American Psychologist, 42,* 565–570.

Rogler, L., & Santana-Cooney, R. (1984). *Puerto Ricans in New York City: Intergenerational processes*. New York: Hispanic Research Center, Fordham University.

Solomon, B. (1976). *Black empowerment*. New York: Columbia University Press.

Swenson, C. (1979). Social networks, mutual aid, and the life model of practice. In C. Germain (Ed.), *Social work practice: People and environments*. New York: Columbia University Press.

Szapocznik, J., Scopetta, M. A., Arnalde, M. A., & Kurtines, W. (1978). Cuban value structure: Treatment implications. *Journal of Consulting and Clinical Psychology, 46,* 961–970.

Szapocznik, J., Scopetta, M. A., & King, O. E. (1978). Theory and practice in matching treatment to the special characteristics and problems of Cuban immigrants. *Journal of Community Psychology, 6,* 112–122.

Triandis, H. (1983). *Allocentric vs. idiocentric social behavior. A major cultural difference between Hispanics and mainstreams* (Tech. Rep. No. 16). Urbana: Department of Psychology, University of Illinois at Urbana-Champaign.

Triandis, H., Marin, G., Lisansky, J., & Betancourt, H. (1984). Simpatia as a cultural script of Hispanics. *Journal of Personality and Social Psychology, 47*(6), 1363–1375.

Valle, R., & Bensussen, G. (1985). Hispanic social networks, social support, and mental health. In W. A. Vega & M. R. Miranda (Eds.), *Stress and Hispanic mental health: Relating research to service delivery*. Washington, DC: U.S. Government Printing Office.

Valle, R., & Vega, W. (Eds.). (1980). *Hispanic natural support systems: Mental health promotions perspectives*. Sacramento, CA: State Department of Mental Health.

Vega, W. A., Hough, R. L., & Miranda, M. R. (1985). Modeling cross-cultural research in Hispanic mental health. In W. A. Vega & M. R. Miranda (Eds.), *Stress and Hispanic mental health: Relating research to service delivery*. Washington, DC: U.S. Government Printing Office.

Vega, W. A., & Kolody, B. (1985). The meaning of social support and the mediations of stress across cultures. In W. A. Vega & M. R. Miranda (Eds.), *Stress and Hispanic mental health* (pp. 48–75). Washington, DC: U.S. Government Printing Office.

Velez, C. G. (1980). Mexican/Hispano support systems and confianza: Theoretical issues of cultural adaptation. In R. Valle & W. Vega (Eds.), *Hispanic natural support systems: Mental health promotions perspectives*. Sacramento, CA: State Department of Mental Health.

Williams, R. M., Jr. (1979). Change and stability in values and value systems. In M. Rokeach (Ed.), *Understanding human values: Individual and societal*. New York: Free Press.

12

WORKING WITH AND UNDERSTANDING GAMBLERS ANONYMOUS

HENRY R. LESIEUR

Gamblers Anonymous (GA) is a self-help group for compulsive gamblers that was started in 1957 in Los Angeles, California. By 1960 (personal communication, Gamblers Anonymous National Service Office, 1988), there were 16 chapters; by 1970, 130; and by 1988, approximately 600 chapters in the United States and more than 1,000 chapters worldwide. There are now groups in Argentina, Australia, Brazil, English and French Canada, England, Germany, Holland, Ireland, Israel, Japan, Kenya, Korea, New Zealand, Panama, Puerto Rico, Scotland, and Uganda, as well as in 46 states in the United States (all but South Dakota, Vermont, Wisconsin, and Wyoming). The organization is based on the Alcoholics Anonymous (AA) structure, with its Twelve Steps and Twelve Traditions. In addition, there are chapters of Gam-Anon (a group for spouses and significant others) in about one-half the locations where GA meetings are held. The coexistence of Gam-Anon and GA is more common on the East Coast of the United States than elsewhere. Gam-Anon itself has about 300 chapters. Although the GA literature has been translated into French, Korean, and Spanish, only one Gam-Anon pamphlet has been translated into Spanish.

GA focuses on gambling as the source of the problem rather than on trying to figure out the "underlying cause" of the problems that the gambler and family are experiencing. The belief is that most problems are a product of destructive gambling.

The author would like to thank Jerome Rothschild and Mary Heineman for their comments on an earlier draft of this chapter.

GA: A TYPICAL MEETING

Most GA meetings are held in church meeting rooms, local YMCAs, or at other nonprofit organizations. Depending on the location, a Gam-Anon meeting is also held in another room at the same time. GA meetings are of two basic types: closed and open. At closed meetings, only members can attend and participate, and each member gets to talk if he or she wishes. Open meetings are open to the public and usually have a limited number of speakers; at these meetings, members of GA and of Gam-Anon and an invited guest or two speak. Some areas of the country have more numerous open meetings than do others. Open meetings are a must for professionals, since it is virtually impossible to get to know about GA unless one attends them.

In a typical GA meeting, held in the basement of a church, for example, about 20 members are present. People notice newcomers right away, ask them how they got there, and tell them that they do not have to speak if they do not want to. A chairperson calls the meeting to order and says, "Anything said in the room stays in the room." New members are introduced. Members are asked, in turn, to read from the meeting booklet. The chairperson then begins the meeting by asking for "therapy."

Therapy frequently proceeds according to the following formula: "I am [Joe or Joan]. I am a compulsive gambler." The person then says how long it has been since he or she made the last bet and tells the story of how gambling interfered with his or her past life (for example, "I lied to my wife and my kids. I stole from my boss. When I came into the room, I owed everybody. I was on the verge of suicide"). The person ends by telling how things are different since he or she joined GA (for instance, "My life has turned around. I am paying off my debts, and my husband and I are back together. Things aren't perfect, but they are 100 percent better than when I was gambling. I'm taking things one day at a time").

Although this format is usually followed in both open and closed meetings, only a few people speak in open meetings but most members speak in closed meetings. Those who do not get a chance to speak one week usually have the opportunity to speak the following week. Whether their story follows the format just described (sometimes called a "war story"), focuses on one of the Twelve Steps, or is centered on feelings depends on the group. The most therapeutic meetings the author has attended have not restricted the discussion to gambling but have ranged from feelings about the past to a here-and-now focus.

HOW IT WORKS

Four concepts describe the keys to success in GA: identification, reference group, spirituality, and relabeling. It is through the identification with a new reference group in a spiritual journey that members of GA reconfigure (relabel) their self-conceptions. The members are no longer "evil" or "stupid"; they are sick people in need of help from a higher power.

In a study of the careers of compulsive gamblers in action and abstinence, Livingston (1974) noted that the following process takes place when one joins GA. Before the first meeting, a crisis typically precipitates the person's entry into GA. Attendance at the first meeting produces relief because newcomers recognize that they are not the only ones with the problem when they meet others who talk to them in a nonjudgmental way. GA members understand because they have had the same problems themselves; as a consequence, the newcomer can be open and honest without fearing a loss of status. GA can become the person's reference group. Members say they "identify" with other members, that is, they see themselves in the stories others tell. After a few weeks, new members float on a "pink cloud" as they come to realize the possibilities that GA offers for reorienting their future. Eventually, their personal biographies are reconstructed to fit the GA conception of self.

Cromer (1978) noted a similar process but one that consists of three stages: (1) status degradation—a recognition that one's identity is in need of transformation, (2) differential association—learning to avoid old acquaintances and replace them with new ones (the GA members), and (3) the usage of time—eventually reorienting one's work and leisure time. Cromer saw two principal barriers to continued attendance at GA meetings: doubts about whether the situation is all that serious and self-deception.

Custer (1982), in a different evaluation of GA, presented seven reasons for GA's success:

a) it undercuts denial, projection and rationalization,
b) identifies the serious implications of gambling,
c) demands honesty and responsibility,
d) identifies and corrects character problems,
e) gives affection, personal concern and support,
f) develops substitutes for the void left by the cessation of gambling, . . .
g) is nonjudgmental. (p. 376)

In an analysis that focused on the spiritual aspects of GA and other self-help groups, Brown (1985) compared the process of recovery in GA with being converted as a "born-again" Christian. Like Livingston (1974) and Cromer (1978), Brown saw the first step as a recognition that the old life is unacceptable (new members are likely to feel that their old life was unmanageable). On the other hand, Brown viewed the process as one of a spiritual conversion. The acceptance of help from "forces greater than the limits of the conscious self" (p. 21) is essential to recovery. Only with acceptance is a reinterpretation of one's past life possible. With acceptance one can forgive and understand oneself. This acceptance is aided by a change to and eventual acceptance of a new reference group.

GA, like other "anonymous" self-help groups, is based on a mixture of medical and spiritual models. It is "nonprofessional" yet accepts a model taken from professionals. The "treatment" is social and spiritual while the relabeling is medical. For some people, the higher power is the group; for others, it is God.

THE ORGANIZATION

Item 9 of the GA Unity Program says that "Gamblers Anonymous as such ought never be organized." While this statement is nominally true, there is an informal organizational structure to GA. Informally, there are three tiers: newcomers, pin holders, and old-timers. In addition, there are the roles of sponsor and trusted servant.

Newcomers are just that. They constantly rely on others for advice and information about the program. Typically, the status of newcomer lasts for almost a year. At the 1-year mark, the newcomer receives a 1-year pin with the letters "GA" on it. This pin is usually worn at open meetings; it signifies that the person has not gambled for at least 1 year. There are also pins for 5, 10, 15, 20, and 25 years. Pin holders can be sponsors or trusted servants. In smaller chapters with few pin holders, those with less than a year of abstinence can and do become sponsors and trusted servants. Old-timers are those members who have been in GA the longest in their chapter. With this status comes some form of recognition at virtually every open meeting.

The roles of sponsor and trusted servant are important for the therapist to know about. Sponsors act as guides and counselors for newcomers. They are on call 24 hours a day and intervene in crises. The best sponsors check on their charges almost every day to give them the moral support they need to resist the impulse to gamble. Sponsors have lived through many of the same problems and typically give advice of the variety, "This is what I did" or "This is what Joe did; why don't you talk to Joe." Sponsors also know how to deal with bookmakers, loan sharks, lending institutions, and other creditors. They have firsthand knowledge of the gambling world in all its complexities. Therefore, they are important allies for therapists who are not familiar with the gambling scene.

The term *trusted servant* in GA encompasses the following roles in the group: secretary, treasurer, public relations representative, rotating chair of meetings, group representative, and chair of pressure groups. These roles are described in the Gamblers Anonymous publication *The G.A. Group* (GA, 1964), which is an essential resource for those who wish to gain in-depth knowledge of GA.

Although GA operates on a group-by-group basis, there is a larger organizational structure. Different regions of the country have "intergroups": organizations of approximately 10 or more chapters that meet once a month to determine GA policy, set timetables, determine who will be responsible for telephone hotlines, and so forth. In addition, there are periodic conclaves, in which open workshops are held for all GA members and interested parties; these conclaves are ideal settings for professionals to learn about the organization. At some conclaves professionals have been invited to speak, sit on panels, or conduct workshops. The topics of workshops have included how to run a step meeting, pressure groups, expressing feelings, the dual addict, and communication.

At the national level, the elected board of trustees sets policy for GA and runs national conclaves. The National Service Office (NSO) produces publications, handles the mail, helps new groups get established, and takes care of other routine operations.

DIFFERENCES BETWEEN AA AND GA

First, it would be easy to believe that GA is a clone of AA. However, those who are familiar with AA will notice that the Twelve Steps are different in GA. God and spirituality are deemphasized in GA's steps and in the overall program, and the Lord's Prayer is not said at the end of each meeting. One consequence is that there are fewer step meetings in GA, which, in the author's experience, works to the detriment of GA members because it is typically at step meetings that members of self-help groups come to express their feelings. (In GA, old-timers who have not been to step meetings frequently still appear to be "big shots.") Thus, some GA groups, especially those whose GA members also belong to AA, tend to hold more step meetings and discuss feelings.

Second, GA meetings are of a longer duration than are AA meetings. It is not unusual to go to a meeting that lasts for 3 or 4 hours, starting at 8 P.M. and ending at about midnight. After the meeting is over, many groups have "aftermeetings" that are held in nearby restaurants. These aftermeetings are an excellent source of camaraderie and help establish social networks that are alternatives to gambling buddies outside the meetings. They are sometimes the only socializing that new GA members can afford.

There are several possible reasons for longer meetings. Some studies (Linden, Pope, & Jonas, 1986; McCormick, Russo, Ramirez, & Taber, 1984) have found high rates of manic and hypomanic disorder among pathological gamblers. Other studies have pointed to evidence of narcissistic personality disorder among pathological gamblers (see Taber & Chaplin, 1988). These disorders may be expressed in lengthy meetings. Alternatively, compulsive gamblers are used to all-night card games and casino ventures and to staying up to listen to sporting events on the radio if they bet on sports; therefore, they may have less need for sleep. Lengthy meetings can be a drawback. Some women do not wish to go to certain meetings because the meetings end too late. Other members use the length of meetings as an excuse to forgo attendance.

Third, Gam-Anon meetings are usually held on the same night and in the same location as are the GA sessions, although most groups hold their meetings in separate rooms. Thus, when the Gam-Anon chapter is strong, the GA chapter is more family oriented than is AA. On top of that, pressure is placed on Gam-Anon members to get the gambler involved in GA. There are differences of opinion as to whether Gam-Anon should focus more on the individual as does Al-Anon. However, the stated purpose of Gam-Anon, like that of Al-Anon, is to help the Gam-Anon member, not to get significant others to quit gambling.

Fourth, unlike AA, GA uses "pressure-relief" groups in which a new compulsive gambler and his or her spouse, parents, or close friends meet with a pressure-group chair or committee (usually one or two GA members who have been in GA for a long time). At the meeting, the new GA member is pressured into revealing all the debt that he or she has. Usually, compulsive gamblers have lied to and conned other people for so long in an effort to obtain money for gambling that their spouses, parents, and close friends no longer trust them. (Most of their lies revolve around finances and financially related illegal activities, such as check forgery, fraud, and theft and embezzlement at the workplace.) Frequently they are pressured to cover bad checks, return misappropriated funds, or provide redress to victims of crime. In addition, loans that are kept secret are a common source of relapse after compulsive gamblers join GA (Lesieur, 1984). Uncovering these activities is probably the most important action of pressure-relief meetings. For GA members who have been lying about money they owe (both legal and illegal), this meeting can be the "push" they need to make a fresh start.

DEMOGRAPHIC CHARACTERISTICS OF PATHOLOGICAL GAMBLERS

Different methods have been used to determine the demographic characteristics of pathological gamblers: surveys of GA members, surveys of persons in treatment, examinations of callers to hotlines, and epidemiological surveys of the general population. Each sample provides different information. From the general population, one can find out who is affected; from the hotlines, one can find out who is informed and concerned about his or her own or someone else's problem; from persons who are in treatment and in GA groups, one can find out which populations are currently being served. When the results of studies of GA members and of pathological gamblers in the general population are compared, it is clear that women, blacks, and Hispanics; those with less education; the unemployed; and young and single people are underrepresented in GA (see Culleton & Lang, 1985; Custer & Custer, 1978; Nora, 1984; Volberg & Steadman, 1988; Wexler, 1986). Therefore, most members of GA are white, middle-aged, married, working- and middle-class men.

WOMEN IN GA

According to the Commission on the Review of the National Policy Toward Gambling (1976), approximately one-third of the "probable" and "potential" compulsive gamblers in the United States were female in 1974 when the survey was conducted. The findings of more recent studies (Culleton, 1985; Culleton & Lang, 1985; Volberg & Steadman, 1988), conducted in the Delaware Valley (New Jersey and Pennsylvania), New York, and Ohio, have been similar. However, research on GA members on the East Coast (Custer & Custer, 1978; Nora, 1984) revealed that 2–4 percent of the members are women. There is a higher percentage of female members on the West Coast, particularly in Nevada, and in the Atlantic City, New Jersey, area where there are casinos. With that exception, the population of female compulsive gamblers is being underserved by GA.

One reason for the failure of GA to attract female members is the stigma that is attached to being a female compulsive gambler. The Damon Runyan stereotype of the "gambler" is male. The female who gambles heavily does not fit this glamorous image. As a consequence, female gamblers are more likely to be closet gamblers than are their male counterparts. They also have fewer social supports than do male compulsive gamblers.

The women who enter GA are less likely to be married than are the men (42 percent versus 83 percent). Therefore, their referral sources are also different from those of men. They are more likely to be self-referred (62 percent were self-referred in one study [Lesieur, 1988]) than men, who are frequently brought in by their wives (Livingston, 1974). This self-referral is reflected in Gam-Anon support. Nora's (1984) study of 186 male and 4 female GA members found that 69 percent had spouses who attended Gam-Anon. However, the author (Lesieur, 1988) found that 48 percent of the women he studied had someone who went to at least one Gam-Anon meeting but only 25 percent went to three or more meetings. A woman may also meet resistance from her husband if she has a male sponsor who calls almost every day to find out how she is doing. In addition to the lack of support, some women tend to feel uncomfortable and out of place in the predominantly male setting. This discomfort is the primary reason for their higher-than-average dropout rate from GA.

MINORITIES, YOUNG PEOPLE, AND GA

Blacks should represent over one-fourth of the GA membership; however, as with females, they are seriously underrepresented. Since there has been no research on this issue, one can only speculate on why this is the case. Blacks, Hispanics, and whites live in segregated communities in the United States. At present, there are no GA chapters in predominantly minority communities. GA members are a reflection of the prejudices, fears, and disjunctures in American society. It is possible that black and Hispanic compulsive gamblers feel uncomfortable about joining GA. It is also possible that they are more resistant to the idea that gambling is a problem. That is, they may be more likely to think that gambling is an external problem, rather than one over which they have some control. Those who are less educated, have a lower income, and are unemployed may hold similar views.

The underrepresentation of the young and single provides several other clues to the nature of GA. The young are probably underrepresented because of the image of the compulsive gambler as a person who has "lost it all." The young are less likely to have experienced bankruptcy, to have been threatened with divorce, or to have seen other serious signs of compulsive gambling. As for single people, they have fewer people who might care for them and pressure them into joining GA.

PERSONS WITH MULTIPLE ADDICTIONS AND GA

A large percentage of GA members have multiple substance abuse problems, are spouses of alcoholics or drug addicts, or are children of addicted parents. In a study of 25 GA members, Linden et al. (1986) found that 52 percent evidenced problems with alcohol, substance abuse, or both. In research on 50 female GA members, the author (Lesieur, 1988) found that 50 percent had abused alcohol, drugs, or both at some point in their lives. Similar findings emerged in Ramirez, McCormick, Russo, and Taber's (1984) study of 51 male compulsive gamblers who were admitted consecutively to the compulsive gambler treatment program at the Veteran's Administration (VA) Medical Center in Cleveland using systematic screening procedures. Thirty-nine percent met the criteria for alcohol abuse, substance abuse, or both in the year before their admission, while 47 percent met these criteria at some point in their lives.

Other addictions also intrude in the lives of pathological gamblers. Adkins, Rugle, and Taber (1985) reported on 100 consecutive admissions to the compulsive gambler treatment program at the VA Medical Center in Cleveland. They found that 14 percent could be judged to have heterosexual addictive patterns following the criteria set forth by Carnes (1983). In the author's study of female pathological gamblers (Lesieur, 1988), 24 percent classified themselves as compulsive overspenders, 20 percent called themselves compulsive overeaters, and 12 percent were possibly sexually addicted. Twenty-two percent of the women were or are currently members of "anonymous" self-help group programs other than GA, including AA, Narcotics Anonymous, Overeaters Anonymous (OA), and Emotions Anonymous. Others went to different types of self-help groups, such as Coke Enders, Weight Watchers, and Take Off Pounds Sensibly. Finally, others went to Al-Anon (the most common), Nar-Anon, and Gam-Anon to cope with a problem that their spouse, lover, or children had.

GA members tell stories about their experiences with other self-help groups. For example, they complain that all-night card games are held after some AA meetings, just as some GA members go to bars after their meetings. Nevertheless, some GA members report being referred to GA as a result of suggestions by members of OA, AA, and other self-help groups. Although most "anonymous" groups ignore other addictions, it appears that the GA NSO recognizes the need for some sort of linkage. In a telephone call to NSO, a GA representative told the author, "We tell people who are trying to start a new meeting to go to AA meetings. About 10 percent of the people in AA usually end up helping to start a new GA group because they have been trying to deal with their gambling in AA but it hasn't been working."

Given their similarities, it is unfortunate that "anonymous" programs still tend to compartmentalize people's problems. For example, GA members have said, "Since they won't allow us to talk about gambling there, there shouldn't be any talk of other addictions here." Although this narrow view is heard less and less in some GA chapters, there is a need for some form of "anonymous" organization that will be able to handle the multiply addicted.

An interesting development has occurred in New Jersey. A new group, Alcoholic, Compulsive Gambler, Narcotic Addicts (ACGNA), has been formed for individuals with multiple addictions. The meetings of ACGNA typically have three speakers, all of whom are dual or triple addicts who talk about each of their addictions.

GAM-ANON AND GAM-A-TEEN

Gambling creates emotional as well as financial problems for the family members of compulsive gamblers. Typically, when Gam-Anon members enter the room, they are concerned with getting their spouse, husband, child, or lover to stop gambling. The focus is on the gambler. Gam-Anon's major goal is to shift the focus to the Gam-Anon member.

There are several major messages in Gam-Anon. The primary message is to get the significant other to stop being an enabler. The principal form of enabling is the "bailout." To bail out the gambler means to pay off debts, cosign loans, or otherwise relieve the financial pressures. Alternatively, it may mean calling creditors, going to a close relative or friend for a loan, or covering bad checks. Gam-Anon members learn that this behavior is like feeding fuel to a fire. With financial pressures relieved, the gambler can go to the race track, casino, or whatever and try to recoup his or her losses. In the end, the bailout means further debt and illegal activities.

Other forms of enabling that Gam-Anon warns against include depriving the family of needed items to make up for lost money, getting a job (or a second job) to pay for the gambling, and lying for the gambler in many ways. Examples of common lies include, "Joe [who just went to the race track] can't come tonight, he's sick" or "Marie can't pay you this week; her car broke down and it will cost a lot of money to fix."

The second major message of Gam-Anon is to "let go." In the process of trying to cope with the situation, significant others attempt to control the gambler and gambling by searching through pockets, questioning where the gambler has been, and otherwise trying to monitor the compulsive gambler's behavior. They frequently believe that "if only I do this, he [or she] will stop gambling." Many believe that all they have to do is go to Gam-Anon for a while and their loved one will stop gambling.

Instead of countenancing enabling and controlling, Gam-Anon follows a Twelve-Step program. The first step, like that for GA members, is to admit that one is powerless over gambling. The journey, like that for GA, is a spiritual one with practical advice.

Children of compulsive gamblers encounter tremendous difficulty in attempting to cope with the problem. Preliminary research indicates that they have fears of abandonment, have deep resentments over money that was "borrowed" by their gambling parent, and are more likely to have problems with substance abuse and addiction.

Unfortunately, attempts to initiate Gam-A-Teen have not been too successful. Periodically, chapters are formed, but efforts to maintain them have had an on-again, off-again success rate. In addition, groups of adult children of compulsive gamblers are being formed. However, it is too early to determine whether they will become as successful as adult children of alcoholics.

PROFESSIONALS AND GA

Both GA members and therapists have been reluctant to rely on each other. Some therapists believe that GA members tell the therapists' patients that GA is the only proper form of treatment for the gambling problem. This reaction by GA members is a result of their experience with therapists who have told gamblers that gambling was not the real problem. Indirectly, these therapists have been telling their clients, "You do not need GA, you need therapy."

Stories of experiences with psychologists, psychiatrists, social workers, and others are part of the GA culture. These stories are told especially by old-timers, who report that they had gone to therapists for years, had conned them, and continued to gamble. Some laugh when they recount that their analyst told them they looked nervous and should relax at a casino or race track. When newcomers relate similar stories, it is no wonder that there is resistance to professional treatment. Some go so far as to say that since the Unity Program says that "Gamblers Anonymous ought to remain forever nonprofessional," professionals should not be part of a gambler's treatment for gambling. This is a minority view, however. More and more GA members accept professionals because they have had some good experiences with professionals who understand and cooperate with GA. That these professionals have had an impact on GA is attested to by group members who have told the author that people who have had experiences with professionals tend to talk about communication and feelings more and concentrate on "war stories" less.

The only way for therapists to overcome the resistance of GA members to therapists is to attend many open meetings. In these meetings, the therapists will meet more GA members and will come to see their point of view. Furthermore, therapists and researchers who have contact with the mass media can help GA by referring media people to GA and Gam-Anon for information.

A therapist can also help a client by understanding that not every GA group will suit every person. Differences in personalities, social class, and style of gambling may influence the client's reactions to GA. Thus, the therapist might suggest that the client attend at least three or four meetings a week for the first 4 months, so the client can be exposed to many different groups. Alternatively, newcomers should be encouraged to go "meeting shopping" until they find a place where they feel comfortable. However, newcomers should have a "home room" where they get to be well known and others wonder where they are when they do not show up.

The therapist should try to meet the client's sponsor and recognize that sponsors are available 24 hours a day for newcomers in GA. Ideally, the therapist and sponsor could act as a team. The therapist should question the client about his or her sponsor and the suggestions the sponsor is making to be sure that the client is attending GA and is growing in that program. The new GA member should feel that he or she can tell the sponsor anything.

The therapist should ask the newcomer to GA about the steps, the pressure-group meeting, and other elements of the GA program. After dealing with addicted clients for a while, it is possible to know where they are in the Twelve-Step program and what progress they are making.

Therapists who use GA as an adjunct to treatment should be aware that although GA is an "anonymous" organization, some groups have been known to provide proof of attendance at GA meetings that judges and other criminal justice personnel may require. This proof can be useful for clients who are on probation or are subject to a sentence review in court.

The client may tell the therapist that he or she does not belong in a GA group. He or she may say, "I'm not like those people. Those people are sick, not me." Such statements indicate that the client is not identifying with GA for some reason. If the client is practicing denial, he or she should be confronted with evidence to the contrary. One benefit of continued attendance at GA meetings is that much of the denial will probably be breached by other GA members.

In another vein, clients may come back into therapy and complain about how GA is run or describe personality clashes with other GA members (Taber & Chaplin, 1988). Taber and Chaplin suggested that such clients should be allowed to vent these feelings, but the therapist should maintain a "wait and see" attitude about the organization.

When they first start to attend GA meetings, members may experience what Livingston (1974) called the "pink cloud": everything seems to be going just fine. They may become complacent and decide that they no longer need GA. It is possible that they are getting bored with the "war stories" and think they are not getting anything out of the meetings. At this point, they should be encouraged to go to step meetings or help start a step-type group.

Since pathological gambling is a family illness, the therapist should work with addicted *families.* Issues frequently arise as a product of having been brought up in an addicted home. At least 25 percent of GA members are adult children of alcoholics (ACOAs), 20 percent are adult children of compulsive gamblers (ACOCGs) (Custer & Custer, 1978; Lesieur, 1988; Lesieur, Blume, & Zoppa, 1986), and at least 20 percent of their spouses are ACOAs and approximately 10 percent are ACOCGs (Heineman, 1987; Lorenz & Shuttlesworth, 1983). One consequence of this high rate of addictive families of origin is that the family of the past will interfere with the treatment of the family of the present. It is essential to know what kind of emotional "baggage" clients are bringing with them. In addition, the children of pathological gamblers need attention so the cycle of addiction can be broken.

WHAT NEXT?

Those wishing to find out more about GA and Gam-Anon should go to open meetings and conclaves; read the literature; contact GA (National Service Office, PO Box 17173, Los Angeles, CA 90017, phone 213-386-8789) and Gam-Anon (Gam-Anon International Service Office, PO Box 157, Whitestone, NY 11357, phone 718-352-1671) for further information; and join the National Council on Compulsive Gambling (National Council on Compulsive Gambling, 445 West 59th Street, New York, NY 10019, phone 212-765-3833) and its state affiliates, which run workshops, train counselors, and are valuable clearinghouses of information. The National Council on Compulsive Gambling publishes a newsletter and a refereed quarterly journal, the *Journal of Gambling Studies* (formerly the *Journal of Gambling Behavior*) that contains articles on the treatment of pathological gambling and research into social as well as pathological gambling (Human Sciences Press, 233 Spring Street, New York, NY 10013, phone 212-243-6000).

REFERENCES

Adkins, B. J., Rugle, L. J., & Taber, J. I. (1985, November). *A note on sexual addiction among compulsive gamblers.* Paper presented at the First National Conference on Gambling Behavior, National Council on Compulsive Gambling, New York.

Brown, R. I. F. (1985). Parallels between behaviour change processes in addiction recovery and in conversion experiences. *Contact: The Interdisciplinary Journal of Pastoral Studies, 86,* 20–22.

Carnes, P. (1983). *The sexual addiction.* Minneapolis, MN: Comp Care.

Commission on the Review of the National Policy Toward Gambling. (1976). *Gambling in America.* Washington, DC: U.S. Government Printing Office.

Cromer, G. (1978). Gamblers Anonymous in Israel: A participant observation study of a self-help group. *International Journal of the Addictions, 13,* 1069–1077.

Culleton, R. P. (1985). *A survey of pathological gamblers in the State of Ohio.* Philadelphia: Transition Planning Associates.

Culleton, R. P., & Lang, M. H. (1985). *Supplementary report on the prevalence rate of pathological gambling in the Delaware Valley in 1984.* Camden, NJ: Rutgers/Camden Forum for Policy Research and Public Service.

Custer, R. L. (1982). Gambling and addiction. In R. Craig & S. Baker (Eds.), *Drug dependent patients: Treatment and research* (pp. 367–381). Springfield, IL: Charles C Thomas.

Custer, R. L., & Custer, L. F. (1978, December). *Characteristics of the recovering compulsive gambler: A survey of 150 members of Gamblers Anonymous.* Paper presented at the Fourth Annual Conference on Gambling, Reno, NV.

Gamblers Anonymous. (1964). *The GA group.* Los Angeles: GA Publishing Co.

Heineman, M. (1987). A comparison: The treatment of wives of alcoholics with the treatment of wives of pathological gamblers. *Journal of Gambling Behavior, 3,* 27–40.

Lesieur, H. R. (1984). *The chase: Career of the compulsive gambler.* Cambridge, MA: Schenkman Books.

Lesieur, H. R. (1988). The female pathological gambler. In W. R. Eadington (Ed.), *Gambling research: Proceedings of the seventh international conference on gambling and risk taking* (Vol. 5, pp. 230–258). Reno: Bureau of Business & Economic Research, University of Nevada.

Lesieur, H. R., Blume, S. B., & Zoppa, R. M. (1986). Alcoholism, drug abuse and gambling. *Alcoholism: Clinical and Experimental Research, 10,* 33–38.

Linden, R. D., Pope, H. G., & Jonas, J. M. (1986). Pathological gambling and major affective disorder: Preliminary findings. *Journal of Clinical Psychiatry, 47,* 201–203.

Livingston, J. (1974). *Compulsive gamblers: Observations on action and abstinence.* New York: Harper Torchbooks.

Lorenz, V. C., & Shuttlesworth, D. E. (1983). The impact of pathological gambling on the spouse of the gambler. *Journal of Community Psychology, 11,* 67–76.

McCormick, R. A., Russo, A. M., Ramirez, L. F., & Taber, J. I. (1984). Affective disorders among pathological gamblers seeking treatment. *American Journal of Psychiatry, 141,* 215–218.

Nora, R. (1984, December). *Profile survey on pathological gamblers.* Paper presented at the Sixth National Conference on Gambling and Risk Taking, Atlantic City, NJ.

Ramirez, L. F., McCormick, R. A., Russo, A. M., & Taber, J. I. (1984). Patterns of substance abuse in pathological gamblers undergoing treatment. *Addictive Behaviors, 8,* 425–428.

Taber, J. I., & Chaplin, M. P. (1988). Group psychotherapy with pathological gamblers. *Journal of Gambling Behavior, 4,* 183–196.

Volberg, R., & Steadman, H. (1988). Refining prevalence estimates of pathological gambling. *American Journal of Psychiatry, 145,* 502–505.

Wexler, A. (1986). *Results of a survey of compulsive gamblers.* Unpublished manuscript.

13

SELF-HELP CLEARINGHOUSES
An Overview of an Emergent System for Promoting Mutual Aid

RICHARD WOLLERT

Several considerations suggest that self-help groups, in which members exchange mutual support for dealing with shared concerns, are an important naturalistic source of human services. For one thing, they serve 5 million to 15 million people in North America and focus on a broad array of problems in living (Academy of Educational Development, 1979). For another, they intervene on several levels—psychological, financial, social, and informational—are usually open to new members, and are less costly than professional alternatives (Hurvitz, 1970). For still another, members of these groups consistently evaluate the quality of the help they have obtained in positive terms (Gottlieb, 1982; Knight, Wollert, Levy, Frame, & Padgett, 1980; Raiff, 1982).

In spite of these and other assets, self-help groups face a variety of problems that limit their potential for affecting personal adjustment. Some cannot recruit enough members to begin meeting, for example, and the recruitment of new members is a chronic challenge for many groups that do become operational. Other groups have difficulty dealing with disruptive members, reaching decisions, or keeping their meetings interesting. Still others do not expand their programs because they lack the resources for such projects as educating professionals, publicizing their group, or writing effective grant proposals. Although the extent of these problems has not been

The research reported in this chapter was supported by grants from the Saskatchewan Health Research Board. The author is indebted to Sharon Miller of the Saskatchewan Self-Help Development Unit for her help in carrying out these projects.

determined, their existence has been amply documented by case histories (Barron, Eakins, & Wollert, 1984; Kleiman, Mantell, & Alexander, 1976; Wollert, Knight, & Levy, 1980). In addition, the destructive impact of organizational difficulties is evident in reports indicating that self-help members often drop out of their groups (Wollert, Barron, & M., 1982) and that a high percentage of self-help groups disband within a short time (Wollert & the Self-Help Research Team, 1987).

These considerations suggest that the realization of the full potential of the naturalistic system of human services that self-help groups represent will, as in the case of such professionally based systems as medicine and social services, require some form of societal investment and stimulation. Although a national funding policy for supporting the self-help approach has not been formulated in either the United States or Canada, many local efforts have been made during the past 15 years to establish clearinghouses for the purpose of promoting the development and use of self-help groups by community residents (Wollert, 1987).

The emergence of clearinghouses on the human services landscape is exciting because clearinghouses advance several ideas that have remained unusually difficult to translate into practice. They encourage a *cross-cutting response* to mental health issues through their support of self-help organizations that address literally hundreds of adjustive concerns. Furthermore, they offer *prevention services* by referring potential members to groups that may help stabilize some conditions, reverse others, or even forestall the development of still others by promoting the effective use of informal resources, such as friends, or formal resources, such as the health care system. Finally, they facilitate an *integration of interest groups* by fostering interdisciplinary working relationships among professionals and collaboration between professionals and members of self-help groups.

In addition, clearinghouse operations have recorded some impressive achievements in the delivery of services. A recent survey of 30 of the approximately 50 clearinghouses serving North American communities found, for example, that their catchment areas included 73 million people (Wollert, 1988). Moreover, these 30 clearinghouses had initiated at least 1,500 new self-help groups, conducted 450 community education projects, and compiled 29 regional and local directories for referring potential members to groups addressing their concerns.

The clearinghouse concept thus represents an innovative approach to supporting the self-help movement. Although a number of writers have dealt with systems that serve specific communities (Borck & Aronowitz, 1981; Hermalin, 1986; Jeger, Slotnik, & Schure, 1982; Madara, 1985, 1986; Wollert, 1985), relatively few have attempted to put the field as a whole into perspective. After founding clearinghouses in Oregon and Saskatchewan (Wollert, 1985; Wollert & Miller, 1985; Wollert & the Self-Help Research Team, 1987), however, this author became so interested in this topic that he submitted a couple of grant proposals to the Saskatchewan Health Research Board to pursue it further. The support he received allowed him to collect and review published and unpublished materials about clearinghouses (Wollert, 1987), to complete a questionnaire survey of most of the clearinghouses in North America (Wollert, 1988), and ultimately to visit 11 sites that typified different organizational and philosophical models. This article discusses the author's findings and impressions with respect to the similarities and differences among clearinghouses and the operational issues and conflicts in values that may challenge the clearinghouses in the future.

SIMILARITIES AND DIFFERENCES AMONG CLEARINGHOUSES

FUNCTIONAL SIMILARITIES

According to both descriptive accounts and the author's observations, clearinghouses serve four general functions: information and referral, consultation, community education, and research. *Information and referral* is perhaps the most readily apparent and widely discussed. To carry out this function, a clearinghouse compiles resource files on self-help groups that are operating in its catchment area. These files typically include information about the purpose of existing groups, criteria for membership, meeting times and locations, and the names and telephone numbers of group members who may be contacted by potential members. Stored on cards or in computerized systems using specially designed software, information about self-help groups is disseminated to human services agencies and other referral sources through printed directories. Telephone switchboards, toll free in some areas, are also maintained to serve the needs of potential members and human services professionals who seek referrals directly from clearinghouses. If groups do not exist to meet the needs of callers, the names and telephone numbers of potential members are recorded and those with similar concerns are eventually placed in touch with one another to stimulate the development of new groups.

As these observations suggest, the collection and maintenance of information on self-help groups in a resource file enables the clearinghouse to conduct many significant activities. Furthermore, these projects often can be undertaken only by clearinghouses because other delivery systems do not collect information on self-help groups in a systematic way. By providing a self-help identity and establishing a domain for the delivery of services, the maintenance of resource files may be considered the core activity on which most clearinghouses rest.

Clearinghouses also provide *consultation* to self-help groups. In some cases, consultation involves providing information on topics that group members identify as being important, such as recruiting new members, dealing with group conflict, obtaining grants, or enhancing meetings. In other cases, it takes the form of making material resources available—meeting space, stamps, computers, video recorders and tapes, or copying machines—that facilitate the achievement of group goals. In still others, it is manifested in spearheading the initiation of self-help groups that are particularly needed in a community and that are unlikely to be member generated because, for example, the conditions they address are either rarely encountered or severely debilitating.

A third cluster of activities is subsumed under the function *community education*. Clearinghouses conduct workshops that describe the self-help approach, the range of groups available in a catchment area, or methods of supporting groups without "co-opting" them for physicians, psychologists, nurses, social workers, members of the clergy, and other human service professionals. To support these workshops, staff members develop teaching resources, including films that depict self-help groups and the achievements of their leaders, books that review the most important issues in the field, and guidelines for organizing groups and providing clearinghouse services. Fairs at shopping malls, libraries, and parks stimulate contact between community residents and group representatives, promote the distribution of information packets and the recruitment of new members, and encourage members from different groups to discuss how common organizational concerns may be overcome. A variety of media techniques—newsletter mailings, billboard advertisements, television appearances, and radio interviews—are used to inform the public at large about self-help topics and events of interest. Because community recognition is essential for a service to be utilized, it is also necessary for clearinghouses to be inventive in using these and other media opportunities to let community residents know about the services they offer and how the residents may gain access to these services.

Of all the functions that clearinghouses serve, *research* is probably emphasized least. Nonetheless, clearinghouse operations invite applied research on issues that may be important for improving services or even achieving financial support that provides for the future delivery of services. From this perspective, research projects have been undertaken to estimate the level of clearinghouse services provided during a given period or the magnitude of self-help resources in a catchment area, to assess the extent to which self-help resources have been developed that address the adjustive concerns of a target population, and to evaluate the satisfaction of consumers with clearinghouse services and to solicit suggestions for their improvement.

Because of the access they have to self-help groups, clearinghouses are also advantageous for conducting basic research. Although this line of research is even less frequently encountered than is applied research, an increased interest in basic research is exemplified in projects that are concerned with identifying personal-change processes that characterize self-help groups and with evaluating the impact that self-help groups have on the moods, attitudes, and coping behavior of their members.

DIFFERENCES

In spite of the recurring patterns in services that are apparent, clearinghouses differ from one another in many significant respects. Developmentally, for example, the *impetus* for establishing services in Denville, New Jersey; Chicago; and New York City was grounded in the individual efforts of the programs' founders, whereas the momentum for the California State Self-Help Center in Los Angeles and most local clearinghouses in New York State came from policy initiatives of legislators and mental health administrators. Clearinghouses, such as those in Westchester County, New York, and Denville have also been supported under the auspices of health or mental health organizations, while others in Portland, Oregon, and Scranton, Pennsylvania, were sponsored by information and referral agencies, and still others were initiated by individuals in Lincoln, Nebraska, and San Diego, California. Finally, being dynamic and outspoken, the founders of many clearinghouses have left the imprint of their *attitudes and work habits* on their programs. As a result, the staffs of some clearinghouses follow a highly formalized set of procedures, work at a hectic pace, and spend a great deal of time on issues—such as preparing budget proposals and maintaining records of the levels of services that are delivered—that are essential for the smooth operation of a professionalized service. In contrast, other clearinghouses are imbued with an air of informality and a relaxed work pace, and their staffs may put as much energy into lobbying for the development of equitable policies for the delivery of human services as they do into actually providing these services.

In addition to such developmental differences, clearinghouses also vary in their contextual characteristics. From 5–10 operations serve either state or provincial *catchment areas*, for example, but most serve local or metropolitan communities. Different types of *settings* have also been selected to house clearinghouses, so that a public library is used in Toronto, Ontario; a tiny storefront, in Pittsburgh, Pennsylvania; a spacious new office building, in Denville; and one floor of a building on a university campus, in Los Angeles. Some of these accommodations are more expensive than are others and, in line with this difference, substantial *budgets* of more than $100,000 are committed annually to a small number of programs—usually those operating under the auspices of health or mental health organizations—although most manage to operate on "shoestring" budgets. Because service delivery efforts are usually determined, in large part, by funding levels, variations in funding are paralleled by *variations in effort* so that the three largest clearinghouses make 7,000–14,000 referrals to self-help groups per year, while their smaller counterparts make anywhere from 200 to 5,000 referrals.

Organizational differences form still a third dimension of heterogeneity. With respect to their *administrative structure,* clearinghouses in St. Joseph, Michigan; Saskatoon, Saskatchewan; Wichita, Kansas; and Los Angeles have been constituted so they operate independently of other information systems. Other programs in Portland and Scranton lack this autonomy, however, since they have been organized as differentiated components—referred to elsewhere as "piggybacked" systems (Madara, 1985)—or more generically focused information and referral agencies. Differences in *intersystem relationships* are also apparent in that the Pittsburgh and New York City operations, in particular, maintain close ties with a large number of self-help groups, whereas the majority of clearinghouses do not. Similarly, the *networking activities* of some clearinghouses, such as those in Denville; Westchester; and Poughkeepsie, New York, have been so successful that they have established strong working relationships with other health and human services agencies. Overall, however, clearinghouses have not connected as thoroughly as they could with other service delivery systems that operate in their catchment areas.

Organizational differences may also be observed in the *specialized services* that clearinghouses are beginning to offer. At Denville, for example, the New Jersey Self-Help Clearinghouse emphasizes the importance of starting as many new self-help groups as possible; therefore, a substantial portion of the staff's effort is directed toward linking potential group members. Other clearinghouses, such as the California State Self-Help Center in Los Angeles and the Westchester County Clearinghouse, have considerable interest in starting groups but spend a relatively greater proportion of their time in training activities because of the elaborate programs they offer for teaching leadership skills to self-helpers. Conceiving of self-help as a force for social change, the staff of the New York City program has emphasized the importance of creating a movement from the self-help network that will advocate for the interests of minority groups. In contrast to all these systems, the Portland and Saskatoon clearinghouses have been concerned primarily with carrying out basic research and program-evaluation projects.

TRENDS AND ISSUES IN THE FIELD

For most directors, the experience of establishing a self-help clearinghouse has brought with it a mixed set of blessings. On the one hand, they are proud of innovating services that support the profound approach to personal adjustment and social change that self-help represents. On the other hand, they are frustrated by a seemingly never-ending struggle to achieve adequate funding to continue their work and to win acceptance of social policies that recognize its value. Overall, however, the rewards of the development of clearinghouses must be compelling, since as many as half the clearinghouses in North America may have been initiated in the rapid-growth period since 1984.

To share their triumphs and to cope with the challenges to their programs, the directors and staffs of clearinghouses have also sought *collegial support.* In the late 1970s, this type of networking was confined largely to the programs that pioneered the clearinghouse concept on the eastern seaboard of the United States. By 1981, however, enough relevant activities were being undertaken throughout the country to support a national conference at New York City (Staff, 1981). This conference was followed in 1985 by a conference in Dallas at which the directors of both Canadian and American organizations endorsed the proposal to form the National Network of Mutual Help Centers (NNMHC) to provide a "forum for the development and exchange of ideas that support the practice of self-help" (Miller & Wollert, 1986, p. 28). Further steps were taken in 1986 when bylaws and an organizational structure for the NNMHC were adopted during another international conference in Minneapolis.

In contrast to the enthusiasm of staff members over their contributions, only weak external recognition of the significance of clearinghouses was evident for perhaps as long as 20 years after the founding of the first clearinghouse in Lincoln, Nebraska, in 1964. Since 1982, however, legislation to fund clearinghouses has been introduced in about five states. From 1986 to 1988, the Canadian Council on Social Development sponsored at least two national conferences of clearing-house directors. In late 1987, the surgeon general of the United States held a 2-day workshop on self-help groups that was organized mainly by representatives of clearinghouses. Therefore, although the re-sponse has not been as strong as advocates of the self-help approach might like, politicians and agencies that are concerned with the development of social policy have shown an increasing interest in clearinghouses.

Since these trends, if they continue, suggest that the credibility and operating resources of clearinghouses may soon be enhanced, they may be regarded as having some positive implications for the future. Other trends appear to augur more negative implications. For example, an increasing emphasis on *specialization*, which may be seen in the limited range of tasks performed by staff members at some of the larger clearinghouses, may eventuate in burnout or low morale among these workers. In addition, the push toward *professionaliza-tion*, evident in the formalized procedures and jargon that have been adopted at some sites, may lead staff members to have a limited appreciation and support for the self-help ethos. Finally, the *low participation of self-help groups* in the administration of clearing-houses, which is now a widespread phenomenon, may prevent clearinghouses from firmly establishing the grass-roots connections that underpin the operation of community-based service delivery systems.

Although none of these misfortunes has yet been documented, the possibility of their occurrence underscores the point that many issues must be anticipated and resolved if clearinghouses are to continue to evolve in the constructive direction that they have thus far taken. Many of these issues seem particularly relevant for program development and the improvement of procedures for delivering services. In view of the limited use of microcomputers (Wollert, 1988), for example, the applications of these and other "high-technology" tools may be more thoroughly studied than they have been. A careful analysis of the advantages and disadvantages of different organiza-tional characteristics, which compares centralized with decentralized information-dissemination systems or freestanding with differentiated administrative structures, may also be useful for gaining an enhanced appreciation of how the achievement of the goals of clearinghouses is facilitated by some characteristics rather than by others. Finally, the utility of formal methods of evaluation research for upgrading services and supporting budgetary proposals may be contrasted with that of the informal methods that are now so widely used.

Other issues are more relevant for clarifying the values that guide the operations of clearinghouses. Surely, the reasons for the weak relationships between most clearinghouses and the self-help groups they serve and the validity of maintaining this separation should be critically analyzed. In addition, leadership training courses that clearinghouses provide to group members could be examined in terms of whether they threaten the naturalistic and nonprofessional qualities associated with the concept of self-help.

Faced with the prospect of confronting this broad array of issues, many of which are emotionally charged, it may seem that the wisest course of action would be to avoid further debate. Doing so would be unfortunate, however, because it would undermine the intellectual vitality that has characterized the development of clearinghouses and that may be responsible for the strong sense of purpose that staff members show in carrying out their work. It would also probably be unnecessary, since the spirit of good will and pragmatism that is pervasive in the field would probably enable those who hold different views either to negotiate a common understanding or to "agree to disagree." The following working definition of self-help groups presents the position that NNMHC has taken on the distinguishing characteristics of self-help groups and is an example of one issue that has recently been resolved. Negotiated in the course of several consultations between an ad hoc committee and directors of clearinghouses, the specificity of these guidelines, approved by the National Steering Committee of NNMHC in September 1987, should be useful for setting boundaries for the delivery of services in the future. The guidelines are as follows:

■ Self-help or mutual support is a process wherein people who share common experiences, situations, or problems can offer each other a unique perspective that is not available from those who have not shared these experiences.

■ Self-help groups are run by and for group members. Professional providers may participate in the self-help process at the request and sanction of a group and remain in an ancillary or consultant role.

■ Activities focus on social support through discussion and sharing of information and experiences, but may extend to other activities and ways of interacting.

■ Self-help groups are open to members of the general public who have experienced the common concern.

■ Self-help groups meet face to face on a regular and ongoing basis. Groups are voluntary and open to new members.

■ There is no charge to participate in a self-help group, although a nominal donation is sometimes requested.

CONCLUSION

This chapter has provided an overview of an emerging service-delivery concept, the self-help clearinghouse. From reading the available literature, surveying directors, and visiting a cross-section of clearinghouses, the author has concluded that clearinghouses have proliferated over the past 10 years and that the vitality of their operations and the professional identity of their staff members have also been enhanced. Clearinghouses may thus be recognized in the near future as the primary vehicle for supporting the development and use of self-help groups at the community level.

Although clearinghouses hold a great deal of promise, they also face a number of obstacles. Some of these obstacles are not within the control of those who are responsible for the day-to-day functioning of clearinghouses. The low level of funding to which most systems must accommodate is undoubtedly the most serious of these. This constraint, in turn, may have arisen because few policymakers understand and value the health and human services contributions that clearinghouses offer. If this hypothesis is correct, further study of the benefits of mutual aid and of the facilitative role that clearing-houses play in increasing the access of community residents to self-help resources may encourage the development of policies that would ensure the ongoing operation of clearinghouses.

Not all the challenges to the successful evolution of clearinghouses are external, however. As this overview has stressed, many technical, philosophical, and interpersonal issues must still be addressed. Engaging these issues may not be an inviting prospect to those human services professionals who wish to deal only with psychopathology and to provide services directly in clinical settings. However, clearinghouses will, it is hoped, attract the involvement of other providers of services who are interested in personal adjustment, small-group processes, community action, consultation, and policy development. They will also certainly continue to welcome the resources that professionals offer—their knowledge of interpersonal behavior, for example, and their expressive abilities and skills for evaluating programs. Finally, clearinghouses will probably provide interdisciplinary rewards to professionals by promoting meaningful collaboration between specialists from such different fields as information and referral, computer technology, media communications and advertising, public health, social work, and psychology.

Overall, self-help groups have the potential to help a great number of people adjust to role transitions and life stresses. Clearinghouses support the realization of this potential. They also are the context within which an existing new practice specialty that integrates service and research activities can be developed. Professionals who are self-help advocates may thus make substantial contributions to both the human services field and the self-help movement through their involvement in clearinghouses.

REFERENCES

Academy of Educational Development. (1979). *The voluntary sector in brief.* New York: Author.
Barron, N., Eakins, L. I., & Wollert, R. (1984). Fat group: A snap-launched self-help group. *Human Organization, 43*(1), 44–49.
Borck, L., & Aronowitz, E. (1981). *Organizing a self-help clearinghouse.* New York: National Self-Help Clearinghouse.
Gottlieb, B. (1982). Mutual-help groups: Members' views of their benefits and of roles for professionals. *Prevention in Human Services, 1*(3), 55–67.
Hermalin, J. A. (1986). Self-help clearinghouses: Promoting collaboration between professionals and volunteers. *Journal of Voluntary Action Research, 15*(2), 64–76.
Hurvitz, N. (1970). Peer self-help psychotherapy groups and their implications for psychotherapy. *Psychotherapy: Theory, Research, and Practice, 7,* 41–49.

Jeger, A. M., Slotnik, R., & Schure, M. (1982). Towards a "self-help/professional collaborative model" of mental health service delivery. In D. Biegel & A. J. Naperstek (Eds.), *Community support systems and mental health: Practice, policy, and research* (pp. 205–223). New York: Springer.

Kleiman, M. A., Mantell, J. E., & Alexander, E. S. (1976). Collaboration and its discontents: The perils of partnership. *Journal of Applied Behavioral Science, 12,* 403–410.

Knight, B., Wollert, R., Levy, L. H., Frame, C. L., & Padgett, V. P. (1980). Self-help groups: The members' perspectives. *American Journal of Community Psychology, 8,* 53–65.

Madara, E. J. (1985). The self-help clearinghouse operation: Tapping the resource development potential of I & R services. *Information and Referral, 7*(1), 42–48.

Madara, E. J. (1986). A comprehensive systems approach to promoting mutual aid self-help groups: The New Jersey Self-Help Clearinghouse model. *Journal of Voluntary Action Research, 15*(2), 57–63.

Miller, S., & Wollert, R. (1986). *Report on the Dallas meeting of self-help clearinghouse directors.* Ottawa: Canadian Council on Social Development.

Raiff, N. R. (1982). Professional attitudes, awareness, and use of self-help groups. *Prevention in Human Services, 1*(3), 79–89.

Staff. (1981, October–November). Clearinghouse directors meet. *Self-Help Reporter,* pp. 6–7.

Wollert, R. (1985). An information and referral model for improving community utilization of self-help groups. *Information and Referral, 7*(2), 1–16.

Wollert, R. (1987). Human services and the self-help clearinghouse concept. *Canadian Journal of Community Mental Health, 6*(1), 79–90.

Wollert, R. (1988). Self-help clearinghouses in North America: A survey of their structural characteristics and community health implications. *Health Promotion, 2,* 377–386.

Wollert, R., Barron, N., & M., Bob. (1982). Parents United of Oregon: A natural history of a self-help group for sexually abusive families. *Prevention in Human Services, 1*(3), 99–109.

Wollert, R., Knight, B., & Levy, L. H. (1980). Make Today Count: A collaborative model for professionals and self-help groups. *Professional Psychology, 11,* 130–138.

Wollert, R., & Miller, S. (1985). Self-help fairs: Promoting mutual assistance at the community level. *Initiative, 2*(1), 4–5.

Wollert, R., & the Self-Help Research Team. (1987). The self-help clearinghouse concept: An evaluation of one program and its implications for policy and practice. *American Journal of Community Psychology, 15,* 491–508.

14

PARTICIPATION IN SELF-HELP GROUPS AND EMPOWERMENT AMONG PARENTS OF THE MENTALLY ILL IN ISRAEL

BENJAMIN GIDRON, NEIL B. GUTERMAN, AND HARRIET HARTMAN

In the theoretical literature on self-help, the concept of empowerment is often used to describe one of the desired outcomes that accrue to the participants in self-help groups. In light of the current lack of clarity about the concept, the authors propose the following as their working definition of empowerment: the process by which an individual acquires strength or mastery that enables him or her to engage in activities or behavioral patterns that were previously beyond the realm of his or her abilities. Furthermore, the authors view personal empowerment as a precondition to social action, especially among those who become involved in self-help groups.

Riessman (1985, p. 2) suggested that empowerment is a critical aspect of self-help:

> When people help themselves—join together with others who have similar problems to deal with their problems, whether they be mental health problems or neighborhood problems—they feel empowered; they are able to control some aspect of their lives. The help is not given to them from the outside, from an expert, a professional, a politician. . . . Empowerment expands energy, motivation, and help-giving power that goes beyond helping one's self or receiving help.

In addition, he noted that an empowered person can go one step further:

> The competencies they develop at the smaller or more immediate level can be applied to the larger political issues. . . . The very process of mutual help begins to develop competencies of working together and sharing,

which can be applied to larger issues. The *beginnings of empowerment emerge as people feel able to control some aspect of their lives.* (p. 3)

Others have also considered empowerment to be a major characteristic of the self-help process (see Battaglino, 1987). In discussing self-help organizations of significant others, Powell (1987) stressed the need for "building confidence" and "developing assertiveness" as components of empowerment. In describing the development of a consumer orientation of the National Alliance for the Mentally Ill, Hatfield (1984, p. 320) noted that the empowerment of consumers of mental health services "can arm individuals with the knowledge and self-confidence needed to make choices which can increase individual satisfaction, marketplace efficiency, and the public good."

Despite the frequent use of the concept of empowerment in connection with self-help, the empirical literature has not yet clearly demonstrated such a relationship. Outcome research on participation in self-help groups has sometimes suggested that such a relationship exists, but most such studies have measured the concept indirectly, through other theoretical constructs, such as "personal strength and resiliency" (Videka-Sherman, 1982), "self-confidence" (Gottlieb, 1982; Shapiro, Possidente, Plum, & Lehman, 1983), and "mastery" (Noh & Turner, 1987).

The study reported here attempted to clarify the issue of self-help and empowerment empirically through an indirect, inductive approach. It compared participants and nonparticipants in self-help groups for parents of mentally ill people in Israel in a number of areas of their lives since the onset of their children's illness. Out of these findings, patterns emerged that suggested conclusions regarding the relationship between participation in self-help groups and empowerment.

METHOD

This study was conducted in conjunction with Enosh—the association for the mentally ill in Israel. It was part of a larger research project that examined stress, coping, social support, and other variables of participants and nonparticipants in self-help groups and organizations of mentally ill people (Gidron, 1989; Gidron & Guterman, 1988; Gidron, Guterman, & Hartman, in press). Enosh is a national voluntary organization comprised primarily, though not exclusively, of family members of the mentally ill. It has branches in approximately 25 cities and towns in Israel. These branches provide services to mentally ill people who live in the community by operating a social club several times a week. They also provide services to parents or spouses of the mentally ill, including support groups, legal advice, and advocacy. The support groups engage primarily in emotional support (discussions about feelings and stresses and about learning strategies to deal with such concerns), but do not engage in more concrete forms of help, such as financial support or advocacy. Finally, Enosh provides information on mental illness to the general public.

SAMPLE

The study was conducted in the five branches of Enosh in which parents were most actively involved. The sample included 50 parents of chronically mentally ill adult children in those five cities; 32 of the 50 parents participated in self-help groups through Enosh, while 18 did not.

The participants' names were provided by the local branches of Enosh. The nonparticipants' names were also obtained either from the same local branches (who were in contact with nonparticipating families through services provided to mentally ill residents living in the community) or from a social worker of the local community mental health clinic.

The majority of the respondents were married (90 percent) and female (62 percent). The age range was 41 to 82, with a median of 61 years. The ethnic makeup of the sample was 74 percent European or American born and 26 percent Asian or African born. With regard to education, 24 percent did not complete elementary school, 20 percent completed 8 years of school, 48 percent had a full or partial high school education, and 8 percent were college educated. It is important to note that although the distribution of educational levels differed from the typical parents of mentally ill persons in other studies, it was similar to the national average in Israel for this age group. Almost half the respondents, primarily the younger ones, were employed outside the home. Slightly more than half considered themselves to be "religious" or "traditional."

In terms of family size, 21 percent had only one child (the mentally ill child), 29 percent had two children, and the remaining 50 percent had three or more children (one respondent had nine children). One-third of the respondents lived in dense housing, with an average of more than one person per room.

The majority (60 percent) of the mentally ill children were aged 26–35 at the time of the interview. Of the remaining 40 percent, 20 percent were 18–25 years, and 20 percent were 36 years or older. At the time of the interview, the diagnoses of mental illness (in most cases, schizophrenia) had taken place within the past 5 years for 10 percent, 6–10 years before for 24 percent, 11–20 years before for 34 percent, and more than 20 years before for 32 percent. All but 6 percent of the mentally ill sons or daughters had been hospitalized at least once, and almost 50 percent were hospitalized four or more times. At the time of the interview, most of the mentally ill sons or daughters lived in the community: 44 percent, in their parents' homes; 24 percent, in their own homes or sheltered homes; and 32 percent, in psychiatric settings.

DATA COLLECTION AND ANALYSIS

After the consent to be interviewed was obtained by a local contact person, a member of the research team contacted the potential respondent for an interview. All the participants in the self-help groups and 46 percent of the nonparticipants who were initially contacted gave their consent to be interviewed.

Descriptive data were collected either in the home or at the office of the local Enosh branch. The interview lasted 1 to 1 1/2 hours. It covered sociodemographic information on the respondent and his or her child. Self-report data on the impact of the child's mental illness on the respondent's life were collected in a number of domains, including perceptions of the life changes since the onset of the illness. The questionnaire used for the interview was adapted from previous surveys that examined the impact of chronic illness on parents (Chesler & Barbarin, 1987). Adjustments were made to account for likely differences in mental illnesses, as well as those in Israeli society.

It was translated into Hebrew and then pretested on a group of parents in an Enosh branch who were not included in the final analysis.

Fifteen items on parents' perceptions of the changes they had experienced in their lives since the onset of their children's illness were included in the survey. These items asked parents to report on their perceptions of these changes, using 3-point scales, anchored with the labels, "worse," "same," or "better." The results were first computed for distributions using percentages. Differences between the participants and nonparticipants in the self-help groups were examined on these items. The items were factor analyzed for data-reduction purposes, using the Varimax method. Chi-square tests of significance were then conducted on the resultant factors with each of the following 12 sociodemographic and situational variables: participation in a self-help group, age, sex, ethnicity, level of education, number of children, religiosity, former knowledge about mental illness, date of the diagnosis, taking an active part in the child's treatment, density of housing, and number of hospitalizations the child had undergone.

RESULTS

Table 14-1 summarizes the individual items on the parents' perceptions of life changes. It is not surprising that the majority of parents reported changes for the worse on key aspects of their lives—such as "satisfaction with life in general," "your mental health," "sense of personal control over your life," "satisfaction with family life," "leisure/recreation time," and "social life"—but reported changes for the better on only two items: "willingness to join others to change things" and "sense of what [I] as an individual can do." The proportions of participants versus nonparticipants who reported changes for the "better" on the first item were 56.3 percent and 16.7 percent, respectively, and on the second item, 38.7 percent and 5.6 percent, respectively.

Table 14-2 reports the results of the factor analysis of the life-change items. These factors included "satisfaction and control over life," "social and family relationships," "health," and "empowerment." The last factor, "empowerment," comprised the only two items on which substantial positive life changes were reported by parents.

Table 14-1

Parents' Perceptions of Their Life Changes That Were Due to Their Children's Illness (percentage, n = 50, except where noted)

PERCEPTIONS OF LIFE CHANGES	WORSE	SAME	BETTER
1. Satisfaction with life in general	70	20	2
2. Your mental health	66	32	2
3. Sense of personal control over your life[a]	59	41	0
4. Satisfaction with family life	56	40	4
5. Leisure/recreation time	52	46	2
6. Social life	50	50	0
7. Your physical health	40	58	2
8. Relationships between family members	36	60	4
9. General standard of living	32	68	0
10. Your work[b]	30	66	4
11. Your physical health compared with others	26	74	0
12. Your sense of what you as an individual can do[a]	25	48	27
13. Division of home/family tasks[a]	22	78	0
14. Your sense of who you are[b]	17	81	2
15. Your willingness to join others to change things	10	48	42

[a] $n = 49$.
[b] $n = 47$.

The results of the chi-square tests between the life-change factors and the 12 sociodemographic and situational variables demonstrated that empowerment was significantly different with regard to the following:

■ Participation, $\chi^2 = 3.67$, $p < .05$; participants reported higher levels of positive changes than did nonparticipants.

■ Education, $\chi^2 = 3.88$, $p < .05$; those who had 8 or more years of formal education reported higher levels of positive changes than did those who had fewer years of formal education.

■ Previous knowledge of mental illness, $\chi^2 = 15.8$, $p < .001$; those with previous knowledge reported higher levels of positive changes than did those without previous knowledge.

Table 14-2

Perception of Life Changes, Factor Analyzed

FACTORS AND THEIR ITEMS	LOADING	COMMONALITY
1. *Satisfaction and Control over Life*		
Satisfaction with family life	.78	.70
Satisfaction with life in general	.78	.74
Sense of personal control	.56	.60
2. *Social and Family Relationships*		
Social life	.76	.72
Division of home/family tasks	.58	.44
Your sense of who you are	.56	.37
Leisure/recreation	.55	.58
Your work	.50	.34
3. *Health*		
Your physical health	.92	.89
Your physical health compared with others	.69	.56
Your mental health	(.47)	(.45)
4. *Empowerment*		
Your willingness to join others to change things	.86	.78
Your sense of what you as an individual can do	.64	.67

The total variance explained was 65.8 percent: Factor 1, 53.4 percent of the explained variance; Factor 2, 19.4 percent of the explained variance; Factor 3, 17.5 percent of the explained variance; and Factor 4, 9.7 percent of the explained variance.
(Factors consist of items of .50 loadings or above.)

■ Taking an active part in treatment, $\chi^2 = 6.55$, $p < .01$; those who took an active part in treatment reported higher levels of positive changes than did those who did not take an active part.

Health was found significantly different with regard to sex, $\chi^2 = 6.75$, $p < .01$; men reported more negative change in health than did women.

DISCUSSION

After becoming acquainted with these parents of mentally ill adult children and their severe and ongoing predicament, which had lasted for over 20 years in some cases, the authors were particularly startled to find reports of any positive changes in the parents' lives. The parents most typically reported feelings of hopelessness and despair in confronting their children's and their own chronic and unpredictable situation. One parent stated, for example, "I feel old, I see no future, nothing interests me any more. I have become apathetic."

The only two items on which parents reported positive changes were "your willingness to join others to change things" and "your sense of what you as an individual can do." These items were the only ones that pertained to the parents' concerns that developed after their children's illness and thus after they would have had the opportunity to participate in self-help groups. Therefore, it is not surprising that the bulk of the parents who reported such positive changes were participants in self-help groups.

These two items appear to have an underlying factor in common, namely, "empowerment." This hypothesis was supported by the factor analysis, which discerned a factor consisting exclusively of these two items. What the factor analysis demonstrated was that those who tended to report positive changes in their willingness to join others to change things also tended to report positive changes in their sense of what they could do as individuals.

Parents' anecdotal responses lend support to the relationship of participation in self-help groups to these aspects of empowerment. For example, in answer to a question about what advice one would give to other parents with a mentally ill child, one parent stated, "Parents should meet with each other and help each other and especially speak about the problem, not try to hide it." Another parent answered, in regard to the same question, "Parents should come to Enosh to leave behind their loneliness and to help each other." A third parent stated, "Parents should learn how to listen to each other in Enosh meetings; parents should not neglect themselves, personally, in light of their problem. They should recruit new parents [to Enosh] and provide help to each other."

Once it was established that there can be positive changes among some parents that are related to empowerment, the question remains, What are the specific characteristics of the parents who report such changes? The authors' third analysis addressed this question. Of the sociodemographic and situational variables that were examined, participation, level of education, knowledge of mental illness before its onset in the child, and taking an active part in the child's treatment were all found to be significantly related to differences in the parents' reported feelings of empowerment. (It is important to note that the empowerment factor was the only one in which significant relationships were found with regard to sociodemographic and situational variables, except the health factor with regard to the parents' sex.)

In earlier analyses of this study (Gidron & Guterman, 1988), it was found that participation in self-help groups was significantly related to the other three variables; that is, participants tended to have a higher level of education and knowledge of mental illness and more frequently took an active part in their children's treatment than did the nonparticipants. Of these four variables, logically speaking, empowerment is most immediately related to participation. However, this relationship seems to be a complex one, and the evidence of the study suggests that it is mediated by the other three variables and possibly by others.

FURTHER QUESTIONS

Although the study suggested that empowerment appears to be an outcome of participation, several unanswered questions remain: What is the specific process through which one goes to achieve empowerment through participation in a self-help group? How do a variety of dispositional and situational variables, not examined here, mediate that process? What is the relationship between personal and social empowerment? Answers to such questions will help researchers clearly identify the specific and unique benefits of participation in self-help groups as well as the type of persons who would most likely benefit from such participation.

REFERENCES

Battaglino, L. (1987). Family empowerment through self-help groups. In A. B. Hatfield (Ed.), *Families of the mentally ill: Meeting the challenges* (pp. 43–52). San Francisco: Jossey-Bass.

Chesler, M., & Barbarin, O. (1987). *Childhood cancer and the family: Managing the challenge of stress and support.* New York: Brunner/Mazel.

Gidron, B. (1989). *Sociodemographic and situational factors in social support for parents of the mentally ill.* Manuscript submitted for publication.

Gidron, B., & Guterman, N. B. (1988). *Stress and coping patterns of parents of the mentally ill.* Manuscript submitted for publication.

Gidron, B., Guterman, N. B., & Hartman, H. (in press). Stress and coping patterns of participants and nonparticipants in self-help groups for parents of the mentally ill. *Community Mental Health Journal.*

Gottlieb, B. H. (1982). Mutual-help groups: Members' views of their benefits and of roles for professionals. In L. D. Borman et al. (Eds.), *Helping people to help themselves* (pp. 55–67). New York: Haworth Press.

Hatfield, A. B. (1984). The family. In J. A. Talbott (Ed.), *The chronic mental patient: Five years later.* New York: Grune & Stratton.

Noh, S., & Turner, R. J. (1987). Living with psychiatric patients: Implications for the mental health of family members. *Social Science and Medicine, 25*(3), 263–272.

Powell, T. (1987). *Self-help organizations and professional practice.* Silver Spring, MD: National Association of Social Workers, Inc.

Riessman, F. (1985). New dimensions in self-help. *Social Policy, 16,* 2–4.

Shapiro, R., Possidente, S. M., Plum, K. C., & Lehman, A. F. (1983). The evaluation of a support group for families of the chronically mentally ill. *Psychiatric Quarterly, 56,* 276–285.

Videka-Sherman, L. (1982). Effects of participation in self-help groups for bereaved parents: Compassionate Friends. In L. D. Borman et al. (Eds.), *Helping people to help themselves* (pp. 68–77). New York: Haworth Press.

15

SELF-CARE, SELF-HELP, AND COMMUNITY CARE FOR HEALTH

BARRY CHECKOWAY, MARK A. CHESLER, AND STEPHEN BLUM

There is widespread dissatisfaction with the medical care system in the United States. Critics charge that the costs are too high, driven up by the expansive medical technology and excess capacity of hospitals (Davis, Anderson, Rowland, & Steinberg, 1990; Ehrenreich & Ehrenreich, 1970; Ensminger, 1975; Fein, 1989; Institute of Medicine, 1976; Kotelchuk, 1976; McClure, 1976; Roemer, 1961; Stevens, 1989) and that higher costs and more expensive technology do not improve the general health of the overall population (Callahan, 1990; Dutton, 1988; Knowles, 1977; McKeown, 1976; McKinley & McKinley, 1977). They further contend that services are unavailable or inaccessible to those who need them most (Davis & Schoen, 1978; De Vise, 1973; Fuchs, 1974; Hiatt, 1989; U.S. Department of Health, Education, & Welfare, 1977, 1979a, 1979b, 1980, 1981); that curative medicine is emphasized at the expense of health education, prevention, and promotion programs (Checkoway, 1989; Jonas, 1978; Knowles, 1977; Navarro, 1986); and that professional dominance and institutional services reduce the responsibilities of individuals and communities for their own care.

Critics charge that ours is not a *health* care system, but a *disease* care system, dominated by providers of medical care who induce demand and have a powerful voice with third-party payers and state and local governments (Duhl, 1986). This system produces a form of triage by which good-quality care is provided for those with money or health insurance and higher mortality and morbidity result for those who are unable to pay or who do not have health insurance. Illich

(1976; see also Berliner & Salmon, 1980; Carlson, 1975) argued that the medical system itself has become a major threat to health, through clinical iatrogenesis (illness caused by physicians and medical institutions) and through social iatrogenesis (which makes people believe they are unable to attend actively to their own well-being).

In response, many people have turned to "alternatives" to the existing system. Some have taken increased personal responsibility for their own health care (self-care). Others have formed "self-help" groups that provide mutual support for individuals in similar situations. Still others have organized or planned programs of "community care," through participation in health planning, social action, neighborhood development, or other methods in which the community is the unit of care. These are not the only alternatives, but they are among the most important. They all incorporate a more integrated view of self and society and, therefore, a more hostile approach to personal and community health than does the traditional health care system. Concern with these alternatives is increasing at a time when the cost of health care is rising, the quality of care is worsening, and further cutbacks in governmental health and human services are being made. This chapter reviews three alternatives, noting some of their strengths or weaknesses in improving health, increasing participation, and creating change.

SELF-CARE

Self-care is an idea whose time has returned. Scarcely a day passes in which the media fail to report some action by an individual, group, governmental agency, or private corporation that is concerned with expanding "personal responsibility" for health. Advertisements and announcements show the variety and range of concerns: personal hygiene, nutrition, exercise, stress reduction, weight reduction, aerobics, jogging, diet, breast self-examination, and so on. These various movements may indicate shifts in beliefs and values, in roles and relationships, and in the central areas of anticipation and responsibility. With self-care, the individual views himself or herself as largely responsible for the development and maintenance of personal health. Self-care challenges people to maintain wellness and to help themselves (Ardell, 1977; Ferguson, 1979; Samuels & Bennett, 1973; Williamson & Danaher, 1978).

People who practice self-care do more than react to mainstream medicine. Studies have found that many of the major correlates of health have little to do with medicine and much to do with living a sensible life, including not smoking, drinking only moderate amounts of alcohol, controlling one's weight, eating a nutritionally balanced diet, exercising regularly, getting a reasonable amount of sleep, driving safely, and wearing automobile seat belts (see, for example, DeFriese & Woomert, 1982; Wildavsky, 1977). Self-care can also contribute to feelings of self-fulfillment, self-worth, and self-confidence. All these can have effects that are rarely the result of established medical and institutional care.

Many individuals and groups have helped themselves to be more healthy. For example, a small group of women met to discuss "women and their bodies" at a conference in Boston in spring 1969. "We had all experienced similar feelings of frustration and anger toward specific doctors and the medical maze in general, and initially we wanted to do something about those doctors who are condescending, paternalistic, judgmental and non-informative" (Boston Women's Health Book Collective, 1972, p. 6), they later wrote. "As we talked and shared our experiences with one another, we realized just how much we had to learn about our bodies" (p. 6).

> These women collected information, discussed in the group what they had learned, and finally presented the results as a course for women on women and their bodies. . . . The process of talking was as crucial as the facts themselves. Over time the facts and feelings melted together in ways that touched us very deeply, and that is reflected in the changing titles of the course and then the book, from *Women and Their Bodies* to *Women and Our Bodies*, to, finally, *Our Bodies, Ourselves*. (p. 6)

This book, and the later book, *The New Our Bodies, Ourselves* (Boston Women's Health Book Collective, 1984), document the ways in which women can increase their participation and improve their health in a male-dominated system. It is only one of several self-care best-sellers across the country.

Many of the techniques of the self-care movement are revivals of older therapies that focused on a holistic concept of health (such as homeopathy, herbalism, folk medicine, and naturopathy) or are drawn from non-Western traditions (massage, spiritual healing, meditation, yoga, acupuncture, and martial arts). Those who use these techniques react against the disease orientation of modern medicine, recast the role of the provider from controller to facilitator and partner, and view themselves as participants, rather than as patients-consumers. They also emphasize principles, such as self-actualization, nutritional awareness, physical fitness, and environmental sensitivity. The common holistic belief is that health and wellness can come about through the search for wholeness of body, mind, and spirit (Gordon, Jaffee, & Bresler, 1982; Hastings, Fadiman, & Gordon, 1980; Kaslof, 1978; Pelletier, 1979a; Salmon & Berliner, 1981; Walker, 1978).

The holistic health movement has experienced rapid growth during the past decade. It is estimated that, as of 1985, there were more than 200 holistic health centers and clinics operating in the United States (Bliss, 1985). Services often mix styles, such as herbal medicine, preventive dentistry, iridology, massage, reflexology, Rolfing, biofeedback, self-hypnosis, meditation, and "inner healing." They expand collaboration in the diagnostic and therapeutic process and provide what many people seek but fail to find in established medicine (Basmijian, 1978; Crasilneck & Hall, 1975; Linn & Lewis, 1979; Luthe & Schultz, 1969; Pelletier, 1979b).

Practitioners of holistic medicine recognize that stress predisposes individuals to a variety of somatic and psychological complaints. They suggest that self-care techniques, such as autogenic training, meditation, and clinical biofeedback, can help a person reduce his or her stresses. In such circumstances, the patient becomes a more active participant in the diagnostic and therapeutic process, often with positive verifiable results.

Other self-care–oriented practitioners appraise personal lifestyles and modify individual behaviors as a means to prevent disease and maintain wellness (Ryan & Travis, 1981; Travis, 1978). They publish community newsletters; design seminars for businesses, universities, hospitals, and professional groups; and consult with individuals on life planning, neurolinguistic programming, gestalt therapy, personal effectiveness, and energy awareness. They do not prescribe medicine or operate curative clinics; rather, they operate as institutions to promote wellness. So popular and fast growing is the demand for such alternatives that big business is stepping up the development, marketing, and production of new participatory tools. "Product development" and "consumer targeting" promise new profits for the wellness entrepreneurs (Jennett, 1986).

Self-care to prevent illness has become increasingly popular in American corporations. Although corporate officers may oppose certain preventive measures, they advocate others with fervor. They recognize that medical care is a costly business expense, that illness and injuries equal large amounts of money and many workdays of lost production, and that stress and heart attacks of executives produce medical bills and require payments for disability compensation and rehabilitation. No wonder the corporations develop physical fitness programs, subsidize preventive measures, and increase the incentives for executives to care for themselves. If they have concentrated on programs for executives and ignored the conditions that affect blue-collar workers, their concern for prevention is prominent nonetheless (Taylor, 1982).

Self-care today is getting a big boost as national policy. Central to the rhetoric of former President Reagan's years in office, for example, was his assurance that the administration would "restore confidence by returning power to the people" (Fisher, 1981, p. 43; see also, Taylor, 1982). He and his health officials advocated the need for individual self-reliance as a major alternative to "government intervention." The result was less money for federal social programs, including health planning, neighborhood health centers, Medicaid, food stamps, and other programs, especially those for the poor and elderly. So far, President Bush has continued this pattern.

Self-care, as national policy, is brilliant politics, seemingly shared by both ends of the ideological continuum: antigovernment conservatives and decentralist progressives and corporate giants and local grass-roots community groups. Who could criticize such a broadly attractive notion?

SELF-HELP

Self-help as a social process is part of the tradition of American voluntary action; it is a core element in the ongoing struggle to achieve a balance between personal initiative and institutional service. Self-help groups are the more or less formally organized expressions of people's desires to meet, work with, and help others who are experiencing similar social or health situations. These groups rely primarily on lay energy or indigenous direction, sometimes initiated or supported by professionals. They add an element of "experiential expertise" to the "credentialized expertise" of the professionals (Borkman, 1976, Chapter 1, this volume; Klass & Shinners, 1982–83; Reinharz, 1981; Rosenberg, 1984). Self-help groups have been defined in various ways, but most of the literature and practice focuses on them as an identifiable group of people, facing a similar life crisis or medical problem, coming together on a voluntary basis, to do for themselves or to help each other.

Health-related self-help groups are increasing in number and scope. There are groups for cancer victims, arthritics, compulsive overeaters, cigarette smokers, parents of babies who died from sudden infant death syndrome, families of ill or disabled children, former mental patients, paraplegics, manic depressives, and those in all 17 disease categories of the World Health Organization (WHO). By the 1980s, Mended Hearts, for those who have had heart surgery, had 12,000 members in 90 chapters and was growing by 250 members a month. Alcoholics Anonymous, formed in the 1930s, claimed more than a million members in 28,000 groups in 92 countries. Indeed, the rapid development and expansion of these groups has led some observers to identify self-help groups as a social movement in and of itself (Katz, 1981).

Self-help groups vary considerably in function and structure, although they contain elements in common. For instance, the most basic function of self-help groups is to provide an arena in which someone with a problem can meet with others in a similar situation. In this setting, information that "only patients know" can be shared. The processes of social comparison and identification with others, shared feelings and coping strategies, and the struggle for mutual empowerment in the face of a disempowering personal or family illness go on. Such processes help create important new social bonds at a time of potential isolation from one's natural system of social support and help counter the culture of silence that often envelops patients with chronic or serious health conditions, particularly those who experience social stigma because of their situation (Bloch & Seitz, 1985; Levy, 1976). In addition to the benefits of personal disclosure and social networking, individuals often feel empowered when they gain new knowledge and give help to others (Dory & Riessman, 1982; Riessman, 1965). The process of helping others may remind partici- pants of their own strengths and coping capacities, even in the midst of illness, emotional pain, and overwhelming tragedy. As patients and their families discover or rediscover their strengths, they may become more assertive health care consumers, standing up for their rights and actively participating in the healing process.

Most groups provide education and information on illness or health conditions and treatment, coping skills, and strategies for action. Educational activities may include lectures and discussions in which essential information is shared by patients or by professionals. Speakers may discuss ways of understanding medical jargon, new advances in treatment, therapeutic equipment, pharmaceutical prepa- rations, and characteristics of medical personnel and how to get along with them. The Candlelighters Childhood Cancer Foundation, a national network of local self-help groups for families of children with cancer, commissioned and (together with the Association for the Care of Children's Health) published a manual (Bogue & Chesney, 1987) for parent-to-parent visitation programs. Utilized by many local groups, some of which deal with childhood cancer and others of which concentrate on one of a variety of childhood illnesses, this manual informs parents (and professionals) how to provide contacts at home or in the hospital, promote the exchange of coping skills and strategies, and develop programs for those who are undergoing the experience for the first time. For example, parents whose child has died may gain understanding, friendship, and mutual support by meeting with those with a similar experience. Persons who are suffering from depressive illness may find relief and encouragement by talking with others who have had the same experience and who can suggest actions they can take and can accompany them to do so (Gussaw & Tracy, 1976).

Some groups raise funds to support research, to provide for needy families, or to augment staffs at local health clinics. The Cystic Fibrosis Foundation, for instance, raises funds nationally to support research to find a cure for the disease and to support families who find it difficult to finance lengthy outpatient treatment. Other illness-related groups provide funds directly to local clinics, such as Leukemia Research Life, of Detroit, Michigan, which supports research on childhood leukemia principally at the Detroit Children's Hospital.

And some groups look outward to the medical system with which they interact, seeking to improve the current state of medical practice by offering professionals feedback on their technical or social services or by submitting collective complaints and grievances. Several parent centers have been funded to provide support for families of health-impaired and disabled children. A central part of their work has been to train parents to advocate for their children's interests and to develop groups and group leaders to advocate collective interests with medical centers, schools, and community agencies (Ayers & Chesler, 1987). Such advocacy may take the form of educational ventures or feedback, but at times, it generates protest and disruptive demonstrations. For instance, in a city in Rhode Island, a group of parents of children with cancer called a meeting with the staff of the local hospital. In a public session, they aired their grievances and complaints with the staff regarding the incomplete and unreliable services their children were receiving. Although the meeting began in the midst of heated exchanges, it quickly moved to a mutual and collaborative problem-solving session, with outcomes agreeable to all parties.

Groups also vary considerably in their structures and operating styles. Some are small and locally based, representing unique neighborhood networks or community responses to individuals involved in a health crisis, such as in a rural area where people recovering from heart attacks meet weekly to drink soft beverages and discuss their coping processes. Such groups may operate informally, without officers or rules for conducting meetings, to share emotions in private and supportive environs.

Other groups operate more formally, with elected officers, committees, and regularly scheduled and planned meetings. In Cincinnati, for example, a chapter of Parents of Murdered Children operates with formal bylaws and regulations for meetings, receives committee reports, and otherwise conducts business like any other local voluntary organization. Part of the chapter's meetings, however, are deeply emotional sessions in which parents share stories about their bereavement and about their experiences with the criminal justice system. Such formalized groups often are affiliated with national organizations, either in loose coalitions such as the Candlelighters Childhood Cancer Foundation, or in formal chapter systems such as the Leukemia Society of America. The American Cancer Society formed Reach for Recovery, which helps two-thirds of the more than 75,000 women who undergo mastectomies each year, and encourages its state and local divisions to work closely with independently organized groups of parents of children with cancer. The American Heart Association officially encourages state affiliates to establish clubs for stroke victims across the country.

Considerable attention and debate have centered on the appropriate roles of health care professionals in this variety of self-help groups. Advocates of their involvement argue that professionals have skills that are relevant for dealing with the informational and emotional needs of patients and family members and can facilitate the patients' access to the medical system. However, advocates of organized groups for patients and their families argue that such professional involvement inherently contradicts some of the vital principles of self-help and transforms such groups into mutual counseling or support sessions. Moreover, they suggest that professional involvement may stifle the patients' expressions of some needs and fails to empower those who require self-initiative and collective identification the most. In contrast, several scholars and practitioners (Borman, 1979; Chutis, 1983; Wollert & Barron, 1983; Yoak & Chesler, 1985) have observed that there are many issues on which professionals and patients may share leadership, create a partnership or a coalition, or divide the labor involved in the initiation and operation of self-help groups in health care.

Critics of self-help groups, especially of those that operate without professional supervision, often express concern about the quality of emotional support and information shared in these settings (see, for example, Mantell, Alexander, & Kleiman, 1976; Ringler, Whitman, Gustafson, & Coleman, 1981; Toseland & Hacker, 1982). They express particular concern about the tendency of groups to promote a uniform style of coping and a distrustful or even resistant attitude toward health care professionals (Mantell, 1983). Others (see, for instance, Withorn, 1980) worry that such groups may encourage patients to concentrate on their own needs for information and support and, as a result, may distract them from the collective and structural problems engendered by the organized health care system—problems that require concerted political action, rather than personal learning. Supporters of self-help groups often argue that many of the problems permeate all aspects of health care and that it is too much to ask these groups to carry the burden of cost, quality, and participation. But several self-help groups do regularly represent their interests on local health planning bodies and testify before state and national legislatures. Indeed, the most vital frontier may involve the formation of partnerships or coalitions between active and energetic patients or family members who are committed to self-help processes, sympathetic policymakers, and compassionate professionals who are willing to help them achieve their goals.

COMMUNITY CARE

Community initiatives to promote health are more important than ever. If self-care views health as an individual responsibility and self-help views health as a responsibility of families, friends, fellow patients, or other sources of social support, community care views health as inseparable from the community of which it is a part. Recent years have witnessed an increase in efforts to improve health by organizing groups for social action, planning programs at the community level, and developing community-based services that are responsive to the community's needs (Checkoway, 1981; Duhl, 1986).

Community initiatives include activities or structures to organize or plan programs or services at the local level. They vary in their scope and structure, roles and responsibilities, organizational capacity, and funding support, but together, they recognize the importance of the community as a unit for health. Community can be defined as an area in which a group of people live, a group of people living in an area, or a group of people who have close ties or common interests. Community thus is more than a physical place; it is also a vehicle for social participation and collective action (Cox, 1987; Lackey, Burke, & Peterson, 1987).

Community initiatives include health planning to assess community conditions and implement programs. In the 1970s, for example, the U.S. Congress created health planning agencies to involve communities in planning for "equal access to quality care at an affordable cost." In addition to having "broadly representative" consumer majorities on planning boards, these agencies were expected to provide for public notice and open meetings, public hearings on plans, and a public record of board proceedings. Although planning practice was uneven overall, some agencies sought community participation with fervor, and some consumers used agencies as vehicles to strengthen their local community organizations (Glenn, 1980; Institute of Medicine, 1981).

Community initiatives also include efforts to organize groups for social and political action around health. In central Illinois, for example, health care consumers conducted an investigation that disclosed the lack of consumer participation in health planning. They conducted a series of community forums to provide information and generate publicity about health care issues, sponsored training workshops for consumer leaders and board members, and formed an organization to take control of the local health planning board. They enlisted providers and consumers to run for the board, and claimed a majority of seats before broadening their agenda and conducting campaigns around other health issues in the community (Checkoway, 1982; Checkoway & Doyle, 1980).

In Wisconsin, citizens with disabilities organized statewide to expand the participation of disabled citizens in personal and public health decisions. More than 6,000 persons participated in projects in rural, urban, and metropolitan areas of the state. They attended leadership training workshops, met personally with public officials, testified at public hearings, conducted telephone and letter-writing campaigns, and placed representatives on key boards and committees. They pressured agencies to provide services for a mother with polio and two children, influenced county board members to override an executive veto of supportive home care, and persuaded officials to fund training for disabled children. They mobilized substantial political resources and had an impact on the planning of policies and the implementation of programs. One participant concluded, "Before the project I felt helpless about the decisions that were affecting my life. But then we visited our legislators at the Capitol and learned that letters and phone calls are taken seriously and can be effective in decisions" (Checkoway & Norsman, 1986).

Community health education includes efforts to increase public consciousness about health problems and their solutions. People come together in small groups to discuss common problems, analyze causes, and build their confidence and competence to create change. They may form adult learning groups, hold leadership training programs for board members of organizations, or conduct educational campaigns in the community. Minkler (1985) described an area of San Francisco in which low-income elderly people lived in isolation and poor health in single-room occupancy hotels. Health educators formed support groups in lobbies of several hotels to encourage interaction and facilitate dialogue on health problems and social issues. They applied Paulo Friere's "problem posing dialogue" and formed support groups for project development. They incorporated as a community organization that continues to address issues of crime and safety, poor access to food and undernutrition, housing, and community development.

Community health programs often develop local resources that are responsive to the needs in underserved rural or urban areas. In rural Mississippi, for example, community health centers have increased the access to affordable health care, involved traditional nonparticipants in leadership positions, and produced political change. Representatives of low-income people on health center boards contributed to program planning and their own social development as a result of participation (Geiger, 1984). In St. Louis, Missouri, a community organization has built and rehabilitated housing, operated social services, attracted new industry and jobs, and formulated plans to boost the local economy. It has operated a senior citizens program that provides meals, transportation, and recreation for elderly residents; run a child care and nutritional program; sponsored youth training and summer vocational activities; and disseminated information about health care and human services through the neighborhood newspaper and local radio station (Checkoway, 1985).

Some established neighborhood groups have expanded their agendas to develop community health services. In Cleveland, Ohio, more than 350 neighborhood residents within a 10-block area interact as a kinship group and take mutual responsibility for the welfare of families in the neighborhood. They now compose the governing board of a multipurpose clinic that also serves as the local unit of a comprehensive community health center (Ross, 1983). In Baltimore, Maryland, a group of residents created an awareness of their neighborhood's needs, strengthened social networks, and linked local groups with outside areas. In addition, they prepared a directory of health resources, formed helping groups and telephone hotlines for persons with special needs, and established community health advocacy groups (Naparstek, Biegel, & Spiro, 1982). In San Francisco, a nonprofit community-based organization was formed to serve functionally disabled and low-income residents in a high-density urban area. It provides multiple services for these semidependent populations, including social, medical rehabilitative, and supportive services like transportation, meals, and personal and home care (Zawadski & Ansak, 1983).

Community care programs promote health, but they also can provide opportunities for people to participate in ways that produce positive psychosocial results. There is evidence that community participation is itself a significant psychosocial factor in the improvement of self-confidence, individual coping capacity, social adjustment, and satisfaction with life. Participation can enhance effective and cognitive support, social contacts and outreach, the maintenance of a social identity, and psychological well-being in health (Cath, 1975; Cutler, 1973; Peirce, 1975). Participation also mediates psychological stress and physical illness that follow major life changes (Cobb, 1976); affect the body's defense system and susceptibility to disease (Cassell, 1974); and correlate with predictors of morbidity, mortality, and other indicators of health status (Cohen & Brody, 1984). In a controlled study of residents in an apartment building in New York City, members of an experimental social activation group significantly increased plasma levels of testosterone, estradiol, and other psychophysiological effects compared with the control group (Arnetz, 1982).

These various community programs represent distinct movements, each with its own approach to the field. But together, they recognize that people can take the initiative to improve health and local health services and that the community can be a unit of solution. This notion has increasing importance in international health and is the basis for a new health-promotion program of WHO (WHO, 1984; see also Hancock, 1987).

The idea of health as a community process gives meaning to health as a form of personal and social well-being, emphasizing the values of an active population at the community level rather than of passive recipients of curative care for illness and disease. As images of health care as curative care give way to views of health as a promotive process involving social support, the community will increase in importance.

LIMITS OF PARTICIPATION: CAUTION AND CRITIQUE

Self-care, self-help, and community care are distinct movements, each with its own approach to health, each motivated by its own background and objectives, roles and responsibilities, strategies and structures. Although some analysts think it would be useful to synthesize the three approaches, there are benefits to emphasizing what is unique to each rather than attempting a grand embracing conception. Self-care is neither self-help nor community care, and each is likely to remain distinct in the future.

Despite their differences, however, these three approaches have some common characteristics. They emphasize people's individual or collective strengths and resources, not only their health problems or social needs. They support personal and social development through knowledge- and skills building, which enables people to help themselves and one another. They strengthen the participation of individuals or groups in planning and implementing initiatives for the promotion of positive health, rather than as a reaction to disease and illness. They give meaning to health as a form of voluntary action and social well-being, emphasizing the positive participation of an active population, rather than the passive receipt of clinical or curative medicine provided by dominating medical professionals.

These three approaches sometimes occur together in mutually reinforcing ways. Since most health problems result from a combination of social, economic, political, and other factors, in addition to physical causes, they could benefit from a mixing and phasing of interventions. In a single situation, for example, it is possible to imagine an intervention involving an individual who takes personal responsibility for improving his or her own health, who organizes others in similar situations to exchange information and build mutual support, and who joins efforts to plan community programs and to develop community services that are responsive to people's needs.

These three approaches also could contribute to a major movement to promote health as a positive personal and social resource. Illich (1976) warned against a medical system that is centered on medical providers and reduces the willingness or ability of people to participate in their own health care. There are growing expectations for a new public health movement that, according to WHO (1986, p. 1), would emphasize the promotion of health as "the process of enabling people to increase control over, and to improve, their health." This movement would include initiatives to develop personal skills, create supportive environments, strengthen community action, reorient health services, and build a more innovative public policy.

It is important to increase individual, group, and community participation in health. However, there are serious dangers when positive aspects of participation are uncritically translated into a national health policy. Under certain circumstances, these aspects may intensify and even worsen the health care problems facing the nation. The following are not the only dangers of the uncritical incorporation of these aspects, but they are among the most important. The problem is not with the ideas of visions of self-care, self-help, or community care, but with their implementation within the political-economic structure of contemporary health care systems.

DANGER TO THE POOR AND PEOPLE OF COLOR

Many federal health programs were originated in response to the special problems that poor people and people of color face. These groups have the least access to competent medical care and the greatest exposure to environmental and social hazards and are among the least healthy Americans. The idea of self-care as a national policy is premised on the ideology that individuals have the ability to pull themselves up by their bootstraps. But this is a strange metaphor, indeed; it is not only physically impossible to accomplish, but as an ideology it is a cruel joke for those without "boots." The benefits that flow from self-care are praiseworthy. But they do little for those without resources and power. Furthermore, poor people and minority group members who *do* participate in self-care may find that their efforts operate as a subtle form of "regulating" the poor (Piven & Cloward, 1971). Self-care may divert attention away from the organization of oppressed groups to recognize the root causes of their problems and to take social and political action on their own behalf.

Self-help groups in the health field seldom include many poor or oppressed people for many complex reasons. First, poor or oppressed people may distrust social situations or the interactive styles of other classes, races, or gender groups. Second, they may have too many responsibilities at home to attend meetings. Third, they may not have the time or be able to afford the costs of transportation to attend meetings in predominantly white and affluent medical facilities or community centers. Fourth, they may be unwilling to subject themselves to the discrimination they fear is practiced by the predominantly white and middle-class members of most self-help groups. Like some of the concerns raised about self-care, differential participation rates also may reflect poor or oppressed people's concerns about initiatives that draw attention to "people like themselves" and away from the health care systems that are serving (or in some cases misserving) them.

Community programs often emphasize resources that are less plentiful in communities in which poor people live. Lacking such resources, the poor are more vulnerable to manipulation, tokenism, or other forms of nonparticipation. In addition, programs often follow the lines of racial and class separation that characterize many other institutions in society. There are serious obstacles to the development of programs across class and racial lines, although such programs have existed, as the history of interracial and interclass initiatives makes clear. But these initiatives are not typical, and they are especially difficult in a service system that allocates resources differentially and when racial and income groups utilize different health care systems.

RETREAT FROM SOCIAL RESPONSIBILITY

In a society that is fueled largely by privatism and competition, the ideas of "social responsibility" and "community" have fallen on hard times. The national policy of self-care leads the country away from these goals. By stressing the importance of *personal* responsibility and *individual* symptoms, it further fragments the individual's social network or the community as a vehicle for social cohesion and mutual and shared obligations and subsumes or denies the sense of shared identity and responsibility. Self-care can be a narrow national policy that has a profoundly antisocial norm. It is the opposite of civilization and adopted only at risk to individuals and the society as a whole.

Although self-help groups are an obvious example of people taking social responsibility for one another, they also may represent retreats from a larger social responsibility. Some observers of local self-help groups state that they focus primarily on internal relationships and resources and rarely reach out to engage others outside the group. Indeed, the very power of small-group and intimate exchanges of information and energy may militate against larger political action organizations or mass membership campaigns. Likewise, few self-help groups focus externally on the structural changes required in the health care system that may make their roles less stressful. The result is an overemphasis on stress buffering as a coping tactic, rather than on stress reduction (see House, 1981), with an acceptance of the health care system as a given rather than as a structure to be changed.

Community initiatives also often sacrifice large-scale social and political mobilization for a piece of the action. Oppressed communities run the risk of becoming involved in the existing system, rather than becoming empowered to change the structures that oppress them. Thus, local and parochial interests in reform may take precedence over national and systemic forms of social responsibility. When individuals care for themselves, when groups of patients care for each other, or when local communities plan programs that are responsive to their own needs, the broader society may have no incentive to take responsibility for increasing the access to high-quality care in the system as a whole.

RETREAT FROM PROFESSIONAL RESPONSIBILITY

While medical providers, physicians, and hospitals have dominated health care, the costs have skyrocketed and many of the problems of quality and accessibility remain. Overspecialization, bureaucratization, and depersonalization may be endemic prices to be paid for the "triumphs" of modern medicine. A national policy of public participation can help deal with these issues, but it may permit professionals to avoid the most innovative aspects of their professional roles. After all, if communities are mobilizing to have an impact on local health care systems, professionals are relieved to some extent from these public and political responsibilities. Instead of seeking allies in the community to transform the health care system, professionals may sit back and "watch" these lay initiatives.

Self-care and self-help, which focus on patients' discovery and use of their own resources, may also contribute to a withdrawal of professional resources and commitment. In addition, they may reinforce an ideology that emphasizes the need for change in individual patients, not for professional change. Just because patients take personal and social responsibility for their care and that of others and promote a more integrated and humane version of care does not mean that professionals can evade their responsibilities to advance a more compassionate and holistic practice of health care.

BLAMING THE VICTIM

The shift in responsibility from federal and public action to the individual (self-care), small group (self-help), or local community (community initiatives) places the burden on individuals to modify their responses, rather than on society to modify the conditions that have created the problems of ill health and inadequate health care. By focusing on individual responses, the current anti-social welfare ideologues and policymakers implicitly argue that individual patients and consumers of health care are the *problem*, rather than the *victims* of the problem. This is bad social science and inept social policy; the forces that create individual and community health problems are not individual; they are largely societal—political, economic, occupational, and environmental. At worst, such efforts become part of a conservative national policy that can, as Sidel and Sidel (1976, p. 68; see also Crawford, 1977) explained,

> all run the danger of diverting from national obligations, of denying the mutuality of class interests, and of subverting dissatisfaction into system-legitimizing do-it-yourself techniques. In effect, we are wisely warned against a clinical version of the blaming the victim rationalization for the status quo: It's your own fault, your own responsibility. The cure is in you—help yourself.

Widespread and uncritical adoption of self-care and self-help can be a mixed blessing under such circumstances: while these approaches help people to solve certain health care problems, they can support a policy of nonbenign neglect of the poor and powerless. When successful, moreover, these options may so dramatize the positive contributions of private initiatives that they are used to justify even further cutbacks in the allocation of public funds, personnel, and other resources.

These cautionary comments are not intended to deny the importance of self-care as one means to improve health. Nor are they intended to discourage self-help groups from forming, helping themselves, and developing a consciousness of the need for institutional change. Nor are they intended to slow the process of grassroots democratization, of local community initiatives that take an embracing view of the participation of multiple-interest groups in health care policy and decisions. Each of these options and all three together make major positive contributions to the quality of health care and to the development of new and more holistic and patient-responsive forms of medical care. But self-care, self-help, and community initiatives alone are not enough. When these democratic options are wedded to conservative and antisocial welfare politics, they become antisocial visions and represent a retreat from expanded services to the poor and minorities, a retreat from societal responsibility, and a retreat from the search for innovative professional responses to health care problems. Participation is good, but not good enough.

REFERENCES

Ardell, D. (Ed.). (1977). *High level wellness: An alternative to doctors, drugs, and disease.* Emmaus, PA: Rodale Press.

Arnetz, B. B. (1982). Social activation of the elderly: A social experiment. *Social Science Medicine, 16,* 1685–1690.

Ayers, T., & Chesler, M. (1987). *Leading self-help groups: A workshop for leaders of childhood cancer support groups.* Ann Arbor: Center for Research and Social Organization, University of Michigan.

Basmijian, J. V. (Ed.). (1978). *Biofeedback: Principles and practice for clinicians.* Baltimore, MD: Williams & Wilkins.

Berliner, H. S., & Salmon, J. W. (1980). The holistic alternative to scientific medicine: History and analysis. *International Journal of Health Services, 10,* 133–147.

Bliss, S. (Ed.). (1985). *The new holistic health handbook: Living well in a new age.* Lexington, MA: Stephen Greene Press.

Bloch, J., & Seitz, M. (1985). *Empowering parents of disabled children.* Syosset, NY: Variety Pre-schoolers' Workshop.

Bogue, E., & Chesney, B. (1987). *Making contact: A parent-to-parent visitation manual.* Washington, DC: Candlelighters Childhood Cancer Foundation.

Borkman, T. (1976). Experiential knowledge: A new concept for the analysis of self-help groups. *Social Service Review, 50,* 445–456.

Borman, L. (1979). Characteristics of growth and development. In M. Lieberman & L. Borman (Eds.), *Self-help groups for coping with crisis.* San Francisco: Jossey-Bass.

Boston Women's Health Book Collective. (1972). *Our bodies, ourselves.* New York: Simon & Schuster.

Boston Women's Health Book Collective. (1984). *The new our bodies, ourselves.* New York: Simon & Schuster.

Callahan, D. (1990). *What kind of life? The limits of medical progress.* New York: Simon & Schuster.

Carlson, R. J. (1975). *The end of medicine.* New York: Wiley-Interscience.

Cassell, J. (1974). An epidemiological perspective on psychosocial factors in disease etiology. *American Journal of Public Health, 64,* 1040–1043.

Cath, S. (1975). The orchestration of disengagement. *International Journal of Aging and Human Development, 3,* 199–213.

Checkoway, B. (1981). *Citizens and health care: Participation and planning for social change.* New York: Pergamon Press.

Checkoway, B. (1982). The empire strikes back: More lessons for health care consumers. *Journal of Health Politics, Policy and Law, 7,* 111–124.

Checkoway, B. (1985). Revitalizing an urban neighborhood: A St. Louis case study. In B. Checkoway & C. V. Patton (Eds.), *The metropolitan Midwest: Policy problems and prospects for change.* Urbana: University of Illinois Press.

Checkoway, B. (1989). Community participation for health promotion: Prescription for public policy? *Wellness Perspectives, 6,* 18–26.

Checkoway, B., & Doyle, M. (1980). Community organizing lessons for health care consumers. *Journal of Health Politics, Policy and Law, 5,* 213–216.

Checkoway, B., & Norsman, A. (1986). Empowering citizens with disabilities. *Community Development Journal, 21,* 270–277.

Chutis, L. (1983). Special roles of mental health professionals in self-help group development. *Prevention in Human Services, 2,* 65–73.

Cobb, S. (1976). Social support as a moderator of life stress. *Psychosomatic Medicine, 38,* 300–313.

Cohen, J. B., & Brody, J. A. (1984). The epidemiologic importance of psychosocial factors in longevity. *American Journal of Epidemiology, 119,* 410–423.

Cox, F. M. (1987). Alternative conceptions of community: Implications for community, implications for community organization practice. In F. M. Cox, J. L. Erlich, J. Rothman, & J. E. Tropman (Eds.), *Strategies of community organization.* Itasca, IL: F. E. Peacock.

Crasilneck, H. B., & Hall, J. A. (1975). *Clinical hypnosis: Principle and applications.* New York: Grune & Stratton.

Crawford, R. (1977). You are dangerous to your health: The ideology and politics of victim blaming. *International Journal of Health Services, 7,* 663–679.

Cutler, S. (1973). Voluntary association participation and life satisfaction: A cautionary research note. *Journal of Gerontology, 28,* 96–100.

Davis, K., Anderson, G. F., Rowland, D., & Steinberg, E. P. (1990). *Health care cost containment.* Baltimore, MD: Johns Hopkins University Press.

Davis, K., & Schoen, C. (1978). *Health and the war on poverty: A ten year appraisal.* Washington, DC: The Brookings Institution.

DeFriese, G. H., & Woomert, A. (1982). The policy implications of self-care. *Social Policy, 13,* 55–58.

De Vise, P. (1973). *Misused and misplaced hospitals and doctors: A locational analysis of the urban health care crisis.* Washington, DC: Association of American Geographers.

Dory, F., & Riessman, F. (1982). Training professionals in organizing self-help groups. *Citizen Participation, 3,* 27–28.

Dubos, R. (1959). *Mirage of health.* New York: Harper & Bros.

Duhl, L. J. (1986). *Health planning and social change.* New York: Human Sciences Press.

Dutton, D. B. (1988). *Worse than the disease: Pitfalls of medical progress.* Cambridge, England: Cambridge University Press.

Ehrenreich, B., & Ehrenreich, J. (Eds.). (1970). *The American health empire: Power, profits, and politics.* New York: Vintage Books.

Ensminger, B. (1975). *The $8 billion hospital bed overrun.* Washington, DC: Public Citizen Health Research Group.

Fein, R. (1989). *Medical care, medical costs: The search for a health insurance policy.* Cambridge, MA: Harvard University Press.

Ferguson, T. (Ed.). (1979). *Medical self care: Access to medical tools.* New York: Summit Books.

Fisher, M. J. (1981). Competition, prevention: Keys to Reagan health strategy. *National Underwriter, 85,* 43.

Fuchs, V. R. (1974). *Who shall live? Health, economics, and social change.* New York: Basic Books.

Geiger, H. J. (1984). Community health centers: Health care as an instrument of social change. In V. W. Sidel & R. Sidel (Eds.), *Reforming medicine: Lessons of the last quarter century.* New York: Pantheon.

Glenn, K. (Ed.). (1980). *Planning, politics, and power: A user's guide to taming the health care system.* Washington, DC: Consumer Coalition for Health.

Gordon, J. S., Jaffee, D. T., & Bresler, D. E. (Eds.). (1982). *Mind, body and health: Toward an integral medicine*. Rockville, MD: National Institute of Mental Health.

Gussaw, Z., & Tracy, G. S. (1976). The role of self-help clubs in adaptation to chronic illness and disability. *Social Science and Medicine, 10*, 407–414.

Hancock, T. (1987). Healthy cities: The Canadian project. *Health Promotion, 26*, 2–4.

Hastings, A. C., Fadiman, J., & Gordon, J. S. (Eds.). (1980). *Health for the whole person: The complete guide to holistic medicine*. Boulder, CO: Westview Press.

Hiatt, H. H. (1989). *Medical lifeboat: Will there be room for you in the health care system?* New York: Harper & Row.

House, J. (1981). *Work, stress and social support*. Reading, MA: Addison-Wesley.

Illich, I. (1976). *Medical nemesis: The expropriation of health*. New York: Pantheon.

Institute of Medicine. (1976). *Controlling the supply of hospital beds*. Washington, DC: National Academy Press.

Institute of Medicine. (1981). *Health planning in the United States: Selected policy issues*. Washington, DC: National Academy of Sciences.

Jennett, B. (1986). *High technology medicine: Benefits and burdens*. Oxford, England: Oxford University Press.

Jonas, S. (1978). *Medical mystery: The training of doctors in the United States*. New York: W. W. Norton.

Kaslof, L. J. (Ed.). (1978). *Wholistic dimensions in healing: A resource guide*. Garden City, NY: Doubleday & Co.

Katz, A. (1981). Self-help and mutual aid: An emerging social movement? *The Annual Review of Sociology, 7*, 129–155.

Klass, D., & Shinners, B. (1982–83). Professional roles in a self-help group for the bereaved. *Omega: Journal of Death and Dying, 13*, 361–375.

Knowles, J. H. (1977). *Doing better and feeling worse: Health in the United States*. New York: W. W. Norton.

Kotelchuk, D. (Ed.). (1976). *Prognosis negative: Crisis in the health care system*. New York: Vintage Books.

Lackey, A. S., Burke, R., & Peterson, M. (1987). Health communities: The goal of community development. *Journal of the Community Development Society, 18*, 1–17.

Levy, L. (1976). Self-help groups: Types and psychological processes. *Journal of Applied Behavioral Science, 12*, 310–322.

Linn, L. S., & Lewis, C. E. (1979). Attitudes toward self care among practicing physicians. *Medical Care, 17*, 183–190.

Luthe, W., & Schultz, H. H. (1969). *Autogenic therapy*. New York: Grune & Stratton.

Mantell, J. (1983). Cancer patient visitor programs: A case for accountability. *Journal of Psychosocial Oncology, 1*, 45–58.

Mantell, J., Alexander, E., & Kleiman, M. (1976). Social work and self-help groups. *Health and Social Work, 1*, 86–100.

McClure, W. (1976). *Reducing excess hospital capacity*. Excelsior, MN: Interstudy.

McKeown, T. (1976). *The role of medicine: Dream mirage or nemesis?* London, England: Suffield Provincial Hospitals Trust.

McKinley, J., & McKinley, S. M. (1977). The questionable contribution of medical measure to the decline of mortality in the United States in the twentieth century. *Milbank Memorial Fund Quarterly, 55*, 405–438.

Minkler, M. (1985). Building supportive ties and sense of community among the inner-city elderly: The Tenderloin Senior Outreach project. *Health Education Quarterly, 12,* 303–314.

Naparstek, A., Biegel, O., & Spiro, H. (1982). *Neighborhood networks for humane mental health care.* New York: Plenum Press.

Navarro, V. (1986). *Crisis, health, and medicine: A social critique.* New York: Tavistock Publications.

Peirce, C. (1975). Recreation for the elderly: Activity participation at a senior citizen center. *The Gerontologist, 15,* 202–205.

Pelletier, K. R. (1979a). *Holistic medicine: From stress to optimum health.* New York: Delta Books.

Pelletier, K. R. (1979b). *Mind as healer, mind as slayer: A holistic approach to preventing stress disorders.* New York: Delta Books.

Piven, F. F., & Cloward, R. A. (1971). *Regulating the poor: The functions of public welfare.* New York: Vintage Books.

Reinharz, S. (1981). The paradox of professional involvement in alternative settings. *Journal of Alternative Human Services, 7,* 21–24.

Riessman, F. (1965). The "helper-therapy" principle. *Social Work, 10,* 27–32.

Ringler, K., Whitman, Gustafson, J., & Coleman, F. (1981). Technical advances in leading a cancer patient group. *International Journal of Group Psychotherapy, 31,* 329–344.

Roemer, M. (1961). Bed supply and hospital utilization: A natural experiment. *Hospitals, 35,* 36–42.

Rosenberg, P. (1984). Support groups: A special therapeutic entity. *Small Group Behavior, 7,* 173–186.

Ross, H. K. (1983). The neighborhood family: Community mental health for the elderly. *The Gerontologist, 23,* 243–247.

Ryan, R. S., & Travis, J. W. (1981). *Wellness workbook.* Berkeley, CA: Ten Speed Press.

Salmon, J. W., & Berliner, H. S. (1981). Alternative health movements: Challenges to health planning. In B. Checkoway (Ed.), *Citizens and health care: Participation and planning for social change.* New York: Pergamon Press.

Samuels, M., & Bennett, H. (1973). *The well body book.* New York: Random House.

Sidel, V. W., & Sidel, R. (1976). Beyond coping. *Social Policy, 7,* 67–69.

Stevens, R. (1989). *In sickness and in wealth: American hospitals in the twentieth century.* New York: Basic Books.

Taylor, R. C. R. (1982). The politics of prevention. *Social Policy, 13,* 32–41.

Toseland, R., & Hacker, L. (1982). Self-help groups and professional involvement. *Social Work, 27,* 341–347.

Travis, J. W. (1978). *Wellness workbook for helping professionals.* Mill Valley, CA: Wellness Associates.

U.S. Department of Health, Education, & Welfare. (1977). *Health of the disadvantaged chartbook.* Washington, DC: U.S. Government Printing Office.

U.S. Department of Health, Education, & Welfare. (1979a). *Health United States.* Washington, DC: U.S. Government Printing Office.

U.S. Department of Health, Education, & Welfare. (1979b). *Healthy people: The surgeon general's report on health promotion and disease prevention.* Washington, DC: U.S. Government Printing Office.

U.S. Department of Health, Education, & Welfare. (1980). *Health United States.* Washington, DC: U.S. Government Printing Office.

U.S. Department of Health, Education, & Welfare. (1981). *Health United States.* Washington, DC: U.S. Government Printing Office.

Walker, M. (1978). *Total health, the holistic alternative to traditional medicine.* New York: Everest House.

Wildavsky, A. (1977). Doing better and feeling worse: The political pathology of health policy. *Daedalus, 106,* 105–123.

Williamson, J. D., & Danaher, D. (1978). *Self care in health.* New York: Neal Watson Academic Publications.

Withorn, A. (1980, May–June). Helping ourselves: The limits and potential of self-help. *Radical America,* 1–9.

Wollert, R., & Barron, N. (1983). Avenues of collaboration. In D. Pancoast, P. Parker, & C. Froland (Eds.), *Social service delivery systems: Vol. 6. Rediscovering self-help: Its role in social care.* Beverly Hills, CA: Sage.

World Health Organization. (1984). *Health promotion: A discussion document on the concept and principles.* Copenhagen, Denmark: WHO Regional Office for Europe.

World Health Organization. (1986). *Ottawa Charter for Health Promotion.* Ottawa, Ontario, Canada: Author.

Yoak, M., & Chesler, M. (1985). Alternative professional roles in health care delivery: Leadership patterns in self-help groups. *Journal of Applied Behavioral Science, 21,* 427–444.

Zawadski, R. T., & Ansak, M. L. (1983). Consolidating community-based long-term care: Early returns from the On Lok Demonstration. *The Gerontologist, 23,* 364–369.

16

THE "DANGERS" OF SELF-HELP GROUPS
Understanding and Challenging Professionals' Views

MARK A. CHESLER

Professionals are often reluctant to trust self-help groups to operate independently, that is, without the guidance and control of professionals. As a result, some members of self-help groups and scholars believe that professionals create subtle barriers to autonomous operations of groups. This chapter explores the dangers that professionals perceive to be associated with self-help groups, highlights the key issues in local group-staff interactions and more broadly in professional-client relationships, and discusses the ways in which professionals and members of self-help groups can collaborate more effectively.

DEFINING SELF-HELP

The literature on self-help groups is complex and often confusing. Although it is often optimistic and enthusiastic, it is full of pros and cons and arguments about the degree of universal or particular utility attributed to self-help groups and processes. The professional literature, moreover, often articulates a series of cautions and dangers that may accompany autonomous self-help activities.

Efforts to define the phenomenon of self-help typically center on informal organizations, composed of and led by people who are suffering from the same condition or situation. In self-help groups, people do "for" and "with" one another, generating an alternative to a reliance only on professional expertise and guidance. Although this definition is standard, the literature often fails to recognize important distinctions; thus, "support groups," "mutual support," "group discussions," "group counseling," and "peer support," often are used interchangeably and carelessly (Killilea, 1976). One has to read carefully to discover which variety of self-help or mutual support is being discussed in any given article.

The core structural distinction among various types of groups concerns the appropriate bases of knowledge and authority for leading self-help groups and processes. Some scholars and practitioners consider professional expertise to be the most effective grounding for group leadership, while others emphasize the experiential wisdom of lay leadership. Searching discussions of the differences between these knowledge bases and the differential authority they convey are contained in Borkman (1976), Klass and Shinners (1982–83), and Reinharz (1981). Partly on this basis, Rosenberg (1984, p. 183) distinguished self-help groups in which the leader's "experience with the problem usually constitutes the authority necessary to lead the group" from support groups in which "authority for leadership emanates from expertise and training in groups or human development." In like fashion, Powell (1985) contrasted "hybrid" self-help groups with "autonomous" ones: the hybrid self-help group is sponsored or supervised by professionals, while the autonomous group is led by people with the condition that causes them to get together. Mellor, Rzetelny, and Hudis (1984, p. 98) created a continuum for categorizing groups on this dimension that extends from the "traditional structured professionally led group" to the "pure self-help group with no professional leader."

A second important distinction stems from the different goals and underlying functions or activities of groups. Thus, Cordoba, Shear, Fobair, and Hall (1984) discussed the differences among self-help, education/discussion, counseling/therapy, and social advocacy groups. These functions may cut across leadership patterns, but they also may be the bases for the choice of professional or lay leaders. For instance, professional leadership is most likely to occur in groups oriented to counseling/therapy and least likely in self-help or social advocacy groups. Killilea (1976) argued that self-help and advocacy groups utilize a "therapeutic process" that is different from traditional psychotherapy and that these different processes require and utilize different leadership expertise/experience and roles. As Yoak and Chesler (1985) demonstrated in their studies of groups for families of children with cancer, formal emotional support is more likely to occur in professionally led groups, while informal sharing and mutual education are more likely to occur in parent-led groups. The resolution of concerns about professional versus lay leadership or control thus is related to conceptions of what does and should occur in different types of self-help groups.

POTENTIAL "DANGERS"

Professional discussions of different types of support groups and of the pros and cons of self-help groups, in particular, often articulate a series of potential dangers or problems. These dangers or problems generally are based on assumptions about or experiences in autonomous organizations that do not rely on professional leaders and those that focus on activities other than supportive counseling or education. Professionals seldom see many dangers in counseling, education/discussion, or mutual-support groups that they run or guide or that have clear goals with which they agree. If some groups are and will continue to be led by members and relate effectively to the professional system of care, it is useful to understand the nature and basis of professionals' perceptions of the dangers of these groups.

Discussions in the professional literature sort these dangers into two main categories: dangers to members and dangers to professionals. To professionals (scholars or practitioners), the dangers that self-help groups pose to members (patients/clients and their families) seem to outweigh by far the dangers they pose to professionals. The dangers usually are identified in the apparent interest of protecting patients/clients and improving support and service; such altruism, of course, reflects the dominant features of a professional ideology of service.

One often-mentioned danger focuses on how lay-led discussions of deeply held feelings may upset some people in the group, escalating anger and anxiety and disrupting individuals' psychological defenses (Belle-Isle & Conradt, 1979; Binger et al., 1969; Heffron, 1975; Johnson & Stark, 1980; Kartha & Ertel, 1976; Ringler, Whitman,

Gustafson, & Coleman, 1981). The possibility that patients may "become terribly depressed, overwhelmingly anxious, even suicidal or psychotic as a result of talking together about having cancer" (Ringler et al., 1981, p. 331) is seen as an inappropriate increase of their already considerable burdens.

The literature also cautions that as fellow-patients or their relatives share information and feelings in an unguided fashion, they may spread medical misinformation and give rise to false fears or unrealistic hopes (Belle-Isle & Conradt, 1979; Deneke, 1983; Mantell, Alexander, & Kleiman, 1976). Peers and lay persons may also give psychosocial advice and in so doing blur the distinction between "therapy" and "therapeutic process" or between "support" and "counseling." As Claflin (1984, p. 125) noted, one root of professional resistance to self-help groups is the "prevalent assumption that peer support groups practice group therapy."

Some professionals have argued that over an extended period, groups may be "habit forming," act as a "crutch," and foster the members' dependence in ways that are inadvisable and inappropriate (Mantell et al., 1976; Toseland & Hacker, 1982). As autonomous groups seek to counter their dependence on professionals and professional orthodoxy, they may create an orthodoxy of their own. When they do so, professionals fear that the groups may place undue pressure on people to join and may urge deviants to conform to the group's ideology or practices regarding ways of thinking about or coping with their situation (Henry, 1978; King, 1980; Rosenberg, 1984).

Some of the typical dynamics of all groups, when they occur in this self-help context, also may be seen as dangerous. For instance, several writers (see, for example, King, 1980) warned of group factionalism or cliquishness and of groups' attempts to solve instrumental problems of management and maintenance that may draw attention away from individuals' personal and familial problems and concerns. In contrast to interpreting individuals' involvement with others in group tasks as a positive development, as a way of gaining distance from intrapsychic stress, this view emphasizes the dangers of escape or diversion from "real" psychological issues.

Many of these conceptions of "danger" are based on assumptions about what is different when a professional "guides" or "leads" a group and the ways in which professionals help groups avoid these problems. For instance, it is argued that professional training and experience leads to a form of expertise that is "objective"—based on scientific knowledge and a degree of distance from immediate and heated feelings (Borkman, 1976; Reinharz, 1981). The lack of objectivity of nonprofessional leaders is sometimes seen to lead to inadequate individual support or counseling, since poorly trained leaders may become overinvolved with peers' dilemmas or lack perspective on individuals' problems. Indeed, Rosenberg (1984, p. 183) argued that it also may lead an entire group to misconceptions of its role, to "heightened sensitivity about marginality," and to "self-fulfilling prophecies and/or delusions."

Commentaries about the differences between professionally led and member-led groups are not only often invidious, they usually are undertaken without sound comparative data. For instance, Lindamood, Wiley, Schmidt, and Rhein (1979, p. 1032) concluded their discussion of their roles in leading a group for bereaved parents with this gratuitous note: "Subsequent discussions with members of a local self-help bereavement group which had no professionals involved supported the conclusion that objective leadership was preferable." Whether the authors were right, they did not articulate the meaning of "objective" in this context or the advantages and disadvantages such a stance may engender among bereaved parents. Moreover, they did not analyze the potential costs, to themselves or to their clients, of their acknowledgment that their own objectivity "does not allow the full experience of the group process" (p. 1033). Finally, they provided no evidence for their conclusion about the local group without professionals, other than that it was based on some form of "subsequent discussion."

The second major reported danger of self-help groups—the danger to professionals—chiefly involves a concern about the development of an antiprofessional or antiintellectual stance among group members (Henry, 1978; Mantell et al., 1976; Rodolfa & Hungerford, 1982; Rosenberg, 1984; Toseland & Hacker, 1982). This stance is seen as working not only to the disadvantage of clients, in that clients do not avail themselves of the necessary or appropriate services (Deneke, 1983), but to the disadvantage of professionals, who encounter resistance to their services. Other forms of antiprofessionalism that are anticipated are the pain and anger that clients direct toward professionals (Ringler et al., 1981) and the clients' direct challenges of the relevance of professionals' expertise and authority (Mantell, 1983; Wollert, Knight, & Levy, 1984).

Still another danger is seen to arise when professionals seek to maintain their roles or the stability of the institutions with which they are involved. For instance, Mantell (1983, p. 47) suggested that some professionals fear that "lay people who adopt professional activities will squeeze professionals out of their jobs." In a somewhat different vein, Silverman and Smith (1984) noted that in a mutual-help group for physically disabled people, a dissatisfied patient was informed that "she could choose her physician, and was not obligated to stay in the clinic. Members gave her the names of several physicians who had worked out well for people with similar problems" (p. 85). The fear that interaction among patients will lead to less of a need for professional services or even to a loss of patients is cited often as a basis of professionals' reluctance to refer people to cancer support groups (Cordoba et al., 1984, pp. 28–29). As an antidote to these fears, the Leukemia Society of America's guidelines for professional facilitators of cancer support groups takes pains to point out that the society is "a neutral organization and does not support one institution in the community over another" (*Family Support Group Guidelines*, undated, p. 10).

Some authors worry about even the positive things that appear to occur as a function of autonomous self-help group activities. For instance, after reporting some of the positive activities in which members engaged in a preventive therapy group they ran for parents of ill children (collecting blood for accident victims, sending cookies to American soldiers in Vietnam, and participating in church functions), Knapp and Hansen (1973, p. 73) noted, "Underlying all these efforts was a need to help others, and do good, perhaps in the hope that it might save their child." However, Knapp and Hansen provided no evidence that the parents' actions were based on this self-interest. Was the hope of saving their children *really* the reason for their involvement and good works? Could it not have been simply a desire to help others and do good? Concerns about danger may lead some professional observers unwittingly to convert positive outcomes and processes into less noble and even negative ones. Riessman (1965) and Dory and Riessman (1982) offered more positive and altruistic interpretations of the motivations of people in crisis in discussing the "helper-therapy" principle that often operates in self-help groups. They argued that one receives benefits from giving to others. In sharing resources, one may learn, grow, develop positive self-esteem and insight, find that one is not totally bereft, and discover spare resources to offer others.

The professional role, as well as clients' activities that may encroach on this role, often are constrained by rules and norms about appropriate behavior in a peer or mutual support group. Chief among these, for professionals, is the need to avoid providing medical advice and therapy. For instance, the Leukemia Society of America's *Family Support Group Guidelines* (undated, p. 8) state explicitly that "a family support group does not provide medical care, medical treatment, medical advice or psychotherapy." What is most interesting about these warnings is that they often are violated in practice: They simply do not make sense in the reality of an informal group setting. People who discuss their common problems *do* give and get medical advice; it is one of the most important things that people share with one another. Although psychotherapy may be performed only by a professional with special training and formal credentials, peers who care for one another, who listen, talk, hug, and cry together, undoubtedly are involved in a therapeutic process if not in "therapy." Unfortunately, a definition of therapy is not offered in most of these discussions—simply the warning that it should not be provided by lay persons. Such unclarity and confusion regarding the reality of interpersonal and group experience suggests that the primary reasons such prohibitions are made may have less to do with meaningful statements about the welfare of clients/patients or with real-life experience than with concerns about protection from malpractice suits, from the resistance of physicians to unwarranted intervention with "their" patients, and from the desire to pacify the notions of professional interest groups about their appropriate "turf." These are potent issues and real dangers for many professionals, but to disguise them as a concern for the welfare of clients/patients further mystifies professional-client interactions.

Given the paucity of systematic empirical research on these issues or with these groups, the extent to which any or all these dangers actually exist is still unclear. It is known, however, that many scholars and professionals perceive these potential dangers to exist. The following sections report on the author's study of the nature and meaning of this professional phenomenon. Fruitful inquiry must explore the systems of meaning that professionals construct with regard to self-help groups and their associated dangers and the ideologies or interests (explicit or implicit) that underlie these interpretations. Such systems of meaning shape attitudes and behaviors and provide the frameworks within which professionals help clients/patients and their families make sense of their experiences and their interactions with the medical care system. The focus on the discovery of ideologies and interests, rather than on the test of a priori conceptions or theories, led the author to use a grounded-theory approach to the study of these issues (Glaser & Strauss, 1967). His derivation of inductive theory to explain these systems of meaning occurred after the systems were discovered and elaborated.

METHOD

The data reported here were gathered and analyzed by the author and his colleagues within the framework of qualitative research procedures conducted in an inductive (nonpositivist or non-hypothetico-deductive) framework. The research was undertaken as part of a larger study of the organization and operation of self-help groups for families of children with cancer (Yoak & Chesler, 1985). Personal interviews were conducted on site with 63 professionals (10 physicians, 21 nurses, 23 social workers, and 9 "others") who worked closely with 35 of these local groups; some groups had no professional working closely with them while others had several. Since the health care professionals were already working in some way with mutual support and self-help groups for parents of children with cancer, one could expect them to be sympathetic to these groups and to the potential for collaboration, perhaps more so than a random or representative sample of health care professionals.

The respondents were asked three standard questions: (1) "Some professionals say that self-help groups can be dangerous: Have you ever heard that stated?" (2) "Have you seen evidence in the local group of such dangers actually occurring?" (3) "What do professionals mean when they talk about the dangers of self-help groups?" The first and third questions do not necessarily focus on the individual respondents' personal views. Since the respondents were asked to report others' views, the researchers assumed that the questions elicited descriptions and analyses of a professional ideology, of beliefs associated with a set of roles. Although all 63 respondents answered Questions 1 and 2, only 48 responded to Question 3.

The first two questions required fairly straightforward "yes-no" answers. To analyze the answers to the third question, the researchers carefully read the transcripts of the interviews with the respondents and underlined all comments naming or related to specific dangers. Then they abstracted these key phrases from the text and organized them into clusters of phrases that seemed to have similar underlying meaning. Several variations of this clustering or coding procedure were utilized, following the "method of constant comparison" articulated by Glaser and Strauss (1967) and Glaser (1978). Finally, 10 clusters were established, and repeated coding by independent observers verified their reliability (for a fuller description of this coding procedure and the set of methods used to analyze this qualitative data set, see Chesler, 1987).

RESULTS AND DISCUSSION

Fifty-seven of the professionals interviewed reported that they had heard that there were dangers associated with self-help groups, but only 15 reported that they actually had seen evidence of such dangers in groups that they worked with or knew about. The fact that the respondents were already working with mutual-support groups or self-help groups may have influenced the low likelihood of their personally experiencing serious dangers; thus, the small number of actual dangers reported may be unrepresentative of what may be seen or felt by a more representative sample of professionals. The same sample bias may have had an impact on these professionals' reports of what they had heard about groups. Perhaps these supporters or advocates of self-help groups emphasized their own marginality in overstating the degree to which their peers have talked about the "dangers," thus ennobling their sacrifices or risks in working with such groups.

However, the dramatic difference between expectations and perceptions has been verified in other accounts of professionals' experiences with self-help groups. For instance, Black and Drackman (1985) reported that 37 percent of the social workers they studied in large hospitals rarely or never referred medical and psychiatric patients to self-help groups; however, the 63 percent who did make referrals reported no harmful outcomes. If this contrast between ideology or assumption and experience is sustained, it is important for several reasons. First, the high prevalence of "knowledge" about the dangers of self-help groups suggests that perceived dangers are not haphazard or trivial; they appear to be part of the belief system associated with a professional role and status. Whether they are learned on the job (from discussions with peers) or as part of preprofessional socialization is impossible to tell from these data, but both possibilities make sense and are mutually consistent. Second, the low prevalence of dangers actually encountered or experienced suggests that self-help groups, at least as far as most of these professionals are concerned, really are not dangerous, or at least not often dangerous. The difference between the number of professionals who "heard about" the dangers ($n = 57$) and the number who "experienced" them ($n = 15$) emphasizes the importance of considering that the roots of professionals' beliefs about self-help groups are in their ideology, rather than in their experience. Such an ideology has an impact on professionals' behavior (and perhaps on clients/patients' and parents' as well), regardless of its congruence with first-hand experiences.

What is the content of this ideology? The various professionals provided a total of 76 comments about the specific dangers they thought that professionals associate with self-help groups. Table 16-1 organizes these comments into 10 clusters of dangers and presents the incidence of each reported danger. Clusters 1, 2, 3, 4, and 5 focus on the dangers that may accrue to parents/members and clusters 6, 7, 8, 9, and 10 focus on dangers that may accrue to professionals who work with these groups. Although this division is undoubtedly arbitrary with regard to some individual comments, it captures the contrasting perceptions.

Table 16-1

Frequency of Reported Dangers of Self-Help Groups

DANGER CLUSTER	FREQUENCY
Dangers to Parents	
1. Create emotional problems for parents	15
2. Parents learn/know too much	11
3. Spread misinformation	8
4. Parents act like professionals	4
5. Group goals and objectives	1
Dangers to Professionals	
6. Challenge the authority of professionals	17
7. Take over professionals' job (social work)	6
8. Transfer doctors or increase physicians' competition	6
9. Question medical authority/judgment	6
10. Emotional attacks on professionals	2

DANGER TO PARENTS/MEMBERS

Among the dangers that professionals see as potentially harmful for members, the possibility that self-help groups may create or escalate emotional problems for parents (cluster 1) is often anticipated in the literature. The respondents' comments focused on parents' release of their emotions in the group setting and on the lack of professional control or direction over this process. Because some parents are overwhelmed by their feelings or their identification with others, they may experience pain and distress.

In general, professionals argue that parents of children with cancer experience enough distress and that it is not advisable (indeed, it even may be dangerous) for them to be involved deeply with others who are so distressed. Some comments in this cluster included the following:

> Doctors discouraged parents from talking with one another because they would intensify problems.

> Groups also cause unnecessary depression and pain.

> Parents with pathology may have that pathology supported by others who don't know how to handle it.

Groups may be dangerous if overreactive parents work up other parents.

Physicians, social workers, and agency executives often refer to this issue as a major reason why trained people ought to lead and direct groups: Untrained leaders may do damage or permit damage to escalate. But untrained people help each other all the time. Moreover, parents have often reported to the author that they are not concerned about this danger. Many say that nothing can happen in a group that is any worse than what has already happened; the information that their child has cancer is worse than anything else, so why worry about the group process?

The knowledge base of leaders of self-help groups becomes an issue in professionals' concern (cluster 3) that discussions among parents may impart misinformation and spread false ideas. Consistent with the literature, professionals fear that sharing ignorance multiplies ignorance and may lead to rumors that encourage false hopes or undermine trust in the medical system. Misunderstandings also may promote confusion. One of the primary stresses of being a parent of a child with cancer involves dealing with large amounts of new information about the diagnosis, treatment, and prognosis of the disease and about the medical system itself (Chesler & Barbarin, 1987). If meetings with other parents provide misinformation, as opposed to information, they are likely to magnify these informational or intellectual stresses. Some comments in this cluster were these:

> There is suspicion they are going to be priming the pump with pathological information.

> Groups can sometimes generate misinformation.

> Doctors don't want a parent giving out misinformation.

A different cluster involving the knowledge base of self-help groups focuses on the danger that parents may learn too much, that is, become too well informed (cluster 2). In this regard, professionals suggest that when parents compare notes and information, they may reach a level of expertise that rivals (or appears to rival) that of professionals. Thus, they may resist professional direction without extensive and time-consuming explanations. This concern was not anticipated in the literature, but is reflected in the following comments:

> Professionals have fears about the sharing/comparing of information.

> _____

> Doctors are worried that parents will get too educated.

> _____

> Professionals are afraid that parents will compare notes, compare protocols, and learn of experiments.

The concern that parents will act like professionals (cluster 4) focuses on parents helping each other in ways that appear to be therapeutic in orientation and intent. When parents attempt things that professionals assume are beyond their skill and training, activities that are normally reserved for professionals, they may be seen as endangering themselves and others, as these comments illustrate:

> Groups may be dangerous if members do things beyond their skill and training.

> _____

> Professionals feel that parents in a group are practicing medicine.

DANGER TO PROFESSIONALS

Among the dangers that appear to threaten professionals' status and role, challenges to their authority (cluster 6) is the single most common example. This cluster focuses on the ways in which peer support may reduce parents' dependence on professionals and when professionals fail to control or guide the activities of parent groups, the power of their role may be compromised. In addition, some parent groups may go outside the normal staff channels to achieve their objectives, perhaps mobilizing the community to pressure the hospital to alter its patterns of service delivery. Examples from this cluster included these comments:

> Professionals fear being challenged.

> _____

> Professionals are concerned with retaining control.

> _____

Doctors sometimes feel threatened by a group because parents gain momentum and power; through the group, parent power increases.

When parents provide important resources to one another, they may be seen as taking over the professionals' role (cluster 7), reducing the necessity for staff involvement. One danger of this competition is replacement; if parents can do what a social worker can do, perhaps physicians will conclude that there is no need for a paid social worker on staff. As one respondent put it, "Social workers are afraid someone is going to step on their space."

A somewhat different danger is involved when parent groups are seen as encouraging the kind of information sharing that escalates competition among physicians, especially competition for patients (cluster 8). It is not a trivial matter for physicians to maintain a patient load that is adequate to guarantee a stable income for the hospital unit, to warrant outlays for new and expensive equipment, or to justify additional staff positions. Moreover, many physicians fear that patients who transfer to other physicians or other forms of treatment will compromise their reputation in the community; they also are concerned that the children may get a less adequate form of care. For example, consider the following comments:

Staff fears parents will encourage each other to use nonconventional medicine.

_____

Groups make doctors struggle to maintain their practice. Patients are money; they may go elsewhere for care.

_____

Local doctors are afraid that the group will give information about other medical centers and that parents may go comparison shopping for doctors.

Another threat arises when professionals fear that parent groups encourage the questioning of medical authority and judgment (cluster 9). The concern again is with knowledge that may challenge professionals' authority and omniscience, especially in an area in which professionals know that uncertainty is the rule. Some argue that for physicians and other staff members to take and proscribe action in an area of great uncertainty, they must have the unquestioned compliance of patients and the patients' families. The practice of medicine in a situation in which the stakes are so high (the life and death of children) often is thought to be difficult enough without parents being encouraged to ask lots of (inappropriate and unnecessary) questions, as these comments illustrate:

> Groups can promote too many questions.

> _____

> Doctors may have to take more time to answer questions . . . they become threatened by questioning.

> _____

> Groups generate questioning of doctor's judgment.

Finally, some professionals mention parents' emotionally inappropriate attacks on them as a potential danger (cluster 10). The primary concern is that when parents are under great stress, their pain or anger may become inflamed by group discussions and may be displaced onto the professionals. Some comments reflecting this danger were these:

> Professionals are worried about the displacement of anger onto them.

> _____

> Groups generate unwarranted criticism of professionals.

This last category is much more prominent in the literature than it was in this sample. One explanation is that the coding process generated a clear distinction between concern about emotional attacks on professionals and concern about challenges to professionals' power and authority, a distinction that has not been clearly made in the literature. Professionals' concerns about emotional attacks were much less prominent in this sample than were concerns about challenges to their authority.

THREATS TO PROFESSIONALS' TRIPLE MONOPOLY

One theme that emerged from these statements and clusters of statements is professionals' concern about authority and control and their perception that autonomous parent self-help activities (and groups) may threaten this authority and control. Authority and control of what? Professionals' administration of various aspects of health and medical care is rooted in the right and power to exercise control of access to the knowledge base on which care is based, control of practice or service in delivering medical and psychosocial care, and control of the moral value frame that suggests how people should behave when they are ill or in contact with illness and the health care system. Threats to this triple monopoly may be the fundamental theme that underlies the various perceptions of danger.

Several scholars (Freidson, 1970; Parsons, 1951; Reiff, 1974) have indicated the extent to which special training and experience are required for access to a professional role and status. Certification in a specialized base of academic and applied knowledge is an essential ingredient of a profession and a necessary basis for according professionals special rights and privileges in a democratic society. Not everyone can get that knowledge and the certification that rests on it, and those who do get them have a virtual monopoly on the assumed expertise. Behavior that challenges the monopoly of knowledge that undergirds the profession of medicine challenges the very basis of the profession, and thus diminishes the power of the professional (Reiff, 1974). Perhaps one root of the perceived danger of self-help groups to professionals is that when parents become well informed, professionals may no longer have (or be seen as having) that edge on expertise and the status and control that accompany it.

Not only is the effective care of patients or clients at stake here, so is the privileged social position of the professional. As Freidson (1970) noted, the professional monopoly to apply medical knowledge and technical expertise often leaks into social and interpersonal status and power. Several perceived dangers reflect professionals' fears regarding ways in which activities of self-help groups may challenge their monopoly of knowledge: clusters 2, 3, and 9. Parents who learn a lot (too much) and who question medical authority are asserting their knowledge base to professionals, and some professionals clearly feel that an independent patient/parent knowledge base threatens them. Concern about parental misinformation further reflects the interpretation that a professional monopoly is necessary to contain the spread of inappropriate knowledge. However vital professional knowledge is to the structure of a profession, and indeed to the effective care of ill children, the preservation of a monopoly, per se, may create problems for autonomous self-help groups.

Direct interviews with parents of children with cancer indicate that highly educated parents report "problems" with the medical staff who serve their children more often than do less educated parents (Chesler & Barbarin, 1984). Perhaps highly educated parents represent a threat to professionals because they know almost as much as the professionals do or because they understand the uncertain knowledge base on which much social work practice and even some medicine rests. Highly educated parents also may be more active copers; they may be more assertive or aggressive and make more demands and even criticisms of professionals. As support groups educate parents, parents may get more active; as parents become more active, they may violate the passive role of patient and become irritants to a smooth-running system. This reasoning certainly links the dangers of information, misinformation, and questioning to that of challenging professionals.

A monopoly of service or practice is another essential ingredient of a profession. If anyone can practice medicine or psychological therapy, why should any practitioner be accorded special rights, pay, and privileges? Moreover, if anyone can practice such arts, how can an unwary or uninformed public be protected against ignorant practitioners, charlatans, quacks, and fakers? In operation, the requirement that professionals have credentials and be certified by the state is the means by which a monopoly of practice is guaranteed—both to the needy public and to the practitioner who has undergone lengthy and expensive training and preparation. Several perceived dangers reflect the concern of professionals about a challenge to their control of practice/service (clusters 4, 6, 7, and 8). A concern about challenges to the power of professionals clearly reflects resistance to the intrusion of patients or parents or undue influence on a role that professionals believe they ought to define. Bliwise and Lieberman (1984, p. 227) supported this interpretation, noting that "service delivery is rarely controlled by the client" and that "self-help organizations are unique among help systems in that the client rather than the professional or an external agency has primary responsibility for care."

Concern about the power to control and maintain accountability over the delivery of services is escalated when professionals perceive that parents are beginning not only to challenge their authority, but to take over their jobs and act as professionals. Claflin

(1984, p. 126) pointed out that it is difficult for professionals to "share treatment responsibilities with patients or patient families." If parents begin to perform what are seen as professionals' jobs, their dependence on professionals is also decreased, which further reduces the professionals' authority. As Hasenfeld (1987) argued in a slightly different context, professionals and professional organizations seek to maintain their authority over clients/patients as a root basis of their general social power and status, often at high cost to their clients/patients.

Patients who "comparison shop" present a slightly different challenge to this service monopoly. Although they do not challenge the monopoly, per se, they do challenge an individual professional's ability to maintain competitive control over his or her service sector—to hold on to his or her clients/patients. This is no idle concern, in a time when federal cutbacks of funds, budget restrictions, and automation and computerization have reduced the resources for human services (LaVoie, 1983; Mantell, 1983). The fear that self-help groups may encourage members to try different health care systems and may encourage competition among physicians and psychosocial practitioners threatens some professionals' economic security.

The third monopoly that professionals often defend is the monopoly of moral values that permit them to define the behavior of clients/patients and the patient-professional relationship. This monopoly is neither as clear nor as firmly entrenched as the other two, but assumptions about medical competence and superior knowledge often are generalized into assumptions about superior values, lifestyles, and coping strategies (Featherstone, 1980). The authority to define and label appropriate and inappropriate coping behavior permits professionals to make (and often enforce) judgments about the moral inadequacy of clients who cope in ways that differ from those that professionals value. As Katz (1984, p. 233) noted, "If consumers do not conform to professional expectations or follow the requirements laid down by the service agency, they are thought to be resistant or refractory." And the promotion of resistant or refractory coping styles is often seen as dangerous—both to those who use them and to the good sense of the expert who "knows" how people should cope. The key here is "resistant" or "refractory," rather than "different"; the conversion of "different" coping styles or preferences for service into "inadequate" or "wrong" styles or preferences is the signal that moral judgments are being made.

Professional assumptions of a monopoly on these matters may not only be intolerant, they may create a "danger" for parents, especially if moral superiority is used (knowingly or unwittingly) as a screen for psychological self-defense. For instance, in a startlingly forthright article, Ringler et al. (1984) discussed their fears and perceptions of the dangers of self-help groups for cancer patients. They admitted that many of their fears were based more on their personal anxieties and defenses than on rational judgments about what went on in groups or what was good for parents. They articulated one of the intrapsychic bases of their fears as follows: "Under the guise of 'protecting the patients,' we were actually projecting our own terror at disfigurement, pain, loss of functioning, and death onto the group members . . . many of the group members were more than ready to look at those terrors" (p. 339). These professionals' moral judgments regarding what patients were or should be ready for differed from those of the patients. Instead of honestly exploring these differences or providing support for different styles, they sought to impose their judgments on patients by controlling the group's agenda and process. Fortunately, they were alert to their attempt, learned from their erroneous judgment, and admitted it—in print! Judgments that represent controls over moral choice are even more dangerous when they are rooted in demographic features that are common to professionals: white racial groupings, male-dominated medical systems or female-dominated psychosocial systems, and middle- and upper-middle-class backgrounds. Then the choices made by members of racial minority groups (women or men, depending on the setting) and less affluent patients and their families are especially unlikely to be tolerated or supported.

IMPROVING COLLABORATION BETWEEN PROFESSIONALS AND LAY LEADERS

Do "real" dangers exist in the operation of self-help and support groups? Certainly they do, and some evaluations of the operations and effects of self-help groups verify precisely the concerns expressed by the professionals interviewed in the study. Certainly self-help groups are dangerous if they humiliate or depress members; if they restrict access to reliable medical care; if they create unthinking conformity to others' styles; if they inappropriately give vent to neurotic rage; if they unwisely escalate parents' fears and fantasies; and if, without cause, they unravel the fragile thread of hope and trust that parents have for their children's physician. However, there is no evidence, here or elsewhere in the literature, that such dangers are real and commonplace. Moreover, there is no evidence that these or other dangers are more likely to occur in an autonomous or lay-led self-help group than in a professionally run or supervised support group. There are some real dangers in all forms of medical and social support, whether conducted on a voluntary or statutory basis, by professionals or lay persons.

It also is clear from these data that professionals' views of the dangers of autonomous parent self-help and support groups more often occur in the abstract than in practice. Furthermore, many of the dangers that professionals encounter represent threats to their own established ways of thinking and acting as health care professionals. Some of these threats to established traditions and historic patterns of control are overtly acknowledged as such; others, however, are cast in the language of protecting parents from themselves.

Finally, these assumptions about dangers are neither accidental nor individualistic; they are rooted in the structure and culture of the health care professions—in the monopolistic organization of professional knowledge, practice, and moral judgment. They are especially likely to occur in the organized operations of highly complex bureaucratic and technical health care systems, such as those involving children with cancer and people with other serious and chronic illnesses. In these circumstances, the high stakes of life-and-death issues and the highly sophisticated knowledge/practice base that is required seem to call for more authority to be exercised by experts and more dependent compliance solicited or demanded from patients and their families. If, as Katz (1984, p. 234) noted, self-help groups often have the "corollary (social) benefit of reducing monopolistic social controls by professionals," it is clear why this "benefit" is often seen by professionals as a danger or as underlying other specific dangers.

To a certain extent, professionals' exaggerated anticipation of specific dangers can be demythologized and disaggregated. Then patients/parents and other self-help group members can educate professionals about the real needs and perceptions of members and about the actual activities of self-help groups. By anticipating professionals' concerns, both with regard to professionals' and their own welfare, they may help reduce fears about emotional volatility and the spread of misinformation (clusters 1, 2, 3, and 10). The efforts of members of self-help groups to educate professionals may involve direct dialogue and a sharing of experience, but it may also take the form of increasing their direct exposure to the operations and activities of self-help groups. Many professionals are unsure of their welcome in patient/family meetings, and others are uncertain of the roles they should play if they do attend. Members can clarify this confusion by explicitly inviting professionals to meetings, or to specific meetings if that is seen as more appropriate. Moreover, professionals can be invited to perform specific tasks and roles, such as giving a talk, leading a discussion, or commenting on the operations of the hospital. In this way, the group can expand its linkages to and liaison with the hospital staff and can engender collaboration in ways that are least threatening and most beneficial to all parties. When self-help groups are able to structure the role that professionals will play in a group, they are helping to design effective collaboration and challenge some of the fears associated with concerns about their goals, turf, and roles (clusters 4, 5, 6, and 7).

Knowledgeable professionals also have a responsibility to educate or reeducate themselves and their peers and to share their actual experiences in ways that help counter the dominant ideology that emphasizes challenges to professional authority, emotional safety, and job security (clusters 5, 6, 7, and 9). Professionals with a collaborative history can go beyond education to advocate for the self-help group with other staff members. Relevant actions may include establishing special staff meetings in which members of a self-help group share what they do and the group's literature with the professionals, create linkages between the group and professionals in the local community, notify new patients of the existence and positive value of the group as a source of help and support, ease the group's effort to gain resources from the medical system (such as rooms and facilities), and convince other staff members of the group's role in a plural service delivery system. In more than one case, staff members who have collaborated with a local self-help group have overtly or covertly gathered lists of clinic patients and shared them with the group, thereby expanding the group's list of potential members.

None of these collaborative options are one-time events; they are best understood as ongoing exchanges that reshape the traditional professional role. Instead of exercising monopolistic leadership, professionals should provide supportive and facilitative coleadership or assistantship with groups of patients and act as advocates with other professionals. Borman (1979, p. 29) suggested that this reshaping involves a shift in the paradigm of professional roles, away "from a principal and solo role to a collaborative one."

Unfortunately, efforts to educate professionals and to share information with them may not always be effective, especially if the roots of professionals' perceptions of the dangers of self-help groups are deeply entrenched in the authority structure and knowledge base of the health care system. Under such circumstances, such efforts may be resisted by the power of the prevailing ideology and the monopolistic self-interests it serves. Then, of course, more challenging or confrontive options must be explored.

The most optimistic scenario for maximum education or reeducation and minimal resistance leads to a hope that changes in professional attitudes and behavior regarding self-help groups can occur and will generate other changes in the organization of staff roles and medical care itself. These changes may encourage nonmonopolistic forms of interaction between professionals and patients/parents—forms that adopt more symmetrical relationships for sharing authority, knowledge, and expertise.

Self-help groups have helped some local medical systems and professionals adopt new and more powerful patterns of shared authority between patients/families and providers, a greater exchange of knowledge and expertise, more mutual problem solving with regard to health care practices, increased pluralism with respect to patterns of family coping, and expansion of patient-to-patient support programs (Chesler, unpublished data base). These innovations are part of a new generation of practices that recognize and expand patient-provider collaboration in medical care. Parents and professionals need to know more about them and about more of them.

REFERENCES

Belle-Isle, J., & Conradt, B. (1979). Report of a discussion group for parents of children with leukemia. *Maternal-Child Nursing Journal, 8*(1), 49–58.

Binger, C., Albin, A., Feuerstein, R., Kushner, J., Zoger, S., & Mikelsen, C. (1969). Childhood leukemia: Emotional impact on patient and family. *New England Journal of Medicine, 280,* 414–418.

Black, R., & Drackman, D. (1985). Hospital social workers and self-help groups. *Health and Social Work, 10,* 95–103.

Bliwise, N., & Lieberman, M. (1984). From professional help to self-help: An evaluation of therapeutic groups for the elderly. In A. Gartner & F. Riessman (Eds.), *The self-help revolution.* New York: Human Sciences Press.

Borkman, T. (1976). Experiential knowledge: A new concept for the analysis of self-help groups. *Social Service Review, 50,* 445–456.

Borman, L. (1979). Characteristics of development and growth. In M. Lieberman & R. Borman (Eds.), *Self-help groups for coping with crisis.* San Francisco: Jossey-Bass.

Chesler, M. (1987). *Professional views of the dangers of self-help groups: Explicating the steps in a qualitative analysis of interview data* (Working Paper No. 345). Ann Arbor Center for Research on Social Organization, University of Michigan.

Chesler, M., & Barbarin, O. (1984). Relating to the medical staff: How parents of children with cancer see the issues. *Health and Social Work, 9*(1), 49–65.

Chesler, M., & Barbarin, O. (1987). *Childhood cancer and the family.* New York: Brunner/Mazel.

Claflin, B. (1984). Mutual support groups in a suburban setting: The opportunities, the challenges. In A. Gartner & F. Riessman (Eds.), *The self-help revolution.* New York: Human Sciences Press.

Cordoba, C., Shear, M., Fobair, P., & Hall, J. (1984). *Cancer support groups.* San Francisco: American Cancer Society–California Division.

Deneke, C. (1983). How professionals view self-help. In D. Pancoast, P. Parker, & C. Froland (Eds.), *Rediscovering self-help: Its role in social care.* Beverly Hills, CA: Sage.

Dory, F., & Riessman, F. (1982). Training professionals in organizing self-help groups. *Citizen Participation, 3*(3), 27–28.

Family support group guidelines. (undated). New York: Leukemia Society of America.

Featherstone, H. (1980). *A difference in the family.* New York: Basic Books.

Freidson, E. (1970). *Professional dominance.* Chicago: Aldine.

Glaser, B. (1978). *Theoretical sensitivity: Advances in the methodology of grounded theory.* Mill Valley, CA: Sociology Press.

Glaser, B., & Strauss, A. (1967). *The discovery of grounded theory.* Chicago: Aldine.

Hasenfeld, Y. (1987). Power in social work practice. *Social Service Review, 61,* 469–483.

Heffron, W. (1975). Group therapy sessions as part of treatment of children with cancer. In C. Pockedly (Ed.), *Clinical management of cancer in children.* Acton, MA: Science Group.

Henry, S. (1978). The dangers of self-help groups. *New Society, 22,* 654–656.

Johnson, E., & Stark, D. (1980). A group program for cancer patients and their family members in an acute care teaching hospital. *Social Work in Health Care, 5*(4), 335–349.

Kartha, M., & Ertel, I. (1976). Short-term group therapy for mothers of leukemic children. *Clinical Pediatrics, 15*, 803–806.

Katz, A. (1984). Self-help groups: An international perspective. In A. Gartner & F. Riessman (Eds.), *The self-help revolution*. New York: Human Sciences Press.

Killilea, M. (1976). Mutual help organizations: Interpretations in the literature. In G. Caplan & M. Killilea (Eds.), *Support systems and mutual help*. New York: Grune & Stratton.

King, C. (1980). The self-help/self-care concept. *Nurse Practitioner, 5*, 34–35, 39, 46.

Klass, D., & Shinners, B. (1982–83). Professional roles in a self-help group for the bereaved. *Omega: Journal of Death and Dying, 13*(4), 361–375.

Knapp, V., & Hansen, H. (1973). Helping the parents of children with leukemia. *Social Work, 18*, 70–75.

LaVoie, F. (1983). Citizen participation. In D. Pancoast, P. Parker, & C. Froland (Eds.), *Rediscovering self-help: Its role in social care*. Beverly Hills, CA: Sage.

Lindamood, M., Wiley, F., Schmidt, M., & Rhein, M. (1979). Groups for bereaved parents—How they can help. *Journal of Family Practice, 9*(6), 1027–1033.

Mantell, J. (1983). Cancer patient visitor programs: A case for accountability. *Journal of Psychosocial Oncology, 1*(1), 45–58.

Mantell, J., Alexander, E., & Kleiman, M. (1976). Social work and self-help groups. *Health and Social Work, 1*(1), 86–100.

Mellor, M., Rzetelny, H., & Hudis, I. (1984). Self-help groups for caregivers of the aged. In A. Gartner & F. Riessman (Eds.), *The self-help revolution*. New York: Human Sciences Press.

Parsons, T. (1951). *The social system*. Glencoe, IL: Free Press.

Powell, T. (1985). Improving the effectiveness of self-help. *Social Policy, 16*(2):22–29.

Reiff, R. (1974). The control of knowledge: The power of the helping professions. *Journal of Applied Behavioral Science, 10*(3), 451–461.

Reinharz, S. (1981). The paradox of professional involvement in alternative settings. *Journal of Alternative Human Services, 7*, 21–24.

Riessman, F. (1965). The "helper-therapy" principle. *Social Work, 10*(2), 27–32.

Ringler, K., Whitman, H., Gustafson, J., & Coleman, F. (1981). Technical advances in leading a cancer patient group. *International Journal of Group Psychotherapy, 31*(3), 329–344.

Rodolfa, E., & Hungerford, L. (1982). Self-help groups: A referral resource for professional therapists. *Professional Psychology, 13*(3), 345–353.

Rosenberg, P. (1984). Support groups: A special therapeutic entity. *Small Group Behavior, 15*(2), 173–186.

Silverman, P., & Smith, D. (1984). Helping in mutual help groups for the physically disabled. In A. Gartner & F. Riessman (Eds.), *The self-help revolution*. New York: Human Sciences Press.

Toseland, R., & Hacker, L. (1982). Self-help groups and professional involvement. *Social Work, 27*, 341–347.

Wollert, R., Knight, R., & Levy, L. (1984). Make Today Count: A collaboration model for professionals and self-help groups. In A. Gartner & F. Riessman (Eds.), *The self-help revolution*. New York: Human Sciences Press.

Yoak, M., & Chesler, M. (1985). Alternative professional roles in health care delivery: Leadership patterns in self-help groups. *Journal of Applied Behavioral Science, 21*(4), 427–444.

17

PROMISES TO KEEP WHEN EXPLORING SELF-HELP GROUPS

VICKI E. KAHL, PATRICIA E. ELLSWORTH, LAURA L. SANDERS, AND CATHERINE A. MURPHY

This chapter is devoted to encouraging you, the helping professional, to acquire first-hand knowledge by visiting self-help groups in your community. We are four graduate students at the University of Michigan School of Social Work who have a wide range of age and life experiences. For a class project, we visited a variety of self-help groups in and around Ann Arbor, Michigan. We addressed the project with enthusiasm and confidence and emerged from it with invaluable understanding and a few unsettling experiences that were more than we had bargained for.

We made mistakes: the kind of mistakes you make when you first approach unexplored territory, when you attempt to bridge the gap between professional treatment and self-help support. Going to the group meetings was more intimidating than we had anticipated. We were concerned about whether we would be welcome and, although we presented ourselves as observers, we were worried about being perceived as eavesdroppers. Once we got over these fears, we felt like explorers on an expedition into the unknown world of self-help.

On the basis of our experiences, we have developed the self-help explorer's "promises"—helpful hints that will prepare you for your journey, so you may sail a little more smoothly than we did through the sea of self-help. This analogy may seem silly, but if you read the community or announcements section of your local newspaper, you will find several or many self-help groups that focus on issues you may never have expected, depending on the size and setting of the community in which you practice or reside. For example, one day, 63 support groups were listed in the Community Calendar of the *Ann Arbor News*. These groups included the usual Alcoholics Anonymous (AA), Overeaters Anonymous, and Al-Anon groups, but also included Emotions Anonymous, Relationships Anonymous, the Recovering Nurses Support Group, Sex Addicts Anonymous, Alcoholics for Christ, Recovery Inc., Shoppers/Spenders Anonymous, the Anxiety Support Group, and on and on. These groups are truly a largely unexplored sea of resources for helping professionals. Together, they make up a movement—a network of people who need and want to give support for a multitude of human problems and concerns.

Begin your expedition by enhancing your awareness of the number and variety of self-help groups available in your community and do some reading on the subject. The self-help explorer's promises will help guide you on your voyage. They are based on our experience, and each promise is illustrated with actual examples from our expeditions. So read them, use them, and good luck in your own mission.

PROMISE 1

I promise to visit at least two groups related to my field of interest or clients' concerns and at least one that has relevance to a personal issue, problem, or concern.

Many helping professionals are skeptical—and understand-ably so—about referring their clients to self-help groups that they know nothing about. Therefore, it makes good sense to check out groups that are appropriate to your clients and to attend a few meetings of each. Pat and Vicki, who are in the field of clinical social work, made a point of visiting groups that serve the special needs of chronically mentally ill people. They found the self-help groups they visited to be invaluable resources for themselves and their clients and plan to continue an exchange relationship with the groups.

Pat observed a meeting of the Manic-Depressive/Depressive Association (MDDA) in Livonia, Michigan. She found that the meetings were helpful not only for clients but for professionals because of the variety of current literature on bipolar and unipolar disorders available at the meeting. In fact, she obtained some information on chemotherapy for bipolar disorders that she had been searching for for some time. As she noted,

> I was very impressed with MDDA of Metropolitan Detroit. The group was well organized and offered a wealth of information on unipolar and bipolar disorders, including diets, medication, and the latest research. I thought that this organization would benefit one of my clients and his family members. A few days after the meeting, I called a member whose name was listed on some of the literature distributed at the meeting to obtain a history of the organization for my research project. This member was unable to provide historical data but gave me the name of the person who had founded the chapter. The founder of the organization sent me information on MDDA's beginnings and a description of its current involvement at the national, state, and local levels. I discovered that a group of MDDA members were meeting each month in the large state hospital where I was completing my social work internship. This group publishes a monthly newsletter and was looking for volunteers to help with the newsletter. Volunteering to help with the newsletter gave me an opportunity to start building a relationship with the group.

Vicki attended a meeting of Recovery, Inc., one of the oldest self-help groups, established in 1937 by Abraham Low, a psychiatrist who advocated a self-help approach for "recovered mental patients." Pat attended Relatives, Inc., the group for relatives of former patients. They both agreed that Dr. Low's approach—a structured self-help program—although successful for many, was not for everyone; thus, they felt much more comfortable deciding which clients it was appropriate to refer to these groups after they observed them.

Pat and Vicki were welcomed into these groups as guests but were not allowed to participate actively in the group process. Recovery, Inc., and Relatives, Inc., generally welcome helping professionals as observers. They believe that helping professionals have something to learn from them; we also believed this to be the case.

Your visit to a personally significant group is of particular value because it brings you closer to the experience of your clients, who may also be visiting a self-help group for the first time. Attend this group as a participant, rather than as an observer, and involve yourself personally in the content of the meeting. Try to relate your feelings during this experience to how your clients may feel when attending a group for the first time. You may even find that you want to become a permanent member of the support group you choose. Catherine found the Ann Arbor Stroke Club to be helpful to her:

> I am in my early twenties, and my parents are in their late sixties. In February 1988, my father suffered a mild stroke. I was naturally concerned about him and wanted to learn all I could not only about the medical aspects of a stroke but about how a stroke affects victims and their families and how people cope with the deficits. What better way to gain this insight than to talk with people who have dealt with or are dealing with the effects of a stroke?
>
> I spoke with a wonderful older woman. She told me the group was open to persons who have had a stroke and to families and friends of that person. I explained why I was interested in attending the group and immediately felt the woman's compassion and understanding over the phone.
>
> The meeting went as well as I had anticipated. In attendance were victims of strokes and their spouses and children. I was introduced and given a chance to express my experiences. The members were emotionally supportive of me at a time when I was concerned about my father. The information they shared about strokes gave me a better understanding of my father's physical disabilities and the types of behavior that can result from a stroke. The experience was positive in all aspects, primarily because I not only gained information about a self-help group but was able to participate in the group as a member. The experience was much different from my experiences in those groups in which I just observed.

Pat attended an epilepsy self-help group. Although she has been seizure free for 10 years, her daughter suffers from seizure disorder. The members of the group greeted Pat in a positive and caring manner and shared their experience of epilepsy with her. The group's leader continues to call Pat to give her information on upcoming conferences and the like. As Pat noted,

> the meeting was held at a local church. Since I was a new member, all the members introduced themselves. I met Alice, a 39-year-old single woman who had suffered from seizures since age 3. Alice works but cannot drive herself to work. She attributed her peace of mind to her supportive family and to therapy. Richard, in his thirties, had suffered from seizures since age 8. Because of the severity of his seizures, he has been unable to hold a job. He is currently involved in a research project at the University of Michigan Hospital on new medications for seizures.
>
> The group shared information about the physicians they used, the medications they found worked best for them, and even hints on how to ride

"defensively" on the city buses (for example, you carry your purse in a paper bag disguised as groceries so your purse will not be stolen). I could understand why one woman in the group later confided to me that the group had been a "lifesaver" for her. I was made to feel at home in this group and I plan to recommend it to my family members as well as my clients.

PROMISE 2

If possible, I promise to notify the group leader that I plan to attend a specific meeting, rather than just show up.

Although the repeated unanswered phone calls and numerous phone-machine messages can be frustrating, be persistent in reaching the contact person for the self-help group you plan to visit. Whether you attend as a participant or as an observer, showing up unannounced and unprepared is anxiety producing or, worse yet, could be perceived as rude. Catherine, for example, could not get in touch with the Relationships Anonymous contact person, so she just showed up, intending only to observe. However, at the meeting, she did not have the heart to tell the group members she was not suffering from a failing relationship, so she lied:

I planned to call to find the time, date, and place of the meeting and to acknowledge that I wanted only to observe the group, not to participate as a member. However, I could reach only the host church's answering machine, welcoming all to the next meeting. The closing remark was "Welcome, friends." It sounded OK, so I jotted down the directions and marked my calendar.

On the day of the meeting, I found the place and slipped in practically unnoticed, thinking that I could sit on the outskirts of the group and just listen. After an opening prayer, however, the group leader asked all newcomers to raise their hands. Not sure what to do, I raised my hand, along with seven other people. The group leader had a great idea. "Let's have the new attendees meet with me, so we can get acquainted with one another!" Before I knew it, I was being herded to a nearby picnic table with no time to explain my intentions of merely observing the group. I felt like bolting in the other direction, but things were moving so fast, I just followed the other people.

The group leader started by saying, "Hello, my name is . . . " and the whole group (except me, of course, because I had no idea of what was going on) chimed back in unison, "Hello, . . ." The leader talked for ten minutes; when he finished, the group chimed in, "Thank you, . . ." Then each person spoke. All I could think about was, "What am I going to say when it is my turn?" I tried to concentrate on what people were saying, but the pounding of my heart was all I could hear. "[Oh God, it's my turn, think fast!] Hello my name is Catherine." "Hello, Catherine," the group members said, smiling warmly. "Well, as you know, this is my first time at this meeting, and I, uh, think—find—it comforting to listen to other people who are experiencing the same thing as I, but, uh, I'm not ready to talk about it yet, so I, uh, I pass." The group members seemed as surprised by my response as I was, but they replied, "Thank you, Catherine." I wanted to slither off that picnic bench on my stomach across the grass and into my car just like the snake I felt like.

After the meeting, I stayed to collect the literature for my self-help file. I was approached by two women who were genuinely concerned about me. The women suggested that we exchange phone numbers to offer support to one another. I thanked them but said that I did not feel comfortable giving out my phone number and was just not ready to talk yet. (Of course, I did not want to do it because I was afraid they would find out that I was just there as an observer.) I felt like a heel—like I was exploiting their trust.

I went home as soon as I could pull myself away from the wonderful, caring people who kept coming up to me and offering their support and understanding of my mental anguish. If only they knew that just my presence at the meeting was causing me anguish. When I got home, I called a colleague to express my anxiety and guilt for what I had done. Even though I had gone to the meeting with full intentions of telling the group that I was just an observer, I still had to face the fact that I had lied to the group and had taken advantage of their trust.

Being the busy person that she is, Laura did not prepare for her visit to Gay/Lesbian AA:

Although I made several attempts through informal networking to identify the meeting's sponsor, no one knew the person's name. Apparently, the sponsorship had changed over the years, and the group operated collectively, independent of the leader. Since I could not acquire permission, I just went.

I arrived a little early and was noticeably nervous, somewhat timid, and overly polite. I told one of the women why I was there. She, in turn, told one of the men, and he directed me to the person who had been in the group the longest—a wise- and gentle-looking man who had established legitimacy through seniority. After I described why I was there, he suggested that I introduce myself and make an announcement at the beginning of the meeting. I said, "Good idea," and my anxiety level shot up like a rocket. Would they kick me out? Would they be offended by my intrusion?

Both Catherine and Laura attended their chosen groups even though they could not make contact with the group leaders or sponsors. Although you may choose to risk attending a meeting without first notifying the group's leader if you fail to make contact, take it from us, preparation reduces put-on-the-spot panic.

PROMISE 3

I promise not to pretend to be a legitimate member if I am not because I am sure to fail, be embarrassed, and create feelings of hostility.

Especially when one is caught off guard, as Catherine was at the Relationships Anonymous meeting, the tendency is to try to fit in—to highlight the similarities rather than the differences between oneself and the members of the group (even if one stretches the truth to do so). We suggest that you avoid this approach, not only by preparing for the experience but by clearly identifying yourself and stating your reason for attending the meeting, especially if you are visiting primarily as an observer. Take it from Vicki, who, determined to attend an Anxiety Support Group meeting even after being told that observers were not allowed, suddenly recalled her mild phobia of elevators. She recalled the anxiety related to this fear and ventured out as a new, one-time-only member of the Anxiety Support Group:

> It was a disaster. To start off, I went to the meeting under a false pretext, which was unethical and made me feel guilty. The group does not generally welcome observers because the members do not feel comfortable doing so. I went anyway because the criteria for attendance included "phobias" and I am afraid of elevators. I figured that because of my phobia, I could go on my own merit and would not have to say I was an observer.
>
> I was not prepared for the experience. The groups I had visited previously had all had a peaceful, warm atmosphere. This meeting was not peaceful. It was held in a small room filled with shaking, sweating people with tremulous voices and nervous tics. The meeting started off as a round-robin, so each person could talk about his or her experiences in the past week for six minutes—*exactly* six minutes (the group leader even had a stopwatch). Then, I was told that there was a session in which everyone set individual goals and that we would work together to overcome our problems. After the meeting, there was to be a social gathering at a local restaurant.

Unfortunately, I missed the last half of the meeting. The guilt I was feeling, combined with being in such a tense atmosphere, made me so anxious that I left early, muttering something about a night class. Luckily, because it is an anxiety group, it has a rule that you can leave at any time with no explanation.

PROMISE 4

I promise to get complete and accurate directions to the meeting place.

An inconvenient result of the informal nature of most self-help groups is that the time and place of a meeting are often subject to change without notice. The last thing a busy explorer wants to do is drive all over town trying to track down a self-help meeting that has changed locations several times since the last announcement or end up, as Vicki did, at the wrong meeting. Pat decided to call the Epilepsy Support Group at the last minute to confirm a group's meeting place and, sure enough, found that one night out of the year the group met at a local restaurant (Pat ate two dinners that night). Catherine set out to visit the Alcoholics for Christ group, whose address she found in the newspaper:

> I left for the meeting geared up for an hour of hymns, personal reflection, and unconditional support. I was sure I would have no problem finding this place, since it was only about two miles from my house. So, I drove to where I thought the place would be. I drove and drove until I *knew* I had passed it. I turned around and went back to the area where the address should have been and started all over again, searching for 45 minutes. As far as I could tell, the address in the newspaper simply did not exist. "Now, how hard could it be to find this meeting?" I thought. "I am on the right street, I have located the addresses on either side of the one I am looking for, but it is nowhere to be found." Needless to say, I never found the meeting.

Just to show that misinformation is sometimes a blessing in disguise, Vicki's stumbling across Families Anonymous was an enlightening experience for her.

> Families Anonymous is a group for parents of children with substance abuse problems. Actually, I did not know about this group; I was on my way to Post-Polio Connection, but the meeting place had been changed, and I ended up at the wrong church. Families Anonymous was meeting there instead, so I attended that group's meet and was impressed with it.

For some reason, meetings that are scheduled at churches seem particularly vulnerable to changes in schedule. Vicki spent several evenings wandering around local churches unsuccessfully trying to locate scheduled meetings. Patience is more than just a virtue when exploring self-help groups; it is a necessity.

PROMISE 5

I promise to attend meetings with an open mind as a learner, rather than as a teacher.

When you walk into a self-help group meeting, leave your assumptions and prejudices at the door. You are there to learn about self-help, not to facilitate, lecture, analyze, assess, scrutinize, instruct, inform, direct, or engage the members.

Some of us definitely thought that some groups were being run differently from the way we would choose to run them. Pat did not approve of the support given those members of the Manic-Depressive/ Depressive Association who chose to discontinue medications or to medicate themselves sporadically without a physician's supervision. Vicki found the tone of the Anxiety Support Group to be negative:

> I thought that limiting everyone to six minutes exactly—with a stopwatch, yet—promoted the anxiety the group members sought to relieve. Also, I found the general tone of the meeting to be defeatist and depressing. In fact, one of the members mentioned that his new social worker had come up with the idea that he concentrate on his nonanxious moments as opposed to his anxious moments and that he had been surprised by this suggestion. He thought it was a good idea, and so did the group. It bothered me that everyone found this to be a novel idea. I was not sure if the group members were really supporting each other or dragging each other down. I kept thinking about how I would run the group differently.

It is possible that the temptation to rearrange or move things around may be greater in smaller self-help groups than in well-established large groups. So keep this in mind when attending groups: It may be difficult *not* to be the authority in the group. Catherine experienced this difficulty firsthand at the Stroke Club:

> When I visited the Stroke Club, it became apparent that someone who is attuned to body language and how it can affect a group might be helpful in

addressing how members relate to one another and to their experience in a group. While at the meeting, I had to keep fighting the urge to turn some people's bodies so they would address the whole group instead of excluding some members.

In this group was a man who had suffered a stroke 10 years earlier and could barely speak. He was, however, fully capable of comprehending all that was going on and being said. However, while the group discussed things that happened to them, this man was being left out of the conversation simply because he could not see the body language of the members who were facing directly toward one another but turning their back slightly to him. It bothered me that no one in the group noticed how important body language is and how it can affect the dynamics of a group. Even though I was an active participant in the group, I would have felt uncomfortable raising this issue on my first visit. I think the members would have thought I was out of line and trying to run their group.

PROMISE 6

I promise to attend at least one minority-specific self-help group, especially if I work with minority clients.

Self-help groups for members of specific minority groups are especially useful to those who are members of a particular ethnic group, religion, race, or subculture. For a minority individual already anxious about attending an initial self-help meeting, the fear of alienation on the basis of a minority status may be enough to deter him or her.

For the moment, let us assume that you, the curious professional, are of the majority culture. If this is the case, your responses to visiting a minority-specific self-help group may enhance your understanding of how a minority client feels when first attending a majority-dominated group. As was apparent in Laura's visit to Gay/Lesbian AA, the fear of being different, stared at, and perhaps misunderstood or ignored evokes extra "jitters" for the explorer and intensifies the already escalating anxiety associated with the visit:

After my rattled speech during announcements, I sat at the "barefoot" table where almost any universal issue that has to do with alcoholism can be discussed. I was warmly encouraged to participate, although I chain-smoked throughout the meeting, and it was a continuous battle to still my shaky knees.

It appears that minority-specific meetings are promoted through informal networking among individuals in the community; therefore, it is difficult for outsiders to obtain information about them. What it means for the explorer is that you have to dig more persistently to find a minority-specific meeting to visit or to use as a referral. Asking friends and co-workers or looking in the announcement sections of periodicals read by members of a particular minority may clue you to a contact. For example, through chatting with a Native American woman from Gay/Lesbian AA, Laura heard of a meeting for women of color that she had not found through any formal source. Laura's experience at Gay/Lesbian AA highlights the purpose and importance of minority-specific meetings:

> At my table, several members mentioned that they also attended "straight" meetings as a means of opening up and becoming less isolated. Also, if a member is truly following the AA program, he or she tries to attend 90 meetings in 90 days. But there are not seven Gay/Lesbian meetings to attend in one week. In fact, in Ann Arbor, there is just one, and in many towns, there are none. Gay and lesbian members use this meeting as a haven in which they are completely understood and do not have to provide any explanations, rather than as the backbone of their AA program.

It should be obvious that advance notification of and permission for you to attend a minority-specific meeting are essential, particularly if you are not a member of that minority. Not only is this behavior considerate of the members and protective of the haven they have purposely created, but it will reduce the additional jitters you may have in visiting a minority-specific group. Laura experienced this kind of nervousness firsthand at the Gay/Lesbian AA meeting:

> During announcements, I spoke nervously, exposed by the frog in my throat and my shaky knees. Trying desperately to fit in, I quickly identified myself as a member of AA (although I had not been to a meeting in two years) and described my interest in the minority experience in AA. I spoke for about five minutes, explaining everything as carefully as possible to win the members' approval. After my speech, I waited anxiously to be ousted, but instead, no one said anything; the meeting went on as usual, and I stayed.

PROMISE 7

I promise to be adventurous in my expedition.

We believe that it is to the explorer's benefit to be adventurous and explore the unknown, in this case, the less conventional self-help groups. Often the less commonplace groups seem intimidating; for example, none of us managed to attend a Sex Addicts Anonymous meeting. Catherine showed her adventurous spirit by attempting to attend Alcoholics for Christ but was unable to find the meeting place. But she did attend a meeting of Dawntreaders, an informal Saturday-night social gathering for mentally ill people. She stayed until the end of the meeting in spite of an atmosphere that some might find disturbing by its lack of structure:

> There was quite a range in the members' emotional stability. For example, one person who seemed to be having a bad day talked about irrelevant topics and rambled. The other members, however, let her talk and even asked her questions to clarify what she was talking about and to include her in the meeting.
>
> The president of the club introduced me to the members as a guest who was there to observe. This seemed to bother a few people. Someone commented, "What is this, the Mickey Mouse Club?" The meeting was informal to the point where there was a lot of cross-talking. This made it difficult for me, the observer, to catch all that was going on. Yet, the members were friendly to and accepting of others and even me as an outsider. This group would be beneficial for a client who is trying to improve his or her social skills and to make new friends.

Other less conventional self-help groups are those that have a function other than self-help. For example, Vicki attended a meeting of the Grey Panthers, which is thought of as both an empowering self-help group for the elderly and a powerful political advocacy group:

> I found the second half of the meeting particularly interesting. A young woman came to the meeting to campaign for Michael Dukakis. She struck me as being an intelligent and well-informed person. Therefore, I was surprised when her campaign speech basically consisted of saying that we should all support Dukakis because she had met him once and he was just the *"nicest"* man. She did not strike me as the dizzy type, and I suspect that she had formulated this particular speech for a bunch of "nice old folks" who did not know too much about the issues but who would be a soft touch for a "nice-guy" approach.

If that was the case, she was certainly in the wrong place. When she finished her speech, an elderly woman stood up and said, "Well, as long as we're on the subject of the presidential campaign, I would like to say a few words on behalf of Jesse Jackson." She proceeded to deliver a concise, well-informed speech about Jesse Jackson in which she addressed specific issues. Other members responded enthusiastically and in a manner that indicated that they were equally informed on the issues. The meeting was called to a close, and the young woman sat down looking a little stunned.

PROMISE 8

I promise not to become a self-help junkie.

Exploring self-help groups can be at once rewarding and frustrating. The conscientious helping professional need not visit every group in town to obtain a working knowledge of self-help groups. In most cases, visiting three or four carefully chosen groups should be sufficient.

Do not become a self-help junkie. Take it from us, exploring self-help groups is a stressful experience; do not overdose, or you may end up a permanent member of self-help anonymous.

PROMISE 9

I promise to prepare myself for the anxiety that may result from my visit to self-help groups.

Throughout this chapter, we have warned that you may feel anxious at various points in your expedition and have tried to give you some "helpful hints" to reduce the occurrence of these uncomfortable moments. But no matter how much you prepare for or are invigorated by your visit (as Catherine was by her visit to the Stroke Club), you are bound to experience unexpected anxieties, so we suggest that you plan for some postvisit help to reduce stress.

Although Vicki did not think to call ahead of time, luckily, her friend with the hot tub was available after her tense experience at the meeting of the Anxiety Support Group. Floating in warm swirling water in a well-ventilated room with a calm friend was the perfect stress reducer for her.

Catherine, in a state of high anxiety from pretending she was suffering from a bad relationship at the meeting of Relationships Anonymous, made a beeline for the local ice cream store in the company of a happily involved friend.

Our point is this: Schedule something relaxing and stress-free after your visit. If you like to discuss experiences, make plans with an understanding friend or co-worker. If you prefer to process things alone or through distraction, watch a mindless television program or a captivating trashy movie. We hope that these basic guidelines will aid you on your expedition and that your adventures in the world of self-help will prove to be as informative and rewarding as ours have been.

INDEX

A

Abstinence, 107, 108
Addicted homes, 251
Addictions. *See also* Alcoholics Anonymous; Alcoholism; Gamblers
  Anonymous; Narcotics Anonymous
  alcoholism as, 106–107, 111–112
  chemical dependence, 32–33
  multiple, 246–247
  sexual, 96–97, 100
Adult Children of Alcoholics, 135
Adult Children of Compulsive
  Gamblers, 248
Affiliation, 159–161. *See also* Group
  composition; Participants
AIDS, 196
Al-Anon Family Groups, 64, 65
  background of, 96
  function of, 97, 132, 135
  linkages with professionals, 114,
    115
  research on, 110–111
Al-Ateen, 96, 135
Alcoholic, Compulsive Gambler, Narcotic Addicts (ACGNA), 247
Alcoholics Anonymous (AA), vii, 33,
  45
  background of, 93–97
  belief systems in, 129
  black chapters of, 196

flexibility of, 64
function of, 97–98
Gamblers Anonymous vs., 242–243,
  247
Gay/Lesbian, 330–331, 334–335
group composition of, 134, 135
literature published by, 100, 109
meeting format of, 99–100
as organization therapy, 59
organized along ethnic and class
  lines, 67, 229
professional linkages with, 113–115
professional opinion and research
  regarding, 106–111
Twelve-Step program in, 93. *See
  also* Twelve-Step programs
Twelve Traditions in, 101–104
women in, 108, 109
Alcoholism. *See also* Addictions
  as disease, 106–107
  stereotypes regarding, 111–112
Alliance for the Mentally Ill, vii, 59,
  187
Altruism, 164, 165
American Cancer Society, 285
American Coalition of Citizens with
  Disabilities, 153
American Heart Association, 285
American Indians, 108–109
Anonymity, 104
Antiprofessionalism, 305–306
Anxiety Support Group, 331–333

CONTRIBUTORS

EDITOR

Thomas J. Powell, PhD, is Professor of Social Work and Director, Center for Self-Help Research and Knowledge Dissemination, University of Michigan, Ann Arbor. One of his special interests, and the focus of the center, which is funded by the National Institute of Mental Health, is self-help programs for people with serious mental illness. Over the years, he has been a member of and supportive professional with numerous self-help organizations. He is the author of *Self-Help Organizations and Professional Practice*, published by the National Association of Social Workers in 1987.

AUTHORS

Stephen Blum, PhD, teaches at the California School of Professional Psychology, Berkeley. He was formerly on the faculty of the School of Public Health, University of California, Berkeley.

Thomasina J. Borkman, PhD, is Associate Professor, Department of Sociology, George Mason University, Fairfax, Virginia. She is principal investigator on two federal-grant studies, one on self-help groups and one on the prevention of drug abuse. She has published various articles and monographs on self-help groups and related alternative forms of health care.

Barry Checkoway, PhD, is Professor of Social Work, University of Michigan, Ann Arbor. His work on community organization, social planning, and health policy has been published in national and international journals. His edited books include *Citizens and Health Care: Participation and Planning for Social Change.*

Mark A. Chesler, PhD, is Professor of Sociology, University of Michigan, Ann Arbor, where he directs the Program on Conflict Management Alternatives, and Vice President, Candlelighters Childhood Cancer Foundation. He is the author of books and articles on health-related self-help and social change and of *Childhood Cancer and the Family*, a book on the psychosocial impact of childhood cancer.

Christine M. Comstock is a therapist in private practice at Horizons Counseling Services, Cleveland, Ohio, specializing in the treatment of survivors of child abuse and dissociative disorders. She writes on the treatment of multiple personality disorder and is the author of *Breaking the Cycle of Child Abuse* and the co-author of *The Nurturing Program for Parents and Children.*

Karin A. Elliott, MSW, is a doctoral candidate in the Joint Program in Social Work and Social Science, University of Michigan, Ann Arbor. Her research interests include the study and formation of personal and community models of empowerment in black and minority communities.

Patricia E. Ellsworth, MSW, has had many years of experience in providing direct-care services to mentally ill and developmentally disabled clients. She is currently developing a training program for providers of adult foster care in conjunction with a community placement agency.

Larry M. Gant, PhD, is Assistant Professor, School of Social Work, University of Michigan, Ann Arbor. He is involved in the development and evaluation of innovative intervention programs for the prevention of AIDS, for foster care, and for community outreach. He is the author of several articles on the prevention of AIDS and on community empowerment.

Benjamin Gidron, DSW, Chair, Spitzer Department of Social Work, Ben-Gurion University of the Negev, Beer Sheva, Israel, is now a visiting professor at the School of Social Welfare, UCLA. He has published numerous articles on self-help and volunteerism and is currently co-editing a book titled, *Government and the Nonprofit Sector: Emerging Relationships in Welfare States.*

Neil B. Guterman, MSW, is a doctoral student in social work and psychology and is working at the National Self-Help Research Center, both at the University of Michigan, Ann Arbor.

Lorraine Gutiérrez, PhD, is Assistant Professor, School of Social Work, University of Washington, Seattle, where she teaches courses on social work practice and in the concentrations on women and minorities. Her practice experience has primarily been with single parents and victims of crime in urban multiethnic communities.

Harriet Hartman, PhD, is a sociologist in the Department of Education, Ben-Gurion University of the Negev, Beer Sheva, Israel. She has published articles on the social support of immigrants and the immigration process, as well as on women's issues.

Vicki E. Kahl, MSW, provides direct-care services in a psychiatric facility in the Detroit area.

Alfred H. Katz, DSW, is Emeritus Professor, School of Public Health and School of Social Welfare, UCLA. His 11 books and over 100 articles have been on chronic illness and rehabilitation and self-help and self-care. He is recognized as a pioneer scholar and analyst in self-help and self-care and has been a consultant to the U.S. government, the World Health Organization, the Ford Foundation, and many other domestic and international organizations.

Linda Farris Kurtz, DPA, is Professor, Department of Social Work, Eastern Michigan University, Ypsilanti. She is the author of numerous articles on self-help, mutual aid groups for substance abuse, and mental illness.

Henry R. Lesieur, PhD, is Associate Professor, Department of Sociology and Anthropology, St. Johns University, Jamaica, New York. He is also a consultant to the South Oaks Foundation, on the board of directors of the National Council on Compulsive Gambling, and editor of the *Journal of Gambling Studies.* He is the author of *The Chase, Career of the Compulsive Gambler,* as well as numerous professional articles on compulsive gambling.

Carl A. Maida, PhD, is Assistant Research Anthropologist, Department of Community Health Sciences, UCLA School of Public Health, and Lecturer, Department of Health Sciences, California State University, Northridge. He has published several articles on chronic illness, natural disasters, and technological displacement with a focus on stress, coping, and social support strategies and has co-authored *The Crisis of Competence: Transitional Stress and the Displaced Worker*, published by Brunner/Mazel in 1989.

Louis J. Medvene, PhD, is Assistant Professor of Psychology, the Claremont Graduate School, Claremont, California. From 1983 to 1985, he was a postdoctoral fellow (National Institute of Mental Health), studying collaborative relationships between self-help groups and mental health professionals. From 1985 to 1989, he was Coordinator of Research Services, California Self-Help Center at UCLA.

Joyce L. Mohamoud, MA, is Adjunct Instructor, Department of Pediatrics, University of Medicine and Dentistry of New Jersey–Robert Woods Johnson Medical School, New Brunswick, where she is Executive Director of the Parents Anonymous of New Jersey State Resource Office. She is a member of the U.S. Advisory Board on Child Abuse and Neglect and immediate past president of Parents Anonymous.

Catherine A. Murphy, MSW, is a social worker in the Chicago area.

Harold W. Neighbors, PhD, is Assistant Professor, Department of Health Behavior and Health Education, School of Public Health, University of Michigan, Ann Arbor, and a member of the Advisory Panel of the National Technical Assistance Center for Mental Health Planning of the National Institute of Mental Health. He is the author of numerous articles on ethnic influences on help seeking, utilization of services, and psychiatric epidemiological field methodology.

Robert M. Ortega, MSW, MA, is a doctoral candidate in the Joint Doctoral Program in Social Work and Social Psychology, University of Michigan, Ann Arbor. He has extensive group work experience in multicultural community mental health settings.

Laura L. Sanders, MSW, provides direct-care services to adolescent clients.

Zulema E. Suarez, PhD, is Assistant Professor, School of Social Work, University of Michigan, Ann Arbor. She teaches courses on social work practice and has extensive experience working in Latino communities.

Lynn Videka-Sherman, PhD, is Dean, School of Social Welfare, State University of New York at Albany. She has studied self-help groups for a variety of life crises, including widowhood and the death of a child.

Richard Wollert, PhD, is Professor and Director of the Graduate Program in Counseling, Lewis and Clark College, Portland, Oregon. His articles on self-help groups have appeared in the *American Journal of Community Psychology, Community Mental Health Journal*, and *Canadian Journal of Community Mental Health*.